PSYCHIATRIC–MENTAL HEALTH ASSESSMENT

PSYCHIATRIC– MENTAL HEALTH ASSESSMENT

BONNIE KAWCZAK HAGERTY, R.N., M.S.

Assistant Director of Nursing,
Psychiatric Nursing Department,
University of Michigan Hospital,
Ann Arbor, Michigan
and
Adjunct Lecturer,
Psychiatric–Mental Health Nursing,
School of Nursing,
University of Michigan,
Ann Arbor, Michigan

Illustrated

The C. V. Mosby Company

St. Louis • Toronto • Princeton   1984

MOSBY

A TRADITION OF PUBLISHING EXCELLENCE

Editor: **Alison Miller**
Assistant editor: **Susan Epstein**
Manuscript editor: **Jennifer Collins**
Design: **Nancy Steinmeyer**
Production: **Carol O'Leary, Patricia A. Carlock, Barbara Merritt**

Printed in the United States of America

The C.V. Mosby Company
11830 Westline Industrial Drive, St. Louis, Missouri 63146

Library of Congress Cataloging in Publication Data

Hagerty, Bonnie Kawczak.
    Psychiatric–Mental health assessment.

    Includes index.
      1. Psychiatric nursing. 2. Mental illness—
Diagnosis. I. Title. [DNLM: 1. Nursing process.
2. Psychiatric nursing—Methods. 3. Mental disorders—
Diagnosis—Nursing texts. WY 160 P97208]
RC440.H25 1984   616.89'075   83-22038
ISBN 0-8016-2012-0

GW/VH/VH/ 9 8 7 6 5 4 3 2 1   02/A/245

To LARRY and JESSICA HAGERTY

for being there

BKH

CONTRIBUTORS

Consultant and Contributor

KAREN L. PACKARD, R.N., M.S., M.B.A.
Clinical Nurse Specialist, Department of Psychiatric Nursing,
Psychiatric Emergency Department,
The University of Michigan Hospitals,
Ann Arbor, Michigan

Contributors

JAY CALLAHAN, M.S.W.
Unit Supervisor, Emergency Services, Washtenaw County,
Community Mental Health and Department of Psychiatry,
The University of Michigan Hospitals,
Ann Arbor, Michigan

JUDITH ANN COSKY, R.N., M.S.N.
Clinical Nurse Specialist,
Fairlawn Center, Child and Adolescent Psychiatric Services,
Pontiac, Michigan

LAURAL GIDMARK, R.N., M.S.N.
Clinical Nurse Specialist,
Group Health Plan of Southeast Michigan,
Warren, Michigan

LISA ROBINSON, R.N., PhD, F.A.A.N., C.S.
Professor of Nursing, School of Nursing,
Assistant Professor, School of Medicine,
University of Maryland,
Baltimore, Maryland

RAMONA RUKSTELE, A.C.S.W.
Psychiatric Social Worker,
Sinai Hospital of Detroit,
Detroit, Michigan

FOREWORD

Psychiatric nursing, like all other specialties within the nursing profession, has greatly expanded its scope and endeavor since the anlages of psychiatric nursing were first recorded. While Man still suffers vicissitudes resulting in a range of responses from indignation to awesome and profound collapse, and nursing maintains its focus on supporting individuals through these developmental and episodic crises, contemporary psychiatric nursing endeavors to do more.

Psychiatric nursing's role in contemporary society is not only to care for the psychologically dysfunctionate but also to evaluate and to assist patients to maintain psychological wellness. This expanded role is quite different from the traditional one that included following physician's orders, transmitting policies, carrying out procedures, and faithfully adhering to supervisory dictates. While there are virtues in such endeavors, contemporary psychiatric nursing has identified a more complex mission. It addresses itself to facilitating the patient's coping and adaptation to life's vicissitudes. It provides an interpersonal, and sometimes a physical, environment, in which patients can be safe, in which they can develop more effective interpersonal skills, and in which they can change and grow.

To address these tasks, both psychiatric nurses and nursing students must be able to identify those processes of the mind that express effective functioning. When deviations from behavioral norms are identified, psychiatric nurses need to recognize the character of that deviation and they must assign to it some type of descriptive label. The latter provides a direction in which to move the therapeutic work. Psychiatric nursing views the patient as an individual evolving into increasing awareness, autonomy, capacity for intimacy, and spontaneity. Therapeutic efforts address these goals, which lead to self-actualization.

Recognition of the patients' selfhood and their needs and psychopathology derives from a data base. A major departure from psychiatric nursing's early efforts is the contemporary thrust toward scientific and organized collection of data from which to understand the patient. No longer is it enough to follow directives of other health care providers in assisting the patient with a psychiatric disorder. From the data base that is gathered by the psychiatric nurse, both nursing diagnosis and direction for nursing care are planned.

Because psychiatric nursing espouses the utilization of data-based practice, it needs the tools to support its mission. Ms. Hagerty has responded to that need. This book provides instrumentation with which to measure patient states and to identify patient needs. In this book practitioners and nursing students alike are offered information about mental function, dysfunction, the current theories of psychopathology, and most importantly, means to assess clinical presentation of psychopathology.

The author has forged ahead, using both assessment tools and nursing's preliminary work with diagnostic classification. For this she is to be commended. In this text Ms. Hagerty offers her colleagues a diverse collection of instrumentation that has been developed through the efforts of many. Her commitment to the continued growth of the profession is evident in this book, which will help its readers to learn and use materials that lead to correct patient assessments in the area of mental illness and mental wellness.

LISA ROBINSON, R.N., Ph.D., F.A.A.N., C.S.

PREFACE

Professional nursing practice is experiencing an increasing emphasis on accountability for its actions and decisions. The nursing process provides a conceptual framework for problem solving and accountability in nursing practice. Assessment, as the initial phase of the nursing process, provides the data and inferences required to plan and implement appropriate and knowledgeable patient care. This demands that nursing assessment be accurate and complete.

The purpose of this text is to provide a comprehensive discussion of the assessment process in psychiatric nursing. Our experiences as clinicians and nurse educators have repeatedly demonstrated the importance of patient assessment as the basis of psychiatric nursing care. A comprehensive psychiatric assessment is the foundation upon which a systematic, therapeutic intervention is formulated. It is essential to accurately collect and record the data necessary to treat patients who may be experiencing disturbed coping behaviors. It is just as essential to make logical conclusions as to the meaning of those data. The practice of psychiatric nursing is often based on abstract psychosocial and developmental concepts. Assessment of human behavior and motivations can be a complex process. Yet there is a need to collect specific, concrete, objective data and to formulate logical inferences about that data. The nurse who has only a comprehensive knowledge base and the ability to utilize the nursing process is not yet fully prepared for clinical practice. The nurse must also possess skills that allow utilization of theory and process, since clinical nursing practice demands integration of theory, process, and skill.

I have observed that psychiatric nursing students and practitioners seem to have difficulty making initial detailed and ongoing patient assessments. Yet existing psychiatric nursing texts present broad overviews of psychiatric nursing concepts. This text specifically focuses on assessment as the foundation for nursing's accountability in providing quality psychiatric nursing care. The structure and content are based on the belief that sound psychiatric nursing assessment requires a framework within which to utilize specific assessment skills. Therefore the book presents three chapters on theoretical foundations for assessment and eight chapters on the clinical assessment of behavioral disorders and disturbed coping patterns.

Chapter 1 delineates basic premises of psychiatric nursing and the nursing process. The American Nurses' Association's Standards of Practice are considered as a basis for accountability and responsibility in providing quality patient care. Chapter 2 describes therapeutic communication and relationships as essential concepts and skills to master for implementing the practice of nursing. Chapter 3 provides a comprehensive structure for conducting psychiatric interviews and details the specific interview skills needed to obtain assessment data. The clinical chapters discuss manifestations of anxiety, disorders of mood, thought disorders, personality disorders, suicidal potential, organic mental disturbances, and substance abuse. The final chapter describes a theoretical basis for assessing children and adolescents with emotional and behavioral problems.

These clinical chapters provide a theoretical overview of the disorders, including definitions, classifications, epidemiology, and causative factors. The particular manifestations of the disorder are described in conjunction with the specific observation and communication skills required to most effectively assess patients' potential problems. Assessment tools are presented for each clinical entity that will assist the clinician in the collection and analysis of data. The assessment concludes with the identification of psychiatric and nursing diagnoses pertinent to the presenting problems. The use of nursing and psychiatric diagnoses is meant to bridge the gap between the present psychiatric classification system using the *Diagnostic and Statistical Manual, Third Edition* and the developing nursing diagnosis model. Each chapter ends with a case study example of a problem discussed in the chapter. Shorter clinical examples throughout the text allow the reader to apply the theoretical information to actual patient situations.

I have chosen to use the word "patient" rather than "client" in this text. Since the text focuses on assisting nurses to identify psychiatric problems, the term "patient" seems most appropriate. "Patient" connotes an individual in need of assistance in identifying and coping with a health care need. In addition, I have tried to avoid sexist language by using third person plural or altering sentence structure throughout the book.

This text is meant to be a clinical guide, a supplement to basic psychiatric nursing texts. Although it focuses on psychiatric nursing, the content has been developed as useful information for nurses in speciality areas. I believe psychiatric nursing is part of the holistic care nursing provides every patient. Problems such as suicide, anxiety, and organic mental disorders occur frequently in medical/surgical populations. Therefore nurses in a variety of clinical specialities should find this text particularly useful. Undergraduate nursing students, practicing clinicians, and graduate students in psychiatric nursing will find this a helpful clinical guide.

I would like to thank those individuals who have contributed to the development of this text. Karen Packard has provided thoughtful consultation and feedback since I first approached her with the idea for this book. She has strengthened its content and structure. The contributors have spent many hours searching for the most appropriate frameworks and content for their respective chapters. George Curtis, M.D. kindly provided input for the chapter on assessing anxiety. Ari Albala, M.D. gave constructive feedback in his review of the chapter on assessing mood disorders. Daniel Pesut, R.N., M.S. reviewed the nursing process chapter. Sigma Theta Tau, Rho Chapter, provided grant funding to assist in the completion of the text. Kathy Hartsell helped with typing the manuscript. Special thanks to Larry Hagerty, Debbie Zies, and Kathy Krone, who provided their own types of encouragement and support. Colleagues and students provided me with the questions and ideas that prompted the conceptualization of this text.

I hope that this text will serve as a helpful basis for clinical psychiatric assessment and future inquiry and research into the assessment concepts presented.

BONNIE KAWCZAK HAGERTY

CONTENTS

CHAPTER 1

PSYCHIATRIC NURSING AND THE NURSING PROCESS

PSYCHIATRIC NURSING

This is a book about psychiatric nursing assessment. Psychiatric assessment, composed of a theoretical base and clinical practice components, is conducted by the professional nurse utilizing a scientific process. The nurse who incorporates theoretical knowledge into a systematic practice must also utilize precise clinical assessment skills in order to identify patient problems and strengths. Psychiatric assessment is the observation and identification of patients' psychosocial health care problems, strengths, and issues. A psychiatric assessment interview may also include physical assessment of the patient. The assessment of a patient's psychosocial status is often the primary focus of the interview, as in the case of a patient arriving at the community mental health center with suicidal ideations. However, psychiatric assessment should be part of any assessment interview, including one with a primary focus on physical examination and health history.

Psychiatric assessment is not limited to the specialty of psychiatric nursing. Nurses in any clinical setting must be cognizant of patients' psychosocial needs and their effect on those patients' total health status. Patients with medical-surgical problems commit suicide, exhibit thought disorders and cognitive deficits, and become depressed. All nurses need psychiatric assessment skills that will assist them to identify patient concerns and stresses. Psychiatric assessment, however, is best understood from the purview of psychiatric nursing. Consequently, any discussion of psychiatric nursing assessment would be incomplete without some understanding of the nature of psychiatric nursing and nursing's use of theory and systematic inquiry.

As defined by the American Nurses' Association, "nursing is the diagnosis and treatment of human responses to actual or potential health problems."[1] Nurses are involved in preventing illness and maladaptation and in promoting and maintaining health. To accomplish this charge, nurses use theory as a basis for intervening in the patient's health concerns and difficulties. The nursing profession is working to develop its own body of scientific knowledge that provides insight into human responses that are of concern to nurses. This effort has promoted the exploration and research of nursing concepts that will provide a unique theory base for nursing care.

With nursing research in its infancy, the profession draws much of its theoretical basis from other disciplines. Nursing, however, modifies concepts from fields such as psychology, sociology, and anthropology and directs their application toward nursing's role in health care. For example, theory and research borrowed from psychology constitutes the basis of the nurse-patient relationship concept.

Psychiatric nursing focuses on people exhibiting maladaptive behavior and experiencing emotional pain. In this respect, all nurses are involved in the practice of psychiatric nursing. Patients in any health care environment are likely to demonstrate fear, anxiety, grief, confusion, isolation, anger, or depression.

Psychiatric nursing is a specialized area of nursing practice that employs theories of human behavior as its science and the purposeful use of self as its art.[2] As specialists, psychiatric nurses focus their practice on persons experiencing psychosocial health care problems. The primary emphasis is to assist the person to develop alternative adaptive coping strategies.

Psychiatric nurses strive to promote, maintain, and restore patients' optimal levels of functioning. This is facilitated when nurses, utilizing themselves as the major therapeutic tools, enter into relationships with patients. This therapeutic relationship is carefully planned to assist the patient in maximizing coping abilities and problem-solving skills. It is this therapeutic use of self that potentiates another human's life experiences.

Hence, psychiatric nursing is an interpersonal process. Peplau describes nursing as an educational, maturing force that promotes creative, constructive, productive, personal, and community living.[3] This maturing force is the nurses' interaction with patients that influences and helps reframe patients' feelings, thoughts, and behaviors. This is accomplished through the development of the therapeutic relationship. Within the context of this relationship, the nurse functions as an advocate, teacher, and consultant.

All psychiatric care professions focus on developing therapeutic relationships and helping the patient improve psychosocial functioning. Most professionals utilize common theoretical bases for their clinical practice. However, psychiatric nursing is different from other psychiatric professions in the focus of its application of concepts. Nurses assess and care for each patient as a holistic being. Theoretically, a holistic approach views individuals as multidimensional, exhibiting needs in the psychological, sociocultural, and physical spheres of their lives. People are more than the sum of their parts. Holism espouses interdependence with each part impacting on the others. Therefore problems in one area have an effect on other dimensions of the individual's life and overall functioning. Psychiatric nurses committed to holism provide care for patients that span their biopsychosocial health care needs.

Psychiatric nursing confronts a professional challenge as it strives to achieve recognition and individuation. Since 1950 when the National League for Nursing stipulated that psychiatric nursing be included in each nursing school curriculum, psychiatric nursing has continued to evolve. Nurses who once assumed the role of caretakers are now fulfilling active, integral, therapeutic roles with patients. The 1973 publication of the *Standards of Psychiatric–Mental Health Nursing Practice* by the American Nurses' Association served to identify psychiatric nursing functions and establish professional standards. The revised 1982 *Standards* further refine psychiatric nursing practice and professional performance standards.

Three requirements for psychiatric nursing practice are reflected in these standards: a process-oriented practice, a scientific knowledge base, and professional accountability. The standards define psychiatric nursing as a process-oriented practice in which problem-solving skills are utilized to provide patient care. The importance of scientific knowledge is emphasized as the basis for clinical practice. Specific standards relating to continued learning and professional development highlight the significance of a theoretical practice base. The standards also address the issues of accountability and responsibility. The health care problems that confront the psychiatric patient create a potential state of surrendered autonomy and vulnerability. Consequently, psychiatric nurses must be cognizant of their accountability for providing safe and effective nursing care.

The *Standards of Psychiatric–Mental Health Nursing Practice* prescribe skills and behaviors that are initiated independently by the professional nurse. These behaviors demand independent thinking, creativity, decision-making skills, and a substantial knowledge base.

Psychiatric nursing has become more complex and demanding because of the impact of other significant professional and social trends. The increased sophistication of psychiatric nursing has come about to accommodate changing social norms. Consumers are increasing their demands for quality care as they become more active in their own health care. As higher education becomes more valued in society and in nursing, the foundations for professional practice improve. The professional practice is based on rapidly expanding knowledge in science and technology. Pharmacology, biochemistry, sociology, psychology, and nursing are advancing new theory and research that affect health care. Nurses must be educated in the most recent advances and trends in order to provide safe and quality patient care.

Professional definition, social trends, the knowledge explosion—all of these issues are pertinent to the understanding of professional, independent, psychiatric nursing practice. As practitioners, nurses are accountable for gathering complete and accurate data about patients' needs, making sound judgments about the data, planning and implementing appropriate nursing care, and evaluating the effects of that care in an ongoing, dynamic manner. This is accomplished by using the nursing process.

OVERVIEW OF THE NURSING PROCESS

The nursing process can be conceptualized as a series of actions that are divided into five steps. Each step involves behaviors and skills that nurses perform to ensure thoughtful, planned care. These steps are depicted in the literature as separate and distinct, yet they do not progress this precisely. The dynamic and flexible nature of the process allows continual flow and overlap among the various components. The nursing process provides nurses with a systematic way of thinking and acting in clinical situations.

In clinical practice it becomes evident that the steps of the nursing process cannot be represented as a hierarchy. The psychiatric nurse is frequently assessing a situation, analyzing that situation, planning interventions, implementing the plan, and evaluating the data all within a short period of time.

> CASE EXAMPLE: A new patient has been admitted to the mental health unit. He is depressed, withdrawn, and unable to leave his room. He was brought to the hospital by police after being found wandering the streets. There is no information about his background. The nurse enters the patient's room to make an initial assessment. While the nurse notes the patient's behavior, appearance, and physical status, she is also planning her approach to the patient, intervening by utilizing therapeutic communication, and evaluating the patient's response.

Although the steps of the nursing process overlap, it is helpful to define the actions involved at each stage. Fig. 1:1 demonstates these stages.

Assessment is the first step of the nursing process. It is the gathering of data about the patient's health status for the purpose of identifying problems amenable to nursing intervention. Assessment is always the

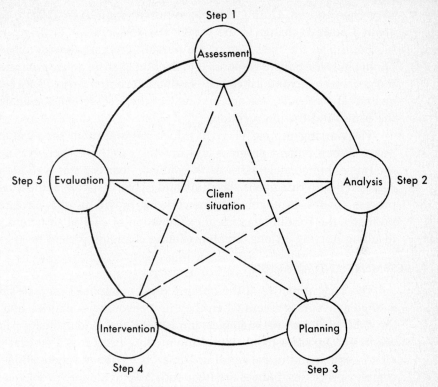

Fig. 1:1 The nursing process.

nurse's initial action. No intervention can be devised from a logical, scientific base unless there are data that provide information about the patient's problems.

Analysis, the second step, is the identification of the patient's health care needs. The nurse sorts through the available data and interprets their meaning. During this phase a nursing diagnosis is formulated when the nurse makes a judgment about the meaning of the data and classifies the patient's health care needs into categories amenable to nursing action. At this point priorities are assigned to the identified problems. The nurse works with the patient to establish goals for improvement or resolution of the patient's problems.

Planning occurs when the nurse creates and examines alternative strategies to meet the established goals, selects those strategies that are most appropriate, and develops a specific plan of care. Throughout the planning phase the nurse involves the patient, family and friends, and other health care personnel in the process whenever possible.

Intervention is the actual implementation of the nursing actions that have been chosen. During this phase nurses apply their skills to bring about a positive change in the patient's health status.

Evaluation, the final step of the nursing process, consists of determining how the patient responded to the nursing care and to what extent the goals were accomplished. The evaluation component will also demonstrate the effectiveness and accuracy of the assessment, the analysis, the plans, and the interventions.

The nursing process (Fig. 1:1) does not stop with the evaluation phase. When patient progress and nursing care have been evaluated, the nurse immediately assesses the patient's current status to identify changed health care needs. The fluid and dynamic nature of the nursing process creates an ongoing framework for providing nursing care. It promotes the continuous critical examination of clinical situations and resulting nursing actions, accommodating changing patient needs.

ASSESSMENT AND ANALYSIS

The cyclical nature of the nursing process implies that assessment is ongoing. Nurses assess when they first encounter a patient, analyze the data, plan nursing strategies, implement care, and evaluate patient progress. The assessment step of the nursing process is a cyclical one.

Assessing and understanding human behavior and motivations are complex processes. Nurses are frequently able to identify problems and write care plans for physically ill patients but have difficulty identifying and categorizing psychological and sociological phenomena. Research suggests that senior nursing students in baccalaureate programs demonstrate less ability to deal with abstract concepts than the average senior college student.[4] This finding is disconcerting in view of the fact that psychiatric nurses are responsible for providing holistic care based on assessment and analysis of abstract concepts.

It has become increasingly difficult for nurses to simply understand scientific theory and apply it to the patient care situation. Professional nursing demands evidence of higher cognitive abilities for complex, creative, critical decision-making and clinical judgment. Nurses need to demonstrate the ability to analyze information and formulate conclusions that will ensure safe and effective patient care.

CASE EXAMPLE: A psychiatric nurse knows that chlorpromazine (Thorazine) is indicated for agitation but has a major untoward side effect of decreasing blood pressure. A patient is admitted to the mental health unit and becomes increasingly restless. There is a physician's order for Thorazine, 50 mg IM prn, when the patient's blood pressure is greater than 100/60. The patient appears to need the medication but her blood pressure is 100/60. At this time the nurse must review all available data on the patient's behavior, determine the emotional climate of the unit, analyze the nursing staff's ability to work individually with the patient, and know the patient's previous reactions to Thorazine. A decision must be made whether to give the Thorazine, call the physician, or institute alternative nursing interventions. Now the nurse must synthesize all relevant data into a complete picture of the patient, the unit, and the staff and make a clinical judgment as to the plan of action that will be implemented.

There are mechanisms that can improve the nurse's ability to utilize abstract concepts in assessing, analyzing, and formulating clinical judgments. These include expanding one's knowledge and application of psychosocial, biophysical, and nursing theory; utilizing an organized system of problem solving; and learning specific assessment skills.

Theory as a basis for assessment and analysis

Standard I of the American Nurses' Association *Standards of Psychiatric–Mental Health Nursing Practice* stipulates that "The nurse applies appropriate theory that is specifically sound as a basis for decisions regarding nursing practice."[5] This standard establishes the expectation that the professional psychiatric nurse utilizes scientific knowledge in practice. It is not sufficient to simply know and understand principles and theories. As practitioners, professional nurses must apply their understanding of selected knowledge in an organized manner and draw valid conclusions upon which action can be predicated.

The process of assessment is one instance where scientific principles and theories provide a basis for nursing action. Empirical knowledge establishes a structure for organizing, collecting, classifying, and analyzing data.

Principles consist of facts that have been proved to be true. Theories are explanations of phenomena that have not been proved. Psychosocial phenomena are difficult to verify because of their abstract nature. Most psychosocial phenomena are theoretical rather than factual. Therefore psychiatric nurses deal more with theories than with principles.

This abstract knowledge base possesses some potential difficulties for psychiatric nursing practice. Some clinicians use intuition and other unrecognized influences as their only bases for assessment and intervention. They rely only on experience and may not possess or apply necessary and useful theoretical knowledge. This omission results in confusion and a lack of rationale regarding nursing interventions for patient care. This can be harmful. When incomplete or invalid data are collected and the nurse relies totally on intuition, erroneous judgments can be made.

In order to establish theory-based practice, nurses need to utilize deductive and inductive reasoning in their assessment and analysis. A deductive, or general to specific, approach is being used when the nurse enters a clinical situation with certain assumptions and theories. These theories act as a framework for collecting specific types of data and drawing conclusions about the patient's needs.

Maslow's hierarchy of needs is one example of a theory that nurses commonly use with a deductive approach to patient care. The nurse who ascribes to Maslow's theory knows that every patient encountered has physical needs that maintain life as well as needs for safety, love and belonging, self-esteem, and self-actualization. Data are collected that demonstrate whether or not the various needs are being met. The data analysis and nursing diagnoses will identify those needs that are problematic and amenable to nursing intervention.

An inductive, or specific to general, approach to assessment involves gathering a wide range of data about the patient situation, classifying that data into logical relationships, and describing the phenomena from a theoretical or conceptual framework. When this is done, the phenomena have been categorized and explained in a sensible way. The manner in which data are categorized and classified is highly complex and based on the nurse's knowledge, past experiences, and cognitive style. With this approach the data have been interpreted and described in conceptual terms as part of a theory or classification system. Once the data have been described in these terms, the nurse can combine deductive knowledge with inductive analysis and formulate hypotheses regarding the potential occurrence of other phenomena.

This can be demonstrated by the case of Mr. Jones, a patient in the mental health unit recently admitted with the diagnosis of a major depressive episode. Mr. Jones will not speak with any staff member. He believes the staff is poisoning his food and plotting to steal his belongings. The nurse collects the data and decides to utilize Erikson's theory of psychosocial development as a means of organizing and explaining this information. Through inductive reasoning, the nurse concludes that Mr. Jones is experiencing difficulty with trust vs. mistrust. The nurse is now able to utilize deductive reasoning to hypothesize as to other possible problem areas for Mr. Jones. Based on Erikson's theory and the conclusion that Mr. Jones is having difficulty with trust, the nurse now predicts that there could be potential problems in areas of autonomy, initiative, industry, identity, intimacy, and generativity. At this point data would be collected to determine if in fact such problems were evident.

Systematic assessment and analysis of patient needs are achieved by integrating deductive and inductive reasoning and incorporating a knowledge base into each approach. This type of synthesis is essential in developing a theory-based practice.

An organized system of problem solving

Nurses utilize the nursing process as a model for problem solving in clinical practice. The nursing process is not an innovation developed by nursing. It is an adaptation of the scientific process utilized by all professions applied specifically to achieving the goals of nursing. The nursing process assumes a major role in distinguishing nursing as a profession utilizing scientific, systematic decision making rather than only performance of technical tasks. It helps ensure patient care based on logical assessment, analysis, planning, implementation, and evaluation rather than intuition, guessing, and random experimentation. Whereas theory provides a framework for clinical psychiatric nursing practice, the nursing process provides a model for the process.

Just as the nursing process has a series of individual steps, so do the individual components of assessment and analysis. Assessment and analysis have their own internal organization that ultimately leads to identification of the patient's health care problems. An understanding of these steps can help nurses scrutinize the manner in which they make clinical judgments.

Assessment. Assessment consists of two steps; data collection and data verification. During assessment, data are collected about the patient's health status. These data are then verified for accuracy.

DATA COLLECTION. Standard II stipulates that "the nurse continuously collects data that are comprehensive, accurate, and systematic."[6]

Data collection is the purposeful gathering of objective and subjective information about the patient's presenting problems and health status. Objective data consist of patient behavior that can be observed by the nurse. Subjective data are information provided by the patient and others. An example of objective data is a nurse's observation that a patient is pacing the floor, whereas an example of subjective data is the patient's statement that she "feels nervous."

Nurses collect data by a variety of methods including palpation, percussion, auscultation, and observation. Observation is the primary means by which psychiatric nurses collect information. Observation involves the utilization of the senses of hearing, seeing, touching, and smelling. Observation occurs during the interview. Interviews are the means by which nurses watch patients' behavior and appearance and listen to their communications. Touch and smell are often overlooked by psychiatric nurses as mechanisms for collecting information about a patient's needs. The nurse may need to touch the patient to inspect the skin, perform procedures such as a brief neurological examination, or respond to the patient's emotional state. Smell may provide information about a patient's personal hygiene, habits, and physiological status.

There are multiple sources for data collection in a clinical setting.

Family, friends, and peers may provide valuable information about a patient's needs. Medical records and health care personnel often reveal important information relevant to the patient's presenting problem. Scientific and professional literature expand the nurse's knowledge of theories and principles that may help establish a model for data gathering or explain a patient's problems. However, it is the patient who is the primary source of information.[7] Secondary sources provide adjunctive data regarding the patient. These sources are particularly important when the patient is unable or unwilling to provide pertinent information.

Data should be collected from all facets of a patient's life. The concept of holism postulates that human beings are comprised of three major spheres of functioning: biophysical, psychological, and sociocultural. Assessment of all these spheres reveals a picture of the patient's state of health that is more accurate and inclusive than examination of only one facet. Because of the interdependence of these various spheres in producing behavior, a patient's presenting problem is never limited to difficulties in just one sphere. Physical illness may cause psychosocial distress and, in turn, psychological distress may result in physical illness.

When collecting data for a psychiatric nursing assessment, the nurse looks for changes in major areas of functioning in the biophysical, sociocultural, and psychological spheres.

The biophysical sphere encompasses anatomical structures and the physiological functions of the human body. This includes all life-sustaining structures and processes. Particular physical manifestations the psychiatric nurse will want to assess include medical and health problems, eating and sleeping patterns, energy level, and sexual activity.

The sociocultural sphere pertains to a person's relationship with the surrounding world, including ethnic, cultural, and religious influences. The nurse should collect data about the patient's family life, social activities, employment, school experiences, and economic status.

In the psychological sphere, cognitive and emotional forces interrelate to produce observed behavior. Cognition is that mental faculty by which knowledge is obtained and intelligence exercised. Specific cognitive functions that should be assessed include thought content, thought process, reality testing, and orientation. The nurse needs to collect data about the patient's affect, mood, and inner emotional experience. Behavior manifestations of patient's problems include the manner in which they present themselves, speech, psychomotor behavior, and impulse control.

Data collection in the above areas is most objective and reliable when specific methods and tools are utilized to measure and collect information. A large number of measurement tools exist for physiological functions. Diagnostic methods such as roentgenograms and blood tests can provide precise, objective data regarding the patient's physical health. Fewer exacting tools exist for data gathering and measurement in the psychological and social spheres. The abstract nature of psychosocial phenomena has slowed the development of objective scientific assessment measures. Specific instruments are available, however, such as behavior rating scales and sociological surveys. Throughout this book, various tools will be presented that can be used for data collection with the patient experiencing a potential psychiatric disorder.

Data collection may be conducted within a few seconds or over a longer course of time depending on the presenting clinical situation. During emergencies the nurse must often act immediately, intervening with a minimal amount of data. A scheduled psychiatric intake evaluation interview, however, provides a more structured situation and a longer amount of time for systematic patient assessment. Murray and Zentner describe two levels of assessment.[8] First level assessment is performed on initial contact with patients to determine immediate needs whereas second level assessment occurs over a longer period of time during which understanding of patient needs is enhanced by an expanded data base.

Every nurse is confronted with a decision about the type and amount of data to be collected. It is impossible in a given clinical situation to gather a total spectrum of information about the patient. The goal of data collection is to identify appropriate facts that illuminate the nature of the patient's presenting problems. Inexperienced clinicians often erroneously believe they must collect as much data as possible from all aspects of the patient's life. This is beyond the goal and scope of assessment. Data collection should be comprehensive in all spheres, as it pertains to the patient's presenting problems.

DATA VERIFICATION. When data have been collected, the nurse should review their accuracy. This review is data verification. Verification is a process that should occur continuously throughout the time the nurse is responsible for providing care to the patient. This often neglected step has been the downfall of many well-intended nursing care plans. Plans based on erroneous data usually do not achieve their intended outcome of improving a patient's health status.

Any data collected should be verified through further inquiry of patients, physicians, families, and so forth. Data should especially be verified when they are conflicting, when the source of the data may not be reliable, and when serious harm to the patient could result from any inaccuracies. To verify data, the nurse obtains additional information from the patient, significant others, nursing colleagues, and other health care personnel who may have knowledge about the patient's difficulties.

Analysis. Analysis consists of the identification of the patient's health care problems. During this step the collected data are sorted, classified, and organized into a pattern of relationships. The data are then synthesized to form judgments or diagnoses regarding the patient's health care problems.

DATA ANALYSIS. Collected data cannot be utilized in clinical practice unless the nurse is able to interpret their meaning and subsequently identify the patient's problems. For instance, the fact that a severely depressed patient has not eaten any meals for 4 days is useless information in its present form. It only becomes significant when the nurse analyzes the data, applies theory, and makes conclusions about the patient's possible needs.

The process of analysis "emphasizes the breakdown of the material into its constituent parts and detection of the relationships of the parts and of the way they are organized."[9] This definition encompasses three diagnostic process activities identified by Marjory Gordon: information collecting, information interpretation, and information clustering.[10]

Information collecting has been discussed as data collection. During data collection, information is described and labeled in objective, behavioral terms. Analysis begins with information interpretation during which the nurse attributes meaning to the data. This is accomplished by inferential reasoning in which the unknown is predicted from the known.[11] When the nurse makes a judgment about the meaning of data, the phenomenon is defined on a more abstract level. An inference is actually a hypothesis, a conclusion that requires additional validation.

Hypotheses are initially generated during data collection. Nurses gather early data that allow them to formulate hypotheses as to the patient's possible health care problems. For example, the day nurse meets a patient who has been admitted the previous evening with the diagnosis of major depressive disorder. The patient immediately says, "You don't want to know me . . . I'm no good." The nurse is able to hypothesize that the patient's words could potentially suggest suicidal ideation and an altered self-concept. These hypotheses are based on the nurse's knowledge of suicidal risk, major depressive disorder, and past experience with similar patients. The nurse would now collect data that negate or validate the hypotheses.

It becomes evident that data collection and analysis are integrally interrelated. As the nurse makes judgments as to the meaning of data, constant validation is required.

Information clustering occurs when cues are organized into meaningful relationship patterns. This is similar to piecing together a jigsaw puzzle. The interpreted data are grouped based on critical cues. Critical cues are important pieces of information that influence decisions. Cues begin to cluster around specific concepts that are meaningful in describing and perhaps explaining the patient's health care problems. At this point the data have been interpreted and grouped and hypotheses or hunches have been generated.

DIAGNOSIS. Standard III states that "the nurse utilizes nursing diagnoses and/or standard classification of mental disorders to express conclusions supported by recorded assessment data and current scientific premises."[12]

When a specific cluster of cues becomes apparent, it is given a category name.[13] This is the diagnosis or problem identification. The data are now synthesized into identified problem statements. These statements may be conceptually formulated by the nurse or taken from a classification system.

Diagnosis signifies a category label and a process leading to clinical judgment. Contrary to popular opinion, diagnosis is not a term specific to medicine. Many professions diagnose, including engineers, dentists, and special education teachers. Psychiatric nurses are involved with two types of diagnoses, nursing diagnoses and psychiatric diagnoses. Psychiatric nurses functioning in traditional roles primarily utilize nursing diagnoses, whereas nurses in expanded roles may be more involved in formulating psychiatric diagnoses.

Gordon defines nursing diagnosis as "a concise term representing a cluster of signs and symptoms describing an actual or potential health problem which nurses, by virtue of their education and experience, are licensed and able to treat."[14] A nursing diagnosis is a conclusion drawn from collected data that classifies a patient's health problems into categories and concepts amenable to nursing intervention. A national classification system of nursing diagnoses is currently being developed. This task is being facilitated by the National Group on Classification of Nursing Diagnoses, a group that coordinates efforts to research and implement nursing diagnoses. This classification system is in its infancy with many of the diagnoses vague and ill-defined or lacking concepts that have not yet been identified. It is, however, a beginning taxonomy that attempts to present a consensus of diagnostic terms nurses can use to describe phenomena amenable to nursing intervention. It is only after diagnosis or problem identification that nurses can then establish appropriate patient-centered goals, plan intervention strategies, and evaluate outcomes.

Psychiatric diagnosis is a term that describes a mental disorder. The *Diagnostic and Statistical Manual of Mental Disorders, Third Edition* (DSM-III), describes a mental disorder as a:

Clinically significant behavioral or psychological syndrome or pattern that occurs in an individual and that is typically associated with either a painful symptom or impairment in one or more important areas of functioning. In addition, there is an inference that there is a behavioral, psychological, or biological dysfunction, and that the disturbance is not only in the relationship between the individual and society.[15]

The diagnosis of a mental disorder can be made by a variety of psychiatric clinicians including nurses, psychiatrists, psychologists, and social workers. Psychiatric diagnoses classified in the DSM-III identify specific mental disorders and their clinical manifestations. The DSM-III presents a behavioral approach to classification of mental disorders, providing specific diagnostic criteria for each disorder. The manual specifies which criteria need to be exhibited by the patient, the number of criteria, and the length of time they must be present. It is atheoretical, making no assumptions about etiology and underlying causes of the problems. The DSM-III presents a multiaxial method of diagnosis where each patient is assessed based on the primary disorder, physical conditions, psychosocial stressors, and past adaptive functioning. A hierarchical organization of diagnostic classification simplifies the process of differential diagnosis.

Although some individuals repudiate the idea of labeling a patient with a psychiatric diagnosis, there are two major advantages to the classification system. First, a diagnosis provides terminology that represents a similar conceptual meaning to all clinicians. This occurs as the result of an agreed upon classification system that facilitates communication among health professionals. Second, a diagnosis provides direction for treatment and outcome evaluation. Clinical practice and research have demonstrated that certain treatment regimens are most appropriate for specific types of psychiatric disorders. Bipolar affective disorder, for example, is often treated successfully with lithium. Once a diagnosis has been established, treatment, based on past therapeutic successes, can promptly begin.

Learning specific assessment skills

The nurse who has only a comprehensive knowledge base and the ability to utilize the nursing process is not yet fully prepared for clinical practice. Knowing the theory and utilizing the process are not sufficient. The nurse must also possess skills that allow utilization of theory and process since clinical nursing practice demands integration of theory, process, and skills.

All of this is analogous to driving a car. A person can own a car and know where to go, how to get there, and even how the car works and yet not be able to drive. Assessment skills, like driving, can be learned.

The skills required in psychiatric nursing include observation, communication, and therapeutic use of self.

Observation skills involve watching patients and listening to their verbal and nonverbal communication. The nurse looks for critical characteristics that might suggest a possible health care problem. It is through communication and interviewing that the nurse obtains data and implements nursing care strategies. Observation, communication, and interviewing are accomplished within the text of the therapeutic relationship. Therapeutic use of self is the ultimate mechanism through which psychiatric nursing care is provided.

Assessment skills can be acquired through education, clinical experience under supervision, and consultation. The nurse, however, must be motivated to learn these skills. Expertise in their use is achieved only through clinical practice and evaluation of their therapeutic results.

CONCLUSION

As the specialty of psychiatric nursing continues to evolve, psychiatric nurses are increasingly accountable for providing systematic nursing care based on scientific knowledge. The science of nursing, however, cannot be separated from the art of nursing. In order to provide sound care, nurses enter into therapeutic relationships with patients. These relationships are the medium through which assessments and plans are made and nursing care is implemented and evaluated. Active involvement of the patient is essential in providing comprehensive nursing care. Through the use of therapeutic communication and the therapeutic relationship, the patient and nurse identify the patient's health care needs, establish objectives, and implement change strategies.

REFERENCES

1. *Nursing: A social policy statement.* Kansas City: American Nurses' Association, 1980, p. 9.
2. *Statement on psychiatric and mental health nursing practice.* Kansas City: American Nurses' Association, 1976, p. 5.
3. Peplau, H. *Interpersonal relations in nursing.* New York: G.P. Putnam's Sons, 1952.
4. Matthews, C.A., & Gaul, A.L. Nursing diagnosis from the perspective of concept attainment and critical thinking. *Advances in Nursing Science* 1979, 2(1), 22.
5. *Standards of psychiatric–mental health nursing practice.* Kansas City: American Nurses' Association, 1982, p. 3.
6. *Standards of psychiatric–mental health nursing practice.* Kansas City: American Nurses' Association, 1973.
7. Campbell, C. *Nursing diagnosis and intervention in nursing practice.* New York: John Wiley & Sons, Inc., 1978, p. 44.

8. Murray, R.B., & Zentner, J.P. *Nursing concepts for health promotion*, ed. 2. Englewood Cliffs, N.J.: Prentice-Hall, Inc., 1979, p. 104.
9. Bloom, B.S., Ed. *Taxonomy of educational objectives*. New York: David McKay Co., Inc., 1976, p. 144.
10. Gordon, M. *Nursing diagnosis: Process and application*. New York: McGraw-Hill, Inc., 1982, p. 13.
11. Gordon, M. *Nursing diagnosis: Process and application*. New York: McGraw-Hill, Inc., 1982, p. 168.
12. *Standards of psychiatric–mental health nursing practice*. Kansas City: American Nurses' Association, 1982, p. 4.
13. Gordon, M. *Nursing diagnosis: Process and application*. New York: McGraw-Hill, Inc., 1982, p. 13.
14. Gordon, M. Nursing diagnosis and the diagnostic process. *American Journal of Nursing*, 1976, 76(8), 1298.
15. American Psychiatric Association. *Diagnostic and statistical manual of mental disorders*, ed. 3. Washington, D.C.: American Psychiatric Association, 1980, p. 6.

CHAPTER 2

COMMUNICATION AND RELATIONSHIPS IN PSYCHIATRIC ASSESSMENT

Whereas the nursing process provides structure for delivering patient care, interpersonal processes are the vehicles by which nurses activate the nursing process. Psychiatric assessment is more than the gathering of data and the analysis of psychiatric problems. It requires the use of therapeutic communication skills and the establishment of a helping relationship whereby maximal information can be obtained that will assist the diagnostic process. An effective psychiatric assessment requires the active participation of the nurse and the patient. A more complete assessment and diagnosis can be made when there is a shared commitment toward, or at minimum a shared acceptance of, the assessment process.

Facilitating a joint effort between nurse and patient in the assessment process requires the use of effective communication skills and relationship-building techniques. Through the use of therapeutic communication skills, relationships are established that permit interactions between patient and nurse that promote improved patient functioning.

COMMUNICATION

Communication is a process we use every day. We talk to one another, smile or frown in response to some incident, move our bodies in ways that allow us to send messages, and are silent during anxious or comforting moments. As social beings, we communicate in an attempt to prevent isolation, fulfill our basic survival needs, and achieve a maximum personal and social growth as human beings. Our advanced ability to communicate allows us to establish structure and organization in our complex environment. The pervasiveness of communication throughout every aspect of our lives permits us to integrate all spheres of our existence.

People communicate using a variety of words, signals, expressions, movements, and other symbols. Communication includes all the processes by which we influence one another.[1] When conducting a psychiatric assessment interview, the nurse needs to be attuned to the nonverbal and verbal communication influencing the interaction.

Nonverbal communication

A student, beginning her psychiatric nursing rotation, was reporting on her interaction with a particular patient. Very frustrated by the patient's silence during the interview, she exclaimed, "He wouldn't communicate with me at all!" In her eagerness to engage the patient in conversation, the student completely ignored the significant messages being relayed to her nonverbally by the patient's silence, dress, posture, facial expressions, and movements.

It is impossible to not communicate. Observe, for example, two persons sitting opposite one another in silence. Although no words are spoken, body positions, eyes, facial expressions, and clothing convey certain impressions to both individuals. Too often, however, these silent transmissions of messages are ignored or discounted by those who give more credence to verbal interactions.

Research has demonstrated that nonverbal communication is our most powerful means of conveying messages to others.[2] Small babies, preverbal in their development, are adept at expressing their emotions, preferences, and dislikes via nonverbal communication. Nonverbally, potent expressions of feelings are conveyed at conscious and unconscious levels. Nonverbal communication has been described as the language of sensitivity.[1] A single gesture, a certain expression, or a glance of the eyes can convey far more meaning than a lengthy verbal interaction.

Nonverbal communication can be a sign such as a gesture or facial expression, an action that involves body movement such as running or dancing, or an object that displays material items such as clothing. Each of these types of nonverbal communications provides clues about the patient's self-image, interests, feelings, social status, and physiological state.

The nurse who is conducting a psychiatric assessment needs to be acutely alert to patients' nonverbal communications. Do patients maintain eye contact? Do they constantly tap their feet? Are patients disheveled or neat in appearance? Are they maintaining large distances between themselves and the nurse? Each nonverbal behavior should be noted as important data that may influence the assessment.

The nurse also needs to be cognizant of incongruent nonverbal behaviors. For example, a patient may describe extreme sadness in reference to the recent death of a parent yet outwardly appear to be exuberant. Because of the complexity of nonverbal communication, each message needs to be examined within the context of its occurrence. The nurse needs to validate meanings of nonverbal behavior with the patient rather than make an interpretation based on assumptions and the nurse's own past experience with nonverbal behavior. A sigh, for instance, can be interpreted to signify boredom, depression, pain, or feelings of being overwhelmed.

The use and interpretation of nonverbal behavior are culturally influenced. Established cultural norms dictate the patterns of nonverbal communication and its meaning. Very early in life, young children model nonverbal behaviors used in their ethnic group, geographical area, and socioeconomic class. Specific behaviors come to represent specific meanings. In Moslem countries, for example, young women learn that direct eye contact with strangers is inappropriate. Oriental groups engage in conversation with minimal space between the parties, whereas in Western countries it is often considered overwhelming and rude to "crowd" someone. The nurse must be aware of patients' cultural backgrounds and their use of nonverbal behaviors within the cultural context.

The nurse's own nonverbal behavior can greatly influence the assessment interview. Patients experiencing emotional and behavioral problems are especially attuned to the nonverbal communication of others. The nurse attempts to utilize nonverbal behavior to convey to the patient caring, interest, and acceptance. Awareness of the impact of the nurse's movement, body positioning, and spatial distancing is necessary in order to establish an environment in which the patient feels safe to share information. Facial expressions, gestures, and movement can be interpreted as discounting and judgmental if the nurse is not aware of such behavior and its effect on the patient.

Verbal communication

The ability to express ourselves through verbal language is our species' distinguishing characteristic. Words, the symbols used to convey information, represent our aptitude for formulating thoughts. Words are arbitrary codes that have come to represent specific meanings.[3] Verbal messages are generated when thoughts are encoded into a symbolic message and conveyed through words to a receiver.

Inherent in the verbal communication process is the chance for misinterpretation of the words or the ascription of a meaning different than that originally intended by the sender. Verbal communication is the process that differentiates human beings from lower life forms, yet it has been estimated that only 35% of our communication is effective for accurate transmitting and receiving of originally intended messages.[3]

It is therefore inaccurate to assume that one's ability to verbally communicate in an effective manner depends on conversational skills and verbiage. The effective verbal communicator must carefully select words that express the thoughts and feelings being shared. The words must be conveyed through appropriate channels, in conducive environments, at the proper time. Receivers of the communications should verify their interpretation of the message in order to prevent incongruent exchanges.

As with nonverbal behavior, verbal communication can best be understood within the context of the individual's sociocultural experiences. Words convey different meanings in various cultures. "Lift," for example, means elevator to the English whereas "lift" connotes the act of raising something to most Americans.

In addition, the expression of feelings is more accepted in some cultures than others. Slavics and Latinos are more open to sharing emotions than American New Englanders. During the psychiatric interview, patients are expected to share feelings and concerns. Cultural norms can significantly influence a patient's desire or ability to participate in an emotional encounter.

When used in a responsible, thought-out manner, verbal communication is invaluable. It allows us to share thoughts as well as feelings. The meanings of nonverbal behaviors can be discussed and openly verified. Verbalization permits us to validate impressions of our surrounding environment, describe personal expressions, and define phenomena that structure our world and our relationships with others.

Therapeutic communication

The crux of interpersonal relationships is the ability of the participants to communicate in honest, direct, and mutually understood ways. Professional psychiatric nursing involves much more than talking to patients and listening to their responses. The basis of psychiatric nursing is the skillful use of therapeutic communication, that is, words and nonverbal behaviors that are consciously planned to direct communication toward predetermined goals. The nurse who effectively communicates with patients uses a process of careful strategizing, choosing the best communication techniques that will promote the goals of the interaction.

The nurse's expertise in the use of therapeutic communication can influence the accuracy and completeness of the psychiatric assessment interview. A major goal in conducting a psychiatric assessment is to obtain information about the patient's biopsychosocial health status that will lead to the identification of health care needs. The nurse, therefore, uses communication techniques that allow for maximal information exchange. Facilitating this therapeutic communication may be more difficult with patients experiencing psychiatric disorders. Recent research indicates that psychiatric patients have a greater amount of dysfunctional communication than persons without psychiatric disorders.[4] This premise poses significant challenges for the nurse conducting a psychiatric assessment interview. Typically, patients requiring psychiatric assessment are exhibiting disruptions in emotional or behavioral functioning that increase anxiety. In addition, the fear and uncertainty surrounding the interview situation compounded by any existing factors such as fatigue, stressful life events, and physical illness can dilute the patient's ability to communicate effectively. The complex process of communication is then often distorted with words and behaviors that are misunderstood or ineffectively expressed.

It is the nurse's responsibility to assure that all communication between patient and nurse is mutually understood. This major task requires nurses to be cognizant of the words and nonverbal behaviors they use, the way these symbols and signs are expressed, and the resulting impact of the communication on the patient.

> CASE EXAMPLE: Mr. Rogers had just been admitted to the mental health unit. Ms. Jones, the charge nurse for the evening, entered his room to conduct an initial nursing assessment. Ms. Jones had spoken with the admitting psychiatrist and knew that Mr. Rogers was exhibiting paranoid ideations and had not slept in 48 hours. When Ms. Jones entered the room, Mr. Rogers was sitting quietly on his bed, hunched over, staring at the floor. Ms. Jones decided to sit in a chair near the door, 5 feet away from Mr. Rogers, so as not to create an environment in which Mr. Rogers felt closed in or trapped. Ms. Jones introduced herself and explained the purpose of her visit. She began asking questions for the nursing data base, including Mr. Rogers' address, telephone number, social security number, and place of employment. Mr. Rogers squinted his eyes and gazed at the floor. He crossed his arms and sat further back on the bed. He then asked, "Why do you need this? Is it for the CIA? Are you getting this information for them?" Ms. Jones leaned toward Mr. Rogers, who promptly stood up and began pacing. Ms. Jones leaned further back in her chair and explained the need for the information, then decided to discontinue collecting the demographic data. She began explaining to Mr. Rogers the need to keep his valuable possessions locked at the nurses' station to avoid loss or theft. Mr. Rogers began screaming, "You're accusing me of stealing. I didn't steal anything!" Ms. Jones explained that she was only trying to suggest he secure his valuables to avoid their loss. By now Mr. Rogers was so agitated that the interview had to be terminated.

The above example depicts the need for nurses to be aware of the impact of their verbal statements and nonverbal behaviors on patients. Mr. Rogers was suspicious and required adequate distancing from the nurse. Although Ms. Jones wisely sat 5 feet from Mr. Rogers, she unfortunately leaned forward as he became agitated about the CIA. Ms. Jones also misjudged the effect that a discussion about valuables and potential theft would have on a suspicious patient's perceptions. The intent of the message was lost as Mr. Rogers became boisterous and defensive.

Communication skills

Nurses who utilize specifically planned communication skills facilitate the purposes of the psychiatric assessment interview. Initially, there is the need to create an environment that is conducive to sharing information. As this is being accomplished, nurses begin collecting data that will delineate and substantiate the existence of psychiatric or other health care problems. In addition, interventions are planned and implemented that reduce patients' anxiety and promote their involvement in the assessment process.

Creating a conducive environment

ACCEPTING BEHAVIORS. As the psychiatric assessment interview begins, the nurse strives to create a climate of support and assistance whereby the patient can begin to feel comfortable in sharing pertinent information. Verbal and nonverbal communication behaviors exhibited by nurses indicate acceptance of patients' current concerns. Frequently, patients requiring assessments for potential psychiatric disorders enter the health care system in fatigued, preoccupied, or distressed states. These compound the usual fears and uncertainties most patients experience when placed in a situation where they are expected to share personal information and describe disturbing events, thoughts, and feelings. Often the patient does not know what to expect from the nurse or the interaction.

The nurse helps the patient to relax by exhibiting caring and interest in what the patient is experiencing. Nonverbally, such attentive behavior is conveyed by the nurse's relaxed posture and seated position, eye contact that is varied rather than intense or indirect, and the use of mannerisms that signal interest and concern. Nods of the head, leaning forward in the chair, and fixed attention on the patient nonverbally demonstrate the nurse's investment in the patient interaction. Nurses have the opportunity to establish initial rapport with patients by introducing themselves and offering a simple explanation as to the nature of the interview. Patients feel more relaxed when they have information about the interviewer and the interview process.

> INTERVIEWER: Hi . . . My name is Amy and I'm a nurse on this unit. I would like to spend the next 20 minutes telling you about our unit routine and finding out how things are going for you here.

In this situation the patient now knows the name and position of the nurse, the purpose and expected length of the interaction, and the general content of the discussion. This information facilitates the patient's participation in the assessment process by providing structure and expectations.

USING SILENCE. The skillful use of silence is a technique that assists in establishing a ripe environment for the sharing of information. Generally, therapeutic use of silence is the most difficult technique to use appropriately. The messages transported between nurse and patient during a period of silence are potentially powerful. Their interpretation depends on how the interview participants perceive the silences. Silence often encourages patients to discuss those matters that are most important to them at that particular moment in time. It represents the nurse's interest in hearing what patients have to say. In addition, silence provides patients with opportunities to gather their thoughts and ponder specific topics. It should be noted, however, that using silence does not mean interrupting or halting communication between patient and nurse. On the contrary, silence allows time for nurses to convey interest nonverbally and to observe the verbal and nonverbal patterns of communications of patients.

Nurses who are skillful in the use of silence are able to assess the indications for its timely use. Silence can escalate anxious feelings in nurses and patients, especially if the interview participants are uncertain as to the expectations of one another. Patients requiring initial assessments are frequently already experiencing a high level of anxiety that needs to be decreased before useful data gathering can begin. In these situations silence must be used with discretion. It may be more helpful for nurses to be directive and active in the assessment interview with highly anxious patients or patients experiencing thought impairment. Patients who seem to need to talk and express their concerns are better able to respond to silence.

LISTENING. Listening is another skill that is used to create a supportive climate for assessment. Effective listening is more than hearing what an individual is saying. It involves three levels of perceiving another's experience: being aware of verbal communications, observing nonverbal behaviors, and analyzing the meaning of these messages in order to prepare a facilitative response. How often we hear another person's words but are unable to paraphrase several minutes later what was actually said. Effective listening is an active process in which nurses perceive all communications being sent by patients. While gathering data for a psychiatric assessment, the nurse listens to verbal content, feelings, behaviors, and covert messages. Generally, the nurse listens for themes that convey the patient's beliefs, ideas, feelings, concerns, and current state. These themes may be obvious, such as the case of a depressed patient who tearfully describes a detailed suicide plan, or implied in covert verbal and nonverbal behaviors. This includes listening for incongruent messages, tone, key phrases, repetitive ideas, value statements, emotional language, silences, and notably absent content. For example, an 18-year-old patient describing his past did not mention his mother throughout the interview. The nurse noted the significance of his failure to discuss such an important person in his life.

Our ability to actively listen can be diminished by a variety of factors. Preoccupation with self and events external to the interview prevents the nurse from concentrating on the patient's communication. Occasionally, the nurse becomes so worried about the progress of the interaction that communication content passes unnoticed. Anxiety aroused by certain topics or by feelings being discussed in the interview often prevents the nurse from perceiving the patient's verbal and nonverbal messages in the manner in which they are intended. Often, nurses react unconsciously to patients' expressions or feelings by blocking out or distorting segments that ignite a personal reaction or bias. Certainly, verbal presentations such as monotone voice, tangential and circumstantial descriptions, and incessant talking serve as obstacles to the nurse's attempt to actively listen. Becoming aware of these barriers to listening and purposefully trying to overcome their impeding effect can greatly enhance the nurse's ability to obtain accurate assessment data, establish rapport, and maintain a therapeutic environment.

Encouraging information sharing. When the nurse has established a supportive climate, the interview progresses to the heart of the matter—the collection of data that illuminate the nature of the patient's health care needs and concerns. Throughout the data-gathering process, communication techniques are used that help obtain necessary information yet do not stifle the patient's expression of feelings or perceptions. The skillful use of questions, following cues, reflecting feelings, and paraphrasing ideas are most apt to facilitate data collection while allowing the patient to air feelings and concerns.

ASKING QUESTIONS. Questions provide structure for information gathering. Initially, questioning appears to be a simple process: ask a question, get a response. Therapeutic questioning demands that the nurse be aware of the types of questions one may ask, the impact of those questions on the patient, and the amount and kind of information the question will elicit.

Open-ended questions invite the patient to share concerns and feelings. These questions cannot be answered with a simple yes or no but usually require a more lengthy explanation. "What brought you to the hospital?" "What was it like being in high school?" "What do you mean when you say that you're upset all the time?" Open-ended questions encourage patients to elaborate on salient points, stimulate discussions of feelings, and present their own perspectives on their presenting problems.

Closed questions require a one- or two-word response. Frequently, they can be answered by a "yes" or "no." "Do you ever feel as though you can't leave the house?" "Have you had this pain for a long time?" Closed questions limit the amount of data the nurse is able to obtain.

An interview in which many closed questions are used can easily become a drill rather than an information-sharing session. Communication between patient and nurse becomes clipped and abrupt. Ultimately, the nurse may have lists of dates, times, "yes's," and "no's" but understand very little about the patient's actual emotional, social, or physical needs. There are times, however, when closed questions are more appropriately used in the interview. One instance is when the patient is extremely anxious or exhibits disorganized thinking. When this occurs it is difficult for the patient to think through an open-ended question that requires a more complex answer. Closed questions provide the necessary structure the patient requires for comprehension and response. Another situation in which closed questions are most useful is when very specific data must be obtained. "What medications were you on last year?" "Are you thinking of hurting yourself?" When nurses find themselves asking many closed questions, they need to determine if it is being done for therapeutic reasons. Often, interviewers ask more closed questions when they are feeling anxious or angry during the interview.

Leading questions provide patients with expected answers. "You were going to the fair, weren't you?" "You don't need to see a doctor, do you?" "Were you feeling sad last night?" Leading questions are embedded with implicit suggestions or commands that may mask the patient's true feelings or responses. When leading questions are used with particularly passive, frightened, or anxious patients, the resulting assessment data reflect the nurse's own biases and perceptions rather than actual patient needs.

FOLLOWING PATIENT CUES. Novices to the art of therapeutic communication often conduct assessments by following strict game plans, obtaining the supposed "necessary" data such as presenting problems, social history, demographics, and past medical history. In general, this strict structure can minimize patients' willingness and ability to provide rich information regarding their concerns. It is most advantageous to avoid skipping from topic to topic and instead relate questions and comments to the content the patient is providing. Nurses should follow cues from the patient that offer direction and substance to the interaction.

This also conveys to patients that nurses understand and are responsive to their concerns. It is usually possible, over the course of the interview, to obtain required data by developing topic areas introduced by the patient.

> NURSE: How are you feeling today, Mary?
> MARY: It was a long night. I'm tired.
> NURSE: You didn't sleep well?
> MARY: No, I was thinking all night.
> NURSE: About anything in particular?
> MARY: My mother. . . . (looks down at the floor)
> NURSE: (Silent a moment) Your mother?
> MARY: They told me she has cancer.
> NURSE: You sound pretty upset, Mary.
> MARY: I am. I can't sleep thinking about it (begins clenching fists, looks out window). I think the doctor has made a mistake.
> NURSE: A mistake?
> MARY: Yes, the wrong diagnosis. So, I really can't talk about it now (begins pacing the room).
> NURSE: Okay, we don't have to talk about it right now.

The nurse in this example discovered that the patient's sleeping difficulty was related to the discovery of her mother's cancer. In addition, the nurse was able to convey caring and concern by following the patient's cues and allowing her to tell her story. When Mary was no longer able to discuss the cancer, the nurse wisely allowed the topic to be dropped.

REFLECTING FEELINGS. The communication technique of reflecting feelings conveys the interviewer's attempt to understand the emotions the patient is experiencing. The nurse responds to a particular statement the patient makes by paraphrasing the salient points back to the patient.

> PATIENT: My son is a jerk. His wife has tried hard to save the marriage.
> NURSE: You're feeling angry about your son's divorce.

This technique encourages patients to continue expressing perceptions and feelings by acknowledging their existence. It also serves as a way to validate if the nurse's understanding of the patient's feeling is correct. Utilization of reflection prevents an assessment interview from becoming a rigid session of questioning for factual information. The nurse who skillfully uses this technique demonstrates empathy and acknowledges patients' rights to have their feelings. The wealth of data that can be obtained regarding patients' opinions, emotions, and perceptions lends an important dimension to the analysis of their psychiatric concerns and needs.

PARAPHRASING IDEAS. Paraphrasing is the reiteration of the patient's ideas by rephrasing the original content expressed by the patient. This technique not only validates the nurse's understanding of the patient's message but also helps crystallize the content the patient hears in the paraphrased expression. The interviewer, utilizing this skill, is able to clarify patient ideas, highlight content areas, and validate perceptions.

> PATIENT: I don't know what to do about my husband's request.
> NURSE: You mean you're undecided about giving him the divorce?
> PATIENT: Yes. And I don't even know how to get a lawyer.
> NURSE: You would like some assistance getting an attorney?

Paraphrasing is similar to reflection of feeling. However, whereas reflection involves restating feelings, paraphrasing emphasizes repeating cognitive content. Both techniques encourage patients to share their perception and experiences by conveying the interviewer's attempt to understand their concerns and issues.

Intervening. In every interview in which therapeutic communication is being used, interventions occur. When assessing a patient's health care status, the nurse should be cognizant of the delicate balance between data collection and patients' needs for intervention. Patients may be too anxious to tolerate a lengthy question and answer session. Others are often too frightened or uncertain to share necessary data until rapport or trust has been established. Frequently, patients may need to tell their story in an uninterrupted, cathartic manner without answering questions about demographic details or specific information needed by the nurse. Essentially, the nurse assesses the patient's readiness to be assessed and makes a clinical judgment as to the amount and type of data that need to be collected for patient safety vs. data that would be nice to have.

The nurse conducting a psychiatric assessment should be skilled with a repertoire of interventions available for a variety of patient needs. However, intervention techniques commonly used during assessment interviews include giving information, generalizing, and offering self.

GIVING INFORMATION. The nurse conducting a psychiatric assessment interview facilitates the process by interpreting events and processes that occur. Information is shared with patients regarding the assessment purpose and process, treatment approaches, the facility, available resources, and any other data that would assist the patients in understanding their problems and care. During the assessment, for example, the patient is usually more comfortable after being told the nurse's name and position and the expected length of the interview.

Information giving can decrease anxiety and fear of the unknown by helping the patient more clearly understand the environment and events. By sharing information and responding to patient questions, the nurse builds rapport during the interview and provides patients with information that will allow them to understand their problems and actively participate in their own care. Sharing information with patients' significant others can decrease anxiety and facilitate their involvement in the patients' care.

It should be, however, with forethought and discretion that the nurse shares information with patients and significant others. People vary in the amount and type of information they want or are able to receive and process. In fact, sharing lengthy, detailed information can alarm patients and increase anxiety levels. A good rule of thumb is to provide information that interprets the patient's environment and answers direct questions.

GENERALIZING. When a patient seems to be having difficulty sharing information or feelings, the nurse can often put the patient at ease by relating the universality of the topic, feeling, or situation: "Many of the people I speak with have financial difficulties." Frequently, a brief parable will demonstrate to the patient that a problem is not unique. "One person I see has had friends question him about his medication. He finally told them it wasn't any of their business."

In this last example the nurse is able to suggest a solution the patient might use to put an end to friends' questions by describing how another patient implemented this technique. Generalizing removes the direct flow of the situation from the patient and allows it to be more safely discussed via the third person.

OFFERING SELF. Perhaps the most useful intervention that impacts patients is the nurses' offering of self. This intervention is nurses' attempts to make themselves available to patients: "I know you're upset. I will sit here with you." This technique communicates to patients that the nurse is concerned about them and is offering to be present or to help with their health care needs. Using this technique, the nurse does not make demands on patients in exchange for availability; the offer is unconditional. The caring and supportive offer can relieve anxiety and provide the patient with a feeling of being anchored to a helping professional. Offering self is a primary technique used to initiate a "caring" relationship and demonstrate support for the patient.

THE THERAPEUTIC RELATIONSHIP

The use of effective communication techniques establishes a climate in which patients can safely share information. The nurse uses these techniques to structure the optimal medium for interaction, an atmosphere in which trust and rapport can emerge. The nurse's ability to engage in interpersonal interactions in a planned way for the purpose of assisting patients with their health care needs is the foundation of nursing practice.

Relationship development plays an important role in the assessment process. Initially, the nurse structures a comfortable environment in which the patient is able to divulge information. This occurs when patients feel the nurse exhibits a true interest in them rather than relating as an information seeker. The quality of the relationship established in the initial interviews can determine whether patients will return for care or seek assistance at a future date. Creating a feeling of relatedness and connectedness during the assessment interview will let the patient know that help is available and will serve as a lifeline in crisis situations. Often, assessment signifies the beginning of a long-term nurse-patient relationship in which the nurse will continue to collect data and diagnose patient needs over a long period of time. Whatever the circumstances, the therapeutic relationship is an important concept to implement in any assessment situation.

Overview

The therapeutic relationship is the medium through which the nursing process is implemented. As the basis for all interactions with patients, it consists of planned, goal-directed encounters between a patient and nurse for the purpose of helping the patient identify and rectify health care problems. In contrast to a social relationship, the therapeutic relationship focuses on the patient's health concerns rather than the personal needs of the nurse.

King describes the therapeutic relationship as a learning experience for both patient and nurse. facilitated by the nurse's utilization of self as a therapeutic tool. She describes a series of four actions that must occur for a relationship to be established in which maximal patient care is achieved[5]:
1. An initial action by the nurse
2. A reaction response from the patient
3. An interaction in which nurse and patient assess patient needs and define goals
4. A transaction in which a reciprocal relationship is finally established to achieve the relationship goals

King hypothesizes that highest quality patient care is achieved when transactions occur between patient and nurse.

Rogers has examined the nature of the therapeutic relationship and describes three elements that promote change and growth in patients: congruence, empathy, and positive regard.[6] Congruence is the art of being genuine. Nurses who are congruent in their therapeutic relationships listen to their internal feelings and reactions and are able to share these with patients. The ability to empathize allows the nurse to get into the patient's perceptual world and understand feelings without losing sight of the nurse's own responses and boundaries. Positive regard demonstrates respect. The patient is viewed and treated as a person worthy of caring and assistance with strengths and achievement potential. These three elements of a therapeutic relationship combine to create an emotional matrix, a design for interrelatedness that facilitates information flow.

The process of relationship development occurs over time. The therapeutic relationship implies a series of encounters during which interpersonal relatedness is established and maintained. There are three phases of a therapeutic relationship: introductory, working, and termination. During the introductory phase, initial trust is established by the nurse's demonstration of caring, concern, objectivity, and respect. The patient and nurse come to know one another in their respective roles as they discuss basic information regarding the patient's needs. A contract is defined in which the purpose, boundaries, time frame, and outcomes of the relationship are clearly delineated. The working phase begins when the nurse and patient set specific mutual goals and openly discuss pertinent issues. The patient is able to share more detailed data, including personal perceptions and feelings that can be examined through reflection and problem solving. During the termination phase, the nurse and patient prepare to say goodbye. They review the patient's accomplishments, future plans, and goals, and they share feelings related to the termination.

Relationship development in assessment

When the nurse is involved in patient assessment, the opportunity for long-term therapeutic relationship development may not exist. The nature of the nurse's relationship with the patient will vary depending on the circumstances of the assessment. Assessment may occur during a one-time encounter, such as a crisis visit to the psychiatric emergency room, or over a longer period of time, such as a 2-month hospitalization on an inpatient unit. The nature of the relationship that is to be built between the nurse and the patient will differ according to the circumstances of the encounter. The nurse will be assessing the patient during one-time only interactions, interactions that begin to establish a long-term relationship, and interactions that occur in the midst of an ongoing relationship.

Initial interviews. An interview is a transitory relationship in which there is limited time to develop the relatedness between the patient and the nurse. Often the nurse is meeting the patient for the first time. The patient may be seeking help in a crisis situation or may be evaluated for therapy referral. Whatever the circumstances, this is not a relationship that will be extensively developed because of time constraints. The purpose of the interview is to assess the patient's psychiatric needs and make appropriate referrals. In some instances the nurse may continue to meet with the patient several more times for further assessment or for crisis intervention therapy.

The intensity and depth of the relationship will be limited when the nurse and patient meet only once or twice. This very limited relationship is actually a therapeutic encounter rather than a relationship. The type of relationship that occurs over several meetings may not be extensive but is often very substantial, making great impact on the patient. Within a brief time, the nurse needs to create a comfortable environment in which the patient can feel safe to share personal information, provide the patient with the feeling of being cared about, let the patient know that help is available, and lay the foundation of trust that will promote the patient's utilization of health care resources in the future.

During an encounter the major goal of the relationship is to establish rapport.[7] With the initial greeting, the nurse demonstrates caring, concern, interest, and availability. By creating an environment in which the patient feels able to share concerns, the nurse increases the patient's confidence and cooperativeness during the interview. The nurse utilizes therapeutic communication skills that permit the patient to speak freely without creating a rigid structure that suppresses the patient's willingness to share. Table 2:1 describes some differences between a long-term relationship and one that is only developed over one or several assessment interviews.

Establishment of a long-term relationship. A nurse often initially assesses a patient with whom a longer term relationship is to be established. In this instance the nurse obtains as much information as is needed to ensure patient safety and comfort in the initial interview but is able to minimize the initial data gathering since there will be additional meetings. A major emphasis will be on establishing trust with the patient in preparation for future encounters. As in any encounter, trust is nurtured by demonstrating congruence, empathy, positive regard, and offering assistance in alleviating the patient's concerns.

The nurse should negotiate a therapeutic contract with the patient that includes the purpose, duration, and nature of the expected relationship. At this time expectations are established for future assessment activities: "Over the next several weeks, perhaps we can talk more about the past several years since your divorce and the kinds of things you think have made it a bad time for you."

The nurse and patient begin to define goals for therapy and the

TABLE 2:1   Comparison of relationship development during brief assessments and long-term relationships

Phase	Brief assessments	Long-term relationship
1. Introductory	Establish rapport Contract: —defines limited nature of relationship —defines purpose as assessment, referral, brief crisis intervention	Establish trust Contract: —sets perimeters for length of relationship —defines purpose as assessment, helping with problems through working together on mutually established goals
2. Working	May never achieve in-depth sharing of feelings, perceptions or patient may share immediate feelings, details if during crisis state	Achievement of patient sharing of issues, feelings Problem solving with nurse's assistance Nurse and patient work toward achievement of patient-centered goals
3. Termination	Less difficult and intense because of limited time together Nurse: —reviews content of encounter(s) —summarizes —makes referrals —establishes future availability —says goodbye	Often intense Patient and nurse: —share feelings —review relationship —review patient accomplishments —review patient plans and goals —say goodbye

relationship. These goals are another basis for assessment. For example, the patient says, "I want to stop feeling so lonely and sad all the time. That's why I came." The nurse knows now that areas for future assessment include the patient's emotional state and events that affect it, past experiences with depression and alienation, and social support systems.

Assessment in a long-term relationship. During an extended relationship with a patient, the nurse has the opportunity to develop the working phase in which the patient discusses feelings and concerns and solves problems around identified problem areas. As the relationship develops, first level assessment continues, with the nurse gathering data about the patient's daily behaviors and needs. Second level assessment, however, becomes more intensified as specific and detailed information is collected that will provide depth to the continued analysis of the patient's problems.

The interaction of the assessment process and development of the working phase of the therapeutic relationship facilitates a mutuality between patient and nurse. Trust is enhanced as the patient shares information to an empathetic, objective interviewer and, in turn, the patient's ability to provide pertinent data and perceptions promotes the alliance between patient and nurse.

As a relationship progresses, the initial emphasis on assessment gives way to a focus on intervention. Although assessment continues with each new encounter to determine current needs or more specific information about problems already identified, the nurse now concentrates on strategies that will assist the patient in achieving defined treatment goals.

Throughout a long-term relationship, it is important to remember that assessment is ongoing. Everyday, stresses that can potentially alter behavior and identified needs impact on the patient. Changing life situations may influence plans for patient treatment. New data may become evident that nullify the nurse's original hypothesis and diagnosis. Therefore assessment should never be an activity limited to initial patient interactions or diagnostic premises.

Values and attitudes

No discussion of therapeutic relationships would be complete without mentioning the values and attitudes that affect nurses' approaches to patients. From birth we are influenced by social, religious, and ethnic behaviors and attitudes that contribute to adult values and biases. As nurses we bring to the profession and, subsequently, to each encounter with patients the sum of our past experiences, preconceived ideas, and established judgments. These color our perception of events and people. We tend to see patients as people entering the nurse's world rather than see the nurse attempting to enter patients' worlds.

Nurses enter assessment situations with preconceived notions about the patient or the type of patient requesting help. How often have we heard, "Oh no, there comes another borderline!" There are some patients the nurse is unable to relate to for a variety of reasons. When this occurs the nurse should be aware of the ideas or attitudes that are influencing the approach and interaction with the patient. Does the nurse disagree with the patient's religious beliefs or feel disturbed by cultural practices? Is the patient raising her children in ways that are contrary to the nurse's philosophy of child rearing? Does the patient's behavior provoke feelings of anger or pity for the nurse?

Whenever the nurse enters into an assessment interview with such attitudes or biases, there is the probability that the assessment will be skewed. Nurses may not collect or pay attention to data that are in conflict with their beliefs. They can misperceive patients' statements or draw conclusions that do not accurately reflect the objective data. Sometimes a strong identification with the patient's problems or personality prevents the nurse from seeing the potential seriousness of the patient's situation. Being frightened of a particular patient will distort the nurse's understanding of that patient's problems.

Nurses' values, biases, and personal feelings will always be evident whenever they care for patients. The nurse, however, has the responsibility to acknowledge that the attitudes do exist and to formulate a plan that minimizes their interference with patient care. Once nurses become aware of the influence of their beliefs on the assessment and decision-making processes, steps can be taken to ensure that they do not interfere with clinical judgments.

First, the nurse needs to acknowledge that personal feelings may be affecting the nurse-patient relationship and the assessment process. Then the effects of these biases can be discussed with a clinical supervisor to determine possible strategies for minimizing their influences.

CONCLUSION

Communicating effectively to develop a relationship that promotes patients' participation in the assessment process is vital in order to ensure accurate analysis of their psychiatric problems. Nurses bring their own belief systems, experiences, cultural influences, and knowledge bases into the process of developing these relationships. Most strikingly nurses exhibit their own styles of interacting during communication exchange and relationship development. We all have our own communication patterns and ways of relating that are most effective in expressing thoughts and feelings and influencing others. Facilitating interpersonal interactions that promote goal achievement is best accomplished when nurses are aware of their personal styles. For example, nurses who tend to talk rather than listen need to be cognizant of this tendency and make conscious efforts to improve listening skills. Clinicians who are able to develop awareness regarding their communication styles and approach to others have the control and ability to alter and improve their methods of relating.

During the assessment process, the nurse attempts to enter the patient's world and elicit issues and concerns while conveying caring, empathy, and positive regard. The initial goals are to gather data and establish rapport and trust. These goals are best accomplished through the nurse's use of the psychiatric interview.

REFERENCES

1. Lewis, G. *Nurse-patient communication*, ed. 3. Dubuque, Iowa: William C. Brown Co., Publishers, 1978, pp. 1, 17.
2. Hall, E., Ruesch, J., & Kees, W. *Nonverbal communication*, Los Angeles: University of California Press, 1956.
3. Pluckhan, M. *Human communication—the matrix of nursing*, New York: McGraw-Hill Book Co., 1978, pp. 11, 43.
4. Heineken, J. Disconfirmation in dysfunctional communication. *Nursing Research*, 1982, *31*, 4.
5. King, I.M. *Toward a theory for nursing*. New York: John Wiley and Sons, Inc., 1971, p. 91.
6. Rogue, C. The interpersonal relationship: The care of guidance. In Rogers, C., & Stevens, B.: *Person to person*. New York: Pocket Books, 1967.
7. Bernstein, L., Bernstein, R. & Dana, R. *Interviewing: A guide for health professionals*, ed. 2. New York: Appleton-Century-Crofts, 1974, p. 31.

CHAPTER 3

THE PSYCHIATRIC INTERVIEW

Our lives are a series of interviews. We interview for jobs, we interview applicants for jobs, we interview clients, we interview teachers when making decisions about schools for our children. Nurses frequently find themselves in positions that necessitate talking with people, getting information, and providing some intervention. Whether it be admitting a patient to a neurology unit, conducting a home health visit, or evaluating the psychological functioning of a patient on an inpatient psychiatric unit, nurses are continually gathering data, sorting and synthesizing the information, and formulating opinions. These tasks make nurses professional interviewers.

Some interviews are directed primarily at collecting data while others are aimed at providing help. Many interviews involve a combination of the two. The psychiatric interview involves both gathering data and providing some form of intervention, whether it be control, support, or interpretation. This chapter focuses on the psychiatric interview as performed by nurses in a variety of health care settings.

The interview is a process or tool used to assess the patient's level of psychological functioning. Interviewing, in general, is an art rather than a science. However, skills can be acquired that will enhance the overall effectiveness of the interview. Proficiency in any clinical skill, such as auscultation, giving injections, or interviewing, develops best through direct work with patients and subsequently through feedback from clinical supervision. Therefore the information presented here is intended to be an adjunct to the actual conduction and supervision of psychiatric interviews. Excerpts from interviews are given to facilitate the acquisition of the basic skills that are requisite for conducting psychiatric assessments. The excerpts are given not as examples of the "correct" or "right" techniques to use but rather as useful examples of how psychiatric interviews might be conducted and organized. The examples are included for your reflection as you develop your own personal style.

DEFINITION

A psychiatric interview is a purposeful interaction between two or more people. More precisely, interviews are chronological reviews of patients' presenting behavioral disturbances, their past physical, emotional, and social histories, and tests of their current mental status. It is a systematic attempt to acquire a broad range of information. Like most interviews the psychiatric assessment involves observation, listening, and questioning. The data generated from the psychiatric assessment should provide the information necessary to formulate initial impressions about the patient's psychopathology and to begin development of a treatment plan.

Interaction and purposeful are key words in describing a psychiatric interview. Interaction implies an interpersonal process or communication between people. Purposeful implies that the interview is more than an arbitrary or random meeting. The interview is goal-oriented for both the nurse and the patient. The specific goals, however, will vary depending on the particular patient, the setting in which the interview occurs, and the circumstances surrounding the interaction. For example, the goal or purpose of a psychiatric interview will be quite different for a patient who is brought involuntarily to a psychiatric emergency room as compared to a patient who voluntarily seeks treatment at the local community mental health center.

For the nurse the purposes of conducting a psychiatric assessment are (1) to assess a patient's current level of psychological functioning, (2) to establish a trusting rapport, (3) to understand how previous modes of coping contributed to the patient's psychosocial development, and (4) to formulate a plan of care.

For the patient the purpose or goal of the interview may not be as clearly defined. The nurse may need to assist the patient to identify the problem and to discover what benefit can realistically result from the interaction. Goals that are mutually agreed upon will enhance and expedite the patient's return to a previous or improved level of functioning. Conflicting goals, on the other hand, can seriously impede the formation of a productive therapeutic alliance.

CASE EXAMPLE: A daughter and son bring their 67-year-old father to the psychiatric emergency room for evaluation for hospitalization. Mr. White has slept only 4 or 5 hours in the past week, has lost about 10 lb in the past several months, bought three cars last week, and has been making numerous long distance phone calls. The nurse determines he is experiencing a mood disturbance and could benefit from hospitalization. Mr. White, on the other hand, feels quite good and the only assistance he wants is help finding garages for all his cars. The patient refuses to sign into the hospital and becomes angry that the nurse cannot find garages for his cars; the family is angry that the nurse cannot convince their father to sign into the hospital; and the nurse is concerned because the patient clearly needs treatment but is not amenable to proposed plan.

GENERAL CONSIDERATIONS

Although there are no strict guidelines or rules under which psychiatric interviews are performed, there are certain conditions that contribute to the overall effectiveness of the assessment. The room, interruptions, the attitudes and behavior of the interviewer, the context of the interview situation, the length of the interview, and note taking all influence the direction and outcome of the therapeutic process. It is worth discussing these factors at this point to help set the stage for the optimal conditions under which assessments should be conducted.

The room

The interview room should be comfortable, quiet, and private. It should look professional in that the design and furnishings should not be overwhelming or distracting and should provide an atmosphere conducive to communication. It should be large enough so that family members can comfortably participate and suspicious or paranoid patients do not feel trapped. The interviewer should never give any patient, especially an agitated one, the opportunity to block the only exit. Ideally a room should have two exits, one for the nurse and one for the patient. Agitated or paranoid patients seem calmer and are more easily interviewed when they have access to an exit. Since most interview rooms do not have two doors, seats should be equidistant from the door.

If the patient is an inpatient on a medical unit, privacy may be very difficult to establish. When there is another patient in the room the curtain should be drawn around the bed and the nurse should sit as close to the patient as possible to afford the greatest degree of privacy.

When interviewing a patient on a psychiatric inpatient unit, it is preferable to hold the interview in an established interview room, activity room, or dayroom. This provides a physically and emotionally neutral area for the patient and the nurse in which information can be more freely discussed. Clinicians should be cautious about interviewing members of the opposite sex in their rooms.

Home health interviews should be conducted in the living room or family room without the noise of televisions or radios. Again it is not appropriate to interview patients in the bedroom of their homes.

Interruptions

Interruptions should be avoided at all cost. A psychiatric assessment is demanding of both the nurse and the patient. It requires attention to and concentration on the situation at hand. The interview can be stressful for a patient who is often relating sensitive information, and interruptions can hinder the therapeutic process and the establishment of trust. The nurse has the responsibility of observing, listening, and concentrating on the patient's verbal and nonverbal behavior.

In addition to external interruptions, it is not uncommon for an inexperienced clinician to interrupt a patient's narrative in order to elicit answers necessary to complete forms. While certain information is essential to obtain, it is more important to allow the patient freedom of expression and to carefully absorb what the patient is relating. Through experience the nurse will become less anxious and better adept at eliciting the necessary demographic information in more subtle ways. Being familiar with conducting interviews, learning to gather factual information through mental status examination questions, and relating questions to topics as they arise are a few ways that nurses improve their proficiency in gathering information.

The interviewer

The use of self is the principal tool the nurse brings to the psychiatric interview. All past experiences, values, attitudes, and feelings influence the nurse's reaction to patients. It is the interviewer who sets the stage, defines the limits of the relationship, and structures the interview in such a way as to obtain maximum benefit for the patient.

In this respect nurses act as participant observers in the psychiatric interview. They not only assess and carefully observe patients' behavior but also structure and guide the interview through the various stages. In other words, nurses play a vital, active role in the interview process. This does not imply that nurses need to do all of the talking. Activity is demonstrated through verbal as well as nonverbal actions. Through their behavior interviewers make their interest continuously felt.

The manner or attitude the nurse assumes sets the climate of the interview and shapes the attitude of the patient toward the examination. If the nurse is accepting, honest, and interested, the patient will feel more comfortable and respond in an open, trusting way. Any ridicule, hostility, or disinterest on the part of the interviewer must be avoided. The patient will sense this and respond accordingly by becoming distrustful and withholding information.

The interview is not the time for disagreement or arguments. The purpose is to gain an understanding of the patient's feelings and current level of psychological functioning, not to debate ideas or thoughts. Some patients may attempt to engage the nurse in controversial discussions. The best response would be to point out how the focus of the interview has changed, restate the purpose of the interview, and redirect the line of questioning.

Previous attitudes, values, and beliefs influence interactions with patients, colleagues, and significant others. It should be remembered that the nurse's chief responsibility is to help patients make adjustments and decisions that are right for them, not the nurse. Ultimately, it is the patient who makes the final decisions and decides which direction to choose. Nurses can share their perceptions and recommendations in the hope of helping patients examine their frustrations, anxieties, inner fears, and alternatives. Nurses cannot, however, impose their own values upon patients or reprimand them for choosing options with which they do not agree.

The interview is unequivocally confidential. Patients come for help assuming they can trust that what they divulge will remain confidential and not be used against them. Care should be taken to ensure that written documents are not accessible to individuals not involved in the patient's care. Patients should never be discussed outside the clinical agency or in elevators or hallways where others may overhear the conversation. Consent forms should always be signed by patients when it is necessary to discuss their cases with individuals outside the agency.

Context and time

The context and length of the interview will be considered together since they are so intimately related. The length of the interview is very much determined by the context or circumstances surrounding the assessment. Most interviews will last between 30 and 90 minutes. Interviews under 30 minutes may be hurried and missing essential information. There are exceptions, though, when a nurse may need to limit a discussion with a patient to just a few minutes. A floridly psychotic or manic patient will be unable to tolerate more than several minutes of structured conversation at a time.

An interview should rarely exceed 90 minutes. If the essential information has not been elicited in 1½ hours, the nurse should step back and reevaluate the purpose and process of the interview. Sometimes patients with personality disorders can manipulate inexperienced clinicians so that interviews tend to drag on for hours. New problems, concerns, or threats are continually brought up whenever patients do not think they are getting enough attention or think the interview may soon end.

Another instance when the interview may exceed the average time span occurs when the patient is tangential in thinking and continues to ramble incessantly. It is counterproductive for the nurse to foster this illogical thinking. The patient should be gently redirected to a more purposeful mode of thinking.

Interviews may be extended in certain circumstances. Interviews with families often take at least 90 minutes to allow each family member a chance to speak. Depressed patients may also require some additional time if there is retardation of speech or motor activity.

Time is money in our fast-paced culture. People pay particular attention to the time afforded them. It is not only courteous to be prompt for appointments and not keep patients waiting, but also it has a powerful influence on the dynamics of the relationship and on the establishment of respect and trust. Patients may begin to fantasize that they have been forgotten or feel that they are not significant if they are kept waiting too long.

It is important that nurses inform patients at the beginning of the interview the amount of time they have to spend with them. Then it is helpful to remind patients 5 or 10 minutes before the session is over that their time is almost up and to begin to summarize and close the session. This provides a framework that helps decrease any anxiety the patient may have about when and how to stop talking.

As mentioned previously, the context of the assessment influences the length of the interview. Psychiatric interviews take place in a variety of settings. Nurses may be called upon to assess the biopsychosocial functioning of a patient during a community health home visit, in a thoracic intensive care unit, in an emergency department, or on a psychiatric unit. The purpose, setting, chief complaint, and subsequent intervention will be different for each of these assessments. This necessitates a flexible approach and the ability to adapt a certain interview style to particular situations. For example, the admission interview of a patient to a psychiatric unit might include a comprehensive mental status examination whereas the psychiatric assessment of a patient in the rehabilitation unit may focus more on the patient's biosocial areas of functioning. A home visit could possibly be less formal and not require detailed mental status testing, unless a problem is suspected.

It is significant whether a patient seeks help voluntarily or has been brought to a clinic or hospital involuntarily. Patients who are brought for help by disgruntled family members or who have been ordered to get help by the court may not even perceive that they have a problem. There is often a disagreement about the purpose or goal of the interview among the interviewer, the court, the family, and the patient.

If the patient is psychotic or there involuntarily, it is best to provide more structure to the interview by clearly stating the purpose of the examination, setting limits on what is talked about and for how long, and carefully guiding the patient through the steps of the interview and the mental status examination.

Note taking

No discussion of interviewing would be complete without some mention of the controversial issue of note taking. The beginning interviewer is often dismayed to learn that considerable variation of opinion exists over whether one should or should not take notes during the interview.

One philosophy purports that jotting down a few reminders will not impede the process of the session. Another philosophy states that anything but active listening interferes with and blocks all attempts at a therapeutic interaction.

If notes are taken it should be done as unobtrusively as possible and should not be so extensive as to interfere with the free flow of the patient's narrative. Notes should be brief reminders of events, dates, incidents, or answers to mental status examination questions related by the patient that need to be documented in the record. For example, documenting specific thought disorders, miscalculations, or interpretations of proverbs is very helpful when interviewing schizophrenic patients. It is also important to note what is *not* said. The nonverbal or metacommunication is often more revealing of the patient's pathology than what is spoken. For instance, it would be important to remember specific tics or mannerisms or any discrepancy between affect and the spoken word.

It is best for nurses to explain to patients at the onset that they may need to jot down a few notes to help them later recall the information as accurately as possible. If the reason for taking notes is presented in a straightforward fashion there is seldom any disagreement from the patient.

The major time note taking is contraindicated is with a suspicious or paranoid patient. Writing comments or responses can be very threatening for these patients and can seriously impede the conduction of the interview as well as the establishment of trust or rapport.

It is important to be extremely careful with any written material to ensure the patient's privacy and confidentiality. The best rule of thumb for nurses to follow is to never write down anything during the interview that they would not want the patient to see. These notes should either be destroyed or kept where the interviewer alone has access to them after the legal record is completed. They should never be left lying out for others' perusal. If the nurse decides not to take notes during the interview, the data should be recorded immediately after the session has ended to prevent any distortion or forgetting of facts.

STAGES OF THE INTERVIEW

The psychiatric interview is comprised of a series of stages or intervals. While these stages are hypothetical and abstract, they are quite necessary for the achievement and development of the therapeutic relationship and for the achievement of the goal of the interview.

Sullivan describes four stages of the psychiatric interview. These stages are formal inception, reconnaissance, detailed inquiry, and termination.[1]

Inception

The inception includes the greeting, formal introduction, and clarification of the purpose of the interview. Although this may sound quite simple, the manner in which a patient is received can enhance and accelerate the therapeutic process or it can impede things from the beginning so that the goal becomes unattainable. The introduction should be handled with respectful seriousness. It is best to address the patient by last name and continue this unless some agreement is reached about using first names. Nurses should give the impression that they are familiar with or aware of the reason for the interview, establish eye contact, and introduce themselves by name and role, for example: "Good morning Ms. Surso, my name is Lucy Baker. I am a psychiatric nurse and Dr. Greyson asked me to speak with you about some concerns you have about your hospitalization."

Inception is also the time to establish a contract with the patient about the purpose of the relationship and to determine the expected length of time it will take to accomplish mutual goals, for example: "Hello, Ms. Goldman, I am Mr. Pesut, a registered nurse on this unit. I will be your primary nurse, which means that I am the person responsible for your nursing care throughout your hospitalization. We will be meeting regularly throughout your stay here to discuss how things are going for you. At this time I would like to ask you a few questions to get to know you better and also give you an opportunity to ask me questions about any expectations or concerns you may have about your hospitalization. Perhaps we could begin by you telling me why you think you were admitted to the hospital."

A brief, yet straightforward, introduction allows patients to begin with some description of why they are here and what they think will happen. Throughout this stage nurses should be aware of how their behavior influences or affects the patient. Likewise nurses should pay particular attention to the immediate impression they obtain from the initial behavior, movements, voice, and mannerisms of the patient and how these in turn influence the patient's behavior. The therapeutic relationship is a cyclical process with each individual influencing the others' behavior. Thus one needs to develop an immense amount of alertness to the work at hand—a sort of watchful clarity as to what happens.[1] Inception ends with the patients disclosing why they are here and with the interviewer and patient both understanding the nature of the presenting problem.

Reconnaissance

The second stage Sullivan describes, reconnaissance, begins with the interviewer obtaining a rough biopsychosocial sketch of the patient. During this stage it is the responsibility of the nurse to make sure that the patient is presenting information that is relevant to the problem at hand. If the patient gets sidetracked or starts describing irrelevant data, the nurse should gently redirect the patient's thinking. Anxious or confused patients have no idea what information is needed and will appreciate some structure at this point.

Areas of information obtained during this stage include education, health, family, and occupational history. This second stage is a time for picking up initial clues that can be useful in envisioning the individual's personality and life-style. At the end of this stage the nurse will have assimilated a great deal of verbal as well as nonverbal behavior that characterizes the patient as a unique person. For example, nurses should take note of the ease with which patients relate the information, their ability to concentrate on the task at hand, their sensitivity to the material, and their overall attitude and behavior. The sum of the information obtained about different aspects of the patient's life gives a more complete picture of the individual as a holistic being.

Detailed inquiry

During the initial stages of the interview the nurse gathers demographic data, observes behavior, and forms basic impressions. The detailed inquiry, or third stage of the interview, is a time to improve and refine those initial impressions. Patients may have misrepresented themselves, consciously or unconsciously, as a result of anxiety, denial, or trying to please the interviewer. The nurse now has the opportunity to eliminate any misconceptions, probe more deeply into critical areas, and refine initial impressions.

By this stage a therapeutic relationship should have been formed and patients should be starting to consider unresolved conflicts, relating a developmental history and beginning to establish new and healthier modes of behavior. In one-time only interviews this stage rarely occurs. Instead, the process moves through a modified version of a combination of reconnaissance and detailed inquiry. There is rarely any working through of conflicts or probing into critical issues during initial assessments. One-time only interviews focus more on information gathering than on clarifying and refining. Detailed inquiry occurs more in the realm of the psychotherapy experience, which involves an established therapeutic relationship.

Reconnaissance and detailed inquiry parallel Murray and Zenter's first and second levels of assessment. First level assessment is performed on initial contact to determine immediate needs and second level assessment occurs over longer periods of time, during which the consideration of a patient's needs is expanded.[2]

Termination

Termination or the closure of the interview is the fourth and final stage. This can be the most difficult and awkward stage for both the patient and the nurse and it is frequently either overlooked or hurried through. It is sometimes easier to avoid termination altogether than to experience the sad and sometimes confusing feelings that accompany leave taking. It is essential that nurses provide the opportunity for termination with their patients. Just as the introduction is very important in setting the climate of the relationship, the last few minutes of the interview can either tie together and solidify what has transpired or do a great deal of damage by leaving the interaction in confusing disarray. The depth or time spent on leave taking will depend on the length of the relationship. If the interview was a 1-hour evaluative meeting, a short summary and recommendation may suffice. On the other hand, if a nurse has been meeting with the patient over a span of several months, a more thorough process of termination will need to be done.

Sullivan describes consolidating the interview in the following four steps: (1) the interviewer makes a final statement to the patient summarizing what was learned during the course of the interview; (2) the interviewer gives the patient a prescription for action in which the patient is now ready to engage; (3) the interviewer makes a final assessment of the probable effects on the life-course of the patient, which can reasonably be expected from the statement and prescription; and (4) there is a formal leave-taking between the two parties.[1]

Another step may be added that allows the patient to offer impressions, describe the benefits, frustrations, and/or accomplishments, and to share any feelings related to ending the relationship.

Termination should not be a time to rehash old material, bring up new material, or become an exhausting turmoil of saying goodbye. The nurse structures this stage carefully and thoughtfully so that it is accomplished in a clear-cut, respectful manner.

CASE EXAMPLE: Ms. Mayne, RN, and Ms. Shapiro have contracted to meet $\frac{1}{2}$ hour every other day to discuss issues and concerns that Ms. Shapiro may have while she is in the hospital. They have met on two occasions and both times Ms. Shapiro brought up an important issue with only several minutes left in the session. What should Ms. Mayne do?

One possibility would be for the nurse to point out exactly what has happened: "You have brought up an important aspect of your treatment just prior to the end of the interview. I am curious about this and thought perhaps you could share your thoughts with me about why this happened."

The nurse may also point out that it is difficult and sometimes painful to bring up the issues that are the most troublesome. Ms. Mayne could also encourage Ms. Shapiro to share her concerns early in the session so there is adequate time for reflection and consideration. If she continues to bring up new issues at the end of the session it would be best to respond with, "I agree that is important, but our time is up. Let's discuss that issue on Tuesday."

THE PSYCHIATRIC ASSESSMENT INTERVIEW

A complete psychiatric assessment consists of two parts, the history and the mental status examination. Together these two parts will reconstruct the patients' behaviors and unravel the stories of their disturbances in light of the information obtained concerning their biological, social, and psychological functioning. The history reveals information about the patient's biological and social spheres and previous psychiatric treatment while the mental status examination provides data about the patient's present psychological condition. The history and mental status examination are not mutually exclusive. These sections may overlap depending on the flow of the content. For purposes of explanation the two parts will be considered separately.

What follows is a schematic representation of the psychiatric interview as it is usually recorded. Examples of certain types of data are included under specific headings, although the nurse need not always proceed according to this format. This data gathering may take place in one interview or over a series of meetings. While the interview itself is conducted in a flexible manner, the recording of the data is best done systematically. The actual interview will flow most easily with the nurse taking cues from the patient rather than following a rigid outline. The following list shows how data collected during the psychiatric interview may be organized*:

1. Identifying information—Name, sex, age, race, marital status, occupation
2. Presenting problem—Brief statement of problem or request from patient or third party

---

*Adapted from Callahan, J. Emergency services case narrative outlined. Unpublished manuscript, Ann Arbor, 1983.

3. Brief recent history—Brief recent history in chronological order beginning a few days to a few weeks ago and ending with the precipitating event
4. Family history—Investigation of the family constellation and any relevant genetic, familial, economic, or social forces
5. Personal history—Exploration of health history, treatment history, childhood, adolescent and adulthood issues, strengths and support systems, previous coping behaviors, occupation, and education history
6. Current presentation and mental status examination—Appearance and behavior, speech, level of consciousness, mood and affect, thought form, thought content, and cognitive functioning
7. Summary and conclusions
8. Plan and disposition

The psychiatric history

Identifying information. A brief initial description of patients' status can usually be obtained from a questionnaire. This includes name, age, sex, race, marital status, occupation, address, and telephone number.

Presenting problem. After the inception, patients should be asked to describe, in their own words, their chief complaint or presenting problem. It is important to pay particular attention to what may already be known about the patient's condition and the manner in which the patient describes the problem. Many times the interviewer's impression of the presenting problem is quite different than what is described by the patient.

> CASE EXAMPLE: A friend brings her roommate, Mary, to the psychiatric emergency room and complains that Mary has been staying up all night, playing the stereo very loudly, spending money she does not have, not attending classes, and wandering around alone at night. Mary begins the interview by screaming that her only problem is her roommate who needs to be committed. She has found peace and love through meditation and only needs freedom to pursue her personal goals.

The patient's chief complaint is unrealistic and untrue. Mary's presentation indicates that she is experiencing a disorder of mood and cognition and the problem is indeed hers and not her roommate's.

The nurse also needs to be aware that although the patient's presenting problem may sound realistic there may also be a hidden agenda in seeking treatment. Individuals with certain personality disorders often appear at mental health clinics and emergency departments complaining of suicidal thoughts or feelings of losing control, and the real problem later turns out to be the need for housing.

Sometimes patients are too shy, uncomfortable, or embarrassed to relate "the real problem" at the onset. A woman may come to the medical walk-in clinic with the chief complaint of anxiety, stomach upset, and trouble sleeping. Through careful and sensitive probing the nurse learns that the real problem is domestic violence and can then proceed with gathering further data upon which to formulate an appropriate treatment plan.

Brief recent history. Questioning should elicit an account of the development of the presenting problem over the past several days or weeks: "How long have you had these thoughts of wanting to hurt yourself?" "What helped you decide to finally seek treatment?" "What difficulties led to your being admitted to the hospital?" This account should include a description of current symptoms and whether these changes have occurred suddenly or insidiously. The nurse should determine when the symptoms were first noticed, their severity, and whether they are persistent or episodic. It is important to obtain a clear description of all symptoms and areas of social functioning that are affected: school, work, church, community, hobbies, sexual activity. What has changed in relation to patients' social spheres? Has anything in particular changed at work, with significant others, in the way they spend leisure time? Have patients been isolating themselves or have they been increasing their contacts and activities? This line of questioning will illuminate any changes in patients' social lives that may be contributing to or the result of the present problems. The current social history provides clues as to how individuals are coping with activities of daily living. Is the 30-year-old housewife able to care for her three children? Has the 48-year-old executive been able to concentrate on his work and manage his responsibilities? Has the 20-year-old student been able to attend class and concentrate on his studies?

In addition to problems in social functioning, support systems and current strengths should be ascertained. When planning an intervention the nurse will want to foster and encourage continuance of any strengths the patient may have. For example, the patient's thinking may be confused, but there may be concerned friends who are willing to be responsible for this patient until medication begins to work or a bed becomes available on the psychiatric unit.

Accounts of the present disturbance must also include the biological functioning of the patient. A health history is extremely important in clarifying the cause of the problem. In-depth questioning should be conducted regarding sleeping and eating patterns, current physical problems, activity level, past medical history, accidents, injuries, and current medications. Questions concerning drug and/or alcohol use are essential in making differential diagnoses. Patients should also be asked about caffeine intake and cigarette smoking. If a patient's chief complaint is anxiety, sleep disturbance, and restlessness, questions about coffee and cola intake may reveal some interesting facts. For instance, if a patient complains of depression and admits to drinking five or six beers a day in addition to taking 10 mg of diazepam (Valium) to get to sleep, it will be impossible to make a definitive diagnosis of depression in view of the chemical involvement. Since different medications can precipitate depressive symptoms, psychosis, and anxiety, exploration about the use of current medications is paramount.

Patients with emotional problems frequently have somatic complaints. It is imperative to rule out organic causes of these complaints. Questioning about headaches, dizziness, palpitations, changes in bowel habits, and sensory alterations should not be glossed over. Careful and detailed inquiry about the patient's current and past health history will assist the nurse in formulating a safe and responsible plan of care.

Family history. The family history reveals important information about the genetic, familial, economic, and social forces that have contributed to the patient's development. An account of the family structure (parents, siblings) will provide cues about issues to be further explored: "Are you close to your family?" "Tell me about your brother's illness." "You mentioned your mother died a few years ago. Tell me what that was like for you." Information generated from this type of questioning will reveal facts about family customs, child-rearing practices, and current support systems. It is important to note the patient's reaction when disclosing family information. How does the patient describe significant events; for example, the parents' divorce, a father's suicide, a sister's graduation from high school? Is there a note of jealousy, hostility, or unresolved grief?

Specific information about the physical and emotional health of relatives should be collected. Is there a family history of substance abuse, alcoholism, suicide, psychiatric hospitalization, or delinquency?

A family history will reveal both environmental and hereditary influences of the patient's emotional problem. There remains today considerable controversy surrounding the impact of environmental and biochemical factors on one's emotional health. In the last decade advanced scientific research has continued to uncover genetic links to certain disorders such as schizophrenia and affective disorders. It is also a fact that much of our behavior is learned and influenced by the family milieu. Therefore both environmental and hereditary factors influence the way in which individuals mature and respond to life experiences. Information about any physical problems of relatives such as diabetes or thyroid disorders may provide clues that will require further investigation to rule out an organic base to the patient's problem.

If the patient is unable to answer questions about physical, social, or family issues, adjunctive interviews with family or friends should be conducted with the patient's permission. Also, if the patient appears to be an unreliable historian, the data should be validated through interviews with significant others.

> CASE EXAMPLE: Mr. Chambers is a 35-year-old male who comes to the mental health clinic complaining of depression. Family history reveals his grandfather had several episodes of depression and subsequently took his own life. His father was an alcoholic who also experienced several episodes of depression throughout his life. Mr. Chambers has lost 10 lb in the past 2 months and reports difficulty falling asleep as well as early morning awakening.

Personal history. After a problem has been clarified and the patient's immediate needs have been met, it is time to begin a more in-depth review of the personal history or maturational process of the patient. This will provide insight into the origin and evolution of the psychiatric disorder. The purpose of the personal history is to obtain a concise picture and historical perspective of the patient's developmental process. The nature of the illness and the meaning of the symptoms will be further understood by securing maximum knowledge of the patient's personality development and the forces that determined it. This includes exploration of events that occurred during childhood, adolescence, and adulthood.

Significant forces to consider during childhood include early childhood memories and dreams, completion of developmental tasks, early issues or conflicts, adaptive and maladaptive behavior patterns, the quality of interpersonal relationships, separation from family, and early expressions of anger and aggression. Any developmental disabilities or physical impairments should be explored. School experiences provide clues to early socialization patterns and intellectual growth. Usual childhood illnesses and injuries are also noted.

Many early symptoms of psychiatric illness first appear during adolescence. Therefore it is necessary to examine the major issues of the patient's adolescent period. Areas of conflict center around issues of peer relationships, sexuality, intimacy, autonomy, independence, physical change, identity, and self-esteem. The patient may be asked, "How was it being a teenager?" Responses may indicate early problematic behavior patterns such as difficulty with peers, inability to achieve intimacy in a relationship, confusion over sexual issues, inability to achieve independence, or lack of self-esteem.

Adulthood issues to explore include establishment of vocation and family relationships. These adulthood issues have been identified in other sections of the psychiatric assessment interview. In addition, an assessment of the patients' ego functioning must not be overlooked. A careful inquiry regarding patients' abilities to cope with internal and external demands will reveal important personality traits. How do patients cope with stress? Are they able to control impulses? Do they demonstrate good judgment? Do they have a solid sense of their own identities? King describes five areas of ego functioning and their related disturbances that are significant to explore.[3] These are (1) relationship to reality, (2) the ability to regulate drives, (3) relationships to other, (4) thought processes, and (5) defensive functions.

Thoughtful, careful exploration of the patient's personal history will help identify the needs, feelings, and motivations manifested in the current symptoms. In reviewing the personal history of any patient, the nurse should pay attention to areas of strength as well as areas of difficulty. Adaptive coping strategies, talents, accomplishments, insights, and support systems are noted.

> CASE EXAMPLE: Mr. Schwebel related several incidents that occurred during his adolescence that still bother him at times. When he was 16 his father was killed in a motor vehicle accident. He had to quit the football team to get a part-time job. He was the oldest male child and he remembers feeling a great deal of responsibility for taking care of his mother and siblings. To this day, he reports that when his mother needs something done around her house she calls Mr. Schwebel, even though he has two strong healthy brothers who could also do the work.
>
> He also reports having had a homosexual experience with an older man when he was 17. He felt confused about the incident at the time and has never before talked about it with anyone. It was soon after this experience that he had his first sexual experience with a teenage girl. He found this quite satisfying but was hurt and angry when the girl rejected him several weeks later. He remembers thinking he must have done something wrong.

The mental status examination

The second part of the psychiatric interview is an assessment of the patient's current mental status. Whereas the first part of the interview reveals a more historical perspective of the social, biological, and psychological factors throughout the patient's life, the mental status examination provides more specific, accurate information about current behavior and mental capabilities. The mental status examination elicits evidence of dysfunction and aids in detecting and identifying etiological factors of psychopathology.

How much of the complete mental status examination is administered and at what point in the relationship with the patient this is done will vary with each individual. In many instances much of the information elaborated below will be elucidated by taking the patient's history. If there is no obvious or serious pathology noted during taking the history no further formal questioning may be necessary. On the other hand, if there are suspicions of organicity or impaired thinking, a more detailed inquiry into certain areas is essential.

A patient may be too ill, physically or emotionally, to be subjected to a prolonged examination of mental functioning. Here again, a great deal of pertinent data can be collected through the history and more thorough questioning can be postponed until the patient is physically and emotionally stronger.

Much of the success and validity of the mental status examination depends on the manner in which the examiner approaches the patient. Care should be taken to alleviate as much of the patient's anxiety as possible. The interviewer needs to present what may seem to the patient to be strange and sometimes silly questions in the same straightforward, decisive way as the rest of the interview.

No matter how scattered are the sources from which the information has been gathered, the data should be recorded in some organized manner. For clarity, the mental status examination should be conducted and recorded in a systematic fashion according to the following categories: general observations and behavior, speech, level of consciousness, emotional state, thought process or form, thought content, and cognitive functioning.

General observations and behavior. The nurse should observe and be astute to all aspects of the patient's behavior. Overall impressions should include a description of physical appearance, dress, grooming, expression, eye contact, motor behavior, posture, gait, and general health.

The nurse should note how the patient enters the room. Are there obvious signs of anxiety or peculiarities in appearance? The patient's appearance should be described in terms of appropriateness to age, sex, climate, and situation. Is the patient neat and clean or unkempt and disheveled? Does the patient appear sad, joyful, or exhibit no expression? Does the patient look directly at the interviewer, around the room, or at the floor? The patient's motor activity may be normal, agitated, or retarded. Is the patient tense, rigid, restless, calm, or relaxed? Are there specific mannerisms such as tics, repetitive gestures, or tremors?

The patient's general health is described in terms of weight, coloring, skin, body build, and obvious physical impairments. Any discrepancy between patients' subjective statements regarding their states of health and the nurse's observations should be noted. People's posture and gait are often indicative of their physical and emotional states. A slumped posture may indicate depression, fatigue, or suspiciousness. An uneven or unsteady gait suggests physical abnormalities or the influence of drugs or alcohol.

A general description of the patient's relatedness is helpful in formulating impressions. Has the patient been cooperative, friendly, mistrustful, embarrassed, hostile, or suspicious in response to the interviewer? Is the general demeanor unremarkable or has the patient been overly revealing or openly defiant?

Likewise, it is helpful at this point if nurses can be aware of their own reactions to patients. The nurse's feelings can provide important information helpful in formulating an impression. Whereas an interviewer may respond with a genuine feeling of sadness and concern for a depressed patient the same interviewer may feel perplexed or angry with a patient with a personality disorder. Angry and hostile patients tend to generate angry and hostile feelings in the interviewer. Whenever a patient generates strong feelings of any kind, the interviewer should attempt to understand their significance.

> CASE EXAMPLE: Ms. Sherry is a 21-year-old female who is casually dressed in jeans and a tee shirt and is neatly groomed. She is slightly overweight with badly blemished skin, but she appears generally healthy. She sat calmly throughout the interview and responded appropriately to questioning, occasionally volunteering information spontaneously and maintaining eye contact. She noticeably began to fidget with her hands when the conversations shifted to the recent death of her mother.

Speech. The quality and quantity of speech can be observed while taking the history. The patient's speech may be unusually fast or slow. Are there any sudden interruptions in the flow of speech? Is the volume of the patient's voice loud or barely audible? Intonation and modulation may be intact or altered. Is there free verbalization, monosyllabic responses, or pressured speech? Is the speech clear or slurred? Is there a noticeable defect? If the patient communicates only with gestures it will be necessary to determine whether the lack of verbalization is an isolated event or merely one aspect of an overall pattern of diminished responsiveness.[4]

Level of consciousness. The nurse should note the patient's sensorium, alertness, and general responsiveness to the environment. Is the patient alert, drowsy, confused, or nonresponsive? Can the patient respond appropriately to questions and follow simple instructions? One method utilized to assess patients' abilities to perform tasks on command is to ask them to touch their noses with a specific finger. States of impairment range from confusion to stupor or unconsciousness. Alterations in consciousness are most frequently caused by organic disturbances that are neurologically, medically, surgically, or drug related. The patient should be referred for a more complete medical examination if alterations in consciousness are detected.

Emotional state. Mood and affect are two emotional states that require assessment. Mood is the feeling a patient experiences. It is determined by a subjective report from the patient. Certain questions can elicit this report of feelings. The questions should be open-ended such as "Tell me how you are feeling" rather than leading as in "Are you feeling depressed?" The patient may express feelings spontaneously or in response to particular questions. Terms commonly used to describe mood are depressed, euphoric, anxious, sad, calm, frightened, angry, or apathetic.

Affect is the emotional display exhibited by the patient. It is observed from the patient's behavior during the interview and can therefore be considered objective data. Affect is described in terms of intensity, appropriateness, lability, and range of emotions. Terms used to describe affect include manic, grandiose, agitated, and flat.

Fluctuations of mood and affect are explored and noted. Are there diurnal or cyclic variations of mood? What part of the day is best or most difficult? Does the affect fluctuate during the interview? Fluctuations of the patient's emotional state can be indicative of psychiatric disorders such as affective illness and schizophrenia.

> CASE EXAMPLE: The patient reported that she was "wonderfully happy" although her affect was flat throughout the interview. Mrs. Ganey continued to insist she felt wonderful while recounting her sister's recent death and her recent loss of a large amount of money.

Thought process—form. It is necessary at this point to repeat that these categories are artificial divisions formulated for the systematic organization of the data collected during the psychiatric interview. Much of the material being described in the mental status examination section will have emerged during the history from either the patient or a significant other. This is particularly true when assessing disorders in a patient's thinking. Special attention is given to the manner in which the patients communicate their thoughts.

Disconnections or disorganization can occur in the patient's stream of mental activity. Schizophrenic patients often have impaired thought processes. In fact, Bleuler regarded disturbances in association as one of the fundamental symptoms of the disease.[4]

Assessing any disorder in thought processes requires the interviewer to be alert to any deviations from rational, logical, organized, coherent thinking. Impairments may be recognized in the productivity and/or associative processes of the patient's thoughts. It is important to notice

TABLE 3:1	Symptomatology involving thought process—form
Symptom	*Definition*
Autistic thinking	Subjective, highly individualized associations that are derived from within the patient
Blocking	Sudden cessation in train of thought or speech
Circumstantiality	Indirect progression of thoughts that contain many tedious and irrelevant details
Confabulation	Unconscious filling in of memory gaps with imagined or fantasized experiences that the patient believes
Flight of ideas	Rapid verbal skipping from one idea to the next but related to preceding content
Fragmentation	Disrupted thoughts that do not result in a complete idea
Loose associations	Thinking that is diffuse and vague with only tenuous connection between contiguous thoughts
Neologism	Coinage of new words not understood by others
Perseveration	Involuntary repetition of the same verbal or motor response
Tangentiality	Digressions in thought unrelated to preceding thought or idea
Word salad	Mixture of words and phrases that lack apparent meaning

the flow of the patient's statements, the relevance and logical progression of thoughts, and the abundance or paucity of ideas. Is the patient's narrative easy to follow or is it tangential, circumstantial, or evasive? Is there a cause-effect relationship between associations? Would the patient ramble on if unchecked? Are words used in their proper context? Does the patient begin to speak and then stop and lose track of the subject?

Problems in association indicate the intrusion of primary process thinking in which there is the use of symbolism and difficulty maintaining a logical thought sequence.[5] A list of common symptoms of dissociation is given in Table 3:1.

CASE EXAMPLE: Peter's story was presented in a loose and tangential manner. He jumped from talking about his grandfather, to Vietnam, to the nuclear power plant by his home. Thought blocking was occasionally noted and his thoughts were irrelevant and often incoherent.

Thought content—theme. During the psychiatric interview, the patient should be encouraged to talk freely and to recount, in detail, the steps that led to his seeking help. It is preferable to allow the patient to give an account of the problem without interruption. Not only can the patient's thought process be assessed, but the nurse is also able to determine the trends or themes of the patient's thinking. The central themes revealed in the patient's thought content are often the presenting problem.

According to psychoanalytic theory, thought content disturbances are the result of major distortions in ego functioning. The ego is the central part of the personality that maintains the individual's contact with reality. It modifies the impulses of the id within the limits imposed by the demands of the environment. Occasionally, these primitive instinctual drives will surface and people find themselves less bound by the conventions of the real world. Defense mechanisms are activated by the patient to ward off these unconscious, unacceptable impulses aroused by conflict situations.

These inner forces originate from the ego and distort perceptions of the external environment in an attempt to minimize the patient's discomfort. The patient begins to rely on mechanisms such as regression, repression, and projection to handle anxiety, anger, or any feeling that seems unmanageable. Unacceptable or ego alien aggressive impulses are turned outward, usually through projection. These unacceptable impulses become evidenced as distorted thoughts and perceptions. The function of the disturbance is usually a protective one in helping the individual cope with feelings that seem overwhelming.

Many psychiatric clinicians no longer adhere solely to the psychoanalytic theory of thought and perceptual disturbances. Causative factors such as biochemical imbalance and learned behavior patterns are being investigated. It is more likely a combination of these factors rather than one specific one that contributes to disturbed thinking.

Disturbances in thought content are manifested in somatic, ritualistic, destructive, or defensive thinking. Somatic themes focus on real or imagined physical symptoms (Table 3:2). Physical symptoms that can actually be observed or hypochondriacal complaints not readily apparent may preoccupy the patient's thoughts. Patients might also experience somatic delusions in which they falsely believe they have physical problems such as the inability to swallow, alterations in the size of body organs, or a corroded digestive system. Somatic complaints such as diarrhea, constipation, headache, weight loss, backache, and sleep disturbance often herald a psychiatric disorder such as depression or anxiety. The severity, location, and type of somatic symptoms the patient is experiencing can provide clues as to the nature of the psychiatric problem. Nurses should listen seriously to the somatic complaints of patients to determine their meaning and cause. Physical complaints need

TABLE 3:2	Symptomatology involving somatic themes
Symptom	*Definition*
Conversion	Intrapsychic conflict converted and expressed in a symbolic somatic symptom
Hypochondriasis	Preoccupation with body symptoms and state of health
Somatization	Physiological complaints (other than conversion symptoms) related to emotional rather than physiological causes
Somatic delusion	A false fixed belief about one's state of health or bodily functions

to be medically investigated to rule out physiological problems that require intervention.

CASE EXAMPLE: A 40-year-old man comes to the medical emergency room complaining of pain in his left arm. Thorough medical evaluation rules out any physical cause of the pain. The mental health nurse discovers during interviewing the patient that the man's father had died 10 years ago this month of a myocardial infarction. The nurse suspects the development of a somatic symptom that mimics his father's pain. Further exploration reveals that the patient is experiencing unresolved grief over his father's death and intervention is planned accordingly.

Ritualistic thought content themes are portrayed through repetitive thinking and behavior (Table 3:3). The patient may describe, or the interviewer might observe, persistent thoughts or acts the patient is unable to control. Repetitive speculation about a topic may interfere with the patient's ability to focus on alternate issues. Phobias, in which the patient describes an irrational fear of an object or situation, may be apparent. Ritualistic themes are evident as secondary symptoms in schizophrenia, affective disorders, and anxiety states.

CASE EXAMPLE: A 36-year-old woman, Ms. Meyers, arrives at the outpatient clinic for a psychiatric assessment requested by her husband. Ms. Meyers enters the room and places two chairs between herself and the nurse. Six times during the interview, Ms. Meyers gets up to straighten out wrinkles in the drapes. She states that she is always checking the stove at home for fear that it has been left on. Throughout the interview, the nurse notes that Ms. Meyers describes constantly checking on everything she has done, including locking the front door, turning off the faucets, unplugging the toaster, and regulating the thermostat.

TABLE 3:3	Symptomatology involving ritualistic themes
Symptom	*Definition*
Compulsion	A repetitive act the patient feels driven to do
Obsession	A persistent thought that the patient is unable to control
Phobia	An irrational, unrealistic fear of objects or situations
Rumination	Repetitive speculation, often circular in nature, that interferes with rational thinking; excessive worrying

TABLE 3:4	Symptomatology involving destructive thinking
Symptom	*Definition*
Homicidal ideation	Thoughts of doing bodily harm to others
Nihilism	Complete destruction
Suicidal ideation	Thoughts of doing bodily harm to self

Destructive thought content themes describe violence, suicide, and homicide (Table 3:4). The patient can be preoccupied with thoughts of violence and destruction and may describe these thoughts with violent imagery. The patient may not recognize the gruesome and destructive nature of his thoughts. The interviewer can comment that the patient sounds angry. This observation often enables the patient to share feelings masked by the violent themes.

Whenever suicidal or homicidal ideation is suspected, the patient should be asked directly about his intentions. The patient is usually relieved that someone has questioned his thoughts because this provides an opportunity to discuss frightening feelings. Any type of violent thought content should be documented by the nurse in the record.

CASE EXAMPLE: Throughout the interview, Mr. Manning describes his life utilizing violent terminology. "My wife stabbed me in the back by telling my employer about my previous job problem. She likes to twist the knife deeper and deeper until my flesh looks like raw hamburger. Life with her isn't worth living." The nurse asks Mr. Manning if he has considered hurting himself. He replies, "Well, sometimes I'd like to run my car off a cliff and crash so that the metal pierces through my body."

TABLE 3:5   Symptomatology involving defensive thinking

Symptom	Definition
Alienation	Viewing one's self as being an outsider
Delusion	Fixed false belief that cannot be changed by an appeal to reason
Depersonalization	Feeling different or strange, loss of sense of identity
Derealization	Feeling that events are unreal or dreamlike; shapes, colors, and objects may appear distorted
Doubting and indecision	Excessive time-consuming uncertainties, ambivalence
Grandiosity	Feeling unrealistically important or overappraising one's ability
Ideas of influence	Thoughts of being controlled or influenced by outside forces
Ideas of reference	Incorrect interpretation of incidents or events as having direct meaning to one's self
Paranoia	Extreme suspiciousness and delusions of persecution; belief of being singled out for unfair treatment
Thought broadcasting	Thoughts transmitted between objects or persons

Defensive thinking is depicted by a variety of symptoms (Table 3:5). These symptoms are behaviors acquired in response to anxiety. The function of defensive thinking is to withdraw from normal communication patterns and to interpret the external world from a more psychologically safe perspective. Defensive thought content may be exhibited overtly or in a more subtle manner by occasional slips or vague clues. The nurse should be alert for persecutory or suspicious thinking, religious references or delusions, thoughts of grandeur and importance, excessive ambivalence, feelings of unreality, or ideas of thought transmission.

The nurse will become aware of defensive thoughts throughout the psychiatric interview by observation and careful questioning. Patients should be questioned about their ideas and how these thoughts affect their lives. However, when it becomes obvious that defensive thinking is impairing a patient's life-style and interactions, questioning should be stopped to avoid reinforcing the patient's illogical thinking.

Defensive thought patterns are often evident in schizophrenia, affective disorders, and organic illness.

CASE EXAMPLE: Mr. Bardwick is admitted to the psychiatric inpatient unit. He describes himself as the "the savior of mankind." Mr. Bardwick is convinced FBI agents are hiding in his attic at home, watching all his movements. He believes the world is about to explode because of FBI arrangements and only he can save it. He states he knows this because the television is sending him thought waves.

Perception is the awareness individuals have of their surroundings (Table 3:6). This awareness originates from different sensory modalities: visual, auditory, olfactory, kinesthetic, and gustatory. Many times patients will experience distortions in one or several sensory modes. These distortions usually take the form of hallucinations and illusions.

The cause of these distortions can be functional or organic. There is a large range of toxic metabolic stressors that can elicit misperceptions as part of their action on the brain. Drugs, alcohol, allergic reactions, metabolic disturbances, and seizures can all produce perceptual distortions. While these organic causes produce the form of the perceptual distortion, the content of the misperception is shaped by the psychological forces that operate within each individual. For instance, toxicity tends to produce visual hallucinations, but the content of the hallucinations is based on all prior experiences and behaviors of the individual. Therefore, although certain perceptual disturbances are more prevalent with certain causative factors (for example, illusions with delirium), each mental dysfunction may be associated with more than one causal factor.

Occasionally, hallucinatory and illusional material may be described

TABLE 3:6	Symptomatology involving perceptions
Symptom	*Definition*
Déjà-vu	Sensation of having experienced current feelings before
Hallucinations	Subjective sensory perceptions that can occur in any sensory modality; a false sensory impression that takes place in the absence of external stimuli (specify type and content)
Hypnagogic	Disorders of perception occurring immediately preceding sleep
Hypnopompic	Disorders of perception occurring immediately after awakening
Illusion	Misinterpretation of a real sensory experience
Jamais-vu	Sensation of looking at a familiar sight or experience and finding it foreign or strange

spontaneously by the patient. He may be frightened by a visual or auditory stimulus and share his concerns and thoughts freely. Most of the time the presence of a perceptual disturbance is uncovered by observation and careful questioning. The patient may be observed to be mumbling, gesticulating, or listening and responding to voices not apparent to the nurse. It is important to be tactful and subtle in eliciting information from the patient if there is a suspicion of hallucinatory or illusionary experiences. Questions such as "Have you experienced any strange happenings recently?" or "Have you had any peculiar thoughts?" may be more helpful than direct inquiry about hearing voices or seeing things. On the other hand, if the nurse has observed behavior indicative or hallucinations or illusions, a direct question such as, "Have you been seeing or hearing things other people do not?" may enable the patient to share his experiences.

If there is evidence of perceptual disturbances, the patient should be questioned further about the content and nature of the experiences. Are voices coming from inside or outside the patient's head? What are the voices saying? What exactly is the patient seeing or smelling? Are misinterpretations of shadows or noises more profound at different times of the day? This information is useful in formulating a differential diagnosis and assessing the severity of the disorder.

> CASE EXAMPLE: Mr. Maher is brought to the psychiatric emergency services department by his brother after he told him he heard their father (deceased for 10 years) tell him he was a bad person and not worthy to live on this earth. The brother states Mr. Maher was responding to his father's voice in the car on the way to the hospital. The voice was telling him to jump out of the car and the brother reports Mr. Maher actually tried to do that.

Cognitive functioning. It is at this point in the interview that more formal testing can occur for patients with obvious or suspected impairments of cognition. Not all patients will require this in-depth or extensive line of questioning. It proves most useful in distinguishing between a functional and organic base of psychosis. For instance, a patient comes to a mental health center after the sudden death of her father and presents her story in a clear, concise, and orderly manner. She should not be subjected to serial sevens or proverb interpretation unless there is some question about her attention and concentration span and capacity for abstract reasoning. On the other hand, a patient may exhibit bizarre behavior and disorganized thinking that requires formal testing. If the results of formal cognitive testing lead to insufficient, confusing, or equivocal data, the patient should be referred for more sophisticated psychological or medical testing.

Orientation, memory, and judgment can be elicited informally while taking the patient's history. If it becomes necessary to pursue a more detailed line of questioning, the purpose of the questions should be explained to the patient, especially the ones that involve calculations. One purpose may be to assess concentration, memory, abstract reasoning, orientation, insight, judgment, or general intelligence. Another purpose is to establish a baseline upon which to evaluate progress and recovery.

It is important to proceed slowly with questions for patients with suspected cognitive deficits. The nurse should take into consideration the patient's age, cultural background, and educational preparation. An 18-year-old may not be able to recall more than two or three of the past presidents and a high school dropout may not do well with digit manipulations. The interviewer should begin with the simple questions and calculations and then proceed with the more difficult tasks.

As a rule, patients should not be given the "correct" answers to mental status examination questions. This could interfere with performance on any subsequent examinations. Chronic schizophrenic patients, for example, often become "test wise" after years of repetitious questioning and will make valiant efforts at providing correct answers. Proverbs and arithmetic functions can be manipulated slightly to check for "test wise" patients. The nurse might ask patients to count forward by sevens rather than backward.

The following subsections are given as a guide for organizing areas of cognition that may require investigation: orientation, attention, concentration, memory, general intelligence, abstract reasoning, judgment and insight, and perception and coordination.

ORIENTATION. Orientation is defined as the ability to recognize one's surroundings. It is also the ability to recognize temporal and spatial relationships to oneself or to appreciate one's relations to the social environment.[4] Disturbances of orientation can occur with time, place, person, or situation. A variety of questions can be asked to determine a patient's general level of orientation.

TIME. Can patients place themselves in time? Do they know the day, month, and year? Frequently hospitalized patients lose track of specific days and dates so errors in these categories are not necessarily indicative of organic brain disease or psychiatric illness. Confusion about the year, though, could be of diagnostic significance.

PLACE. Can patients tell the nurse where they are? Do they know they are in a hospital? If patients correctly answer that they are in the hospital and there remains some suspicion about their orientation, nurses should ask them for the name of the hospital and the city in which it is located. This additional probing is often quite revealing of disturbances in orientation that may be missed with only general questioning. Brain-injured or delirious patients are frequently confused about where they are and may mistakenly believe the hospital is a hotel or restaurant. Schizophrenic patients may also be disoriented to place, but this is usually of a delusional nature.

PERSON. Can patients state their complete names? Generally, orientation to person will remain intact even after orientation to time and place is lost.[4] Disorientation to person should be considered a serious symptom of pathology and is usually associated with some form of organicity. Disorganization of ego functioning may cause individuals to mistakenly believe they are someone else. This delusion is usually related to an underlying conflict. For example, an unhappily married woman may give her maiden name in an attempt to deny the marriage.

SITUATION. Do patients know the context of the situation? Can they accurately relate why they are in the hospital or seeking help? The ability or inability of patients to do this is often overlooked by clinicians. If there is any suspicion of disorientation, asking the patient about the nature of the visit provides additional substantiating data for the assessment.

ATTENTION AND CONCENTRATION. There are certain exercises that patients should be asked to perform to determine a general level of attention and concentration. The "digit span" exercise consists of having patients repeat, first forward and then backward, a series of numbers read to them. The nurse begins by reading two or three numbers and then proceeds to a more difficult series of five and six numbers. The digits should be given at a rate of about one per second. An acceptable level of performance for most adults consists of five to eight correct digits forward and four to six correct digits backward. Less than five forward or three backward is indicative of some impairment. Age, educational preparation, and anxiety can influence the performance of this exercise and should be considered if the patient's performance is questionable.

DIGITS FORWARD	DIGITS BACKWARD
6, 3, 2	2, 4
4, 7, 5	6, 9
3, 4, 1, 2	4, 3, 1
6, 7, 1, 5	6, 2, 8
6, 3, 1, 4, 2	6, 4, 7, 2
7, 2, 5, 9, 7	9, 3, 5, 6
5, 2, 9, 5, 7, 1	4, 5, 7, 9, 2
7, 3, 4, 6, 9, 3	6, 7, 5, 3, 1

Serial sevens (or serial threes) is a test of concentration in which patients are asked to subtract sevens (or threes) from 100 in serial fashion, audibly and as fast as they can. Serial subtraction continuously taxes the ability to attend and concentrate and is valuable in detecting slight changes in both. The patient may have difficulty, evidenced by heightened effort, increased length of time of performance, hesitation, numerous errors, asking to start over, or refusing to do the test altogether. The average performance time for serial sevens (or threes) is approximately 90 seconds. Seven or more errors is considered poor and four to seven errors is considered fair. Some patients become proficient at this task by virtue of experience and practice. If the clinician suspects this is the case the patient should be asked to start subtracting seven from 102 or 103 instead of 100.

If patients appear unable to perform this task, they should be asked to perform tasks of lesser difficulty, namely counting forward by sevens or threes, reciting the alphabet, or performing simple arithmetic calculations such as "What is one plus two?" It is important to proceed slowly with these exercises and to move from the simple to the more difficult tasks.

MEMORY. Both recent and remote memory need to be assessed. Recent memory can be checked by asking patients to report events of the last 24 hours or recent news events. Another check would be to give patients the names of three objects or cities and ask them to recall the three objects or cities after approximately 5 or 10 minutes. Was the patient able to recall one, two, or all three objects or cities? Remote memory can be ascertained by asking the patient for telephone numbers, birth dates, grades in school courses, names of former teachers, or past dates of hospitalizations. If there is any suspicion the patient is confabulating, the answers should be validated with a relative or significant other.

When impairment in memory is observed, the nurse should note the attitude of the patient toward the impairment. Are efforts made to cope with or hide any memory deficits? Is the patient oblivious to any mistakes made?

GENERAL INTELLIGENCE. The patient's fund of information and vocabulary are two good indicators for a nonstandardized assessment of intelligence. How well are patients attuned to what is going on in the environment? Can they relate recent news stories? Can they recall the past five presidents? Can they name the five largest cities in the United States? The nurse should look for the patient's ability to present factual information in a comprehensive, meaningful way.

Some questions that may be useful in determining general intellectual level are as follows:

How many days are there in a week?	Seven
Name the four seasons of the year.	Summer, fall, winter, spring
How many ounces in a pound?	Sixteen
Where does the sun set?	West
What is the name of the nation's capital?	Washington, D.C.
Who invented the telephone?	Alexander Graham Bell
What is habeas corpus?	Legal writ to be brought before a court or set free

The questions should become increasingly more difficult. An individual of average intelligence should be able to answer at least 75% of the questions.

The patient's vocabulary is a good indicator of intelligence and can be observed and evaluated throughout the interview. It can also be tested by asking patients to define certain words. Examples are:

Apple	Kind of fruit
Donkey	Domestic animal
Shilling	Form of money
Armory	Place where arms are stored
Microscope	Instrument for magnifying minute objects
Plural	Word form used to denote more than one
Recede	To withdraw or to move back from
Chattel	Movable personal property (slave)

The patient's answers must be interpreted in relation to life experiences and education. An individual with an eighth grade education may not be able to answer the same questions as a college graduate.

Again, the task should move from easy to more complex words. Patients should be expected to give reasonable definitions or meanings of the words. From 50% to 75% of correct definitions would indicate average intellectual ability.

ABSTRACT THINKING. The ability to reason abstractly is sometimes impaired in organic disturbances and in certain psychotic states, particularly schizophrenia. The nurse should be able to assess the patient's capacity to generalize, to find meaning in symbols, and to conceptualize objects and events. Two ways to test for the patient's capacity for abstraction are through the interpretation of proverbs and similarities. The tests are designed to evaluate current reasoning ability, not prior performance.

The use of proverb interpretation is subject to criticism because patients frequently become accustomed to the questions and learn acceptable responses. Other patients may not understand what a proverb is. It is helpful to begin the questioning by explaining that a proverb is a saying and then asking the patient what people generally mean by the following saying. Some proverbs frequently given include:

Don't count your chickens before they are hatched.
(Don't anticipate the outcome before it happens.)

A stitch in time saves nine.
(Prevention is more efficient than repair.)

Don't put all your eggs in one basket.
(Don't rely too exclusively on one resource.)

People who live in glass houses shouldn't throw stones.
(Don't criticize others for what you may do yourself.)

There is no use crying over spilt milk.
(There is nothing to be gained in dwelling on past happenings.)

An adequate interpretation of a proverb is one that conveys the general idea or principle of the saying. Specific examples could be used as well as a broad applicability to people and life. An abstract interpretation of the spilt milk proverb would be "There is no use ruminating about what has already happened." A concrete interpretation of the same proverb might be "Mary spilled her milk and didn't cry over it."

The nurse could also ask the patient to describe in what way certain pairs of objects are alike. Here the nurse is concerned with the patient's ability to see objects and concepts in terms of general classes. Examples of certain similarities are:

Rum and scotch	Alcoholic beverages
Cat and mouse	Animals
Guitar and violin	Stringed musical instruments
Nine and sixty-four	Numbers, perfect squares
Pound and mile	Units of measurement

A correct or abstract interpretation of how a cat and a mouse are alike would be that they are both animals. A concrete and less abstract interpretation would be that they both have four legs. The emphasis is on classifying items according to classes or categories. Again, the nurse needs to consider the patient's experience and educational background when assessing abstract reasoning.

INSIGHT AND JUDGMENT. Insight can usually be determined at the onset of the interview when the patient relates the presenting problem. The clinician should attempt to determine whether patients recognize the significance of the present situation. Do they feel there is any need for treatment? Do they recognize the seriousness of the situation? Frequently, patients with psychological disturbances deny they have any problems and it is family members or friends who recommend treatment. It is this situation that causes the difficult dilemma of attempting to treat patients who do not realize they require treatment. There are degrees of insight. For example, a patient may agree he has a drinking problem but blame it on his wife. Insight is usually described in terms of being good, fair, or poor.

Judgment is defined as the ability to compare and evaluate facts, ideas, and choices, to understand their relationships, and to draw appropriate conclusions.[6] Has the patient acquired an understanding of common modes of behavior, social mores, and conventions? Defects in judgment usually become apparent while the patient is relating current and past history. How has this patient been handling interpersonal, occupational, and economic activities?

There are specific questions that can be asked to objectively test the patient's judgment. Patients should be asked to predict what would happen or what they would do in imaginary situations. For example, two frequently asked judgment questions are "What would you do if you found a stamped, addressed, sealed letter on the street?" "What would you do if you smelled fire in a theater?" Examiners should be particularly careful to correct for their own biases and values.

> CASE EXAMPLE: The patient had little if any insight into her problem. She described the problem as being her sister's. If she wanted to spend $1,000 on long distance phone calls, that was her decision, even if it was on her sister's phone. When asked what she would do if she found a stamped envelope on the ground, she replied that she would open it because it was probably meant for her anyway.

PERCEPTIONS AND COORDINATION. A thorough psychiatric assessment would not be complete without at least a brief examination of the patient's perceptual and visual motor functioning. To assess these areas patients should be asked to write their names on a piece of paper. The clinician should observe for ease, speed, coordination, correctness, and presence of tremors. The patient could also be asked to copy certain figures the nurse would first draw on the paper. Common figures are a circle, a square, a diamond, and a clock. The nurse should watch for the patient's ability to correctly reproduce the design with a reasonable degree of speed and dexterity. Inability to perform these simple tasks point toward impairment of the visual, motor, and perceptual processes and is suggestive of neurological impairment or mental deficiency. The patient should be referred for a more thorough examination if aberrations are observed.

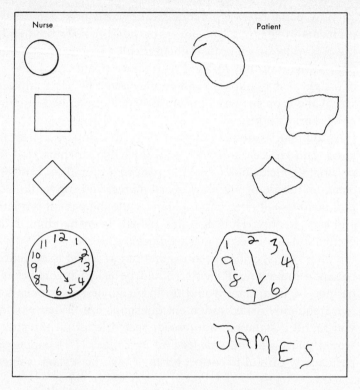

CASE EXAMPLE: Impairment noted in the patient's perception and co-ordination.

Summary and conclusions

The important psychopathological findings identified during the history and mental status examination should be summarized and clearly stated. Findings rather than interpretations should be recorded. The data collected and recorded should provide a picture of the patient's psychological functioning.

Overall impressions of the patient's deficits, performance, behaviors, and mental organization constitute the formulation of a nursing diagnosis. The psychiatric classification currently used by the American Psychiatric Association is presented in the *Diagnostic and Statistical Manual of Mental Disorders, Third Edition* (DSM-III).[7] The DSM-III is atheoretical with regard to most etiologies and pathophysiological processes. Instead it describes the behavior or manifestations of mental disorders. The DSM-III also uses a multiaxial classification system to ensure that all essential information is included in a diagnosis. Axis I and II cover the mental disorders. Axis III is used to describe any physical conditions the patient may be experiencing. Axis IV describes the severity of the psychosocial stressors and Axis V describes the highest level of adaptive functioning during the past year. Nurses may find the DSM-III a helpful tool in formulating diagnostic impressions.

Plan and disposition

The final part of the psychiatric assessment involves recording the disposition. It is important to note that most assessments involve some degree of intervention. The intervention may be clarification of the problem, identification of resources, admission to a hospital, support, or activation of healthy coping strategies. Assessment without some form of intervention only benefits the nurse. The patient should actively participate in planning the disposition. The rationale for the disposition should be explained to the patient especially if hospitalization or commitment is the plan of choice.

CASE EXAMPLE: Assessment of Mr. Howard

Identifying information. Mr. Howard is a 35-year-old male, unemployed factory worker. He is brought to the psychiatric emergency room by the police.

Presenting problem. Mr. Howard states that the police brought him in because they know he has the power to solve all the unsolved crimes in the world and that they are going to make him a chief detective. The police report he refused to leave the police station and interrogated people as they walked in and out of the building.

Brief recent history. The police report Mr. Howard started calling the police department 2 weeks ago volunteering his services and recommending plans for catching criminals. He gave several leads, which all turned out to be false. Yesterday evening he showed up at the second precinct office and refused to leave. He did not sleep at all last night. He ate only when food was offered. He has been verbally assaultive to individuals he suspected were criminals and today he attempted to physically assault a police officer he accused of impersonation.

Family history. Mr. Howard reports both his parents are deceased and that he has an older brother who lives in Tuba City, Arizona on an Indian reservation. He denies any family history of emotional problems except to say his father "drank too much." The patient is very confused and disorganized in his thinking and does not appear to be a reliable historian.

Personal history. Mr. Howard reports he was hospitalized in 1968 and 1976 in psychiatric hospitals. He cannot state the reasons for hospitalization. He denies any current health problems. He had a cholecystectomy in 1979. He admits to taking psychotropic medication in the past but denies current medications. Mr. Howard reports he finished the eleventh grade. He has had various construction jobs in the past but has not worked for several months. He receives Social Security Disability. Mr. Howard denies drug or alcohol use/abuse, but the police report states that they found a marijuana cigarette in his possession when they searched him at the police station. Mr. Howard states the police planted it on him because they are jealous that he is such a good crime solver. A developmental history was not obtained because Mr. Howard's thinking was too disorganized.

Current presentation and mental status examination. Mr. Howard is a sloppily dressed and poorly groomed cachectic-looking male who appears older than stated age. He has several objects pinned to his clothing as well as a false FBI identification card. His speech is loud and somewhat pressured. His mood is both euphoric and irritable. His affect is labile, giddy, and inappropriate. He denies suicidal or homicidal ideation, stating he only hit the police officer to protect the country from impersonators. Thoughts are expressed in a loose and tangential manner with flight of ideas and occasional blocking. He is generally suspicious and reports delusions of grandeur and ideas of influence. He denies hallucinations.

Cognitive functioning. Mr. Howard is not oriented to time or place. He is able to give his correct name and address, but he is confused as to the context of the situation. He feels he is at FBI headquarters for a job interview.

He performs three digits forward and none backward. He gives 100-97-87-77 for serial sevens. Short-term memory is impaired. He recalls zero out of three objects after 5 minutes. He can recall past events such as birthdate, place of birth, and address. He appears to be of average intelligence. He can list Presidents Reagan, Carter, Ford, Nixon, Johnson, Kennedy, and Eisenhower. Abstractions are concrete and suspicious. His replies to proverbs are as follows: glass houses—"The police throw bombs at houses"; rum and scotch—"Both cost money, but don't tell anyone." Insight is poor and judgment is severely impaired. He would call the FBI if he smelled smoke in a theater and he has a mission to replace all police officers.

Summary. The patient appears to be experiencing a disorder of congition and possibly of mood. His thinking is delusional in nature, he is suspicious, his mood is labile, and his orientation, as well as his insight, and judgment are impaired.

Nursing diagnosis. 1. Impaired thought processes
2. Ineffective individual coping with impaired cognitive abilities and social functioning

Psychiatric diagnosis. 295.12—Chronic disorganized schizophrenia

Plan. Based on his psychotic thinking and his potential dangerousness Mr. Howard was committed to the state hospital. The police did the application and Dr. Babcock did the first certificate.

CONCLUSION

The psychiatric interview is the basic tool used to assess all types of mental health disorders. It is conducted by nurses working in a variety of different settings. Nurses gather and record the information obtained during the interview. They then evaluate and synthesize the data and begin formulating a nursing plan of care with the ultimate goal being to improve the patient's overall level of psychological functioning.

REFERENCES

1. Sullivan, H.S. *The psychiatric interview.* New York: W.W. Norton & Co., Inc., 1970, pp. 39, 72, 210.
2. Murray, R.B. & Zentner, J.P. *Nursing concepts for health promotion,* 2nd ed. Englewood Cliffs, N.J.: Prentice-Hall, Inc., 1979, p. 104.
3. King, J. The initial interview: Assessment of the patient and his difficulties. *Perspectives in Psychiatric Care,* 1967, *5,* pp. 256-261.
4. Freedman, A.M., Kaplan, H.I., & Sadock, B.J. *Modern synopsis of comprehensive textbook of psychiatry,* Baltimore: Williams & Williams, 1972, pp. 191, 351, 548.
5. Stuart, G.W., & Sundeen, S.J. *Principles and practice of psychiatric nursing.* 2nd ed. St. Louis: The C.V. Mosby Company, 1983, p. 149.
6. Reynolds, J.I., and Logsdon, J.B.: Assessing your patient's mental status. *Nursing '79,* 1979, *9*(8), 26-33.
7. American Psychiatric Association. *Diagnostic and statistical manual of mental disorders,* 2nd ed. Washington, D.C., 1968.

CHAPTER 4

ASSESSING MANIFESTATIONS OF ANXIETY

All people have experienced the feeling of anxiety at some point in their lifetimes. Every day we are bombarded with stresses and threats that create unpleasant feelings. The subjective experience of anxiety causes the individual to feel apprehension, dread, uneasiness, and alarm. The reader may recall waking up in the morning and feeling upset without knowing the reason or sitting in a classroom and suddenly feeling nervous and uneasy with no specific precipitant. When this occurs, the person feels "pitted" against the unknown, tackling forces that are not understood.

The discomfort created by anxiety causes individuals to respond in conscious and unconscious ways. Consciously, they may attempt to ignore the anxiety, accepting its waxing and waning so long as it does not interfere with activities. People may try to maintain busy schedules or plan a variety of activities to disperse or mask the unpleasant feelings. Participating in sports often helps reduce the tension associated with anxiety. As the anxiety continues or increases in intensity, people may decide to confront the upsetting feelings and sensations by seeking help from professionals or friends, while others may withdraw and become increasingly anxious. Some individuals attempt to allay the anxiety with drugs and alcohol. Unconscious mechanisms such as directing anxiety into physical symptoms or displacing it onto external events may temporarily relieve overt anxious feelings.

Anxiety is pathological when it becomes a predominant focus in an individual's life that results in maladaptive coping. Maladaptive coping occurs when the strategies used to reduce tension and inner conflict are no longer useful. At this point, the person's daily functioning becomes impaired in some way. The mechanisms utilized by individuals to decrease the anxiety adversely affect their lifestyles or mental well-being. The severity of the person's impairment depends on the type, duration, and intensity of the coping strategies used. For example, some people are able to utilize alcohol for a short period of time to help them get through a difficult week. For others, the use of alcohol might become habitual and problematic.

When anxiety or the mechanisms utilized to cope with the anxiety become disruptive to individuals' lifestyles, they may be experiencing a psychiatric disorder. Disordered psychological function is ultimately attributed to some aspect of anxiety in almost every clinical disturbance.[1] The nature of the psychiatric disorder that results depends on the severity of the anxiety, the types of mechanisms or strategies used to deal with the anxiety, and the resulting symptomatology. This chapter discusses assessment of anxiety that is manifested through physical and ritualistic symptoms.

DEFINITION

Anxiety is a state of dread, worry, or apprehension. It is a response that occurs when the individual's sense of self is threatened. When the threat becomes overwhelming, the anxiety is channeled into some form of expression to maintain an intact sense of self. Anxiety cannot be directly observed. A state of anxiety is implied through its observable expressions or the person's description of vague nervousness and worry.

When anxiety is expressed directly through physical symptoms, people experience dread and apprehension. They are aware of uncomfortable feelings. The autonomic neuroendocrine system is stimulated and the individuals experience physiological sensations such as perspiration, palpitations, shortness of breath, and urinary urgency.

Anxiety can be channeled through physical symptoms that are not related to autonomic neuroendocrine stimulation such as back pain. In these instances, a physical examination does not reveal a physiological cause for the symptoms or their severity. Patients focus on the symptom, expressing concern about their state of health, but are not cognizant of the underlying anxiety.

Ritualistic symptoms are behaviors that individuals are unable to control. These include repetitive or recurring behaviors such as compulsions and phobias. These symptoms directly prevent patients from feeling anxious. If individuals stop these behaviors or are prevented from carrying them out, they will experience increased anxiety.

Individuals experiencing indirect ritualistic symptoms demonstrate sudden changes in identity or motor behavior. People are unable to control these behaviors and may not necessarily feel anxious during the incidents. Often they are not aware that these changes are occurring.

Anxiety should be differentiated from the emotion of fear. Anxiety is an emotion that occurs in respond to an intangible threat or conflict. When the feeling of apprehension is triggered by an external, specific threat, it is called fear. The feeling of anxiety is diffuse whereas fear is directed toward an object or situation. Anxiety may persist over long periods of time but fear is an acute response. Physiological studies suggest that anxiety increases heart rate and blood pressure while fear decreases these vital signs.[2] Therefore, although anxiety and fear are unpleasant, uncomfortable emotions, there are distinct differences in their clinical presentations.

CLASSIFICATION

Historically, pathological expressions of anxiety have been discussed as neuroses. Definitions of neuroses are derived from loose clinical groupings of symptoms that cluster together.[3] The term neurosis has created a great deal of confusion among psychiatric clinicians with multiple interpretations of its meaning and characteristics. In addition, neurosis is associated with psychodynamic constructs, a theoretical approach with which some clinicians do not agree.

The DSM-III attempts to classify psychiatric disorders based on observed symptomatology rather than theoretical conjecture. This classification does not recognize causes of anxiety such as unconscious conflict, learned behavior, physiological alterations, or severe psychosocial stress. Therefore the former neurotic classification of anxiety is now divided into three categories of disorders grouped by behavioral manifestations: anxiety disorders, somatoform disorders, and dissociative disorders.

Anxiety disorders

The major feature of anxiety disorders is the direct expression of anxiety. This anxiety may be the primary disturbance or it may be experienced if the patient attempts to control the symptoms.[4] Anxiety disorders include phobic disorders, anxiety states, and obsessive-compulsive disorder. The patient with a phobic disorder experiences irrational fear when exposed to a specific object, activity, or situation. The predominant feature of anxiety states is the direct physical and emotional expression of anxiety. The patient exhibits autonomic neuroendocrine symptoms and feels a sense of apprehension and nervousness. When anxiety is expressed through obsessive-compulsive behavior, the individual experiences obsessions or compulsions that interfere with routine functioning. Attempts to ignore or confront these symptoms create anxiety.

Somatoform disorders

The patient experiencing a somatoform disorder demonstrates physical symptoms that cannot be explained by physical examinations and diagnostic laboratory tests. Types of somatoform disorders include so-

TABLE 4:1	Classification of manifestations of anxiety as having physical, ritualistic, direct, and indirect expression	
Expressions of anxiety	*Physical*	*Ritualistic*
Direct	Panic attacks Generalized anxiety Hypochondriasis	Obsessive-compulsive disorder Phobic disorder
Indirect	Conversion disorder	Dissociative disorder

matization disorder, conversion disorder, psychogenic pain disorder, and hypochondriasis. The primary features of somatization disorder are multiple somatic complaints for which no physiological cause can be found.[4] With conversion disorder, the patient exhibits impairment of sensorimotor functioning that has no identifiable organic basis. The symptoms seem to serve some psychological need. The patient with psychogenic pain disorder experiences severe and long-standing pain that is not explained by medical examination. The major feature of hypochondriasis is the patient's excessive preoccupation with symptoms and state of health.

Dissociative disorders

Dissociative disorders involve sudden, temporary changes in consciousness, identity, or motor behavior. Psychogenic amnesia, psychogenic fugue, multiple personality, and depersonalization disorder are included in this classification. The patient with psychogenic amnesia is suddenly unable to recall personal information. The essential feature of psychogenic fugue is sudden, unexpected travel away from home with the inability to remember the past. With multiple personality, the patient experiences personality changes involving new identities and behaviors. The primary feature of depersonalization disorder is the experiencing of depersonalization episodes during which the patient feels a sense of unreality.

EPIDEMIOLOGY

It is difficult to obtain valid and reliable information about the incidence and prevalence of psychiatric disorders involving manifestations of anxiety. Individuals experiencing symptoms of anxiety usually do not require hospitalization and may not even seek treatment unless the problem becomes seriously incapacitating. In addition, the lack of objective diagnostic criteria for neuroses has interfered with past attempts to gather accurate diagnostic statistics. It is therefore difficult to identify the actual prevalence of disorders involving anxiety symptoms. It is possible to describe treated prevalence rates based on patients seen privately by clinicians or treated in hospitals.

Statistics compiled in 1975 by the National Institute of Mental Health show that out of all admissions to state and county mental hospitals, 2.8% had some type of diagnosis involving neurotic disorders.[5] Similar statistics compiled from private mental institutions demonstrate that 5.6% of those admitted suffered a neurotic disorder.[6] Discharge data from nonfederal general hospital psychiatric inpatient units in 1975 suggest that 6.2% of the patients experienced a neurotic disorder.[7]

There is little information about the prevalence of disorders involving manifestations of anxiety in the general population. These disorders do seem to occur more frequently with women. Persons of all ages, from teens to the elderly, may experience these disorders. According to the DSM-III, approximately 2% to 4% of the general population has experienced an anxiety disorder.[4] Statistics on somatoform disorders are extremely difficult to obtain, although most are seen more commonly than thought by family physicians and specialists. Dissociative disorders occur infrequently.

CAUSATIVE FACTORS

Manifestations of anxiety that result in maladaptive coping strategies or behaviors do not constitute well-defined diseases or pathological processes. Rather, the clinical classifications of anxiety manifestations represent clusters of symptoms that depict states of being. It is therefore difficult to discuss the bases of anxiety states without referring to the many diverse theoretical explanations. Each explanation presents a narrow perspective on the cause of anxiety since it is most likely that a combination of factors are involved. At the present time there is only sparse understanding of the contribution of different etiological factors on the development of anxiety. Therefore it is only possible to postulate the general likelihood of their contributions to the predisposition to anxiety.[8]

Three major theoretical foundations of anxiety and its manifestations are described in this chapter: psychodynamic theory, behavioral theory, and biological theory and research.

Psychodynamic theory

Psychodynamic theory utilizes dynamic constructs to explain the basis of anxiety. The major premise is that anxiety is the result of intrapsychic conflict where mental forces or impulses seeking expression are regulated by various psychological mechanisms. This hypothesis has been described most prominently by Freud and Fenchil.

According to this perspective, the individual encounters traumatic experiences at some point during childhood. This trauma may be an actual disturbing experience or the child's instincts being unable to attain satisfaction.[9] The child represses the forbidden, unsatisfied instinct into the unconscious rather than incorporating it into actual behavior.

Anxiety is experienced at a later time in life when environmental stress or a reenactment of the original trauma causes the repressed event to threaten the consciousness, signaling new danger.[10] The resulting intrapsychic conflict is analogous to steam forcing the lid off a cooking kettle. The ego attempts to control the forceful, threatening, unconscious impulses by invoking various mechanisms. In some instances the anxiety is directly expressed through the development of physical symptoms and subjective distress. The individual may not be aware of or understand the nature of the intrapsychic conflict, feeling only the tension and apprehension of anxiety.

Other manifestations of anxiety occur when the ego begins to utilize defense mechanisms to distort reality and reduce the patient's feelings of anxiety. Tables 4:2 and 4:3 illustrate the psychodynamic structures of the mind and major defense mechanisms that control anxiety. The defense mechanisms control anxiety by converting direct anxiety to physical or ritualistic symptoms. The types of defense mechanisms utilized and the nature of the resulting symptoms depend upon the individual's stage of development at the time of the original trauma and subsequent effective use of those mechanisms.

The physical and ritualistic symptoms that result from the use of defense mechanisms prevent the patient from acknowledging the in-

TABLE 4:2	Psychodynamic constructs illustrating structures of the mind
Structure	*Function*
Id	The part of the mind that harbors instincts, drives, and unconscious material
Ego	The part of the mind that comprises the individual's sense of self and a sense of reality, maintains contact with the external world, and develops and utilizes psychological defense mechanisms
Superego	The part of the mind that dictates limits, morals, and values

TABLE 4:3   Major defense mechanisms utilized in manifestations of anxiety

Defense mechanism	Action	Symptoms
Repression	Places thoughts, emotions, and sensations out of awareness into the unconsciousness	Inability to recall thoughts, emotions, sensations
Conversion	Converts anxiety into a symbolic sensorimotor body symptom	Paralysis, blindness, hearing loss, voice loss
Dissociation	Alters consciousness and identity to avoid reality and anxiety	Loss of memory, loss of identity, disorientation
Reaction formation	Replaces original attitude or feeling with an opposite one	Intense insistence on a particular viewpoint or theme
Undoing	Channels psychic energy into physical activity to neutralize a wish or action	Repetitive or symbolic actions
Displacement	Unconsciously transfers emotions from one object or situation to another	Intense feelings directed toward a benign object or situation
Projection	Attributes own feelings or thoughts to other persons or objects	Inappropriate blame, suspicion, fear of other person or object

trapsychic conflict. The duration and intensity of the symptoms will depend on how much environmental stress patients are experiencing and their ability to repress the threatening impulses. Therefore manifestations of anxiety may vary in their duration and severity. Some symptoms may occur sporadically whereas others may be chronic. A patient may exhibit a variety of symptoms such as phobias, panic attacks, and preoccupation with physical health.

Horney, May, and Sullivan expand the psychodynamic understanding of anxiety to include consideration of social and interpersonal factors.[11-13] Horney suggests that anxiety results from growing up in an environment in which there is a lack of parental ability to provide genuine warmth and affection. The child learns anxiety and helplessness by repressing hostility toward the parents. May considers changes in society and their impact on the individual as contributing to the development of anxiety. Sullivan proposes a more interpersonal theory on the development of anxiety. He believes anxiety results from conflicts in interpersonal relationships rather than only intrapsychic processes. As children interact with significant others, they construct a sense of self. Anxiety is the result of disapproval from significant others and subsequent feelings of apprehension and insecurity.

Theorists disagree as to whether mental or interpersonal factors are the cause or the effect of anxiety symptomatology. However, a continuum of psychodynamic theory presents behavior as a product of internal and socially determined processes.

Biological theory

The development of biological research regarding the basis of anxiety and its manifestations has been slower than with other types of mental disorders. This is due, in part, to the long held psychodynamic belief that anxiety was the result of intrapsychic forces.

The amount of biological research on anxiety has increased, but scientists have been unable to trace these disorders to specific organic causes. It is unknown if the biological changes that are becoming evident precipitated anxiety or whether the emotional state prompted the physiological changes.

Researchers are well aware of the mind-body connection. "Evidence suggests an intimate connection among mental states; biochemical, physiological, and endocrine systems."[14] The emotion of anxiety is manifested through actual physical changes in all body systems via the autonomic nervous system. Hans Selye's reknowned work on stress discusses biological reactions that lead to the general adaptation syndrome.[15]

Historically, physical manifestations of anxiety have been attributed to unconscious mental processes. However, new data reveal that, when followed up years later, a large number of patients diagnosed as having organic complaints with a psychogenic basis are found to have serious somatic disease that was undiagnosable during its prodromal phase.

There is an increasing awareness that various manifestations of anxiety may be related to physiological abnormalities. Recent research, for example, has demonstrated that actual cardiac abnormalities are significantly more frequent in patients diagnosed as having anxiety neurosis and panic disorders than patients in control groups.[17] A common cardiac abnormality often evident is mitral valve prolapse.

Other research has shown that an intravenous infusion of sodium lactate will trigger a panic attack in patients diagnosed as having a panic disorder but not in normal subjects.[16] It has also been reported that relaxation training for anxious individuals decreases plasma catecholamines and platelet monoamine oxidase activity.[18]

All of the above research demonstrates an integral link between anxiety and physiological functioning. It has yet to be determined whether abnormal biological processes constitute a cause of anxiety.

Behavioral theory

Behavioral theory presents human behavior as a series of learned activities. According to this premise, behavior results from a system of responses to specified stimuli. Over time, the individual develops habitual responses to those stimuli.

Wolpe postulates that manifestations of anxiety are learned, conditioned responses.[19] Symptoms are provoked by exposure to the original stimulus or a stimulus similar to the original one. Thus the symptoms of anxiety are viewed as the major problems requiring attention. This is in contrast to the view of the psychodynamicist who perceives psychological and interpersonal difficulties as primary causative factors in anxiety.

Behaviorists agree that symptoms of pathological anxiety cannot be reduced by intellectual processes since anxiety is an emotional response served by a primitive level of neural organization.[19] Therefore anxiety and its symptoms can only be eliminated by a process of relearning where the stimulus will no longer evoke the symptomatic response.

CLINICAL PRESENTATION

Patients experiencing anxiety often do not appear to have an overt psychiatric problem since they are able to function in most circumstances and are oriented to reality and demonstrate no major affective disturbance. When the anxiety symptoms become uncomfortable, many patients recognize that they do have a problem and voluntarily seek treatment. Few patients are admitted to psychiatric hospitals with anxiety symptoms as the primary problem since manifestations of anxiety are usually not severe enough to warrant such hospitalization.

Patients who have physical symptoms of anxiety may be seen by the nurse after admission to a medical-surgical hospital unit or the emergency department or following contact with a private family physician. These patients know that they have a problem but generally believe it is organic in nature. They may be unaware of any psychosocial components relating to the physical symptoms. Many have had physical examinations and medical testing that failed to reveal a cause for the symptom or its severity. The patient is then advised to consult a psychiatric clinician.

Individuals who express anxiety through ritualistic symptoms usually have some understanding of their problem. Many are able to accurately define the nature of their disorder. These patients contact a psychiatric clinician rather than medical personnel as a result of their insight. Patients with identity problems or altered states of consciousness, such as those seen in dissociative disorders, may be brought in by significant others who are concerned about their wandering or strange behaviors. Patients with ritualistic symptoms may not understand the cause of their problem, but they do admit that it interferes with normal activities. Sometimes, the problem of interference with daily activities may be the initial presenting problem. A patient may state, "I haven't been able to go to work" rather than, "I'm afraid to drive my car" or "I was fired from my job" instead of "I have periods of time I can't recall." The nurse should question patients about their decision to seek treatment: "What was happening that caused you to come in today?" Further exploration of the patients' responses will reveal the exact nature of their presenting problems: "What happened that caused you to be fired from your job?"

Common presenting problems of physical expressions of anxiety can be listed as follows:

SYMPTOMS	EXAMPLES OF STATEMENTS
Chest pain and palpitations	"I think I'm having a heart attack or stroke."
Shortness of breath	"I can't breathe."
Perspiration	"I get light-headed, nauseated, and faint."
Tingling of extremities	"I have seizures and black out."
Nausea and vomiting	"I can't move my legs."
Increased blood pressure	"I can't see anymore."
Increased pulse	"I feel like things aren't real."
Fatigue	"I know there's something seriously wrong. Am I going to die?"
Headache	
Diarrhea	"I have a long history of medical problems and my doctor suggested I see you."
Seizures	
Paralysis, muscle weakness	"My body is falling apart."
Hearing loss	
Blindness	
Speech loss	
Gynecological problems	
Memory loss	
Feelings of unreality	
Sexual problems	
Blurred or double vision	
Fainting, loss of consciousness	
Vague complaints of pain	

Common presenting problems of ritualistic expressions of anxiety include the following:

SYMPTOMS	EXAMPLES OF STATEMENTS
Repetitive, uncontrolled acts	"I'm afraid of elevators."
Fear of crowds	"I haven't left the house in six months
Fear of being alone	except to come here."
Fear of public scrutiny	"I keep checking on my child even when
Irrational fears of objects or	he's sleeping."
situations	"I get up every night to shower at
Repetitive, uncontrolled thoughts	1 a.m."
Loss of memory	"I'm afraid everyone will laugh at me."
Assumption of new identity	"I don't remember anything except
Feelings of unreality	winding up in California."
	"I feel like I'm in a dream."
	"My name is Mary, not Lucy."
	"I'm afraid I'll faint in public."

Physical manifestations

Anxiety disorders. Physical symptoms that occur with anxiety disorders are the result of autonomic nervous system activity. In addition to the subjective feelings of anxiety and fear, the patient experiences direct physical expression of anxiety. These physical symptoms include shortness of breath, palpitations and chest pain, perspiration, tingling of extremities, nausea, increased blood pressure and pulse, faintness, dizziness, trembling, diarrhea, dry mouth, and cold, clammy hands.

Phobic patients experience these symptoms when exposed to the threatening object or situation. Patients with obsessive-compulsive disorder usually demonstrate autonomic symptoms of anxiety when they are not able to continue the repetitive thinking and behaviors. During a panic attack, the patient directly exhibits these physical symptoms. The symptoms may be accompanied by feelings of death and doom. With generalized anxiety disorder, these physical symptoms persist for at least one month. In addition, the patient may describe fatigue, muscle aches, insomnia, and restlessness.

Patients express concern and apprehension regarding their physical symptoms. The nurse may hear, "I'm having a heart attack" or "I feel constricted around my throat; I can't breathe." When the physical symptoms are acute, the nurse needs to decrease the anxiety before attempting to interview the patient. The patient should be reassured that people are available to help. Interventions such as walking the corridors and breathing into a paper bag to combat hyperventilation help the patient regain control.

Physical symptoms of anxiety resemble a variety of physical illnesses including cardiac impairment, stroke, pulmonary embolus, and hyperthyroidism. Patients often arrive at the emergency room or the family physician with their complaints. In these situations, it is difficult to differentiate between manifestations of anxiety and potentially serious illness. Therefore a thorough health examination should always be conducted to rule out the presence of any medical problem.

The nurse should question the patient about substance abuse. Patients frequently use drugs and alcohol as a means to allay feelings of anxiety. Many physicians prescribe medications such as tranquilizers and pain relief agents to anxious patients, thus increasing the possibility of drug abuse. It has been suggested that 25% of people with anxiety neuroses are heavy drinkers and 15% are dependent on alcohol.[20] The nurse needs to ask, "How much alcohol do you drink daily?" and "What drugs are you taking?" Early symptoms of alcohol withdrawal, including shakiness, perspiration, upset stomach, insomnia, and increased pulse rate, mimic symptoms of anxiety.

> **CASE EXAMPLE:** Panic attack
> Mr. Howe was brought to the emergency room by his wife after she found him sitting on the sofa trembling, having difficulty speaking, perspiring, and experiencing chest pain and tightness in his throat. He requested to be taken to the emergency department, frightened that he was having a heart attack. Mr. Howe told the nurse he felt as though he would die. A thorough physical evaluation indicated there was no organic cause for the symptoms.

Somatoform disorders. Physical symptoms are the central focus of the somatoform disorders. These are not necessarily related to autonomic activity. The patient describes various physical complaints, yet medical examinations fail to reveal any physiological cause of the symptoms or their severity.

The symptoms of somatization disorder and hypochondriasis have insidious onsets and persist over time. The nurse discovers that the patient's current physical symptoms are just the most recent on a long list of physical ailments. The patient may describe recent visits to internists, surgeons, and other medical specialists in an attempt to find causes and cures for the symptoms. Although no organic cause for these illnesses can be found, the patient actually experiences the symptoms. They are not voluntarily controlled.

Physical symptoms that occur with somatization disorder and hypochondrias span the various body systems. Neurological symptoms include visual impairments, seizures, loss of consciousness, and muscle weakness. Gastrointestinal complaints are nausea and vomiting, diarrhea, or abdominal pain. Shortness of breath, chest pain, and heart palpitations are frequent cardiopulmonary symptoms. Menstrual and sexual difficulties may also be described by the patient.

Patients experiencing conversion disorders suffer a loss or impairment of sensorimotor functioning. Common symptoms include impaired hearing, vision, and speech and paralysis and seizures. These symptoms seem to enable the patient to avoid activities and receive extra support and attention from others. They are not under voluntary control. Often these symptoms occur suddenly after the patient confronts a stressful event. One interesting aspect of conversion symptoms is that the patient frequently exhibits an attitude of indifference towards them. Patients experiencing somatization disorder and hypochondriasis, on the other hand, are quite concerned about their symptoms.

The primary physical symptom for psychogenic pain disorder is pain. The pain may be in any anatomical location. Medical examinations do not reveal an organic cause for the pain or its severity. Usually, the patient complains of severe pain over a long period of time, although the pain may subside temporarily. As with conversion symptoms, the pain allows the patient to avoid activities and obtain support from the environment.

> CASE EXAMPLE: Conversion disorder
> Mrs. Smith was told that her 10-year-old daughter might have a serious illness. The following day Mrs. Smith experienced a grand mal seizure as she was preparing to visit her daughter in the hospital. Mr. Smith was at home when the seizure occurred. Mrs. Smith was not injured. She was not incontinent during the seizure or confused afterwards. She seemed unconcerned about the event and went to see her daughter later in the day.

Dissociative disorders. The major physical symptoms of dissociative disorders is altered levels of consciousness. The patient experiences memory loss or feelings of unreality. Dizziness and clouding of consciousness may also be apparent. These physical symptoms can be indicative of serious neurological impairment, including epilepsy, organic mental disorders, and tumors. However, a patient experiencing a dissociative disorder will have normal neurological examinations. In addition, the altered states of consciousness are precipitated by psychosocial stress.

Emotional manifestations

The emotion of anxiety exists at three levels as a neuroendocrine response, a motor-visceral response, and a level of conscious awareness.[1] The patient may be conscious of feeling nervous and apprehensive. However, the individual might only be aware of the unpleasant physiological symptoms caused by the anxiety. Not every person exhibiting anxiety symptoms subjectively feels anxious.

The feeling of anxiety is most strongly experienced by those individuals with anxiety disorders. These patients will describe their mood as "upset," "nervous," "on edge," or "frightened." They speak of vague feelings of dread or specific feelings of panic and fear. Often, the physical sensations that result from the anxiety response create more intensified feelings of nervousness, fear, and doom. The patient's affect is usually appropriate to the circumstances and the subjective feelings.

In somatoform disorders, patients' emotions are strongly focused on states of health. Most evident are worry, concern, and preoccupation with the physical impairments. The patient attributes subjective feelings of anxiety and fear to concern regarding the physical symptoms. Patients experiencing somatoform disorders often demonstrate pronounced emotional expression. The nurse may observe a labile affect with the patient's dramatic recounting of past and present problems. One noticeable exception to the exaggerated emotions and excessive concern for physical symptoms occurs with conversion disorders. The clinician will frequently observe the patient exhibiting a relative lack of concern toward the impaired sensory or motor function. Apparently, the acquisition of the physical symptom is less disconcerting than directly acknowledging anxiety and inner conflict.

Dissociative disorders occur in response to psychosocial stress. Before the onset of the change in behavior, patients may not be aware that they are stressed or anxious. During these dissociative reactions, patients can exhibit outbursts of anger and irritability. When personality changes occur, new emotional reactions often become apparent. For example, an individual may appear more open and inhibited in the new personality than in the predominant one.

The nurse should not underestimate the effect that anxiety has on patients' emotional states. In addition to feeling upset and apprehensive, people often become irritable, tense, and emotionally drained. The intense emotionality can interfere with perceptions of other people, situations, and the meaning of events. Entwined in the maze of anxiety, patients interpret environmental events in ways that explain and justify their feelings. Patients experiencing anxiety symptoms are often tense, on-guard individuals.

A depressed mood and flat affect frequently accompany anxiety symptoms. Depression is especially evident with patients experiencing obsessive-compulsive disorder, somatoform disorders, and phobic disorders. Depressive symptoms, however, are secondary to the expressions of anxiety. The disturbance of mood has not colored the patient's life and actions as have the anxiety symptoms.

Cognitive manifestations

The patient exhibiting symptoms of anxiety has, in general, minimal cognitive impairment. However, anxiety does affect problem-solving, learning, and communication by distorting perceptions and impairing the ability to process information from the environment. As anxiety increases, these cognitive functions become more difficult to perform. The ability to abstract, which is usually not significantly impaired in mild or moderate anxiety states, gives way to more concrete thinking as anxiety escalates. Extremely anxious patients such as those experiencing panic attacks or phobic reactions may describe thoughts that are tangential, rambling, or circumstantial. Severe anxiety can prompt thought blocking in which the patient is unable to complete a sentence or phrase.

Most patients are oriented and able to state their name and the date and to provide the necessary demographic data. A major exception is the patient who is experiencing a dissociative disorder. If the episode occurs during the interview, the individual may be disoriented, giving the nurse a false name or being unable to describe the date and place. Memory is impaired in dissociative disorders. The patient may have amnesia or only vague recollections of specific past events.

The thought content of patients exhibiting manifestations of anxiety revolves around somatic complaints, subjective feelings of anxiety, obsessions, phobic reactions, and uncontrolled behaviors. A patient may appear to be delusional in regard to certain themes, particularly the meaning of somatic symptoms and phobic reactions. However, the experienced clinician will recognize that the false or seemingly irrational beliefs are not true delusions since the patient realizes that the thoughts are illogical and irrational. Suicidal and homicidal ideation, defensive thinking patterns, and hallucinations and illusions occur infrequently in the thought content.

Obsessional thinking is often seen in various types of psychiatric disorders, including schizophrenia. In obsessive-compulsive disorder, the patient is lucid, coherent, and able to reality-test yet describes uncontrolled, recurrent thoughts or images. However, with schizophrenic disorders, the obsessions are only one aspect of the thought disorder. Obsessions also occur with mood disturbances but are secondary to the affective changes the patient exhibits.

The degree of insight the patient exhibits regarding the anxiety symptoms depends on the nature of the psychological disorder. Most patients with anxiety disorders have some insight into their problems. They are aware of their experience of anxiety and may seek treatment. When anxiety is expressed indirectly through physical symptoms such as in the somatoform disorders, patients are apt to view their physical complaint as the major problem affecting their lives. Many patients experiencing dissociative disorders are unaware of their changes in identity and behavior.

CASE EXAMPLE: Psychogenic fugue
Ms. Rarick was being interviewed by the nurse during admission to a psychiatric unit. Suddenly, she began using foul language, pacing the room, and shaking her head vehemently. Mr. Rarick left the room and began telling other patients that she was leaving on a trip to Philadelphia. Twenty minutes later, Ms. Rarick returned to her usual, subdued self with no recollection of the episode.

Social manifestations

Symptoms of anxiety are responses to stress. This stress may be caused by internal psychological conflict or environmental stressors. The astute nurse will usually be able to ascertain, over a period of time, psychosocial stressors that are related to the anxiety. However, it is sometimes difficult to determine which actually occurred first, the stressors or the symptoms.

The symptoms of anxiety adversely impact on social functioning. As symptoms become more pronounced in duration and intensity, stress is placed on marital and family relationships. The patient finds it more difficult to be productive at work or school. Many individuals, however, continue to fulfill their social responsibilities and never seek professional help. When a patient does contact a clinician, it is because family, work, social, or school activities have been impaired.

Anxiety symptoms channel anxiety and distant inner conflicts into more manageable expressions. In addition, they allow the patient to gain added support from significant others and to be relieved of expected activities and responsibilities. Symptoms such as physical impairments are viewed as socially acceptable reasons for altered social functioning. It is important to note that these symptoms are not voluntarily controlled by the patient. The behaviors occur naturally and spontaneously with no premediated planning.

The available data on the familial patterns of anxiety suggest a possible increase in incidence of anxiety symptoms among family members. Physical expressions of anxiety seem to occur over a period of time in familial patterns.[21] These data, however, are not conclusive and further research is needed.

ASSESSMENT TOOLS

Tools 4:1 through 4:3 have been developed as guides for assessment of anxiety symptoms. These tools are designed to assist with data collection and classification. They are not intended to be definitive diagnostic criteria. They span each of the three major DSM-III diagnostic categories that describe expression of anxiety. Part I on each tool describes prominent signs and symptoms that are reflective of the disorder. Any yes response on Part I indicates that the patient may have a psychiatric disorder in that category. If there are one or more yes responses in Part I, the nurse should complete Part II, responses to signs and symptoms. A yes response in Part II is additional evidence that the patient is experiencing a psychiatric disorder. The nurse should validate the data and refer to the DSM-III for specific diagnostic criteria.

TOOL 4:1   Brief assessment for anxiety disorders

PART I.   SIGNS AND SYMPTOMS

Does the patient:	Yes	No
1. Avoid being alone in public places?	____	____
2. Avoid situations in which the patient will be scrutinized by others?	____	____
3. Avoid specific objects or situations?	____	____
4. Describe feeling anxious, fearful, or worrisome or anticipating misfortune?	____	____
5. Exhibit or describe signs from any of the below categories?	____	____
a. Shakiness, muscle aches, eyelid twitch, strained face, startling easily, fidgeting, inability to relax, furrowed brow?	____	____
b. Sweating, pounding heart, cold and clammy hands, dry mouth, dizziness, upset stomach, tingling of extremities, diarrhea, faintness	____	____
c. Insomnia, difficulty concentrating, irritability, impatience, distractibility, fear of losing control	____	____
d. Chest pain, shortness of breath, choking sensations, lump in throat	____	____

PART II.   RESPONSES TO SIGNS AND SYMPTOMS

Are the patient's symptoms:	Yes	No
6. Interfering with daily life activities?	____	____
7. Causing subjective distress?	____	____
8. The reason the patient is seeking help at this time?	____	____

Adapted from American Psychiatric Association. *Diagnostic and Statistical Manual of Mental Disorders*, 3rd ed. Washington, D.C.: American Psychiatric Association, 1980.

TOOL 4:2   Brief assessment for somatoform disorders

PART I.   SIGNS AND SYMPTOMS

Does the patient: *Yes*   *No*

1. Exhibit or describe physical symptoms in any of the following groups for which no apparent physiological cause can be found?   ____ ____
   a. Pain   ____ ____
   b. Impairment of sensory functioning   ____ ____
   c. Impairment of motor functioning   ____ ____
   d. Seizures, dizziness, furrowed brow   ____ ____
   e. Chest pain, palpitations, shortness of breath   ____ ____
2. Appear preoccupied with state of health?   ____ ____

PART II.   RESPONSES TO SIGNS AND SYMPTOMS

Are the patient's symptoms: *Yes*   *No*

3. Interfering with daily life activities?   ____ ____
4. Enabling the patient to gain added support or avoid some activity?   ____ ____
5. The reason the patient is seeking help at this time?   ____ ____

Adapted from American Psychiatric Association. *Diagnostic and Statistical Manual of Mental Disorders*, 3rd ed. Washington, D.C.: American Psychiatric Association, 1980.

TOOL 4:3   Brief assessment for dissociative disorders

PART I.   SIGNS AND SYMPTOMS

Does the patient: *Yes*   *No*

1. Exhibit or describe sudden memory loss regarding important personal information?   ____ ____
2. Exhibit or describe having more than one personality or identity?   ____ ____
3. Travel away from work or home suddenly with inability to recall the past?   ____ ____
4. Exhibit or describe feeling unreal or changed in some way?   ____ ____

PART II.   RESPONSES TO SIGNS AND SYMPTOMS

Are the patient's symptoms: *Yes*   *No*

5. Interfering with daily life activities?   ____ ____
6. The reason the patient is seeking help at this time?   ____ ____

Adapted from American Psychiatric Association. *Diagnostic and Statistical Manual of Mental Disorders*, 3rd ed. Washington, D.C.: American Psychiatric Association, 1980.

TOOL 4:4   Hamilton rating scale for anxiety states

Item	Symptoms	Grade
Anxious mood	Worries, anticipation of the worst, fearful anticipation, irritability	
Tension	Feelings of tension, fatigability, startle response, moved to tears easily, trembling, feelings of restlessness, inability to relax	
Fears	Of dark, of strangers, of being left alone, of animals, of traffic, of crowds	
Insomnia	Difficulty in falling asleep, broken sleep, unsatisfying sleep and fatigue on waking, dreams, nightmares, night-terrors	
Intellectual (cognitive)	Difficulty in concentration, poor memory	
Depressed mood	Loss of interest, lack of pleasure in hobbies, depression, early waking, diurnal swing	
Somatic (muscular)	Pains and aches, twitchings, stiffness, myoclonic jerks, grinding of teeth, unsteady voice, increased muscular tone	
Somatic (sensory)	Tinnitus, blurring of vision, hot and cold flushes, feelings of weakness, pricking sensation	
Cardiovascular system	Tachycardia, palpitations, pain in chest, throbbing of vessels, fainting feelings, missing beat	
Respiratory system	Pressure or constriction in chest, choking feelings, sighing, dyspnea	
Gastrointestinal system	Difficulty in swallowing, wind, abdominal pain, burning sensations, abdominal fullness, nausea, vomiting, borborygmi, looseness of bowels, loss of weight, constipation	
Genitourinary system	Frequency of micturition, urgency of micturition, amenorrhea, menorrhagia, development of frigidity, premature ejaculation, looseness of bowels, loss of weight, constipation	

Adapted from Hamilton, M. The assessment of anxiety states by rating. *British Journal of Medical Psychology*, 1959, *32*, 54.

TOOL 4:4	Hamilton rating scale for anxiety states—cont'd	
Item	*Symptoms*	*Grade*
Autonomic system	Dry mouth, flushing, pallor, tendency to sweat, giddiness, tension headache, raising of hair	
Behavior at interview	Fidgeting restlessness or pacing, tremor of hands, furrowed brow, strained face, sighing or rapid respiration, facial pallor, swallowing, belching, brisk tendon jerks, dilated pupils, exophthalmos	

Grades:	0 Not Present	1 Mild	2 Moderate	3 Severe	4 Very Severe

Tool 4:4 was devised by Max Hamilton to help the clinician gather data about anxiety states.[22] The symptoms listed on the Hamilton Scale will provide useful information that will help collect and classify data related to anxiety symptoms. The nurse can assess whether or not the patient exhibits symptoms in any of the item areas and the degree of their severity.

DIAGNOSIS
Nursing diagnoses of anxiety

After collecting data about the patient's health care concerns, the nurse organizes that data into meaningful patterns and analyzes the meaning. Patients manifesting anxiety exhibit problems that span the biopsychosocial dimensions. Therefore diagnostic judgments as to the meaning of the data will reflect a variety of problems amenable to nursing care.

The boxed material on the following page presents a beginning taxonomy of nursing diagnoses that particularly pertain to patients experiencing anxiety symptoms. Each nursing diagnosis shown in the box can be further subdivided and made more specific to each patient situation. The nurse can develop the taxonomy on increasingly specific levels to accurately describe the patient's individualized problems. Additional nursing diagnoses not listed in the outline may be required to describe additional psychosocial or physical concerns. The reader is referred to Kim and Moritz, *Classification of Nursing Diagnosis,*[23] for further diagnostic information.

**TAXONOMY OF NURSING DIAGNOSES FOR
MANIFESTATIONS OF ANXIETY**

1. Fear
   1.10 Fear of specific object
   1.20 Fear of specific situation
   1.30 Nonspecific feelings of dread
2. Ineffective individual coping
   2.10 Ritualistic behaviors
        2.11 Interference with employment
        2.12 Interference with relationships with significant others
        2.13 Interference with social activities
        2.14 Interference with activities of daily living
   2.20 Physical symptoms
        2.21 Interference with employment
        2.22 Interference with relationships with significant others
        2.23 Interference with social activities
        2.24 Interference with activities of daily living
3. Disturbance in self-concept
   3.10 Unaware of own identity
   3.20 Change in usual ability to function
   3.30 Concern with inappropriateness of own behavior

Psychiatric diagnoses of anxiety

Expressions of anxiety are classified in three major DSM-III diagnostic categories. Since manifestations of anxiety are often exhibited in physical symptoms, the clinician will need to make careful differentiated diagnoses between anxiety states and physical illnesses. Physical examination and laboratory tests assist to discriminate between physical and anxiety diagnoses. Anxiety, dissociative, and somatoform disorders are not diagnosed when the anxiety and resultant behavior are secondary to other psychiatric disturbances.

The clinician arrives at an appropriate diagnosis based on the specific diagnostic criteria presented for each disorder. The DSM-III is quite specific as to the type and number of criteria that need to be present before a diagnosis can be made. There will be only one primary diagnosis although several diagnoses can be derived based on the DSM-III multiaxial method. The outline* opposite lists the selected psychiatric diagnoses discussed in this chapter. The reader is referred to the DSM-III for specific diagnostic criteria.

*Adapted from American Psychiatric Association. *Diagnostic and Statistical Manual of Mental Disorders*, 3rd ed. Washington, D.C.: American Psychiatric Association, 1980.

I. Anxiety disorders
  A. Phobic disorders
    1. Agoraphobia
    2. Social phobia
    3. Simple phobia
  B. Anxiety states
    1. Panic disorder
    2. Generalized anxiety disorder
    3. Obsessive-compulsive disorder
II. Somatoform disorders
  A. Somatization disorder
  B. Conversion disorder
  C. Psychogenic pain disorder
  D. Hypochondriasis
III. Dissociative disorders
  A. Psychogenic amnesia
  B. Psychogenic fugue
  C. Multiple personality
  D. Depersonalization disorder

CASE EXAMPLE: Assessment of Mrs. Carroll

Identifying information. Mrs. Carroll is a 30-year-old housewife, mother of two children. She is a patient on a medical unit of University Hospital and has been referred for a psychiatric consultation.

Presenting problem. Mrs. Carroll states she was hospitalized 5 days ago with complaints of abdominal pain, diarrhea, headaches, and muscle weakness. She does not understand the need for a psychiatric consultation and states that she has no "emotional problems." Mrs. Carroll's physicians state they are unable to find any physiological explanation for her symptoms.

Brief recent history. Mrs. Carroll states she has not been "feeling well" for several months. She has had numerous physical illnesses in the past 15 years. This most recent episode occurred shortly after Mr. Carroll lost his job 3 months ago. Since that time Mrs. Carroll's physical complaints have become progressively more frequent and currently prevent her from working as a cocktail waitress. She was hospitalized last week when she appeared in the emergency room in a state of moderate dehydration. Her private physician, Dr. Greene, reports that results of all physical examinations and tests have been normal. Mrs. Carroll is taking no medication at the present time. She denies sleep disturbance or weight loss. She also denies use of alcohol but smokes two packs of cigarettes per day.

Family history. Mrs. Carroll is an only child. Her mother died in an auto accident when she was 3 years old and she was raised by her father and grandmother. She married at age 18 and has two children, ages 10 and 8. Mrs. Carroll denies any family history of emotional problems but states that according to her father, her mother had always been "sickly." Mrs. Carroll states her marriage is "usually okay" but has recently been "difficult." Mr. Carroll, an auto worker, is currently unemployed. The family is having financial difficulties and soon will not be able to pay their numerous loans.

Personal history. Mrs. Carroll's childhood was unremarkable until she was 3 years of age when her mother was killed in an auto accident. Her father apparently was unable to raise her alone because of his long work hours and Mrs. Carroll's paternal grandmother moved into the home. Mrs. Carroll states she had some friends throughout school but no close ones. She received C's in high school and married immediately following graduation. She describes herself as having had health problems since high school such as menstrual difficulties, urinary tract infections, fainting, and abdominal pain. She had exploratory surgery for abdominal pain 10 years ago. Findings were normal. She has been employed as a part-time waitress for the past 4 years. She currently has few friends and spends much of her time "watching soap operas, reading magazines, and cleaning the house." She and her husband have recently stopped socializing with friends because of her poor health.

Mental status examination. Mrs. Carroll was lying in bed throughout the interview. She appeared thin with a drawn face. She smoked a cigarette during the interview and would occasionally fidget with the bedsheets. Her speech was soft and calm, although it became more rapid when her husband was mentioned. Eye contact was good. Her mood was slightly depressed. Her affect was appropriate, showing concern for her symptoms. Mrs. Carroll's thoughts were logical and coherent. Her major concerns focused on her physical problems. There was no evidence of suicidal ideation. There was little mention of her husband's unemployment. Mrs. Carroll was alert and oriented and she appeared to be of average intelligence. She was unable to equate her physical symptoms with any stress. She saw no need for psychiatric care. A thorough test of cognitive functioning was not performed.

Summary. Mrs. Carroll is exhibiting a variety of physical symptoms as evidenced by her smoking, fidgeting, drawn face, and depressed mood. She appears slightly anxious and depressed. She was functioning at home and at work until last week when her physical symptoms prevented her from working. She resists discussing her husband's unemployment and the financial strain it is causing in the family.

Psychiatric diagnosis. Somatization disorder

Nursing diagnosis. Ineffective individual coping with physical symptoms preventing employment and social activities.

Plan. Mrs. Carroll refuses any recommendation for outpatient psychiatric treatment. She is unable to relate stress to her physical problems. I provided her with the number of Community Mental Health and several other agencies for her future reference. I recommended she seek professional help because of the impairments her physical problems are now making on her life.

REFERENCES

1. Lief, H. Psychoneurotic disorders. I: Anxiety, conversion, dissociative, and phobic reactions. In A. Freedman and H. Kaplan, Eds., *Comprehensive textbook of psychiatry.* Baltimore: Williams & Wilkins, 1967, pp. 857, 859.
2. Gellhorn, E. The neurophysiological basis of anxiety: A hypothesis, *Perspectives in Biological Medicine,* 1965, *8,* 488.
3. Nemiah, J.C. Psychoneurotic disorders. In A. Nicholi, Ed., *The Harvard guide to modern psychiatry.* Cambridge, Mass.: Belknap Press, 1978, p. 173.
4. American Psychiatric Association. *Diagnostic and Statistical Manual of Mental Disorders,* 3rd ed. Washington, D.C.: American Psychiatric Association, 1980, pp. 225, 253, 341.
5. Mayer, N.G. Diagnostic distribution of admissions to in-patient services of state and county mental hospitals, U.S., 1975. DHEW Publication No. (ADM) 77-158. Rockville, Md.: Department of Health, Education and Welfare, 1975.
6. Distribution of admissions to private mental hospital inpatient units by primary diagnosis, race, and sex, U.S., 1975. Table 4c. Bethesda, Md.: National Institute of Mental Health, 1975.
7. Faden, V. Primary diagnosis of discharges from non-federal general hospital psychiatric inpatient units, U.S., 1975. DHEW Publication No. (ADM) 77-158. Washington, D.C.: Department of Health, Education and Welfare, 1977.
8. Schecter, D. Early developmental roots of anxiety. *Journal of the American Academy of Psychoanalysis,* 1980, *8*(4), 539.
9. Fenchil, O. *The psychoanalytic theory of neurosis.* New York: W. W. Norton & Co., Inc., 1945, p. 132.
10. Freud, S. *New introductory lectures on psychoanalysis.* New York: W.W. Norton & Co., Inc., 1933, p. 84.
11. Horney, K. *The neurotic personality of our time.* New York: W.W. Norton & Co., Inc., 1937.
12. May, R. *The meaning of anxiety.* New York: Ronald Press Co., 1950.
13. Sullivan, H.S. *The interpersonal theory of psychiatry.* New York: W.W. Norton & Co., Inc., 1953.
14. Gray, M. *Neuroses: A comprehensive and critical view.* New York: Van Nostrand Reinhold Co., Inc., 1978, p. 51.
15. Selye, H. *The stress of life,* rev. ed. New York: McGraw-Hill Book Co., 1976.
16. Klein, D., et al. *Diagnosis and drug treatment of psychiatric disorders: Adults and children,* 2nd ed. Baltimore: Williams & Wilkins, 1980, pp. 503, 519.
17. Venkatesh, A., et al. Mitral valve prolapse in anxiety neurosis. *American Heart Journal,* 1980, *100* (3), 304.
18. Mathew, R.J. Catecholamine and monoamine oxidase activity in anxiety. *Acta Psychiatrica Scandinavica,* 1980, *63,* 245.
19. Wolpe, J. *The practice of behavior therapy,* 2nd ed. Elmsford, N.Y.: Pergamon Press, Inc., 1973, pp. 7, 25.
20. Sartorius, N. Epidemiology of anxiety. *Pharmakopsychiatrie Neuro-Psychopharmakologie,* 1980, *13* (5), 253.

21. Goodwin, D. & Guze, S. *Psychiatric diagnosis*, 2nd ed. New York: Oxford University Press, 1979, p. 60.
22. Hamilton, M. The assessment of anxiety states by rating. *British Journal of Medical Psychology*, 1959, *32*, 54.
23. Kim, M., & Moritz, D.A. *Classification of nursing diagnoses*. New York: McGraw-Hill Book Co., 1982.

CHAPTER 5

ASSESSING DISORDERS OF MOOD

Nurses assume an important role in the recognition and detection of mood disorders. They frequently have extended opportunities to observe and evaluate the mood or emotional status of their patients. These observations of emotional behavior combined with the patient's history and physical status provide the clinical evidence necessary to accurately diagnose and treat a mood disorder. A change in mood can be a primary psychiatric disorder or it can be precipitated by a particular physical illness or medication. In addition, it is now thought that 13% to 20% of the population suffers from "depressive symptoms" at some time during their lives. Therefore, because of the high prevalence of mood changes and because these changes are observed in a variety of clinical settings, all nurses should be proficient in assessing for disorders of mood. This chapter is devoted to providing nurses with the assessment skills necessary to detect mood disorders exhibited by their patients.

Descriptions of affective disorders* date back to the fourth century B.C. when Hippocrates first wrote of "melancholia" (depression) resulting from the influence of black bile and phlegm on the brain. Throughout history there continued to be numerous references to melancholia by Aristotle, Aretaeus of Cappadocia, Plutarch, Pinel, and James.[1-3] Associations were made between melancholia and mania as far back as the second century A.D. There was even mention of these disorders being attributed to "humoral imbalances," a beginning argument in favor of the biological theories of affective disorders. Although these writings were sometimes centuries apart, there is a relative consistency in describing a condition that remains strikingly similar to current descriptions of mood disorders.

In the latter part of the nineteenth century, a major contribution to the classification of affective disorders was made by Kraeplin. He separated the functional psychoses into two groups, dementia praecox and

---

*The terms affective disorder and mood disorder will be used synonomously in this chapter.

manic depressive psychosis. Dementia praecox (schizophrenia) was thought to be chronic with a poor prognosis, while manic depressive psychosis was episodic with periods of good or "normal" functioning between episodes. Kraeplin felt very strongly that manic depressive psychosis was innate (biological) and not governed by social or intrapsychic forces.

Freud, on the other hand, postulated the opposite conviction. In his classic work, *Mourning and Melancholia*, he outlined his theory of the psychodynamic genesis of depression based on the loss of a love-object.[4] Although the theories of the organization of depression and mania differed, the symptoms and clinical descriptions described were similar and provided a solid foundation upon which current ideas and research are based.

DEFINITION

Mood is often referred to as a spectrum of feelings extending from elation at one extreme to despair at the other. Disorders of mood are characterized by two primary abnormalities or extremes, depression and mania. Both can be visualized as occurring along a continuum ranging from normal to pathological, as follows:

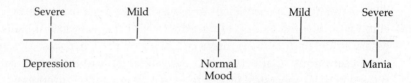

The pathological or severe range is clearly out of proportion to the patient's usual demeanor, either too intense or too prolonged. These discrete syndromes of pathological mood are referred to as affective disorders.

The boundary between normal and abnormal mood is not always easily defined. All individuals experience highs and lows or mood swings that are not considered abnormal. What is it then that distinguishes "normal" mood changes from the severe forms of mania and depression? Generally, if the episode or behavior is more intense and prolonged than usual, interferes with activities of daily living, and pervades an individual's thinking and emotions, the disorder should be considered pathological and in need of intervention.

The emphasis in assessing affective disorders should be on the change that occurs in individuals. What is different now about a particular patient? What is the patient not able to do or enjoy today that was routine 2 months ago? A central feature in affective disorders is the deviation in mood, but there are many other clinical features unique to both depression and mania that should be investigated. Associated with alterations in mood are such symptoms as insomnia, fatigue, anorexia, self-reproach, psychomotor retardation, agitation, hyperactivity, suicidal ideation, and flight of ideas. Most notable, true affective disorders differ from "normal" mood changes in that they have a specific onset, course, duration, and outcome.

CLASSIFICATION

A method of classification is necessary to understand mania and depression. There are as many different classifications of affective disorders as there are articles and books written about the syndromes. Historically, the attempt has been made to classify mood disorders in terms of dichotomies: endogenous vs. reactive, psychotic vs. neurotic, agitated vs. retarded, mild vs. severe, bipolar vs. unipolar, and primary vs. secondary. These subtypes were devised based on various clinical and research criteria.

Unfortunately, not one of the many classification systems is consistently utilized. The result has been a sharp division by those health care personnel who do research and those in clinical practice. The two groups have different classification needs. Clinicians must find a category for every patient seen. Therefore they prefer categories that tend to be broad and generalizable. Researchers, on the other hand, like to narrowly define their investigative scope and require more stringent guidelines for classification in an attempt to control variables.

Because of the confusion, ambiguity, and controversy surrounding the classification issue, the DSM-III was designed to meet the needs of both researchers and clinicians. It categorizes mood disturbances based on observed symptomatology rather than theoretical conjecture. The affective disorders are divided into three main categories: major affective disorders, other specific affective disorders, and atypical affective disorders. This chapter will use the DSM-III's classification scheme, discussing major affective disorders.

Major affective disorders

The category of major affective disorder includes both major depression and bipolar disorder. These two categories are distinguished by whether or not there has ever been a manic episode. Major depression is diagnosed when the patient experiences only depressed episodes. Bipolar disorder is diagnosed if the patient has had at least one manic episode with or without an episode of depression. Bipolar patients would be subclassified as manic if they were in a manic state; depressed if they were depressed but had a history of a manic episode; or mixed if they showed symptoms of both mania and depression or were seen to rapidly shift moods.

Other specific affective disorders

Two subcategories are included under other specific affective disorders: cyclothymic disorder and dysthymic disorder. Patients would typically show symptoms similar to those in the major affective disorder category only less severe and less comprehensive. A cyclothymic disorder is characterized by alternating episodes of depression and hypomania not severe enough to be labeled bipolar. With a dysthymic disorder the degree or severity of depression is considerably less and the patient would have a history of a depressive character style.

Atypical affective disorders

This category is a residual one for disorders that are "atypical" or do not meet the strict requirements of the previous two. For example, a patient's manic symptoms may not be severe enough to warrant a diagnosis of bipolar affective disorder and would instead be classified under atypical bipolar disorder. This category should be used sparingly for only those cases that do not fit neatly into the major or other specific affective disorder category.

EPIDEMIOLOGY
Major depressive disorder

Studies have shown that the prevalence of non-bipolar depression in industrialized countries is about 2.0 cases per 100 for men and between 2.0 and 9.3 cases per 100 for women. Interestingly, the highest rates are reported in Africa: 14.3 for men and 22.6 for women.[5]

The incidence of non-bipolar depression in women is between 247 and 7800 per 100,000 per year and the incidence for men is approximately 82 per 100,000 per year.[5] These estimates are thought to be low since as many as one quarter of all people with depressive episodes may go untreated.

Research suggests there are certain risk factors associated with a non-bipolar, major depressive episode. Current information and statistics indicate those in the general population who are more prone to depression. Familiarity with these factors helps nurses in their clinical practice to identify patients at risk. Several risk factors worth noting are sex, age, family experiences, personality characteristics, recent life stresses, and the postpartum and menopausal periods.

Sex. It has long been known that women appear to suffer from depression roughly twice as often as men. It was often speculated that this statistic could be attributed to the help-seeking behavior of women.

Recent studies have proven this sex difference is real and not just the result of women seeking help more often.[6]

Age. Depression has no age limit. Studies now show depression may be a major cause of behavior disorders in children as well as the cause of behavioral and organic changes in older adults. Depression can strike at any age but usually occurs after age 30. The rates tend to increase with increasing age.

Family experience. An important risk factor to consider is that a family history of depression or alcoholism increases the likelihood of depression in offspring. First-degree relatives of depressed probands are twice as likely to be depressed or alcoholic as relatives of controls.[7] Although the evidence for the genetic transmission of bipolar disorder is becoming increasingly strong, the transmission of unipolar depression is still uncertain and the focus of considerable debate. Is depression genetically, culturally, or environmentally passed on from one generation to the next? The question remains to be answered.

Orvaschel[8], however, concluded that environmental forces do play a part in adult depression. Case studies reveal that hostile, chaotic, negative family environments produce more depressed adults than do control environments. The complexity of a retrospective evaluation of childhood experiences considerably clouds the prospect of producing reliable data. More longitudinal studies are needed that follow individuals and their families throughout their life spans.

In the same study, Orvaschel refutes the evidence of a correlation between early parental death and subsequent depression. He found no difference between depressed adult patients with an early parental loss and control subjects. Many clinicians still believe, however, that the loss of a parent or parental figure in the oral or genital phases of development predisposes individuals to depression. The risk factor of early loss and adult depression needs further exploration, but it is certainly worth investigating and should be questioned when taking a family history.

Personality characteristics. Whenever a mood disorder is suspected the patient's underlying personality style should be determined. Although most research is inconclusive and needs replication, preliminary data reveal certain personality traits that are more prominent in people who become depressed. These individuals tend to be shy, insecure people who worry a lot and cannot handle a lot of stress. They tend to internalize their feelings, take things very personally, and lack assertive behavior. They more often have an external locus of control (see themselves as being controlled by the environment) and are frequently described as obsessive-compulsive individuals.

While taking a personal history, patients should be asked to describe their behavior at work and at home. It is useful to give patients certain situations and ask them how they would respond: "What would happen if another salesperson with less experience were promoted over you?" "How do you spend your time on the weekends?" "How would your friends describe you in social situations?" The answers to these questions will provide you with substantial data to determine a premorbid personality style. Often it may be necessary to obtain this information from family members if the patient is severely depressed.

Recent life stresses. Frequently patients will seek treatment after a major life event. These life events are often negative ones such as the death of a loved one, dissolution of a meaningful relationship, job loss, financial difficulties, or trouble with the law. Many times an event like retirement, although viewed as a positive experience, significantly changes an individual's pattern of behavior and can confuse and overwhelm even those who have carefully planned for it. The absence of a recent stress or precipitating event should not preclude ruling out a major depression. It is not a prerequisite nor is it included in the DSM-III criteria for a major depressive episode, but individuals with recent life stresses seem to be at risk for an affective disorder.

Postpartum and menopausal periods. While there is evidence of increased risk of depression during the postpartum period (up to 6 months), several recent reports refute the correlation between depression and menopause. Although the incidence of depression is high for women over age 45, it is more likely related to age and not to menopause.[5,9] During the postpartum period depression is thought to be caused by endocrine changes, role changes, stress, or a combination of these.

Bipolar affective disorder

A bipolar disorder includes the presence or history of mania. Unipolar or major depression involves depression alone. The criterion for inclusion in this category then is either a current or past manic episode. There is evidence that about 1 in 10 affectively disordered patients is bipolar. The incidence is about 9 to 15.2 new cases per 100,000 for men per year and about 7.4 to 32 new cases per 100,000 women per year.[3-5]

Just as there are known and proven risk factors associated with a major depressive episode, there are certain factors that place people at risk for bipolar illness. Several of the more important factors include sex, age, social class, and family experiences.

Sex. Just as with major depression, the prevalence of bipolar depression is greater in women, but the ratio of bipolar women to men is not as great as that in unipolar depression.

Age. Age-specific factors provide no better source of agreement among researchers than many of the other risk factors. There is disagreement as to the age of first onset, but a modal age of several studies is around 32 years old. The interval between episodes tends to decrease with increasing age and the length of each episode increases.[10]

Social class. A link between bipolar mood disorder and the upper socioeconomic class has been suggested.[11] It is thought that the disorder affects those who are high achievers, highly creative, ambitious, and energetic people who strive for success. These individuals tend to achieve higher levels of education and obtain more prestigious positions than control subjects.

Family experience. The importance of genetic factors in the transmission of a bipolar disorder is well documented.[12,13] A more complete description of genetic transmission will be described in the Causative Factors section of this chapter.

Just as with major depression a family history of bipolar affective disorder increases the likelihood of mania and depression in offspring. A complete family history should yield information about the emotional health of first-degree relatives as well as their substance abuse history. It is also important to ascertain the nature or circumstances surrounding marital separation or divorce. There is evidence that bipolar mood disorder is found more often in people who are either single or divorced. The fact that bipolar illness can be so disruptive leads one to believe that the disorder contributes to divorce rather than divorce being a precipitant for the disorder.

CAUSATIVE FACTORS

Exciting new discoveries are being made every day that support the biochemical theories of affective illnesses. Recent advances offer promising evidence that supports the neuroendocrine and biogenic amine involvement in affective disorders. These findings alone, however, do not account for the clinical diversity found with depression and mania. Intrapsychic factors also contribute to the complexity of mood disorders. While causative theories of many disorders tend to be incompatible, the biological and intrapsychic theories of affective disorders are interdependent. It is likely that affective disorders result from a combination of a wide variety of influences. Mood is a complex phenomenon and changes in mood most likely reflect changes in both biochemical and psychological processes.

The following theoretical conjectures regarding mood disorders will be described: genetic, the amine hypothesis, neuroendocrine abnormalities, electrolyte imbalances, intrapsychic factors, and miscellaneous causes of affective illness.

Genetic

There is compelling evidence of the genetic influences in affective disorders. Data from studies of twins, people who were adopted, and families show that as many as 20% of first-degree relatives can expect to exhibit symptoms of major depression or bipolar illness. The twin studies are perhaps the most remarkable, with concordance rates from affective disorders in monozygotic twins ranging from 33% to 92.6% depending on the study.[14]* There is also supportive data for the hereditary link from twins raised apart, but there is, understandably, a limited number of these cases available for study.

Numerous family studies reveal that bipolar probands can have both bipolar and unipolar first-degree relatives, a predominance of them being bipolar. Unipolar probands tend to show a high rate of only unipolar depression in their family history. These statistics are consistent with comparisons of morbidity rates in the general population.

An association between major depressive disorder (unipolar) and alcoholism has long been postulated. There is a higher prevalence of mood disorders and alcoholism among first-degree relatives of affectively ill patients than among psychiatric or normal controls.

Although genetic evidence remains inconclusive, it is doubtful that random environmental forces could account for the predominance of affective illness observed in families. It is possible that heredity determines the potential for mood disorders, biological forces subsequently trigger them, and environmental factors influence how symptoms and behaviors are exhibited.

The significance of genetic vulnerability necessitates the need for genetic counseling for persons at risk. Patients with a mood disorder should be educated about the familial nature of their illness.

Biogenic amines

Zis provides a comprehensive review of the importance of the monoaminergic systems in appetitive, endocrine, emotional, psychomotor, and cognitive functions.[15] The amine hypothesis associates affective disorders with either excessive or insufficient availability of one or more neurotransmitter amines at critical adrenergic receptor sites in the brain. Recent evidence points to the significance of abnormalities in certain brain amines, especially norepinephrine (NE) and serotonin (5-HT) in affective disorders. In depression there is usually a deficit of one or more of the neurotransmitters while mania seems to be related to neurotransmitter imbalances.

---

*Dizygotic twins tend to have a concordancy rate of about 20%.

Since it is impossible to directly measure brain NE levels, the metabolites of NE in the cerebrospinal fluid (CSF) and urine are monitored. A major metabolite of NE, 3-methoxy-4-hydroxyphenylglycol (MHPG), is excreted in the urine and CSF. It is found in significantly lower levels in the urine of some depressed patients. Bipolar patients tend to have the lowest 24-hour urinary MHPG excretion.[15] The data are inconclusive for altered MHPG levels in the CSF. These metabolites are also influenced by such variables as age, sex, diet, activity, and phase of illness. Recent research now controls more closely for these factors yielding more consistent findings.

Additional support for the amine hypothesis is offered by the mechanistic action of the tricyclic antidepressants, the monoamine oxidase inhibitors (MAOI), and electroconvulsive therapy (ECT). The tricyclics prevent the reuptake of NE into the presynaptic neuron and thus increase the amount of the neurotransmitter available. ECT also increases the level of brain NE. The MAOIs (such as phenelzine and tranylcypromine) interfere with the enzyme that aids in the breakdown of NE. These three major treatments of choice all help to restore normal levels of NE at brain receptor sites, thereby relieving depression.

Neuroendocrine abnormalities

For many years there has been a known association between certain endocrine dysfunctions and affective disorders. Depression and mania are both cyclical phenomena and may be related to the ebb and flow of hormonal factors. During the past two decades there has been remarkable progress in exploring the role that endocrine functioning plays in mania and depression. Appetite, mood, libido, sleep, and autonomic activity are all functions that may be disturbed in depressed patients. These functions are regulated and mediated through the limbic system, which also regulates neuroendocrine activity. Sophisticated measurement tools have documented abnormal levels of cortisol, human growth hormone (HGH), and thyroid-stimulating hormone (TSH) in depression.

Many of the hypersecreting corticosteroid findings in depression are similar to the changes associated with Cushing's disease. Individuals with Cushing's disease exhibit mood changes of euphoria and depression. In addition, the administration of steroids for therapeutic purposes frequently produces severe mood swings. Although it is often difficult to distinguish Cushing's disease from depression based on clinical laboratory data, the cortisol production in depressive patients is not nearly as severe as in those with Cushing's disease, and depressive patients never exhibit any of the tissue changes associated with Cushing's disease.

Depressed patients tend to exhibit increased total cortisol secretion and a loss of the normal circadian pattern. One way researchers have discovered this is by administering the synthetic glucocorticoid, dexamethasone, to depressed patients. In normal subjects, there would be a subsequent suppression of cortisol secretion. Depressed patients, however, are resistant to cortisol suppression and instead exhibit an escape manifested by increased levels of post-dexamethasone cortisol secretion. A cortisol value over 5 μg/dl is abnormal after an ingestion of 1 or 2 mg of dexamethasone.[16] The dexamethasone suppression test is discussed further in the section on Assessment Tools.

Patients with hypothyroidism tend to exhibit symptoms similar to depression. Prange[17] and others have shown a deficient thyroid-stimulating hormone (TSH) response to an infusion of thyrotropin releasing hormone (TRH). Gold et al.[18] reported that unipolar patients are more prone to deficiencies than are bipolar patients.

Human growth hormone (HGH) responses are more difficult to accurately measure because they are affected by estrogen and testosterone levels, obesity, and nutrition. Nevertheless, Carroll[19] established that there is a deficient HGH response in depressive patients to insulininduced hypoglycemia as compared to normal subjects. What is interesting is that 5-HT and NE are neurotransmitters that are believed to mediate the HGH response to hypoglycemia. This evidence supports the theory of a connection or some interdependence among all the biochemical networks. The different amine systems, electrolytes, and hormones can all influence the activity of endocrine functioning. It has been suggested that cycles may be established in patients with mood disorders resulting from consecutive disturbances in multiple systems.[20]

Electrolyte metabolism

It has already been stated that mania and depression may result from the malfunction of neuronal activity. Electrolytes play an important role in normal neuronal functioning. They are responsible for maintaining the normal resting states of nerves and for the carrying of the current responsible for the transmission, storage, and release of the key neurotransmitters associated with mood disorders.

In persons suffering from depression there is a disturbance in the distribution of sodium and potassium across the cell membrane. Studies have shown an excess of sodium within the nerve cells of depressed patients. Upon recovery, these electrolytes return to normal levels.[20] It is interesting that lithium, used in the treatment of affective disorders, interferes with the cellular exchange of sodium and regulates the level according to whether the patient is manic or depressed.

Psychodynamic theory

In 1917 Freud published his classic work, *Mourning and Melancholia*, in which he compares the conditions of melancholia (a major affective disorder) and grief. He described mourning as a reaction to the loss of a love-object or to the loss of an abstraction such as fatherhood, liberty, freedom, or career. Although mourning involves a temporary departure from the normal way of a person's life, it is viewed as normal and in fact necessary for "working through" the grief and resolving the loss.

Melancholia, on the other hand, occurs only in certain people. It has some features similar to mourning, but there are also distinguishing differences. Like mourning, melancholia is the result of the loss of a love-object. The similar feelings include dejection, loss of interest, and emptiness. The feature that is missing in mourning but usually present with melancholia is the loss of self-esteem. There is an inhibition and constriction of the ego on a grand scale. In mourning, individuals view life as empty and the world as poor, but with melancholia it is the self that is impoverished. It is the self that the melancholic person hates. Anger becomes self-directed or internalized rather than externally directed. Freud postulated that "if one listens patiently . . . one cannot in the end avoid the impression that the most violent self-accusations are hardly at all applicable to the patient himself . . . but rather reproaches against a loved object which have been shifted on to the patient's own ego."[4] He described this as a regression from the object cathexis to the still narcissistic oral phase of the libido. Freud postulated that the difference between whether mourning or melancholia results from a loss may rest with the presence of ambivalence in the person's relationships. The hostile part of the ambivalence gets directed toward the ego in self-reproaches. After experiencing a loss, individuals frequently develop defenses that serve to recapture or retain the lost object. Several defense mechanisms commonly associated with Freud's theory of melancholia are described in Table 5:1.

Abraham[21] believed that ungratified sexual desires stimulate feelings of hatred and hostility, which diminish an individual's capacity for love. This repressed hostility results in emotional impoverishment.

Melanie Klein[22] saw the melancholic process as hinging on the mother-child relationship in the child's first year of life. An infant reacts to frustration with rage. The weakness of the infantile ego leaves the child afraid of being destroyed by these impulses. Children resolve these feelings when they feel assured of their mother's love. If that assurance never develops there will always be a predisposition to feelings of sadness, helplessness, and guilt.

TABLE 5:1	Defense mechanisms associated with melancholia
Defense mechanism	*Definition*
Identification	Process of modifying selected areas of one's self in accordance with the image of another person
Denial	Logical facts or implications of reality are denied in favor of internally derived, more comfortable fantasies
Introjection	Fixed mental representation of a lost loved one; internalizing the image of another person
Repression	Thoughts, emotions, and sensations are involuntarily taken out of awareness into the unconscious

Others who have written extensively on intrapsychic theories of depression include Bebring, Jacobson, Rado, and Kohut.

Miscellaneous causes of affective disorders

In addition to the causative factors already described, mood disorders have been associated with numerous toxic and pharmacological agents as well as with certain physical diseases. Any condition that impairs the normal functioning of the central nervous system may produce a change in mood, namely mania or depression.

Mood changes can occur as a result of medications administered for unrelated conditions. Some of the more common drugs that may potentially elicit a mood change are:

Sedatives:	Alcohol
	Barbiturates
	Benzodiazepines
Antihypertensives:	Reserpine
	Propranolol
Steroids:	Corticosteroids
	Oral contraceptives
Other:	Marijuana
	Cocaine
	Cimetidine
	Isoniazid
	Levodopa
	Antidepressants
	Amphetamines

Many times patients will begin to use drugs such as diazepam (Valium), marijuana, and alcohol in an attempt to alleviate depressive symptoms. Most often these drugs only intensify the problem instead of alleviating it.

Mood changes may precede, accompany, or follow a larger number of medical conditions. Several of the more common conditions frequently associated with concurrent mood fluctuations are:

Viral infections:	Influenza, mononucleosis
Metabolic disorders:	Diabetes, hypothyroidism
Endocrine disorders:	Cushing's disease, Pick's disease
Central nervous systems disorders:	Parkinson's disease, subdural hematoma, Alzheimer's disease, multiple sclerosis
Malignancies:	Pancreatic, hepatic
Anemias:	Pernicious anemia

A complete medical workup and a thorough nursing assessment is indicated for every patient with a suspected mood disorder. Nurses working in medical and surgical areas should take special care in observing their patients for fluctuations in mood resulting from physical illness or pharmacological treatment.

CLINICAL PRESENTATION

For purposes of clarity in describing how patients with affective disorders exhibit symptomatology, major depression and bipolar illness will be described in terms of the symptoms of depression and mania, respectively. Nurses should keep in mind, however, that these categories are used solely to facilitate the description of the pathological symptomatology and are not meant to represent the accepted descriptive categories of DSM-III as described earlier in this chapter.

There is a wide array of situations where nurses have excellent opportunities to observe and assess patients for symptoms of affective disorders. Clinics, home visits, medical/surgical units, emergency rooms, and psychiatric units are examples of the numerous places nurses can be astute to changes in the patient's mood. Depressive symptoms usually develop more insidiously and it may not be the patient who first recognizes something is wrong. Often family members, friends, or co-workers will observe changes in the patient's behavior that warrant concern. For example, a wife may observe that her husband has lost his appetite, is not sleeping well, and is isolating himself from the family. The husband himself may report he just had a lot on his mind and was not even aware of his change in behavior. A teacher may notice the increasing acting out behavior of a fourth grader or the declining grades of a high school student. It is often significant others who first confront patients about the observed behavior rather than patients volunteering that they feel depressed. Again, this description applies to major depressive disorders and not to reactive depressions that we all experience from time to time.

Manic symptoms, on the other hand, usually develop more rapidly and are more pronounced, and there is seldom any doubt that the patient is in need of treatment. The patient may exhibit pressured speech, an eccentric appearance, dangerous and/or grandiose behavior, and the inability (or the felt need) to sleep. Manic patients often deny any problem and in fact will report that they have never felt better. Again, it is usually significant others, or the police, who will bring patients experiencing symptoms of mania to the nurse's attention. Because manic symptoms are usually so dramatic it is usually a hospital or clinic where the nurse will first observe this behavior.

Only the clinical manifestations for the more severe range of affective disorders will be described in the following section. Milder forms of depression and mania (hypomania) are usually less intense, less pronounced, and less prolonged versions of what is depicted. Two obvious differences between the mild and severe forms of affective illness are the absence of a thought disorder in milder forms of depression and mania and the lack of need for hospitalization.

Physical manifestations

Depression. The physical or vegetative symptoms of depression are considered by some to be evidence supporting the biochemical theories of affective disorders. The specific physiological functions that are often disrupted are regulated and mediated through the limbic system. This system also regulates neuroendocrine functioning, which is believed to play a significant role in the pathogenic development of mood disorders.

The most common complaints include a sleep disturbance, loss or decrease of appetitive functions, and fatigue. Sleep disturbances usually involve both initial and middle insomnia and early morning awakening. Occasionally, a sleep disturbance is marked by increased sleep. Overall, patients report never feeling rested no matter how much sleep they get. Investigators have solid evidence based on direct observation and interpretation of electroencephalogram (EEG) recordings that depressed patients sleep less than normal controls. The studies also show an excessive amount of restlessness and movement during the night among depressed patients.[1]

The patient's sleeping pattern is a good topic to initially use when assessing for suspected mood disorders. Many people do not associate sleep difficulties with psychiatric illness. It is a safe, nonthreatening topic that patients will usually freely discuss. Some useful questions the nurse should ask include:

Tell me how you are sleeping.
Is this a normal sleep pattern for you?
Do you wake up during the night? How often?
Are you able to fall back to sleep?
What time are you waking up in the morning?

Loss of appetite is one of the earliest signals of a depressive episode. Anorexia with some weight loss is usually reported by approximately 75% of depressed patients. Weight loss of up to 40 lb can occur within several months. Again, questioning about changes in appetite should reveal such information as detailed weight loss, length of time in which the weight loss occurred, and do patients fix their own food or do they wait for others to fix meals for them.

Loss of interest in sex (decreased libido) is also a frequently mentioned symptom of depressed patients. Another is fatigue, which patients describe as loss of energy, listlessness, or exhaustion. The depressed patient may also be preoccupied with bodily functioning. This preoccupation can range from hypochondriacal thinking to frank somatic delusions. Other frequently reported physical manifestations of depressions are listed in Table 5:2.

TABLE 5:2   **Common presenting manifestations of physical expressions of depression**

System affected	Manifestation
General	Sleep disturbance
	Appetite change
	Decreased libido
	Fatigue
	Pain of any nature
	Dizziness
	Dry mouth or a burning, unpleasant taste
Cardiovascular	Tachycardia
	Dyspnea
Gastrointestinal	Nausea
	Vomiting
	Constipation
	Diarrhea
	Indigestion
Endocrine	Menstrual irregularities
Neurological	Blurred vision
	Paresthesia

Mania. Manic patients tend to report an overall good feeling. They experience an increased amount of energy and usually exhibit an increase in sexual interest and activity. The sleep disturbance tends to be the same as for depressives—diminished. Their physical appearance usually deteriorates and is often eccentric and flamboyant in nature.

Because none of these symptoms are specific to affective disorders, nurses need to carefully document subjective reports from their patients about physical concerns or changes. It is also important to document these reports, because just as a report of loss of appetite is associated with depression so is a report of return of a normal appetite an indication that the depression may be lifting.

> CASE EXAMPLE: Mr. Maglocci was brought to the psychiatric clinic by his wife because she had noticed her husband had lost weight, was not sleeping well, was no longer interested in sex, and was spending more time alone. She had initially insisted he see their family doctor who, after extensive testing, found nothing physically wrong with Mr. Maglocci. She referred him to the psychiatric clinic for evaluation. Mr. Maglocci began the interview by saying "He was not sure what was wrong, but he knew he was not himself." He no longer felt physically capable of continuing in his job as chief executive officer of a local manufacturing firm.

Emotional and cognitive manifestations

Depression. Emotional expressions of depressive symptoms offer additional key information nurses can utilize in assessing disorders of mood. Depression is a disorder of mood; therefore subjective reports of how patients feel are of paramount importance. Nurses can begin by asking the patient, "Tell me how you've been feeling lately?" Depressed patients typically describe their feelings as "blue, sad, low, hopeless." Profound unhappiness, boredom, loneliness, emptiness, and desperation are other common reports. Nurses should remember that individuals who are depressed actually feel tremendous emotional anguish that can be just as crippling as any physical pain. Their despair and intense suffering is real. Depressed patients usually exhibit a constricted or flat affect, decreased motivation, and report a diminished sense of pleasure in activities they formerly found pleasurable. For example, a patient may volunteer that she no longer enjoys her Friday afternoon bridge club that she organized 2 years ago.

A diurnal variation often characterizes depression. Typically, patients report feeling worse in the morning and better as the day goes on. Occasionally, though, no particular pattern is discernible.

Depression also distorts patients' perceptions of themselves and their surroundings. Predominant themes of the distortions center around guilt, pessimism, and negativism. Depressed patients often express feelings of guilt over what may seem to be trivial events. There is a strong feeling of self-reproach and self-criticism. The feelings may progress to the point where patients hate themselves and feel disgusting. These self-deprecating feelings are related to egocentric notions of causality. Patients may express feeling responsible for the country's economic or unemployment situation or a particular world crisis. They often view themselves as criminals and worthy of punishment.

There can be increased concern about one's physical appearance and depressed patients will often report feeling ugly and repulsive. A woman may wear a veil over her face to hide her appearance while a man may believe he has grown quite fat even with evidence to support this is not true.

Depressed patients may also experience a sense of derealization or depersonalization and see themselves as apart or different from others. The passage of time slows down and they feel pessimistic about the future, and about their own prognosis. It is interesting that of 150 patients interviewed, only 25% of the bipolar affected group thought they would get better as compared to 61% of those with a medical illness. Most patients can be expected to recover from a bipolar episode while there are numerous incurable medical problems.[1] This speaks to the truly desperate sense of hopelessness and pessimism depressed patients experience.

Depressed patients are preoccupied with themselves. As mentioned previously the preoccupations often center around bodily functions and self-image. They worry and ruminate about past and present events. There is little concern for the future. One young man kept expecting the police to arrest him for a minor traffic violation that had occurred several years ago. The cognitive processes, as well as thought content, are distorted. The quality and quantity of thoughts may be diminished and there may be impaired memory and difficulty concentrating for more than a minute or two.

Suicidal and, to a lesser extent, homicidal thoughts have historically been associated with depression. The thoughts may take a variety of forms from a fleeting thought to a carefully detailed plan. Suicidal wishes may also take the form of the patient taking unnecessary risks such as driving an automobile at a high rate of speed. Or the patient may pursue a more passive method of self-abuse by not eating, not taking prescribed medications, or mixing drugs and alcohol. Specific questioning of self-destructive thoughts should occur to ascertain the seriousness of the risk. Assessing a patient's potential for violence is covered more thoroughly in Chapter 8 of this book.

Sometimes depression is so severe that patients will experience delusions (fixed false beliefs), hallucinations (false sensory perceptions), or other manifestations of impaired reality testing. Nihilistic and somatic delusions are the most common. In a nihilistic delusion patients believe the world is empty, all is lost, and may in fact believe they are dead. Somatic delusions are hypochondriacal in nature as evidenced, for example, by the patient who believes he has an incurable disease or that his intestines are rotten.

Few depressed patients report hallucinations. When they do occur, however, patients frequently report hearing voices telling them they are bad or they deserve to die. Others may include seeing dead people or hearing the voices of deceased relatives.

Mania. The emotional manifestations of mania are mostly opposite those for depression. Manic patients emotionally feel happy, carefree, and euphoric, but because they are also emotionally labile, that euphoria and cheerfulness can quickly change to irritation and hostility. Their

TABLE 5:3	Emotional, perceptual, and cognitive manifestations of affective disorders	
	Depression	*Mania*
Emotional	Sadness, gloom, dejected mood, loneliness, despair, flat or constricted affect, crying spells, diminished sense of pleasure, diurnal variation, anxiety, tension, irritability, hopelessness, hostility, ambivalence, decreased motivation, indifference	Happiness, carefree mood, humor, elation, euphoria, irritability, anger, crying spells, heightened sense of pleasure, increased motivation, unrealistic hopefulness, expansive mood, extreme lability
Perceptual	Feelings of guilt, self-reproach, self-criticism, worthlessness, evil, distorted body image, pessimism, slow passage of time; underestimates abilities, overestimates problems	Feelings of grandiosity, inflated sense of self, distorted self-image, optimism; interest in all activities, overestimates abilities, underestimates problems; heightened sensory perceptions
Cognitive	Impaired memory, difficulty thinking and concentrating, preoccupation with self, ruminations, worrying, slowed thoughts, diminished quality and constriction of thoughts, poor judgment, delusions and hallucinations, suicidal and homicidal ideation	Difficulty concentrating, flight of ideas, distractibility, thought rushing, poor judgment, hallucinations, delusions of grandeur

moods tend to be expansive and they enjoy a heightened sense of pleasure with even mundane tasks.

Manic patients also experience perceptual distortions, but instead
of feeling worthless, they experience feelings of grandiosity and an inflated sense of self. They frequently report heightened sensory perceptions and will underestimate or completely deny any problems. In one
example, a man on the inpatient unit told the nurse that he needed an
overnight pass to fly to California to appear on the Johnny Carson Show.
He reported that he was considered to be the best comedian in the world.

Patients who are manic also experience problems with cognition.
They will have difficulty concentrating, be easily distractible, and exhibit
flight of ideas. This flight of ideas differs from that of schizophrenic
patients in that with manic patients the ideas, although sped up, are
still understandable. They may experience delusions of grandeur and
hallucinations that tend to be either sexual or religious in nature. Manic
patients are normally not suicidal, but their feelings of grandiosity may
lead to inflated notions about their power. For instance, a woman may
believe she can fly and attempt to do so by jumping off a tall building.
Nurses should take care to assure that manic patients are afforded the
same safety and protection as depressed patients since their judgment
can be so severely impaired.

> CASE EXAMPLE: Mr. Davidson is a 20-year-old male who was brought to
> the emergency room by the police after being found standing on the
> railroad tracks and refusing to move. He wanted to prove that he was
> the strongest man alive and had supernatural powers by proving he
> could stop a train with one arm. Mr. Davidson could not understand
> why he had been brought to the hospital; he didn't feel sick. During
> the interview he exhibited flight of ideas and consistently performed
> poorly on judgment questions. When questioned about drug use, Mr.
> Davidson reported that he had taken several amphetamines earlier that
> day, but he had not noticed any effect from the pills.

Table 5:3 summarizes the more frequent emotional and cognitive
manifestations of affective disorders.

Behavioral manifestations

Depression. There is some overlap between features already described and what are considered observable behavioral manifestations
of depression. The picture of a classically depressed individual is not
hard to define. The sad expression, disheveled appearance, poor eye
contact, stooped posture, slow speech, and either agitated or retarded
motor behavior are pathognomonic expressions of depression. Agitated
motor activity alone can be so overwhelming that other symptoms go

unnoticed. The patient feels restless and there is considerable pacing and wringing of one's hands. Purposeful behavior is diminished. Retarded behavior is characterized by slowed responses and movements. Routine tasks may take hours to perform and speech may slow to where the patient is mute or even stuporous. There is a lack of spontaneity and patients move as though their bodies are weighed down. Other adjectives used to describe depressive behavior include forlorn, melancholic, dejected, and pathetic. Some patients in the early stage of a depressive episode will attempt to hide their sad feelings behind a cheerful facade. If other symptoms are observed and depression is suspected, careful probing and the development of trust will eventually unmask the patient's true despondent feelings.

Social relationships are impaired as well. The depressed person becomes isolative, feeling unable to reach out to others. There is a loss of social and emotional attachments and those relationships that survive are impoverished. Depressed patients will usually withdraw unless otherwise encouraged or directed. They will choose passive solitary activities often because of lack of energy and the anxiety felt in social situations, and yet at the same time there is an increased desire for dependency. It is not so much the need, but the desire, to be helped with activities that the patient would normally be capable of handling alone that characterizes depression. For example, many depressed patients require assistance feeding and bathing themselves and others often refuse to leave the treatment room or their hospital bed.

Mania. Having interviewed or even just having observed a manic patient, one is unlikely to ever forget the experience. The atmosphere becomes intense and highly charged. The patient's behavior is hyperactive and there is an accelerated pace of psychological activity. Patients may be extremely verbose and in a festive, playful mood that can quickly change to anger and hostility if their desires are thwarted. Manic patients are considerably uninhibited and will frequently embarrass those around them. Speech is pressured and often accompanied by rhyming and punning.

Their behavior is typified in particular by poor impulse control. Patients in a manic episode may spend a large amount of money with a reckless abandon and lack of discrimination that characterizes an impairment in their sense of reality. They behave peccantly, engaging in senseless and risky adventures. One woman bought a new car when hers ran out of gas and a college student began making phone calls trying to order several hundred personal computers for all his fraternity brothers.

Manic patients are described as gregarious and often increase their social contacts. Their behavior is provocative and sexual activity in-

TABLE 5:4	Common behavioral manifestations of affective disorders	
	Depression	*Mania*
Interpersonal	Loss of attachments Impoverished relationships Isolative behavior Passive activities Increased dependency	Increased social contacts Increased sexual activity Manipulative behavior Gregarious and aggressive behavior

Intrapersonal	Agitated or retarded motor
	  behavior
	Disheveled appearance
	Slow speech
	Stooped posture
		Poor impulse control
		Uninhibited behavior
		Senseless, risky endeavors
		Impaired reality testing
		Eccentric, bizarre appear-
		  ance

creases, especially with women. They become so busy with superfluous activities that they begin to neglect their personal hygiene and appearance. They may be observed being carelessly or insufficiently dressed. Women tend to wear an excessive amount of makeup and provocative clothing. Overall, manic patients appear bizarre and eccentric.

> CASE EXAMPLE: Ms. Manning is a 36-year-old secretary who was brought to the hospital by three friends. The patient was sprawled on the floor reading quite loudly from a Reader's Digest. She informed me she was a vice-president "and a darned good one at that. I made a million dollars last year. How much do you make, honey?" She was basically hostile and uncooperative with the interview and would make up words to rhyme with whatever last word I would say. She had difficulty sitting still. Her friends report she had made numerous long distance phone calls, but as of today she had done nothing dangerous. She was sloppily dressed and poorly groomed. Her lipstick was bright red and stretched almost clear across her face.

Table 5:4 summarizes the most common behavioral features of patients experiencing affective disorders.

ASSESSMENT TOOLS

Moods and feelings cannot be measured precisely. Scores from rating scales can only reflect the mood or feeling state as described by the patient or an observer. Many rating scales are not intended to be used as diagnostic instruments but rather as tools to assess severity or improvement. There are numerous rating scales available to clinicians that can be of assistance in collecting data. Only several of the more commonly used tools will be described. The reader is referred to the additional reference section at the end of this chapter for a more comprehensive list of scales and tools.

Dexamethasone suppression test

One commonly used laboratory test for assessing somatically treatable depression is the dexamethasone suppression test (DST). The test is easy to administer and there is minimal risk to patients. The DST is a standardized, indirect marker of melancholia. It assists in diagnosing, quantifying severity, predicting outcome, and monitoring treatment.

The probable site of dysfunction in depressed patients is the hypothalamic-pituitary-adrenal system (HPA). The administration of synthetic dexamethasone presumably marks the pathophysiological disinhibition of the limbic system. In normal subjects there would be a suppression of cortisol secretion. Depressed patients are resistant to this cortisol secretion and fail to maintain the suppressive response.

The current standardized procedure consists of the administration of 1 mg dexamethasone, orally, at 11:30 PM. Plasma cortisol concentrations are determined the following day at 1600 and 2300 hours. Outpatients are usually limited to the 1600-hour blood draw. If either post-dexamethasone cortisol level exceeds 5 μg/dl, the test is considered abnormal. The test may be readministered as often as every 7 to 10 days to monitor progress. The overall diagnostic confidence for melancholia associated with a positive DST ranges from 83% to 95%.[23]

Numerous medications can skew the results of the DST. Hypnotics, antianxiety drugs, anticonvulsants, and beta blockers can all interfere with obtaining accurate results. Alcohol also interferes with the test and certain narcotics are suspected to as well. When a DST is going to be performed nurses need to ask patients about medications, alcohol, and drug use. They should not forget to ask about the use of steroid creams. Patients often forget to mention their use when asked about medications and these creams do skew the DST results.[24]

Several medical factors that can interfere with the DST are outlined as follows*:

I. False-positive tests
   A. Pregnancy
   B. Cushing's disease
   C. Weight loss, malnutrition, anorexia nervosa (body weight less than 80% of ideal weight)

---

*From Carroll, B.J., et al. A specific laboratory test for the diagnosis of melancholia. *Archives of General Psychiatry*, 1981, *38*, 16.

    D. Hepatic enzyme induction (phenytoin sodium, barbiturates, meprobamate)

    E. Uncontrolled diabetes mellitus (hypoglycemia, acidosis)

    F. Major physical illness, trauma, fever, dehydration, nausea

    G. Temporal lobe epilepsy (possible), reserpine (possible), narcotics (possible)

    H. Acute withdrawal from alcohol

  II. False-negative tests

    A. Addison's disease

    B. High-dose benzodiazepines (greater than 25 mg/day of diazepam), cyproheptadine hydrochloride (possible)

 III. Uncertain exclusion criteria

    A. Other endocrine disease

    B. Spironolactone

Observer rating scales

Observer rating scales are dependent on the information obtained and perceived by the observer and are subsequently influenced by observer bias. The observer should take note of both the verbal answers to the questions and the patient's behavior and appearance. Observer bias can be decreased and reliability can be improved by the use of two independent observers.

Tools 5:1 and 5:2 were designed as guides for the assessment of affective symptoms. Any yes response may be indicative of a mood disorder and needs further investigation. Patients' progress can also be measured using these tools. If more specific diagnostic criteria are necessary the nurse should refer to DSM-III or other diagnostic tools.

TOOL 5:1   Brief assessment for major depressive disorder

Does the patient:	Yes	No
1. Exhibit or describe a dysphoric mood?	——	——
2. Describe a disturbance in appetite?	——	——
3. Describe a disturbance in sleep?	——	——
4. Exhibit or describe psychomotor retardation or agitation?	——	——
5. Describe feelings of worthlessness, self-reproach, or guilt?	——	——
6. Exhibit or describe impaired ability to think or concentrate?	——	——
7. Describe thoughts of suicide or homicide?	——	——
8. Describe loss of interest, pleasure, or energy?	——	——

TOOL 5:2   Brief assessment for manic episode

Does the patient:	Yes	No
1. Describe one or more distinct periods with a predominantly elevated, expansive, or irritable mood?	___	___
2. Exhibit or describe an increase in activity, restlessness, or distractability?	___	___
3. Exhibit excessive talkativeness?	___	___
4. Exhibit flight of ideas?	___	___
5. Exhibit inflated self-esteem?	___	___
6. Exhibit decreased need for sleep?	___	___
7. Exhibit an increase in dangerous, bizarre, or inappropriate behavior?	___	___

TOOL 5:3   The Hamilton Rating Scale for Depression

Item number	Score range	Symptom	Score
1	0-4	Depression mood	___
2	0-4	Depression guilt	___
3	0-4	Depression suicide	___
4	0-2	Insomnia (initial)	___
5	0-2	Insomnia (middle)	___
6	0-2	Insomnia (delayed)	___
7	0-4	Work and interests	___
8	0-4	Retardation	___
9	0-4	Agitation	___
10	0-4	Anxiety (psychic)	___
11	0-4	Anxiety (somatic)	___
12	0-2	Somatic symptoms G.I.	___
13	0-2	Somatic symptoms general	___
14	0-2	Somatic symptoms G.U.	___
15	0-4	Hypochondriasis	___
16	0-2	Loss of insight	___
17	0-2	Loss of weight	___
		TOTAL	___
18	0-2	Diurnal variation$_E^M$ A	___
19	0-4	Depersonalisation etc.	___
20	0-4	Paranoid symptoms	___
21	0-2	Obsessional symptoms	___

From Hamilton, M. *Development of a rating scale for primary depressive illness.* British Journal of Social and Clinical Psychology, 1967, 6, 278-296.

0, Absent; 1, mild or trivial; 2 and 3, moderate; 4, severe; 0, absent; 1, slight or doubtful; 2, clearly present.

Tool 5:3 was designed by Max Hamilton[25] specifically for rating symptoms of depression. The Hamilton Rating Scale for Depression (HRSD) contains 21 variables. The sum of the scores of these variables will assist in quantifying the severity of depressive symptoms.

Tool 5:4 is the 26-item Manic-State Rating Scale[26] designed for use primarily with hospitalized patients. The scale provides a method for measuring manic symptomatology.

TOOL 5:4   Manic State Rating Scale

PART A   FREQUENCY (how much of the time?)

The patient	None 0	Fre- quent 1	Some 2	Much 3	Most 4	All 5
1. Looks depressed						
2. Is talking						
3. Moves from one place to another						
4. Makes threats						
5. Has poor judgment						
6. Dresses inappropriately						
7. Looks happy and cheerful						
8. Seeks out others						
9. Is distractible						
10. Has grandiose ideas						
11. Is irritable						
12. Is combative or destructive						
13. Is delusional						
14. Verbalizes depressive feelings						
15. Is active						
16. Is argumentative						

From Beigel, A., et al. The manic state rating scale. *Archives of General Psychiatry*, 1971, 25, 257.

Continued.

TOOL 5:4   Manic State Rating Scale—cont'd

PART A   FREQUENCY (how much of the time?)

The patient	None 0	Fre-quent 1	Some 2	Much 3	Most 4	All 5
17. Talks about sex						
18. Is angry						
19. Is careless about dress and grooming						
20. Has diminished impulse control						
21. Verbalizes feelings of well-being						
22. Is suspicious						
23. Makes unrealistic plans						
24 Demands contact with others						
25. Is sexually preoccupied						
26. Jumps from one subject to another						

PART B   INTENSITY (how intense is it?)

The patient	Very mini-mal 1	Mini-mal 2	Moder-ate 3	Marked 4	Very marked 5
1. Looks depressed					
2. Is talking					
3. Moves from one place to another					
4. Makes threats					
5. Has poor judgment					
6. Dresses inappropriately					
7. Looks happy and cheerful					

TOOL 5:4   Manic State Rating Scale—cont'd

PART B   INTENSITY (how intense is it?)

The patient	Very minimal 1	Minimal 2	Moderate 3	Marked 4	Very marked 5
8. Seeks out others					
9. Is distractible					
10. Has grandiose ideas					
11. Is irritable					
12. Is combative or destructive					
13. Is delusional					
14. Verbalizes depressive feelings					
15. Is active					
16. Is argumentative					
17. Talks about sex					
18. Is angry					
19. Is careless about dress and grooming					
20. Has diminished impulse control					
21. Verbalizes feelings of well-being					
22. Is suspicious					
23. Makes unrealistic plans					
24. Demands contact with others					
25. Is sexually preoccupied					
26. Jumps from one subject to another					

Self rating scales

Numerous scales have been devised for patients to complete themselves. The two most frequently used self-rating scales that measure depression are the Beck Depression Inventory (BDI)[27] and Zung's Self-Rating Depression Scale (SDS).[28]

The BDI, Tool 5:5, is an easily administered questionnaire that can be completed by the patient in about 10 minutes. Scoring consists of adding up the encircled numerical values. The total score provides an estimate of the degree of severity of depressed mood. The mean scores can be interpreted as follows:

	MEAN	STANDARD DEVIATION
Not depressed	10.9	8.1
Mildly depressed	18.7	10.2
Moderately depressed	25.4	9.6
Severely depressed	30.0	10.6

TOOL 5:5   The Beck Depression Inventory

A. (Sadness)
  0 = I do not feel sad
  1 = I feel sad
  2 = I am sad all the time and I can't snap out of it
  3 = I am so sad or unhappy that I can't stand it

B. (Pessimism)
  0 = I am not particularly discouraged about the future
  1 = I feel discouraged about the future
  2 = I feel I have nothing to look forward to
  3 = I feel that the future is hopeless and that things cannot improve

C. (Sense of failure)
  0 = I do not feel like a failure
  1 = I feel I have failed more than the average person
  2 = As I look back on my life all I can see is a lot of failures
  3 = I feel I am a complete failure as a person

D. (Dissatisfaction)
  0 = I get as much satisfaction out of things as I used to
  1 = I don't enjoy things the way I used to
  2 = I don't get real satisfaction out of anything anymore
  3 = I am dissatisfied or bored with everything

From Beck, A.T., et al. Inventory for measuring depression. *Archives of General Psychiatry*, 1961, 4, 561-571.

TOOL 5:5	The Beck Depression Inventory—cont'd

E. (Guilt)
    0 = I don't feel particularly guilty
    1 = I feel guilty a good part of the time
    2 = I feel quite guilty most of the time
    3 = I feel guilty all of the time

F. (Sense of punishment)
    0 = I don't feel I am being punished
    1 = I feel I may be punished
    2 = I am disgusted with myself
    3 = I hate myself

G. (Self-dislike)
    0 = I don't feel disappointed in myself
    1 = I am disappointed in myself
    2 = I am disgusted with myself
    3 = I hate myself

H. (Self-accusations)
    0 = I don't feel I am any worse than anybody else
    1 = I am critical of myself for my weaknesses or mistakes
    2 = I blame myself all the time for my faults
    3 = I blame myself for everything bad that happens

I. (Self-harm)
    0 = I don't have any thoughts of killing myself
    1 = I have thoughts of killing myself but I would not carry them out
    2 = I would like to kill myself
    3 = I would kill myself if I had the chance

J. (Crying spells)
    0 = I don't cry any more than usual
    1 = I cry more now than I used to
    2 = I cry all the time now
    3 = I used to be able to cry but now I can't cry even though I want
       to

K. (Irritability)
    0 = I am not more irritated now than I ever am
    1 = I get annoyed or irritated more easily than I used to
    2 = I feel irritated all the time now
    3 = I don't get irritated at all by the things that used to irritate me

L. (Social withdrawal)
    0 = I have not lost interest in other people
    1 = I am less interested in other people than I used to be
    2 = I have lost most of my interest in other people
    3 = I have lost all of my interest in other people

M. (Indecisiveness)
    0 = I make decisions about as well as I ever could
    1 = I put off making decisions more than I used to
    2 = I have greater difficulty in making decisions than before
    3 = I can't make decisions at all anymore

Continued.

TOOL 5:5   The Beck Depression Inventory—cont'd

N. (Self-image change)
  0 = I don't feel I look any worse than I used to
  1 = I am worried that I am looking old or unattractive
  2 = I feel that there are permanent changes in my appearance that make me look unattractive
  3 = I believe that I look ugly

O. (Work difficulty)
  0 = I can work about as well as before
  1 = It takes extra effort to get started at doing something
  2 = I have to push myself very hard to do anything
  3 = I can't do any work at all

P. (Sleep disturbance)
  0 = I can sleep as well as usual
  1 = I don't sleep as well as I used to
  2 = I wake up 1-2 hours earlier than usual and find it hard to get back to sleep
  3 = I wake up several hours earlier than I used to and cannot get back to sleep

Q. (Fatigability)
  0 = I don't get any more tired than usual
  1 = I get tired more easily than I used to
  2 = I get tired from doing almost anything
  3 = I am too tired to do anything

R. (Anorexia)
  0 = My appetite is no worse than usual
  1 = My appetite is not as good as it used to be
  2 = My appetite is much worse now
  3 = I have no appetite at all any more

S. (Weight loss)
  0 = I haven't lost much weight, if any, lately
  1 = I have lost more than 5 pounds
  2 = I have lost more than 10 pounds
  3 = I have lost more than 15 pounds
        I am purposely trying to lose weight by eating less
        Yes _____
        No _____

T. (Somatic preoccupation)
  0 = I am no more worried about my health than usual
  1 = I am worried about physical problems such as aches and pains; or upset stomach; or constipation
  2 = I am very worried about physical problems and it's hard to think of much else
  3 = I am so worried about my physical problems, I cannot think about anything else

U. (Loss of libido)
  0 = I have not noticed any recent change in my interest in sex
  1 = I am less interested in sex than I used to be
  2 = I am much less interested in sex now
  3 = I have lost interest in sex completely

TOOL 5:6   The Zung's Self-Rating Depression Scale

	None or little of the time	Some of the time	Good part of the time	Most or all of the time
1. I feel downhearted, blue and sad	1	2	3	4
2. Morning is when I feel the best	4	3	2	1
3. I have crying spells or feel like it	1	2	3	4
4. I have trouble sleeping through the night	1	2	3	4
5. I eat as much as I used to	4	3	2	1
6. I enjoy looking at, talking to and being with attractive women/men	4	3	2	1
7. I notice that I am losing weight	1	2	3	4
8. I have trouble with constipation	1	2	3	4
9. My heart beats faster than usual	1	2	3	4
10. I get tired for no reason	1	2	3	4
11. My mind is as clear as it used to be	4	3	2	1
12. I find it easy to do things I used to	4	3	2	1
13. I am restless and can't keep still	1	2	3	4
14. I feel hopeful about the future	4	3	2	1
15. I am more irritable than usual	1	2	3	4
16. I find it easy to make decisions	4	3	2	1

Continued.

TOOL 5:6	The Zung's Self-Rating Depression Scale—cont'd			
	None or little of the time	Some of the time	Good part of the time	Most or all of the time
17. I feel that I am useful and needed	4	3	2	1
18. My life is pretty full	4	3	2	1
19. I feel that others would be better off if I were dead	1	2	3	4
20. I still enjoy the things I used to do	4	3	2	1

The SDS, Tool 5:6, is also easily administered and scored. It is designed so that the less depressed patient will have a lower score and the more depressed patient will have a higher score. An index score is derived by dividing the sum of the values obtained by 80, the maximum possible score. The index scores range from .25 to 1.00.

DIAGNOSIS
Nursing diagnosis of mood disorders

Patients experience disorders of mood along a continuum from mild to severe. The symptoms of mood alterations are manifested physically, behaviorally, emotionally, and cognitively. Many of these symptoms can have a far-reaching impact on the patient's ability to function. Mania and especially depression are frequently masked by other symptoms. A careful nursing assessment provides both diagnostic and evaluative information about the patient.

The boxed material opposite describes the major nursing diagnoses that apply to patients experiencing mood disorders. The numbers are used as a means of delineating levels of classification. Each diagnosis can be broken down further to make each patient's situation more specific. The reader is referred to *Classification of Nursing Diagnosis* by Kim and Moritz[29] for additional nursing diagnostic information.

Psychiatric diagnosis of mood disorders

Affective disorders are classified in DSM-III according to three major categories (see the outline on p. 130).[30] The nurse arrives at one particular

TAXONOMY OF NURSING DIAGNOSES FOR MOOD DISORDERS

1. Disturbance in self-concept
   1.10 Impaired self-esteem
       1.21 Feelings of worthlessness and guilt
       1.22 Feelings of grandiosity or omnipotence
   1.20 Impaired role-performance
   1.30 Impaired body image
2. Ineffective individual coping
   2.10 Impaired social functioning
   2.20 Impaired relationships with significant others
   2.30 Impaired occupational functioning
   2.40 Impaired cognitive abilities
   2.50 Impaired activities of daily living
3. Dysfunctional grieving
   3.10 Denial of loss
   3.20 Identification with lost object
   3.30 Prolonged grief
4. Alteration in nutrition
   4.10 Inadequate food intake
   4.20 Lack of interest in food
5. Sleep pattern disturbance
   5.10 Excessive sleep
   5.20 Inadequate amount of sleep
       5.21 Insomnia
       5.22 Early morning awakening
       5.23 Perceived lack of need
6. Self-care deficits
   6.10 Impaired ability to maintain personal hygiene
   6.20 Impaired ability to maintain adequate grooming
   6.30 Impaired ability to adapt in environment

diagnosis based on the symptoms of the patient and the particular diagnostic criteria presented for each affective disorder. DSM-III is quite specific as to the type and number of criteria that need to be present before a definitive diagnosis can be made.

Two diagnoses that have affective symptomatology are organic disorders and schizophrenia. Hyperactivity, memory loss, or inability to concentrate are just a few examples of symptoms that may be indicative of organic impairment. A thorough physical examination should be conducted when the nurse suspects there may be an organic insult. Schizophrenic patients may also exhibit affective symptoms. However, the diagnosis of schizophrenia is usually made when a thought disorder is predominant.

According to DSM-III, the essential features of a major depressive episode are a dysphoric mood, a disturbance in any appetitive function, psychomotor retardation or agitation, feelings of worthlessness and guilt, and suicidal ideation. There may be a loss of interest in usual activities and the patient may or may not exhibit an impaired ability to think or concentrate.

Bipolar affective disorder necessitates having experienced at least one manic episode with or without ever having experienced an episode of depression. Manic patients are best characterized by their expansive mood, increased activity, grandiose ideas, and bizarre or eccentric behavior. Again, patients may or may not exhibit an accompanying thought disorder.

I. Major affective disorders
   A. Major depression
   B. Bipolar affective disorder
II. Other specific affective disorders
   A. Cyclothymic disorder
   B. Dysthymic disorder
III. Atypical affective disorders
   A. Atypical depression
   B. Atypical bipolar disorder

CASE EXAMPLE: Assessment of Dr. Parker

Identifying problem. Dr. Parker is a 36-year-old Ph.D. psychologist. She is divorced and is working at a clinic that does psychological testing. She has a 14-year-old daughter.

Presenting problem. Dr. Parker is brought to the psychiatric emergency room by three friends for evaluation and possible hospitalization. The friends report she has not slept in several days, is not eating well, is spending money quite freely, is making long distance phone calls and is making reservations for exotic vacations. Most of the information is obtained from her friends since Dr. Parker is uncooperative during the interview.

Brief recent history. The friends report that Dr. Parker has had a manic episode on at least two other occasions that they know of—6 months ago and 2 years ago. She was hospitalized both times and treated with phenothiazines. She has been depressed on at least one occasion but was not hospitalized. She is not currently in treatment nor is she taking any medication. This episode began about 6 days ago.

Her friends report she is generally a healthy person who takes good care of herself and her daughter. This week she has been drinking a great deal of coffee and alcohol. They do not believe she uses drugs.

Dr. Parker has been working as a psychologist doing psychological testing at student services. Her friends deny any problems at work until this week. She has also been frequenting bars and attempting to pick up men. She put money down on a new car, booked a Caribbean cruise, and has been calling all her old college friends. Dr. Parker is uncooperative answering my questions and will only say that she is the world's best psychologist. She states she has no problems except the three people who brought her in: "They are a pain."

Family history. The family history is sketchy. The friends report that both Dr. Parker's parents are deceased. They think her father was an alcoholic and they believe she has a brother who lives in California who has been hospitalized once or twice for depression. Her 14-year-old daughter attends junior high school and is currently staying with friends. Dr. Parker states she has no family, "never had any, never will."

Personal history. The personal history was obtained from the friends. Dr. Parker graduated in 1972 with a Ph.D. in psychology from the University of Virginia. She married during graduate school. She and her husband moved to Michigan upon her graduation. He worked in business and they were divorced after seven years of marriage. They have one child, the 14-year-old daughter. The ex-husband lives in New York and rarely has contact with Dr. Parker or their daughter. Her work history has been good except during her manic episodes.

Mental status examination. Dr. Parker appears much older than her stated age. She is disheveled and wearing eccentric clothing and jewelry. When I entered the room she was sprawled in the chair reading quite loudly from a religious book. Her speech was quite rapid and when I attempted to interrupt her reading she would talk louder. She had difficulty sitting still and would frequently cross and uncross her legs. She was hostile and uncooperative during the interview. Her affect was quite labile and fluctuated between agitated and irritated. Her thought processes were difficult to follow and she would quickly jump from one topic to the next.

Thought content centered around her friends "being crazy" and her religious readings. She exhibited grandiosity in her thinking and there was a hint of ideas of reference when she related that several of the Biblical readings specifically referred to her. There was no evident disturbance in her perceptions.

Dr. Parker was oriented to time, place, and person. She refused all attempts at formal cognitive testing, but it was obvious that her attention span was quite short and she was unable to concentrate on the issues at hand. Her insight and judgment were poor.

Summary. Dr. Parker is exhibiting symptoms of heightened mood and affect. She is not sleeping, refuses to eat, and has been spending money excessively. Her work became affected this week when she began not showing up. Her insight and judgment are poor, although she has not done anything dangerous and she appears to be able to still take minimal care of herself. She is currently not psychotic.

Psychiatric diagnosis. 296.42 Bipolar affective disorder, manic without psychosis

Nursing diagnosis. 1. Ineffective individual coping
2. Disturbance in self-concept
3. Sleep pattern disturbance
4. Self-care deficit

Plan. Dr. Parker refused all offers of medication and/or hospitalization. Her friends confiscated her car keys and her credit cards. The friends will continue to monitor her behavior. They will bring her back to the hospital for admission if she agrees. Otherwise, the three friends were instructed to observe for any committable behavior and to call community mental health for assistance.

CASE EXAMPLE: Assessment of Mr. Klamer

Identifying information. Mr. Klamer is a 36-year-old married schoolteacher and administrator. He is the father of three children.

Presenting problem. Mr. Klamer called the clinic this morning and although his problem did not sound emergent he was asked to come in this afternoon because he sounded delusional about some events at work. He now reports he is here because he is fearful about what has happened at work and believes he is being framed in hopes that he will resign.

Brief recent history. Mr. Klamer decided to seek help at the encouragement of his wife. Although he is convinced there is a plot against him at work, his wife believes this is not true. He is the language department chairperson at the local high school and is responsible for ten other language teachers. He believes this plot against him started 2 months ago after he gave mediocre performance evaluations to several of the teachers. He now believes the principal thinks he was wrong and he goes to work every day waiting for the principal to fire him. His wife reports he has been isolating himself at home. He spends hours alone in his study going over these past evaluations ruminating about whether he was fair and accurate in his assessments. He reports his sleep has been disturbed. He has trouble falling asleep (thoughts keep racing in his head) and wakes up every morning about 5:00 and immediately begins to worry about work. He thinks he has lost about 8 lb and his wife reports he probably would not eat if she didn't put food in front of him. He describes experiencing frequent headaches and stomachaches the past 2 months. He has lost interest in running and no longer feels enjoyment from most activities. He denies any known medical problems, takes no medication, and admits to an occasional use of alcohol, mostly at social events.

Family history. Mr. Klamer's parents are both alive and live nearby. They are in relatively good health. His father was hospitalized twice for depression, once after the sudden death of a younger brother and once right after retirement. He was treated and responded well to antidepressant medication. Mr. Klamer never knew this information until about 4 days ago when his father told him in an attempt to get him to get help. He really has not thought much about what his father told him because he has been too preoccupied trying to save his job.

He has one brother (a real estate agent) and one sister (an accountant). He is unaware of any physical or emotional problems with them. He denies any alcoholism in his family.

Personal history. Mr. Klamer relates having a happy childhood. He did well in school, played sports, and had many friends. He graduated from The Ohio State University with a degree in secondary education. He was a member of Delta Tau Delta fraternity, played intramural sports, and met his wife, Anne, at a party. They were married shortly after college. She teaches nursing at a nearby university and they have three children, ages 8, 6, and 3. He has taught French for 10 years and during the summers he received a masters degree in French. He and his wife have taken several groups of students on tours to Europe. Two years ago he was named department head, being promoted over several other teachers with more experience. He now relates he probably didn't deserve to be promoted. "They" have realized their mistake and are trying to correct it now. He cannot remember ever being depressed and his wife verifies she has never observed this behavior before.

Mental status examination. Mr. Klamer was neatly dressed and groomed. He was wearing a sport coat and tie. He appeared tentative and his shoulders were a little slumped. He looked at the floor during much of the interview. He appeared tired and stated he had only slept 2 hours last night. He was not spontaneous with information but was cooperative answering questions. Mr. Klamer's speech was slow and he sometimes mumbled answers. He described his mood as dejected. His affect was flat and constricted. He was able to understand questions and answered in a logical manner, but there were major deficits in his thinking manifested in somatic, ritualistic, and defensive thinking. He complained of headaches and stomachaches and had been to see his family doctor who found nothing wrong with him. He ruminates about work and his wife states he can barely talk about anything else. There was considerable evidence of persecutory and suspicious thinking. He described feeling unable to make even simple decisions about what to wear to work. There were considerable themes of guilt, worthlessness, and pessimism noted in his story. He was not experiencing any perceptual distortions. He denied feeling suicidal and said that although he was feeling somewhat desperate he did not want to die.

Mr. Klamer was oriented to time, place, and person. His attention and concentration were impaired. He performed four digits forward and three backward. He did serial sevens to 65 with no mistakes and then shook his head and apologized saying, "he just had too much on his mind." He recalled 2 out of 3 objects after ten minutes. His intelligence appears above average. He was able to think abstractly yet his answers had depressive overtones. His response to "Don't put all your eggs in one basket" was "Don't count on only one resource, because you may get fired and will need to look for another job." His insight and judgment are impaired. He is considering resigning before he is fired, and he is incapable of any reality testing around this issue.

Summary. Mr. Klamer is preoccupied with his job, appears delusional about what is going to happen at work, and relates considerable themes of worthlessness and guilt. His sleep and appetite are decreased. He has lost interest in most activities, his memory is impaired, and his insight and judgment are fair.

Psychiatric diagnosis. 296.24 Major Depressive Disorder, single episode with psychotic features

Nursing diagnosis. 1. Disturbance in self-concept
2. Ineffective individual coping
3. Sleep pattern disturbance
4. Alteration in nutrition

Plan. 1. DST—take 1 mg dexamethasone (Hexadrol) tonight at 11:30 PM and have blood drawn tomorrow at 4:00 PM.
2. Per Dr. Greyson begin trazodone hydrochloride (Desyrel) 100 mg and loxapine (Loxitane) 10 mg hs. Increase Desyrel 100 mg each night for two nights to a total of 300 mg hs.
3. Follow up visit tomorrow at 4:30 PM.
4. Patient and wife given 24-hour emergency telephone number.

REFERENCES

1. Beck, A.T. *Depression: causes and treatment.* Philadelphia: University of Pennsylvania Press, 1967, pp. 4, 10, 34.
2. Burton, R.: *The anatomy of melancholy,* ed. by Dell, F., and Jordon-Smith, P. New York: Tudor, 1927.
3. Goodwin, D.W., & Guze, S.B. *Psychiatric diagnosis.* New York: Oxford University Press, 1979, pp. 4, 8.
4. Freud, S. *Mourning and melancholia.* London: The Hogarth Press Ltd., 1957.
5. Boyd, J.H., & Weissman, M.M. Epidemiology. In E.S. Paykel, Ed. *Handbook of affective disorders.* Edinburgh: Churchill Livingstone, 1982, pp. 115, 117, 120.
6. Weissman, M.M., & Kleinman, G.L. Sex differences in the epidemiology of depression. *Archives of General Psychiatry,* 1977, *34,* 98.
7. Winokur, G. Unipolar depression: Is it divisible into autonomous subtypes? *Archives of General Psychiatry,* 1979, *36,* 47-52.
8. Orvaschel, H., et al. Children and depression: The children of depressed parents, the childhood of depressed patients, depression in children. *Journal of Affective Disorders,* 1980, *2,* 1-16.
9. Weissman, M.M. The myth of involutional melancholia, *JAMA,* 1979, *242,* 742-744.
10. Klerman, G.L. & Barrett, J.E.: The affective disorders: Clinical and epidemiological aspects. In S. Gershon and B. Shopsin, Eds. *Lithium: Its role in psychiatric research and treatment,* New York: Plenum Press, 1973, pp. 201-236.
11. Krauthammer, C., & Klerman, G.L. The epidemiology of mania. In B. Shopsin, Ed. *Manic illness.* New York: Raven Press, 1979, pp. 11-28.
12. Nurnberger, F.I., & Gershon E.S. Genetics. In E.S. Paykel, Ed. *Handbook of affective disorders.* Edinburgh: Churchill Livingstone, 1982, pp. 126-144.
13. Lidd, K.K., & Weissman, M.M. Why we do not yet understand the genetics of affective disorders. In J.O. Cole, et al., Eds. *Depression: biology, psychodynamics, and treatment.* New York: Plenum Press, 1978, pp. 107-121.
14. Allen, M.G., et al. Affective illness in veteran twins: A diagnostic review. *American Journal of Psychiatry,* 1974, *130,* 1234-1239.
15. Zis, A.P., & Goodwin, F.K.: The amine hypothesis. In E.S. Paykel, Ed. *The handbook of affective disorders.* Edinburgh: Churchill Livingstone, 1982, p. 183.
16. Carroll, B.J. Neuroendocrinology and depression. *Medicographia,* 1981, *3,* 12-14.

17. Prange, A.J., et al. Effects of thyrotropin-releasing hormone in depression. *Lancet,* 1972, *2,* 999-1002.
18. Gold, M.S., et al. Distinguishing unipolar and bipolar depression by thyrotropin release test. Lancet, 1979, *2,* 411.
19. Carroll, B.J. Neuroendocrine function in psychiatric disorders. In M.A. Lipton, et al., Eds. *Psychopharmacology: A generation of progress.* New York: Raven Press, 1978, pp. 487-497.
20. Frazier, A. Biological aspects of mania and depression. In A. Frazier, and A. Winokur, Eds. *Biological bases of psychiatric disorders.* New York: Spectrum Publications, Inc., 1977, p. 221, 222.
21. Abraham, K. The first pregenital stage of the libido. In *Selected papers on psychoanalysis.* London: The Hogarth Press Ltd., 1927, pp. 248-279.
22. Klein, M. A contribution to the psychogenesis of manic-depressive states. In *Contributions to psychoanalysis,* London: The Hogarth Press Ltd., 1948, pp. 282-310.
23. Carroll, B.J., et al. A specific laboratory test for the diagnosis of melancholia: Standardization, validation and clinical utility. *Archives of General Psychiatry,* 1981, *38,* 15-22.
24. Ritchie, J. Personal communication, January 1983.
25. Hamilton, M. Development of a rating scale for primary depressive illness. *British Journal of Social and Clinical Psychology,* 1967, *6,* 278-296.
26. Beigel, A., et al. The manic-state rating scale. *Archives of General Psychiatry,* 1971, *25,* 256-262.
27. Beck, A.T., et al. Inventory for measuring depression. *Archives of General Psychiatry,* 1961, *4,* 561-571.
28. Zung, W.W.K., & Durham, N.C. A self-rating depression scale. *Archives of General Psychiatry,* 1965, *12,* 63-70.
29. Kim, M., & Moritz, D.A. *Classification of nursing diagnoses.* New York: McGraw Hill Book Co., 1982.
30. American Psychiatric Association. *Diagnostic and Statistical Manual of Mental Disorders,* 3rd ed. Washington, D.C.: American Psychiatric Association, 1980.

ADDITIONAL REFERENCES

American Psychiatric Association. *Diagnostic and statistical manual of mental disorders,* 2nd ed. Washington, D.C.: American Psychiatric Association, 1968.

Carroll, B.J., Fielding, J.M., & Blashki, T.G. Depression rating scales: A critical review. *Archives of General Psychiatry,* 1973, *28,* 361-366.

Endicott, J., & Spitzer, R. A diagnostic interview: The schedule for affective disorders and schizophrenia. *Archives of General Psychiatry,* 1978, *35,* 837-844.

Hamilton, M. Rating depressive patients, *Journal of Clinical Psychiatry,* December 1980, *41,* 12, Sec. 2.

Lyerly, S.B. *Handbook of psychiatric rating scales,* 2nd ed., DHEW Pub. No. 73-9061. Washington, D.C.: U.S. Government Printing Office, 1973.

Wing, J.K., Cooper, J.E., & Sartorius, N. *Description and classification of psychiatric symptoms.* Cambridge, England: Cambridge University Press, 1974.

Zung, W.K., & Durhan, N.C. Factors influencing the self-rating depression scale, *Archives of General Psychiatry,* 1967, *16,* 543-547.

CHAPTER 6

ASSESSING THOUGHT DISORDERS

The mind has remained largely a mystery since people began to record their history many centuries ago. In the past 100 years medicine and other disciplines have made fantastic strides in identifying the anatomy of the mind, but little is really known about its physiology. It is agreed that the mind is responsible for feeling, thought, memory, and decision making—to name but a few of its functions. However, the processes underlying these functions are not known.

For instance, intelligence is a concept that is related to thought, or so some believe. In 1929 Harold Lashley wrote, "The whole theory of learning and intelligence is in confusion. We know at present nothing of the organic basis of these functions . . . The concepts are so poorly defined that it has not been possible even to imagine a programme of physiological research which seemed likely to reveal more than superficial relationships."[1] Since 1919, much research has been reported but still the mind has not revealed its secrets. A scientist wrote that "Scientists studying brain function from the inside out simply have not even approached a stage in which the investigation of complex thought processes is either reasonable or possible. We are not even sure whether thinking is a function of neurons."[1] This exquisitely complex process that seems to tap the whole brain is thought by some to be concerned primarily with the cerebral cortex and the midbrain, but even this observation is unproved.

The process of thinking is so complex that it continues to defy the efforts of neuroscientists all over the world. The ability to think clearly and communicate those thoughts is very much accepted and taken for granted by human beings who have normal intelligence (whatever that really is) and who are not troubled in other areas of their lives.

But what of those persons who are troubled? There are human beings who can envision but cannot "find words" to characterize and express their thoughts. There are persons whose brain tissue has been injured. They are apparently able to "know" the meaning of images but they relate or think incorrect terms to describe what they know. Some people experience extreme fatigue, stress, or sensory alterations that impair their thought processes. There are individuals who suddenly laugh or scream obscenities that are completely out of their control, and it is not known what stimulates their brains to dictate such behaviors. There are also many people who seem to have normal cerebral tissue, but who, for reasons not yet clearly known, do not act as if they have processed cues from the environment. These persons are frequently of normal and above normal intelligence. If we accept intelligence as being related in mysterious ways to knowledge, it can be said that these persons can take concepts and organize them into schemata. They seem also to have intact reservoirs of memories upon which to draw. However, some linkage in the thought process is altered.

Functional, disordered thinking is usually termed schizophrenia, although other mental disorders such as reactive psychosis and paranoid states also demonstrate disordered thinking. The term schizophrenia, which has no inherent meaning, has been called a wastebasket term that stigmatizes people for their entire lives. Menninger wrote on this topic:

The name and the naming of . . . an instance of schizophrenia implies a hopelessness of outcome which has a derogatory effect on the patient. To be told that one has cancer is discouraging, I concede, but the designation of cancer, the psychological effect of being told that one has it, does not in itself materially affect the disease (in most cases) and may lead to corrective steps. In a psychological disease, on the other hand, the individual is nearly always negatively affected by the knowledge and the tendency toward the establishment of a self-fulfilling prophecy develops. The name spells great knowledge and great pessimism, neither of which the doctor may have. But the patient, knowing the prevalent opinion about such a disease, begins to feel pessimistic. So do those about him and all begin to fulfill these expectations.[2]

It can be concluded that schizophrenia, a group of thought disorders, is a collection of symptoms and presentations. People from all walks of life, from every country in the world, suffer from it. It is known that approximately 25% of those who are so diagnosed in their first episode obtain a complete remission of symptoms.[3] The remainder either become chronically ill or they enter a remission, only to suffer future acute exacerbations. These facts indicate that this thought disorder is prevalent, that those who suffer it are stigmatized as well as crippled by their impairment, and that the majority of them will likely remain ill and needful of psychiatric nursing care. For these compelling reasons, the nurse as a psychiatric care-giver is enjoined to learn as much as possible about the disorder that so many human beings suffer from and to conceptualize and implement strategies for improving their quality of life.

DEFINITION

For many years, clinicians have noticed that some people exhibit a disruption in their thought processes. Thought processes are cognitive functions that permit individuals to perceive stimuli, process that stimuli in an organized conceptual manner, and respond with an adaptive, problem-solving mode. Bellak describes thought processes as specific ego functions that include memory, conceptualization, attention, and communicative language.[4] Additional ego functions defined by Bellak that relate to our thinking ability are listed in the outline below. These processes are influenced by psychological, social, and biophysical variables. Persons exhibiting disordered thinking processes may be experiencing a functional mental illness or a response to organic or environmental insults.

Ego functions and their components*

1. Reality testing
   a. Distinction between inner and outer stimuli
   b. Accuracy of perception of external events
   c. Accuracy of perception of internal events
2. Judgment
   a. Anticipation of consequences of intended behavior
   b. Manifestation of this anticipation in behavior
   c. Appropriateness of behavior to external events
3. Sense of reality
   a. Extent of derealization
   b. Extent of depersonalization
   c. Self-identity and self-esteem
   d. Clarity of boundaries between self and world
4. Regulation and control of drives, affects, and impulses
   a. Directness of impulse expression
   b. Effectiveness of delay mechanisms
5. Object relations
   a. Degree and kind of relatedness (narcissistic attachment or symbiotic object choices)
   b. Primitivity versus maturity
   c. Degree to which others are perceived independently of self
   d. Object constancy
6. Thought processes
   a. Memory, conception, and attention
   b. Ability to conceptualize

---

*From Bellak, L., & Sheehy, M. The broad role of ego functions assessment. *American Journal of Psychiatry*, 1976, *133*, 1263.

   c. Primary versus secondary process as reflected in communicative language
7. Adaptive Regression in the Service of Ego (ARISE)
   a. Ability to regressively relax cognitive acuity
   b. Ability to allow new configurations to emerge in thinking
8. Defensive functioning
   a. Weakness or obtrusiveness or defenses
   b. Success or failure of defenses
9. Stimulus barrier
   a. Threshold for stimuli
   b. Effectiveness of management of excessive stimulus input
10. Autonomous functioning
   a. Degree of freedom from impairment of primary autonomy apparatuses
   b. Degree of freedom from impairment of secondary autonomy apparatuses
11. Synthetic-integrative functioning
   a. Degree of reconcilation of incongruities
   b. Degree of active relating together of events
12. Mastery-competence
   a. Competence (how well a person performs in relation to his or her capacity to actively master and affect his or her environment)
   b. Feeling of competence as measured by person's expectations of success on actual performance
   c. Discrepancy between actual competence and feeling of competence

Dementia praecox was a term used by Emil Kraeplin in an attempt to aggregate all the syndromes of rapid intellectual deterioration that had been observed in the early and mid-1800s. He observed that the persons who suffered the symptoms of thought disorders usually first evidenced these symptoms at a young age and they had a poor prognosis. Eugene Bleuler, a Swiss psychiatrist, troubled by the rigidity of Kraeplin's conceptualizations, believed that the process of deterioration was not assured in all cases. In his attempts to categorize cases by their outcomes to show that perhaps some did not belong in the broader group called dementia praecox, Bleuler concluded that dramatic hallucinations and delusions were not necessarily schizophrenic. What the latter group had in common, according to Bleuler, was a disturbance of mental associations and a loosening of the linkages between thoughts. Bleuler based the diagnosis of schizophrenia on symptoms rather than on course of the disease. He wrote "By the term 'schizophrenia' we designate a group of psychoses whose course is at times chronic, at times marked by intermittent attacks, and which can stop or retrogress at any stage, but does not permit a full restitutio ad integrum. The disease is characterized by a specific alteration of thinking, feeling and relation to the external which appears nowhere in this particular fashion."[5]

In recent years investigators have been trying to be more specific in the area of psychiatric diagnoses. Their studies suggest that there are subgroupings of schizophrenia with different degrees of genetic factors, different prognoses, and different responses to treatment. These studies have resulted in the development of more specific criteria, many of which are now included in the third edition of the *Diagnostic and Statistical Manual* (DSM-III). According to that document, schizophrenia is a group of disorders involving severe disorganization of functioning with certain characteristic disturbances of thinking, feeling, and behavior. Because the disorder is viewed as chronic, the diagnosis is not made unless symptoms have been present continuously for at least 6 months.

Schizophrenia involves impairments in thinking. Some clinicians diagnose schizophrenia on the basis of form rather than content of the thought disorder. Essentially,

Patients speak in ways that do not follow conventional semantic rules so that a listener cannot understand what is being said. In extreme cases patients are incoherent and will invent new words (neologisms) . . . There is a loosening of associations so that the connections between statements are tangential or sometimes nonexistent. Even when the connections are superficially reasonable, there may be a poverty of content. A patient may speak at length but in such vague, abstract or stereotyped way that little if any information is conveyed. Schizophrenics often display thought blocking, their flow of speech stopping abruptly as if the timing process had been paralyzed.[5]

The term psychosis indicates gross impairments in reality testing and other thought processes. When people are psychotic they do not correctly evaluate the accuracy of their perceptions and thoughts. Consequently, incorrect inferences are made about external reality.

Schizophrenic individuals may be psychotic sometimes and not psychotic at other times. Nonschizophrenic persons can be psychotically impaired and exhibit thought disturbances. This can occur with individuals who experience extreme fatigue, severe situational stress, or sensory overload or deprivation. Patients in intensive care units are especially prone to psychosis because of the altered sensory environment. All of us have the potential to exhibit impaired thought processes to varying degrees. The nurse needs to be alert to clues of impaired thinking and reality testing with patients in any health care setting.

CLASSIFICATION

Thought disorders are exemplified in a series of diagnostic classifications, including schizophrenia, reactive psychosis, schizoaffective disorder, organic mental disturbances (see chapter 9), and paranoid disorders. In all of these categories, patients demonstrate impairments in cognitive functioning resulting from functional or organic causes.

Schizophrenia

The thought disturbances in schizophrenia are pronounced. Schizophrenia can be grouped into types based on clusters of symptoms observed during an acute illness. The current subgroupings include disorganized (which was formerly called "hebephrenic"), catatonic, paranoid, and undifferentiated types.

Disorganized type. In this subgrouping, patients are noted to be markedly incoherent, "flat," undemonstrative of affect, withdrawn, and silly in their behavior. These patients do not have well-developed delusions, though they may demonstrate fragmentary ones or hallucinations. Such patients may grimace a great deal, demonstrate odd mannerisms and behavior, complain hypochondriacally, and exhibit extreme social withdrawal.

Catatonic type. Patients who fall into this category demonstrate marked psychomotor disturbances. They may appear stuporous or just the opposite, rushing about in aimless excitement. They tend to posture a great deal, to be rigid in their bodies, and to be negativistic. Many times the catatonic patient is mute.

Paranoid type. Unlike the disorganized group of patients, these persons are highly organized in their delusional systems. In fact, the prominent symptom that these patients display is persecutory or grandiose delusions or hallucinations reflecting such content. Impairment in social functioning may not be readily apparent. These patients may display unfocused anxiety, anger, and argumentativeness.

Undifferentiated type. Patients in this subgrouping demonstrate psychotic behavior, but their symptoms are mixed so that they cannot be clearly classified in any of the above groupings. Thus they have prominent delusions, hallucinations, incoherence, or grossly disorganized behavior. Their symptoms, however, do not fit any category predominantly.

Reactive psychosis

Persons who do not suffer from schizophrenia but exhibit psychosis may be experiencing a brief, reactive psychosis. This type of thought disorder is differentiated from schizophrenia by its sudden onset with eventual return to the premorbid level of functioning. The psychotic symptoms emerge immediately after the presentation of a recognizable psychosocial stressor. Emotional turmoil is evident with perplexity and feelings of confusion. The behavior of such a patient may appear like typical schizophrenic behavior, such as bizarre behavior with peculiar postures, strange dress, screaming, or muteness. Speech may be incoherent or repetitious nonsense. Affect may be inappropriate or explosive. Indeed, delusions and hallucinations may emerge. Disorientation and loss of recent memory may be demonstrated. While all of these symptoms appear identical to schizophrenia, the difference is in the duration of the illness and its outcome. Usually the psychotic symptoms clear in a day or two, but they always do so within 2 weeks. Eventually there is a complete return to the premorbid level of functioning.

> **CASE EXAMPLE:** Mr. Long, a 38-year-old engineer, was admitted to the medical service for evaluation of his chronic myelogenous leukemia, which was in an acute exacerbation. The nurse-consultant from psychiatry was called to evaluate the clinical situation because Mr. Long was extremely anxious. He defended against his anxiety by being overcontrolling, charting on his steno pad the people who entered his room, what time they came, and what they did. This patient also chained his clock, television, and radio to the over-bed table. When Mr. Long's medications were not administered exactly on time, he complained loudly. It was recommended that he be permitted to keep his prn medications at his bedside, taking them when needed, and charting accordingly on his steno pad. His report would be transferred to his chart by the nurse on each shift. It was believed that this added control would help decrease Mr. Long's anxiety. In addition, the consultant was certain that because of this engineer-patient's compulsive nature, he would chart efficiently. All went quite well until Mr. Long's attending physicians decided to prescribe a course of prednisone and vincristine for him. The second day of this regimen he was found by the nurse turning off the volutrol attached to his IV apparatus. The staff told him that he could not do this. Mr. Long expressed his anger and frustration at his loss of control over his own comfort. Within 24 hours he became floridly psychotic. About 10 days later his disorientation and delusions of persecution cleared.

Schizoaffective disorder

This category of illness includes persons who exhibit psychoses but who suffer both impaired reality testing and symptoms of an affective illness. This means that there is a mood incongruence associated with the delusional or hallucinatory material. This is demonstrated as either marked depression or mania in conjunction with the thought disorder.

Paranoid disorder

Paranoid disorders are characterized by delusions of persecution, jealousy, or influence. The delusions are stable and fixed and behavior is appropriate to the content of the delusions. The individual does not usually experience hallucinations or other gross indicators of psychosis such as loose associations and disorientation.

EPIDEMIOLOGY

It has been noted that despite many advances in knowledge about schizophrenia during the past 25 years, epidemiologists still experience difficulty in developing reliable and valid estimates of incidence and prevalence rates of this disorder, specific for age, sex, race, and various demographic factors for the United States and different countries of the world. The basic problem that still impedes obtaining such data on schizophrenia is the absence of sensitive and specific case finding techniques for this disorder that can be applied uniformly.

Nonetheless, it is known that the schizophrenic psychoses are found in all cultures in which mental disorders have been studied. According to Kolb and Brodie, cultural forces appear only to modify the symptoms in terms of the content of delusional and hallucinatory material.[7] These psychoses are observed in all socioeconomic groups, although several epidemiological studies indicate that there is a correlation between higher prevalence of illness and lower socioeconomic status. At this time, the schizophrenias are the most prevalent of the major psychoses. Findings of various studies defining morbid risk as "the total risk of becoming manifestly ill for all persons surviving the age period of 15 to 45 years" suggest that the morbid risk of being diagnosed with a schizophrenic illness is 1%.[7]

The number of schizophrenic patients in the public mental hospitals of the United States rose during the early part of the century, leveling off at the rate of approximately 150 per 100,000 population during 1955. Since then, the number has declined continuously. The first admission rate to mental hospitals for schizophrenic patients rose from 18% per 100,000 in 1950 to almost 20% in 1962. These figures fluctuated later as community mental health centers were developed and identified patients were treated without hospitalization in the deinstitutionalization effort. Currently, the age-group of schizophrenic individuals with the highest first admission rate falls between 25 and 34 years. This group has two times the overall rate for first admissions to hospitals as others.[7]

Data compiled by the National Institute of Mental Health indicate that in 1975, 33.7% of people admitted to state and county mental health hospitals were diagnosed as schizophrenic.[8] This is the largest category of patient types, followed by a 27.7% for alcohol disorders. Males outnumbered females with this diagnosis. Discharge diagnoses from general hospital psychiatric inpatient units in 1975 indicate 24.1% of the patient population exhibited schizophrenia.[9]

Hospital readmission rates of schizophrenic patients have doubled since the number of patients hospitalized for long periods of time has decreased. Despite research and developments regarding the care and treatment of schizophrenic patients, the incidence and prevalence remain the same, with over 600,000 schizophrenic persons in the United States.

It is difficult to study the prevalence of other thought disorders such as reactive psychosis and paranoid disorders. Reactive psychosis follows the onset of a significant psychosocial stressor. Frequently, the patient is not diagnosed by a clinician since the duration is less than 2 weeks. Paranoid disordered patients usually continue to function in daily activities and do not seek psychiatric assistance.

CAUSATIVE FACTORS

The causes of schizophrenia are widely studied and equally disputed. While literature on the subject abounds, there is little agreement among its authors. Broadly speaking, the theories of causality may be grouped into the following categories: psychological, social, biological, and internal and external stressors.

Psychodynamic theory

It is not possible to clearly separate the social from the psychological factors that are descriptive of the illness that we call schizophrenia. Retrospective studies and histories of patients indicate that these patients had psychological problems even in their developmental years. Parents have reported awareness that their babies were "different" than their other children. The child may have been inert, inattentive, passive, slow to develop, or unable to interact with the mother in the ways usually observed.

Freud did not specifically address schizophrenia in his theories and writings. However, certain psychodynamic concepts aid in our understanding of the schizophrenic issues. During the oral gratification period, the infant is fused with the love-object, the primary care-giver. As infants develop, they begin to differentiate themselves from the love-object, and the ego, or sense of self, begins to form. Infants who have received nurturing and gratification of needs are more able to separate their boundaries from the love-object's boundaries. Thus in the schizophrenic person in the oral stage of development, a defective sense of self, or weak ego, is established. The infant has not learned to trust the world, that is, trust that basic needs will be met. The infant then uses basic, early defense mechanisms such as repression, introjection, and projection to deal with the anger and frustration over the dependence of the love-object. These serious conflicts interfere with the development of the ego's thought processes. All of these characteristics—lack of sense of self, mistrust, repression, and projection—are also characteristics of the schizophrenic adult.

According to Scheflen, as children, schizophrenics may be prone to attacks of panic and delusions.[10] During the school years, these children tend to be underachievers. They may be described by teachers as inattentive, poorly motivated, and not participating in class. They may be extremely religious or very rigid within a narrowly defined set of moral values. The schizophrenic individual tends to live in one-to-one or one-to-none relationships. From a majority of reports, the predominant symptoms of psychological difficulty observed before the first psychotic episode are withdrawal and isolation. These symptoms are often associated with the schizophrenic person's distrust of self and others. Low self-esteem and fear of failure are also noted. These terms are descriptive of a psychological set; they are not necessarily synonymous with psychological cause.

Paranoid disorders have their dynamic basis in the infant's inability to develop trust in others. The young child becomes angry and attempts to deal with this inner anger and aggression by denying its existence and projecting it onto others in the environment. The individual thus comes to externalize feelings of aggression by creating delusions of persecution by others.

Social theory

Social issues that appear to be associated with schizophrenia may be divided into smaller categories, such as the family, communications, and dyadic relationships. The latter is most often characterized as the mother-child relationship. Mahler described the relationship between mother and future schizophrenic child as one of excessive symbiosis, or need for one another.[11] In symbiotic conditions, the mother and child are unusually close and one or both may believe that they have intimate knowledge of the other that does not require consensual validation. Symbiotic relationships are characterized by the loss of boundaries between the principals. Mahler and others who are interested in this condition as it is associated with schizophrenia have noted the high degree of attachment and affiliation between schizophrenic children and their mothers. The twosomes are disturbingly aware of one another. They often "know" what each is thinking, feeling, and needing. It is as if the two persons shared one brain, with one system of thought.

Scheflen addressed family relationships and their associations with schizophrenia. He divided the family theories into three groups: theories of excessive interdependence among family members, theories of family homeostasis or stalemated conflicted, and the "double bind theory."

Bowen claims that families of schizophrenic people discourage self-differentiation and autonomy.[12] He and other investigators believe that such families become closed off from others, excessively interdependent and unable to benefit from inputs from others. Wynne describes these attachments as less binding and genuine than appear at first observation. They call these relationships "pseudomutuality."

Theories of homeostasis and stalemate describe a situation in which members of schizophrenic families, especially the parents, are stuck in a stalemate in which growth and maturation cannot occur. The schizophrenic member reflects the family's illness, expressing the group inertia. The parents in these families have unshakable beliefs about the welfare of the family; unfortunately, the adults in the system do not agree on the family's best course of action so that no action is taken. The result is absolute stalemate.

The double bind theory was proposed by Bateson et al.[14] In their view, the potential schizophrenic person was subjected to contradictory messages all through the developmental years. To act upon one set of them was to disobey the other. According to this theory, these contradictions in experience make it impossible for the growing child to distinguish important sorts of social cues and cognitive distinctions. This inability, according to double bind theory, is schizophrenia.

Biological theory

Biological theories of schizophrenia address the genetic and physiological causative factors.

It is no longer questioned whether genetics play a part in the incidence of schizophrenia, rather the research question has become "How do genetics influence the occurrence of these disorders?" There are two points that are clear to a geneticist concerning this question. The first is that genes are involved in determining who becomes schizophrenic and who does not. Kety and Heston have provided conclusive evidence that some biologically transmitted genes increase the risk of an individual becoming schizophrenic.[15] These studies reviewed the incidence of schizophrenia in adopted children as compared to the biological parents. Also supporting the genetic theory are studies on familial clustering of schizophrenia. It has been demonstrated that environmental factors may produce a lifetime liability or susceptibility to the disorder, but environmental factors do not act to precipitate an episode of illness.

Rosenthal found a high rate of schizophrenia in relatives of schizophrenic people.[16] To be exact, the rate was 5 to 15 times the incidence found in the general population. The risk is greatest for children whose fathers and mothers are both schizophrenic. Approximately 50% of this group became schizophrenic.

There is much research centered on the physiology of schizophrenia. Ornstein has demonstrated that "normal" persons integrate complex linear activities with the use of the cerebral hemisphere in which the functions of speech are well developed.[17] This is typically the left hemisphere. Ornstein uses the term "left cerebral dominance" to describe this skill. According to Scheflen "Such performance requires the following activities to be coordinated: images or memories must be evoked, a set of steps must be remembered, and an image of achievement, that is, a picture of the finished task, must be recalled."[17]

The schizophrenic patient demonstrates a relative inability to accomplish linear tasks. Some of the physiologic investigations focus on cerebral laterality and on integration of the two hemispheres. It appears likely that schizophrenic people have difficulties in unit-context relation, that is, difficulty in perceiving a relationship between two phenomena, for instance, seeing an object as separate from the sky. Another line of investigation indicates a possible abnormality in the reticular activating system that is also under the regulation of the limbic system. This subsystem acts to regulate arousal, alertness, and consciousness. It modulates sensory inputs to the cortex and is, in turn, modulated by the cortex by the way of the limbic system. Scheflen writes that in the schizophrenic patient, there is a disturbance in the modulation of these corebrain subsystems. It is possible to explain this failure on modulation by positing an insufficient or excessive temporal lobe cortical activity.[17] Yet another area of interest to neuroscientists studying schizophrenia is the temporal lobe. This portion of the brain is vital to limbic-corebrain connections for those pathways being in the medial and underside of this region of the cerebrum. The temporal lobe is the anatomic origin for some pathways to the motor area, pathways to the sensory nuclei, and the limbic to corebrain projections. Evidence suggests that the temporal lobe is instrumental in the projection of sensory experience in paranoid states. Flor demonstrated that 90% of patients who had tumors of the left temporal lobe also had auditory hallucinations and delusions. Thus it can be conjectured that the temporal lobe is critical to this process, which is an aspect of thought disorders.[18]

Research also indicates that there is a disturbance in neurotransmission in schizophrenia. This focus falls within those theories on information processing. Dopamine and norepinephrine, two kinds of catecholamine neurotransmitters, are critical in the corebrain and in parts of the cerebrum for the transmissions of impulses across neurosynaptic junctures. It has been shown that increased elevations of these substances are found in the brains of schizophrenic persons on postmortem examination.

These citations represent only the barest review of the physiological theories and research into the causes of schizophrenia. While these studies will ultimately lead to a unified theory of the etiology of schizophrenia and to either prevention or effective treatment or both, it is premature to look to that body of literature for those answers now.

Internal and external stressors

An individual diagnosed as schizophrenic experiences remissions and exacerbations that relate to perceived stress in the patient's life. A simple cold, difficulty at work, or a change in daily routine can initiate the psychotic symptoms.

Persons who are not schizophrenic also exhibit disordered thinking and communication under stressful conditions. The degree of disturbed thought and communication will vary depending on the premorbid personality and coping mechanisms of the individual and the onset, course, and duration of the stressor. Examples of conditions that contribute to impaired thinking are listed as follows:

Fatigue
Starvation
Disrupted sleep
Physical pain
Physical illness, altered body systems
Drug/alcohol use
Brain injury
Sensory overload
Sensory underload
Losses of relationships, finances, status, role

CLINICAL PRESENTATION

Patients experiencing thought disorders present a wide array of signs and symptoms. Although difficulty with cognition and subsequently communication are primary features, these impairments impact on the individual's ability to function in relationships, daily activities, and employment or school situations. The disruptions in thinking alter the patient's mood, behavior, and sensorimotor functioning.

The onset of schizophrenia occurs in adolescence or early adulthood. Paranoid disorders may appear in the 30 to 40 age-group. Many persons with schizophrenia are marginally functioning in society. Between exacerbations, they can maintain jobs, fulfill daily living routines, and occasionally engage in relationships. Patients exhibiting catatonic and disorganized types of schizophrenia have the most difficulty maintaining day-to-day living responsibilities and often do so at a minimal level, precariously awaiting the next maladaptive episode. Paranoid schizophrenic people are most successful in their routine functioning. Schizophrenic people in general continue to have difficulty thinking and communicating even when they are functioning at their maximum.

During periods of exacerbation, patients decompensate and experience a breakdown of control over their cognitive, emotional, interpersonal, and behavioral spheres. The patient seems to literally fall apart. This occurs during a prodromal phase in which the exacerbation begins and increases in intensity. The manifestations of the disorder appear to distance the individual from the external world. However, the psychosis also serves to reconstruct reality, as though the symptoms substitute for a barren or denied external world.[19] As anxiety increases, the symptoms become more pronounced. As the patient improves, a residual phase occurs in which the symptoms slowly subside.

Persons who become psychotic because of causative factors such as stress, fatigue, drugs, or sensory deprivation also appear in decompensated states. These individuals may exhibit insidious or acute onset of symptoms, depending upon the nature of the precipitant. Occasionally, these people are aware of their decline in functioning and seek assistance from doctors, nurses, friends, or family. It is quite frightening to experience impaired thinking, hallucinations, or delusions, and many are uncertain or embarrassed by their sensations and difficulties. College students, for example, who study or party for several days with no sleep describe sensations of unreality, paranoid thinking, illusions, and auditory hallucinations. Often, the individual experiencing the problem or the person providing assistance can recognize the precipitant and work to remove or reduce its effect. Persons may be hospitalized or closely followed in clinics to monitor and reduce the psychosis. Nurses in medical-surgical settings, particularly intensive care areas, should observe for early signs of disordered thinking and communication evidenced by patients with the knowledge that organic insult and sensory deprivation may initiate such behaviors.

Schizophrenic patients may never voluntarily seek help for their problems. Many continue to function in isolated roles, relating to their own internal reality. As long as their basic needs are met and there are no social or legal disruptions, these individuals can maintain their mode of living. A great many, however, enter the health care system when they are no longer able to care for themselves or when their behavior has created social or legal disruptions. Then family members, employers, police, or social agencies bring the patients to psychiatric clinics, emergency departments, or psychiatric hospitals for assessment and treatment. The actual presenting problems vary. Listed below are some of the more common ways in which individuals with thought disorders enter the health care system.

Exhibits bizarre behavior in public areas

Creates a social disturbance

Frightens significant others with bizarre behavior

Withdraws and isolates self

Unable to meet basic needs: food, hygiene, self-care

Unable to maintain job, school, social activities

Seeks psychiatric help as a way of achieving social relatedness

Becomes frightened and seeks assistance

Attempts suicide

Cognitive and perceptual manifestations

Deficits in cognitive and perceptual functioning are the primary features of thought disorders. In the initial stages, some cognitive alterations may appear to be within a range of normal functioning. As the individual continues to decompensate, the signs and symptoms of dysfunction become increasingly apparent.

Acutely ill schizophrenic patients and those persons who are not yet acutely ill are hypersensitive to visual and auditory stimuli. Attention and scanning efforts are altered, usually in the direction of increase. In fact, these persons are usually hyperreactive to aspects of the sensory fields that would typically be disregarded by others as marginal or totally irrelevant. Schizophrenic patients frequently see objects and people change their dimensions, their outlines, and their brightness from minute to minute as the sense of boundaries is distorted. Mrs. Anders, for example, felt as though she were shrinking and changing in size from day to day. She approached the nurse asking how much shorter she had become overnight. Mrs. Anders looked in a mirror and saw herself shrink and completely disappear.

The most typical symptoms of distorted thinking are those phenomena known as hallucinations and delusions. Actually, they are two aspects of the same event. The delusion is a false belief that is within the individual. The hallucination is perceptual, a projection to the external field of the delusion. According to Horowitz "Hallucinations are mental experiences that: (1) occur in the form of images, (2) are derived from internal sources of information, (3) are appraised incorrectly as if from external sources of information, and (4) usually occur intrusively."[20] Thus hallucinations occur without corresponding external stimuli. They are a common symptom of schizophrenia. Auditory hallucinations are most frequently experienced. The voices are those of God, the devil, relatives or neighbors, or persons unknown to the patient. Auditory hallucinations often begin with friendly voices and progress to threatening, per-

TABLE 6:1	Development of auditory hallucinations

Phase	Behavior
I	The individual retreats into a private, internal world as anxiety increases.
II	The individual recalls a helping person, and thinks and speaks to that person. There is relief from anxiety.
III	The pattern in Phase II is repeated and becomes more organized. The voice reassures, confirms opinions, provides reasons for not following logic.
IV	The individual withdraws further with decreased attention control and begins to doubt the reappearance of the hallucinatory voice.
V	The individual's loss of attention becomes apparent to others, creating embarrassment and further withdrawal.
VI	The voice becomes blaming and threatening toward the individual who is feeling high anxiety and decreased self-worth.
VII	The voice now begins to influence behavior. The individual feels controlled and changes behavior accordingly.

Adapted from Field, W.E., & Ruelke, W. Hallucinations and how to deal with them. *American Journal of Nursing*, 1973, *73*, 638-640.

secutory, and frightening messages and commands as the person continues to decompensate. The nurse needs to ask the patient experiencing auditory hallucinations about the nature of the voices, including who is speaking and what messages are being given. Questions, such as "Have you ever heard voices that other people didn't hear?" "Who are the voices?", and "What are the voices saying to you?", help elicit this information. At times, these voices command the psychotic person to perform harmful acts, including suicide and homicide. Table 6:1 depicts development of auditory hallucinations.

Visual hallucinations occur less frequently. They almost always occur with hallucinations in other sensory modalities. Freedman, Kaplan, and Sadock indicate that schizophrenic individuals "often experience kinesthetic hallucinations, sensations or altered states in body organs without any special receptor apparatus to explain the sensations: for example, a burning sensation in the brain, a pushing sensation in the abdominal blood vessels, or a shutting sensation of the heart."[22] When hallucinating individuals are occupied with these phenomena, they may seem oblivious to the external environment. They may react with laughter, anger, or fear, or they may converse at length with the voices. The patient experiencing visual hallucinations should be thoroughly assessed for organic illness since these hallucinations are most indicative of organic mental disturbances, including drug-induced psychosis.

Delusions are false beliefs that cannot be corrected by reasoning. They may be simple and focused or detailed and involved. Although delusions may appear grotesque and meaningless, they are never without meaning. These aberrant ideations are specific and adapted to the individual's particular psychological needs and situation. They are in keeping with the individual's particular life experiences. The schizophrenic person's delusions tend to be grotesque, to be loosely organized, and to center on themes of persecution, grandiosity, sex, bodily functioning, and control by others. According to Kolb and Brodie "He may believe that his thoughts are withdrawn and others inserted from outside and that they are being broadcast, are very loud, or are different from those he believes he owns. He may subjectively believe that his will is replaced by that of others, that he is forced to move or act or have wishes which he disowns as his own, and that even his spoken words and handwriting are controlled from outside."[7]

Delusions of persecution are most frequent. In such delusions, patients feel that they are being persecuted or followed by powerful agencies or specific persons. Ideas of reference are seen in which patients suspect that conversations, glances, and behaviors of others are referring to them. Delusions of grandeur, in which the patient feels important or assumes the identity of a famous or important individual, are also common. Patients may believe they are Napoleon, Jesus Christ, or the President of the United States. With sexual and somatic delusions, patients believe they are being approached by others in a sexual way, are of a different sexual gender, or experience false beliefs about their physical status. Delusions of thought transmission dictate that other beings or forces are controlling them. Nihilistic delusions herald the end of the world, a complete destruction of being.

The nurse assesses the patient's delusions by inquiring about their content: "You say people are following you . . . Who is following you? Why would they follow you?" It is important to initially assess the delusional content in order to understand the nature of the patient's conflicts and concerns. However, the clinician must be cautious about discussing the delusion on a continuing basis because this only serves to reinforce the false beliefs. Patients who are encouraged to recite the delusions begin to develop even more complex themes. Nurses do not dispute the patient's delusions or agree with them since these interventions will concretize the content. Rather, nurses listen to the patients, state their perception of reality, and refocus the direction of the interview. Simple statements, such as "I have no reason to believe the CIA is after you," state the nurse's own perception of reality without disagreeing with the patient.

Primary process thinking is most evident in patients with thought disorders. This thinking is concrete, lacks logical cause and effect connections, and assumes an unconscious direction. Magical thinking occurs, in which patients believe that wishing for something makes it happen. Schizophrenic patients frequently cannot arrive at conclusions based on reality or universal truths. Problem solving is impaired as the ability to differentiate stimuli, analyze, and generalize is lost. Insight and judgment are lacking. The nurse can ask questions such as "What would you do if you found an addressed, stamped envelope on the street?" The patient with a thought disorder may respond, "Look at the address to find out who is trying to spy on me by putting the letter under my feet." The patient may respond in a bizarre manner to questions regarding similarities and differences. Thinking can be concrete or overly abstract and extremely bizarre in content. Responses to proverbs are often bizarre or concrete. "People shouldn't cry over spilled milk because it is white." Frequently, patients exhibit automatic knowing and are unable to consensually validate thoughts or communication. Autistic thinking is evident, in which the patient's thoughts evolve from an isolated inner world. There is a bareness of thought. Thought blocking occurs when patients lose their stream of thought in mid-sentence. Thought processes are often loose, tangential, circumstantial, repetitive, and symbolic of inner turmoil. Thinking is subsequently reflected in language and speech. During the interview, the nurse will see evidence of impaired thought process form by the patient's inability to connect ideas, the invention of new words or neologisms, and digressions in the conversation. Paranoid-disordered patients generally do not demonstrate such generalized disruption in thought processes. The focus of their disturbance is paranoid or persecutory delusions, not generalized thought impairment. The reader is referred to Chapter 3 for review of symptoms of impaired thought processes.

It can be quite difficult to interview a patient with a thought disorder. The interview should be short and focused on here and now issues. The nurse can assess the patient's cognitive and perceptual difficulties without resorting to in-depth questioning.

CASE EXAMPLE: Mr. Cohen was brought to the Emergency Department by his landlord. He was found rummaging through the trash in the basement of his apartment building. When the landlord asked him about his behavior, he responded, "I know you . . . you're part of them trying to get me the letters . . . Letters like A, B, C . . . see the sea, see the sea . . ." Mr. Cohen was so agitated and incoherent that the landlord brought him to the Emergency Department. The nurse was unable to obtain any information from Mr. Cohen.

Emotional manifestations

Emotional disturbances are closely associated with thought disorders. An alteration in thinking subsequently affects the patient's ability to feel and respond in the usual ways. With schizoaffective patients, it is difficult to differentiate between affect and thought as the primary disorder. Problems in both areas are nearly equally evident. In other thought disorders, cognitive impairment is the focal deficit with secondary disturbances in affect. Schizophrenic patients tend to evidence either a dulling of their emotions or a heightening of them. There is often a high degree of ambivalence with contradictory emotions flaring simultaneously. According to Kolb and Brodie, there is an apparent poverty and a disharmony of feeling tone.[7] The patient's affect is incongruent with the external situation, although it is usually appropriate to the patient's internal reality. A dulling feeling is accompanied by an insidious narrowing of interests. Patients experience themselves as unable to regulate their own emotions properly. Some may complain of not even being able to feel. As the condition worsens, the patient becomes indifferent to fundamental comfort needs. Whatever feelings are experienced may lack depth or focus. Particularly noticeable is the schizophrenic patient's anhedonia, or incapacity for pleasurable affect.

Emotional expression seems unrelated to reality. Responses to social situations may be inappropriate or opposite of what might have been expected. Often, whatever emotional expression is evidenced is stilted and unnatural. The nurse often experiences feelings of uneasiness and estrangement in the interview. This serves as an indicator as to how others feel in the presence of the schizophrenic individual and the resultant lack of emotional attachments. It is believed by some that schizophrenic individuals do not lose their capacity for emotionality but withdraw it from the social world and invest this aspect of self in highly personalized events that cannot be observed by others. The patient reports feelings of vagueness, of unreality. This is described as "feeling like a spectator of life" instead of taking part in it. If any feeling is demonstrated that is robust and not fragmented, it is that of guilt. Feelings of guilt usually emerge as by-products of the patient's delusional system and sometimes this feeling leads to self-destructive acts.

A patient experiencing a thought disorder exhibits a range of emotions, including rage, anger, irritability, apathy, fear, apprehension, terror, omnipotence, and emptiness. Paranoid individuals are particularly prone to anger and argumentativeness whereas disorganized types of schizophrenic patients tend to be flat and undemonstrative. Persons demonstrating thought impairments resulting from stress or organic insults also exhibit blunted affect dispersed with a wide variability of emotions. The nurse may note emotional lability as the patient fluctuates between moods.

> CASE EXAMPLE: Mrs. Pell is a patient on the mental health unit. She is detached, spending much time sitting in a chair in the day room, rarely conversing with other patients. Periodically, Mrs. Pell becomes agitated and waves her arms in an accusing manner at nearby patients, mumbling incoherent phrases, with no apparent provocation. Mrs. Pell'saffect is usually flat with little expression of emotion or relatedness.

Social and behavioral manifestations

Most schizophrenic persons are deviant, finding it difficult to interact face to face and are often disinclined to make the effort to interact. It is typically found that as children, schizophrenic people did not have many friends and were not popular in grade school. Girls are commonly said to have been passive and overcompliant to authority, while boys were more often passively defiant or uncooperative. These children did not participate in extracurricular events and usually went right home after school to withdraw into the solitude of their rooms.

Another prepsychotic type identified by Scheflen is the impeccably proper and hypermoral child. This student has strong attachments to the family and to some overriding ideology, often a religion. Such children achieve in an exemplary manner while in school. However, when their socializing patterns are explored, it is seen that they do not interact or engage others in social processes.

A large percentage of schizophrenic patients have their first psychotic episode as adolescents. Their anxiety increases as they are stressed not only by normal events of adolescence, such as dating, other social relationships, and changes in their physical bodies, but also by those stressors that are aspects of schizophrenia. Both normal and preschizophrenic adolescents alike tend to be lonely and perhaps a little depressed at various times. The need to be close to parents is in conflict with the need to move apart. Schoolwork makes increasing demands as well. The premorbid picture may also be complicated by the use of alcohol and drugs that either arouse or sedate the anxious individual. Sometimes schizophrenic patients seem preoccupied. They may appear "far away." If the patient is in school, the schoolwork may deteriorate and the persons withdraws from social contacts. There may be an apparent shift to laziness and loss of spontaneity, of ambition, and of interest in competition with the peer group. The patient may become restless and silent.

When the school years are over, these individuals may attempt to leave home to go away to college or to work. A large percentage of the prepsychotic will become acutely ill at this time. Those who do not may extend their high school adjustment, that is, doing what they have to do to meet requirements and coming home to be recluses in their rooms. Those who are able to work often take employment that is much below their qualifications.

Scheflen has examined the schizophrenic individual's microbehavior on the wards and finds vast differences in them vs. other patients. He finds that the schizophrenic patients are notably rude and asocial as reflected in their lack of manners. Scheflen portrays this as a statement of lack of social competence.

While the majority of other patients who are acutely ill in a psychiatric setting appear flat with expressions that are unchanging, schizophrenic patients are different. They gaze beyond the speaker, that is to say, the eyes focus perhaps a foot beyond the object. "He seems to be looking through and beyond: conversely, the gaze is focused in front of the conversational partner. Many such patients also invariably avoid gaze contact. A few gaze fixedly, and make you uncomfortable."[10] The pupils may be overly dilated or constricted, giving the patient a look of coldness and distance. Gazing at the ceiling or glancing around the room may indicate the presence of hallucinations. The nurse noting this behavior should assess further hallucinations.

Schizophrenic patients' greeting behavior is stilted and cold. They rarely touch others. These characteristics, coupled with the deviant focusing of the eyes, combine to create an aura of unsociability in the patient. This lack is both a resistance and a lack of ability. Schizophrenic persons are characteristically unskilled at conversation, courtship, and confrontation. They appear to have difficulty understanding the social significance of behavioral cues and there is a failure to distinguish patterns of behavior.

Interestingly, while schizophrenic patients are typically observed to be distant, defensive, and withdrawn, they may also be markedly attached and dependent on one partner or family member or a staff member in the hospital. The dependent relationship is usually very strong. If it is not with a family member, the patient tries to structure the same symbiotic relationship enjoyed with the partner in the family system. Within this relationship, the patient may be highly rigid and resistant to change. This characteristic may be a need for constancy in a field of cues to prevent psychotic disorganization.

Overall, schizophrenic individuals are typically avoidant, overly dependent on another, and rigid in their need to maintain constancy. While most of these people are cold, distant, and aloof, some are extraordinarily creative, especially in the arts. Some have concerns with power and dominance while others adjust by becoming passively subservient and obsequious.

Physical and motor manifestations

There are few major physical markers that are associated with thought disorders. Early on in schizophrenia, the patient may complain of various physical symptoms, including headaches, muscle pains, and indigestion. Later, schizophrenic patients are less likely to develop psychosomatic disease and allergies than the average person.[23]

Patients experiencing somatic delusions describe physical symptoms that either do not exist or are exaggerations of actual maladies. One man, for example, believed that a mole on his arm was seeding cancer throughout his body, despite pathology reports that indicated the mole was benign.

Schizophrenic patients often have difficulty caring for their health needs. Personal hygiene and grooming may be neglected and early symptoms of illness ignored. Their general appearance tends to be unorganized and unkempt. These individuals exhibit a general lack of spontaneity and initiative. Scheflen noted that some schizophrenic people appear robust and vital. Young paranoid patients in their first episodes of manifest psychosis are such an example. But even in these persons, Scheflen noted a subtle deviation. "There is an excessive brightness of the eye, and the appearance of vitality begins to take shape as a poorly controlled restlessness and a marked increase in muscular tonus and arousal."[10]

Abnormal motor behavior is commonly seen with strange mannerisms such as scratching, grinning, grimacing, or echopraxia (imitation of movements of another person). Deficits in motor skills and lack of coordination may be present. The schizophrenic patient may appear stiff and awkward or in a catatonic, stuporous state. Occasionally, the nurse will see waxy flexibility in a catatonic patient in which movable body parts can be placed in positions that remain stable for hours. On the opposite side of the spectrum, patients can be agitated and hyperactive, particularly catatonic patients during a catatonic excitement. During most psychotic episodes, patients exhibit dilated pupils, elevated heart rate and blood pressure, and perspiration, indicative of sympathetic excitation.[23]

Minor neurological abnormalities are commonly seen in schizophrenia.[24] These include "soft" neurological signs and electroencephalographic abnormalities. Soft signs are evidenced by motor nonpersistence, hyperreflexia, disturbed balance and gait, stereogenesis, graphesthesia, movement disorders, control sensory abnormalities, speech defects, poor auditory-visual integration, choreiform movements and tremor, and cranial nerve abnormalities.[24] EEG testing often indicates nonspecific changes, particularly with catatonic patients.

While the pituitary adrenal pathways are not typically abnormal in schizophrenic people, there are often abnormalities of other neurohormonal pathways. In women, these are evidenced by hirsutism and amenorrhea. Sometimes the hair is lacking in luster and order. Skin may be sallow, dry, or waxy. There may be a marked deviation in body tonus, with either an elevation or a marked reduction.

ASSESSMENT TOOLS

Assessment of thought disorders is accomplished through the use of the psychiatric interview, particularly the mental status examination. The nurse should quickly be able to elicit cognitive impairments, perceptual disturbances, and psychosocial difficulties. Individuals experiencing problems with thinking will manifest those in their speech, nonverbal communications, and behaviors.

Tool 6:1 lists signs and symptoms indicative of four types of thought disorders. A patient exhibiting any of these signs and symptoms should be assessed carefully for the presence of the thought disorder. The reader is referred to Chapter 9 for information regarding assessment of organic cognitive impairments.

Schneider devised a set of symptoms he postulated were useful in identifying schizophrenia and differentiating it from other disorders.[25] Research on these symptoms provides mixed results as to their validity in identifying schizophrenia, yet many clinicians find them useful assessment criteria. Schneider's first ranked symptoms are presented on Tool 6:2.

Bleuler's fundamental symptoms of schizophrenia are listed in Tool 6:3.[26] These classic symptoms, often referred to as the "four A's," reflect basic symptoms that are indicative of schizophrenia. Although the diagnosis of schizophrenia is more complex than identification of these four signs and symptoms, the four A's do provide an initial framework for recognizing schizophrenic disorders.

Tool 6:4, the New Haven Schizophrenia Index (NHSI), was developed by Astrachan, et al. during an attempt to devise utilization review procedures for evaluating psychiatric treatment.[27] Definitions of the symptoms were delineated in order to promote more reliable scoring among clinicians. The patient needs to receive a minimum score of four to be considered schizophrenic. *Text continued on p. 164.*

TOOL 6:1	Brief assessment for thought disorders		

	Yes	No

1. Schizophrenic disorders

Does the patient exhibit:
a. Delusions _____ _____
b. Hallucinations (usually auditory) _____ _____
c. Loose associations _____ _____
d. Circumstantial thinking _____ _____
e. Illogical thinking _____ _____
f. Concrete or abstractly bizarre thoughts _____ _____
g. Incoherence _____ _____
h. Flat or inappropriate affect _____ _____
i. Withdrawal and isolation _____ _____
j. Neglect of self-care _____ _____
k. Odd mannerisms _____ _____
l. Disorganized behavior _____ _____
m. Deterioration in daily functioning _____ _____

2. Paranoid disorders

Does the patient exhibit:
a. Persecutory delusions _____ _____
b. Ideas of reference _____ _____
c. Absence of generalized thought impairments _____ _____

3. Schizoaffective disorder

Does the patient exhibit:
a. Diagnostic symptoms of schizophrenic disorders _____ _____
b. Prominent affective disturbances _____ _____

4. Brief reactive psychosis

Does the patient exhibit:
a. Diagnostic symptoms of schizophrenic disorders _____ _____
b. No previous psychiatric history of psychosis _____ _____
c. Acute onset of symptoms with clearing within 2 _____ _____
   weeks
d. An identifiable stressor _____ _____

TOOL 6:2   Schneiderian First-Rank Symptoms

Symptom	Evidence of symptom
1. *Audible thoughts.* The patient experiences auditory hallucinations.	_____
2. *Voices arguing.* Two or more hallucinatory voices disagree, usually about the patient.	_____
3. *Voices commenting on one's action.* The auditory hallucination describes the patient's activities.	_____
4. *Influence playing on the body, somatic passivity.* Bodily sensations are imposed upon the patient by some external force.	_____
5. *Thought withdrawal.* The patient describes thoughts being taken from his or her mind but by an external force.	_____
6. *Thought broadcasting.* Patients believe thoughts are not contained in their own minds but escape into the external world.	_____
7. *Delusional perceptions.* A perception arises that has private, irrational meaning for the patient, followed by the development of an elaborate delusional system.	_____
8. *Feelings, impulses, and volitional acts experienced as the work of others.* The patient feels controlled by external forces.	_____

Adapted from Schneider, K. Clinical psychopathology. Trans. M.W. Hamilton. New York: Grune & Stratton, Inc., 1959.

TOOL 6:3   Bleuler's Fundamental Symptoms of Schizophrenia

Symptom	Definition
1. Loose associations	Absence of logical connections between thoughts
2. Impaired affect	Limited emotional expression or incongruency of affect and external situation
3. Ambivalence	The experience of contradictory emotions occurring simultaneously
4. Autism	Retreat into an internal world and preoccupation with an inner life

Adapted from Bleuler, E. *Dementia praecox or the group of schizophrenias.* New York: International Universities Press, Inc., 1950.

TOOL 6:4   New Haven Schizophrenia Index Checklist

CHECKLIST OF SYMPTOMS

A. Symptoms

1. (a) Delusions (not specified or other than depressive) ____
   (b) Hallucinations (auditory) ____
   (c) Hallucinations (visual) ____
   (d) Hallucinations (others) ____

2. Crazy thinking and/or thought disorder. Any of the following:
   (a) Bizarre thinking ____
   (b) Autism or grossly unrealistic private thoughts ____
   (c) Looseness of association, illogical thinking, overinclusion ____
   (d) Blocking ____
   (e) Concreteness ____
   (f) Derealization ____
   (g) Depersonalization ____

3. Inappropriate affect ____

4. Confusion ____

5. Paranoid ideation (self-referential thinking, suspiciousness) ____

6. Catatonic behavior ____
   (a) Excitement ____
   (b) Stupor ____
   (c) Waxy flexibility ____
   (d) Negativism ____
   (e) Mutism ____
   (f) Echolalia ____
   (g) Stereotyped motor activity ____

SCORING SYSTEM

To be considered part of the schizophrenic group, the patient must score either Item I or Items 2a, 2b, 2c and must attain a total score of at least 4 points.

He can achieve a maximum of 4 points on Item 1: 2 for the presence of delusions, 2 for hallucinations.

On Item 2, he can score 2 points for any of symptoms (a) through (c), 1 point for either or both symptoms (d) through (e), and 1 point each for (f) and (g). He can thus score a maximum of 5 points on Item 2.

Items 3, 4, 5, and 6 each receive 1 point.

Note: Where the 4th point is necessary for inclusion in the sample is provided by 2(d) or 2(e), these symptoms are not scored.

Continued.

TOOL 6:4   New Haven Schizophrenia Index Checklist—cont'd

I. Definitions

A. *Bizarre or idiosyncratic thinking* is defined as inconsistent, confused or contradictory statements which do not make sense, statements which dramatically demonstrate an unexplained gap in the reasoning process, logically coherent statements which are unrelated to the topic at hand, strange or socially inappropriate statements, etc. Bizarre thoughts refer to the form that thoughts take when they are expressed.

B. *Illogical thinking, looseness of associations* refer to the content and form of a person's expressed thoughts. Thoughts are not continuous, thinking is illogical, not oriented to any goal and operates with ideas and concepts which have little or no connections with the main idea.

C. *Autism or grossly unrealistic thoughts* is defined as the interpenetration of outer reality and inner thoughts and the tendency not to distinguish between the two. Objectified facts become obscured, distorted or excluded in varying degrees and there is a detachment from reality with the relative predominance of inner life.

D. *Blocking* refers to the sudden cessation in the flow of thought or speech, or the interruption of a train of thought due to emotional factors.

E. *Overinclusion* is used as originally defined by Cameron as difficulty in maintaining the usual conceptual boundaries and a tendency to include many elements irrelevant to the central idea in thinking.

F. *Concreteness* is defined by Vygotsky as the loss of ability to think in abstract concepts. This has been further elaborated by Goldstein and Benjamin in terms of reacting in too literal a way, without considering the relationships of particular thoughts or ideas.

II. *Delusions and/or hallucinations*

Although often considered to be secondary symptoms of schizophrenia (Bleuler, 1950), they are still generally regarded as evidence of the patient's break with reality. Delusions occur in many syndromes and thus must be considered as generally indicating a psychotic condition.

Delusions were rated as if they were depressive or if other than depressive.

Delusions are false beliefs out of keeping with the individual's level of knowledge and cultural background. They may be viewed as a manifestation of the individual's misinterpretation or misconception regarding the self or the external world. In keeping with current American practice, we did not specifically exclude depressive delusions or

From Astrachan, B.M., et al. A checklist for the diagnosis of schizophrenia. British Journal of Psychiatry, 1972, *121,* 529-539.

TOOL 6:4   New Haven Schizophrenia Index Checklist—cont'd

hallucinations, but we rated them separately so that we could separate out those patients who might have predominantly depressive psychotic symptoms.

Hallucinations are defined as manifestations of an individual's misperception of the self or world, a false sensory perception in the absence of actual external stimuli. Hallucinations are separately categorized as auditory, visual or other.

III. *Minor symptoms*

Investigators and clinicians have described a number of other symptoms as frequently being associated with the schizophrenic syndrome, but at present there is some controversy about most of these symptoms.

We used the following definitions to rate these symptoms.

A. *Disturbance of affect* is defined as a lack of depth and consistency of affect, a lability of affect and inappropriate affect. Opinions as to its importance as a symptom of schizophrenia are quite diverse, yet its consistent appearance in most psychiatric textbooks throughout the years merits its inclusion in our checklist (Kolb, 1968; Shanfield et al., 1970). We did not consider a description of flat affect as in itself sufficient to rate as a disturbance of affect.

B. *Confusion* is defined as a disturbed orientation with respect to either person, place or time. The literature is quite mixed as to the consistency with which this symptom is described as well as to its specificity to schizophrenia. We recognize that it would seriously confuse the diagnosis of an organic state, but nonetheless included in this item in our overall checklist as a more global measure of functioning (Vaillant, 1962; 1964).

C. *Derealization, depersonalization and dissociation* are symptoms which some theoreticians (Brauer et al., 1970; Federn, 1952; Gurland et al., 1969) have related to the schizophrenic syndromes. There is a great deal of dispute as to whether they occur with any frequency, and—even more importantly—with any specificity, in a schizophrenic syndrome.

1. *Derealization* is a mental phenomenon characterized by the loss of the sense of reality concerning oneself in relationship to one's surroundings, that one's circumstances have somehow changed so that the real environment is in some way no longer what it used to be.

2. *Depersonalization,* to which derealization is closely related, is a sense of unreality or estrangement from oneself. Everything seems dream-like and the actions of oneself or others are watched with detachment.

Continued.

> **TOOL 6:4   New Haven Schizophrenia Index Checklist—cont'd**
>
> 3. *Dissociation,* particular amnestic or fugue states (personality dissociation characterized by amnesia, actual flight from the immediate surroundings), though rare, are sometimes described as schizophrenic. Dissociations are psychological separations or splitting off where emotionally significant thoughts and affects are detached from awareness.
>
> D. *Paranoid ideation* specifically referred to the presence of paranoid thoughts, other than delusions, specifically including suspiciousness and self-referential thinking. Although it occurs in many conditions other than schizophrenia, the consistency with which it is identified in schizophrenic patients led us to include this symptom in our checklist (Bleuler, 1950).
>
> E. *Catatonic behavior* was rated when symptoms of stupor, waxy flexibility, negativism, echolalia, stereotyped motor behavior, reduced motor activity or excitement were described.
>
> IV. *Object relations*
>
> A tendency towards social isolation and a history of chaotic interpersonal relationships have been cited in the sociodynamic (Phillips, 1953; Stephens et al., 1966; Harrow et al., 1969; Vaillant, 1962, 1964) and psychodynamic (Bateson et al., 1956; Bellak, 1970; Lidz et al., 1965; Singer et al., 1965; etc.) theories of schizophrenia.
>
> A. The tendency towards *social isolation* was rated whether it occurred only in the past year or long-term. It is defined as withdrawal from contact with others, an avoidance of people and of situations in which contact with others might be expected.
>
> B. *Chaotic interpersonal relationships* was defined as evidence of extremely disturbed, often intensely ambivalent relationships to significant others in at least two role areas (e.g., work performance, family role, school, relationship with friends. etc.).

DIAGNOSIS
Nursing diagnoses of thought disorders

Thought-disordered persons experience difficulties ranging from mild to severe in their social and work-related activities. They typically misperceive important social cues in their environments or they assign irrational meaning to them. As a result these persons respond in inappropriate ways and are consequently "out of synch" with those around them. To protect themselves from all the above-mentioned problems, thought-disordered patients often seclude themselves, becoming

TAXONOMY OF NURSING DIAGNOSES FOR THOUGHT DISORDERS

1. Alterations in thought processes
    1.10 Impaired reality testing
    1.11 Delusions
    1.20 Impaired ability to abstract
    1.30 Impaired ability to reason logically
    1.40 Disorganized thinking
    1.50 Bizarre thought content
    1.60 Impaired judgment and insight
    1.70 Impaired problem-solving
2. Impaired verbal communication
    2.10 Inability to speak logically and coherently
    2.20 Inability to express thoughts and feelings
    2.30 Inappropriate verbalizations
3. Sensory-perceptual alterations
    3.10 Hallucinations
    3.20 Agitation and restlessness
    3.30 Change in usual response to stimuli
4. Ineffective individual coping
    4.10 Impaired social functioning
    4.20 Impaired relationships with others
    4.30 Impaired occupational functioning
    4.40 Impaired cognitive abilities
    4.50 Impaired ability to carry out daily activities
5. Self-care deficit
    5.10 Impaired ability to maintain personal hygiene
    5.20 Impaired ability to maintain adequate grooming
    5.30 Impaired ability to adapt in environment
6. Fear
    6.10 Hypervigilance

progressively autistic and unable to take care of their own basic needs. The nursing diagnoses most applicable to thought-disordered patients reflect impairments in communication, thinking, coping, and self-care. These are listed in the box above. Patients demonstrating thought disorders may have a number of nursing diagnoses that are descriptive of their difficulties maintaining themselves in society.

Psychiatric diagnosis of thought disorders

According to the DSM-III, the essential features of the schizophrenic disorders include psychotic episodes, with the first acute illness occurring before age 45, illness of at least 6 months duration, deterioration from a previous level of functioning, and disturbances of content and form of thought, perception, affect, sense of self, volition, relationships to the external world, and psychomotor behavior.

The schizophrenic disorders are to be differentiated from organic delusional syndromes, especially those caused by amphetamine or phencyclidine. Some affective disorders may also appear with withdrawal and deterioration of functioning. However, in the latter case, the development of delusions or hallucinations follows a period of affective disturbance. The diagnosis of schizophrenia is made only if the affective syndrome appeared after the psychosis or was brief in duration relative to the duration of the psychotic symptoms.

Patients with paranoid disorders experience delusions of a persecutory and paranoid nature. They generally do not, however, exhibit incoherent thinking or bizarre thought form. The diagnosis of schizoaffective disorder is made if the patient demonstrates the diagnostic symptoms of schizophrenia in addition to highly prominent, continual affective disturbances. The patient with a brief, reactive psychosis manifests schizophrenic symptoms but has an acute onset of those symptoms in relation to an identifiable stressor. The episode usually clears within 2 weeks. A list of potential psychiatric diagnoses is presented below. The reader is referred to DSM-III for specific diagnostic criteria.[28]

1. Schizophrenic disorder
   a. Disorganized type
   b. Catatonic type
   c. Paranoid type
   d. Undifferentiated type
2. Paranoid disorder
3. Brief reactive psychosis
4. Schizoaffective disorder

CASE EXAMPLE: Assessment of Peter W.

Identifying information. Peter W. is a 24-year-old high school dropout. He works off and on as a night watchman at a building site. He is admitted to the locked ward from a police van. He was picked up by the latter from an Emergency Room where he had been committed on two certificates.

Presenting problem. Peter appears dazed. He does not know his last name. He was brought to the Emergency Room by a "friend" who rents a room in the same house where Peter rents. The friend reports that Peter returned to the house from his midnight to 8 AM shift and his eyes looked glazed. He did not recognize his friend nor the place where he had rented a room for the past 6 months. Upon interview Peter sits politely and stares into space. Occasionally he looks just beyond the interviewer and answers her questions haltingly. The patient claims that he does not know what the problem is. In fact, he does not really know where he is or why.

Brief recent history. The informant is the accompanying friend. Peter has lived in the boarding house for the past 6 months. He spends most of his time in his room. He is known to drink beer "up there" sometimes with the door shut. He owns a small black and white television set and it is turned on most of the time. The friend knows only that the patient is 24 and is a high school dropout.

Mental status examination. The patient sits quietly, if somewhat rigidly, in his assigned chair. His eyes appear unfocused except for transient moments when he looks just beyond the interviewer while she speaks to him. His voice is soft. His speech is at times incoherent. Occasionally, the patient seems to gather himself together, tilts his head slightly, and then smiles furtively. When asked if he is hearing voices he denies this. He reports that from time to time he believes that his thoughts are being clocked by someone. He states he is convinced the interview is an attempt to "brainwash" him by the FBI.

The patient is dressed in dirty, wrinkled overalls and a shirt. He wears socks and tennis shoes. One of the socks is pulled down under his heel. He patient's speech is sometimes retarded and continuously stilted. His affect is blunted. He is disoriented to time, place, and person. He expresses delusional ideation and appears to be hallucinating. His memory is impaired, judgment is poor, and he is unable to carry out serial sevens.

Summary. Peter exhibits impaired thinking. He is disoriented and lacks insight into his present problem. His affect is blunted. He expresses concern about external control of his thoughts, and he appears to be hallucinating. No other data are available about Peter's living situation or family.

Psychiatric diagnosis. Schizophrenia, paranoid type.

Nursing diagnosis.
1. Alteration in thought processes, disorientation, distractibility, incoherent speech
2. Ineffective individual coping with impaired social, occupational, and cognitive functioning and inability to carry out daily activities

CASE EXAMPLE: Assessment of Cindy H.

Identifying information. Cindy H. is a 19-year-old college student. She is a transfer student who spent her freshman year at a distant university but did not successfully complete more than one half of her program there. The reason for the underachievement was apparently Cindy's numerous small crises and ensuing trips home for comfort and support.

Presenting problem. Cindy is seen in the walk-in clinic of the Psychiatric Institute because she feels "out of myself, strange, like I'm watching me."

Brief recent history. This appropriately dressed, somewhat immature-looking college student describes herself as feeling progressively more alienated from self. These feelings, which began about 3 weeks ago, have gotten to the point where the patient "does not feel real." Cindy says that she has a roommate whom she does not particularly like but that the other girl doesn't bother her a lot, except when she gets the green glob going in the corner of their room. When asked to describe more about this, the patient says that she cannot and she appears anxious and angry. She also reports missing her mother quite a bit. Her mother is in the city, living in the family home with Cindy's father; however, Cindy has been "encouraged" by her father to spend more time at school and less at home.

Family history. This patient has one sibling, a brother. Both parents are living. They own a home that is approximately 20 miles from Cindy's present school. The brother attends a boarding school. Cindy has not informed her family of her appointment at the Psychiatric Institute.

Personal history. Cindy is the oldest of two siblings. Her parents enjoy a comfortable marriage, though her father drinks occasionally and then becomes "loud and scary." This patient, who sits rather primly and answers the interviewer's questions obediently, describes herself as someone who feels adrift and is moving farther away from her own core everyday. She says that she misses her mother's advice and that she is sure that her mother wants her to come home again but that her father does not want her. She has never done well in school and does not have any real friends. She denies dating, saying that boys are "strange." She has never smoked, denies the use of chemical substances, and occasionally drinks a small amount of wine.

Mental status examination. Cindy is a quiet, immature-appearing 19-year-old college student. Her clothes were appropriate, though dull in color and style. She sat obediently, like a small child, in her chair and answered all questions in a soft, monotonous tone. Cindy's speech was normal. Her mood may have been slightly depressed. She denied affective problems. This young woman described herself as afraid. She inferred a sense of dread about the future as she grew more distant from herself. Cindy was oriented ×3. She was able to perform serial sevens and to remember an object pointed out at the beginning of the interview. She seemed to describe her illness trajectory in chronological order. She described an hallucinatory experience but did not report or appear delusional in other aspects of her presentation. While this patient performed within acceptable limits on the examination, her responses were always slightly vague and tenuous. Occasionally her speech would become very circumscribed. Cindy does not foresee any dire prognostications, but it is evident to the interviewer that this girl has decompensated and is in need of rigorous intervention, including antipsychotic medication.

Summary. Cindy demonstrates some fear of an unclear future but definitely one in which she becomes less and less capable of coping. Her mood is slightly depressed and she is fearful. This student is having difficulty functioning in her college work. (She has always underachieved in school and she left her original college setting, having failed much of her first year's work there.) It is inferred that her mother has been overly involved in the past with her child's problems, while her father is characterized as trying to maintain some distance. Cindy's present problem has been developing over the past 3 weeks. While imminent decompensation is not in the patient's awareness, it is the interviewer's concern that this process has begun and prompt supportive measures must be taken if this patient is to be maintained outside of a residential treatment facility.

Psychiatric diagnosis. Possible schizophrenia (further assessment required)

Nursing diagnosis. Alteration in thought processes, inaccurate interpretation of environment, hypervigilance, egocentricity.

REFERENCES

1. Taylor, G. *The natural history of the mind.* New York: Dutton Press, 1979, p. 260.
2. Menninger, K. Syndrome, yes: Disease, no. In R. Canco, Ed. *The schizophrenic reactions.* New York: Brunner/Mazel, Inc., 1970, pp. 71-78.
3. Mendel, W. *Supportive care: Theory and technique,* 2nd ed. Los Angeles: Mara Books, 1975, p. 11.
4. Bellak, L., & Sheehy, M. The broad role of ego functions assessment. *American Journal of Psychiatry,* 1976, *133,* 1263.
5. Snyder, S. *Biological aspects of mental disorder.* New York: Oxford University Press, 1980, pp. 49, 51.
6. Wynne, L., et al. *The nature of schizophrenia: New approaches to research and treatment.* New York: John Wiley & Sons, 1978, p. 545.
7. Kolb, L., & Brodie, K. *Modern clinical psychiatry.* Philadelphia: W.B. Saunders Co., 1982, pp. 347, 348, 361.
8. *Diagnostic distribution of admissions to inpatient services of state and county mental hospitals.* Bethesda, Md: National Institute of Mental Health, 1975, p. 11.
9. *Primary diagnosis of discharges from non-federal general hospital psychiatric inpatient units.* National Institute of Mental Health, 1975, p. 14.
10. Scheflen, A. *Levels of schizophrenia.* New York: Brunner/Mazel, Inc., 1981, pp. 59, 73, 129-130, 136.
11. Mahler, M. Autism and symbiosis. *Internatonal Journal of Psychoanalysis,* 1958, *39,* 77.
12. Bowen, M. *Schizophrenia as a multi-generational phenomenon.* In M. Berger, Ed. Beyond the double bind theory. New York: Brunner/Mazel, Inc., 1978.
13. Robinson, L. *Psychiatric nursing as a human experience,* 3rd ed. Philadelphia: W.B. Saunders Co., 1983, p. 382.
14. Bateson, G., et al. *Toward a theory of schizophrenia.* New York: Behavioral Books, 1956.
15. Kety, S., et al. Mental illness in the biological and adoptive families of adopted individuals who have become schizophrenic: Prevalence of mental illness and other characteristics. In L. Wynne, et al., Eds. *The nature of schizophrenia.* New York: John Wiley & Sons, Inc., 1978.
16. Rosenthal, D. *Genetics of psychopathology.* New York: McGraw-Hill Book Co., 1971.
17. Ornstein, R. The psychology of consciousness, 2nd ed. New York: Harcourt Brace Jovanovich, Inc., 1977.

18. Flor, H. Schizophrenia-like reactions and affective psychoses associated with temporal lobe epilepsy. *American Journal of Psychiatry*, 1969, *136*, 400.
19. Arieti, S. *Interpretation of schizophrenia*, 2nd ed. New York: Basic Books, Inc., Publishers, 1974, p. 20.
20. Horowitz, M. A cognitive model of hallucinations. *American Journal of Psychiatry*, 1975, *132*, 8.
21. Field, W.E., & Ruelke, W. Hallucinations and how to deal with them. *American Journal of Nursing*, 1973, *73*, 638-640.
22. Freedman, A., Kaplan, H., & Saddock, M. *Comprehensive textbook of psychiatry*. Baltimore: Williams & Wilkins, 1979, p. 229.
23. Gregory, I., & Smeltzer, D.J. *Psychiatry—essentials of clinical practice*. Boston: Little, Brown & Co., 1977, pp. 233, 234.
24. Pincus, J.H., & Tucker, G.J. *Behavioral neurology*, 2nd ed. New York: Oxford University Press, 1978, pp. 108, 109.
25. Schneider, K. *Clinical psychopathology*, trans. M.W. Hamilton. New York: Grune & Stratton, Inc., 1959.
26. Bleuler, E. *Dementia praecox or the group of schizophrenias*. New York: International Universities Press, Inc. 1950.
27. Astrachan, B.M., et al. A checklist for the diagnosis of schizophrenia. *British Journal of Psychiatry*, 1972, *121*, 529-539.
28. American Psychiatric Association. *Diagnostic and Statistical Manual of Mental Disorders*, 3rd ed. Washington, D.C.: American Psychiatric Association, 1980.

CHAPTER 7

ASSESSING PERSONALITY DISORDERS

Every individual is unique and differs from every other human being. In turn, each of us resembles one another in a variety of ways. The sum of who we are is generally called our personality and reflects a unique arrangement of common characteristics or traits. The term personality in professional practice is a more precise concept denoting a consistent and idiosyncratic style of thinking, feeling, and interacting with the world. In working with patients and staff, it is important to develop an understanding of patients' personalities and to be able to communicate to staff the relevant aspects of a patient's personality. Clinical impressions and an assessment of personality trends should direct every aspect of the treatment and nursing care plans to follow.

Psychological literature provides guidance for clarifying our thinking about personality. To the psychologist McNeil,[1] the term personality is used to describe ". . . a person's objectively observable behavior as well as his inner experience." In other words, we glean from our observation and inquiry information that tells us about observable behavior (patterns of interpersonal relationships, behavior, moods and affects, social and occupational behavior, relation to reality) and inner experience (thoughts and feelings, self-image and sense of self, perceptions, and attitudes). A study of the information gathered results in an understanding of a personality composite that not only directs the planned work with patients but also provides an ability to anticipate behavior and responses in the course of treatment.

There is a large population of patients whose personality, the constellation of genetic, biological, emotional, and intellectual facets, is troublesome. They are locked into a characteristic style of "being" that is self-defeating or disturbing to people around them. Their disturbance is not manifested in distinct symptoms as is the case with patients in the diagnostic categories of anxiety, affective, thought, and organic disorders. Their difficulties are less related to what they do (the signs and indicators of disturbance) than to who they are. They appear to be unable to behave, feel, or think differently despite the personal or social penalties involved. Their disorder is evidenced by patterns of long-standing personality characteristics rather than discrete symptoms. It is this category of individuals who are diagnosed as "personality disorders." This chapter discusses the assessment of this group of patients. It is the enduring personal design—the patient's fundamental character—that is manifesting difficulty and will be the focus of attention.

DEFINITION

It is not difficult to recall situations where we behaved in ways that we consider to be "unlike us" or "out of character." We are also aware of circumstances or cultures where "normal" behavior seems extraordinary to us and where standard rules of behavior seem irrelevant. We may, for example, recall crisis periods where we responded to stress by insulating ourselves from social interactions and becoming very isolative. Or we may have been in social situations where a typically reserved and quiet person became lively, dramatic, and obnoxious. Both of these situations are examples of what we might casually label "personality changes," yet the manifestations are transient, time limited, and relegated to a very specific set of circumstances; the isolative person returns to regular socializing and relationships after the crisis has been alleviated and the "life of the party" returns to a more introverted manner. The demonstrations of unusual behavior do not reflect a characteristic style. Personality-disordered patients, on the other hand, manifest behavioral, emotional, cognitive, and interpersonal features that are consistent over time, inflexible, and maladaptive. The maladjusted trends are typically not anxiety-provoking for the patient, nor are they utilized as modes of coping with particular circumstances. They are a person's fixed approach to life.

The degree of maladaptiveness may be determined by the milieu, the culture, or by the patient's experience of unhappiness. The patient's source of unhappiness may also vary. Many personality-disordered patients are more distraught about the outcome of their maladaptive behavior and not at all disturbed by the behavior itself, for example, thieves who are distressed by their arrest but not by their criminal behavior. Other patients may be very uncomfortable and aware of their problems but seem incapable of changing despite a desire to do so. Such is the case of a woman who repeatedly marries abusive husbands and suffers tremendous physical and emotional pain but feels unable to make different choices. These maladaptive patterns can be traced back to adolescence in the personality disorder. The characteristics are stable over time and not related to particular life situations or stress.

The term personality disorder as used here reflects current diagnostic as well as nosological trends. One of the goals of the DMS-III is to increase diagnostic specificity. With the DSM-III major diagnostic group of personality disorders, there are eleven distinct types of disorders that have been identified.[2] Each type is representative of a particular style or combination of behavioral, emotional, cognitive, and social features. The eleven types are the paranoid, schizoid, schizotypal, histrionic, narcissistic, antisocial, borderline, avoidant, dependent, compulsive, and passive-aggressive personality disorders. We can generalize about typical stylistic manifestations of each personality disorder and use this understanding in the therapeutic approach as well as in the care plan.

These diagnostic and nosological distinctions are very important. In the past, the terms personality disorder and character disorder were used to refer to what is now considered to be one specific type of personality disorder. A review of the older psychiatric literature indicates that a diagnosis of personality disorder in the past referred to some of the focal diagnostic criteria now indicative of the antisocial personality. Increased study in the field has refined one general category into eleven distinctive subtypes. The nurse is encouraged to take advantage of these developments and to clarify with peers and other professionals exactly what is intended by their use of the term personality disorder. Despite advances, less precise usage continues.

CLASSIFICATION

The DSM-III seeks to increase the amount of consistency in the use of psychiatric diagnoses. For the personality disorders, as in the other diagnostic categories, objective criteria have been developed to support diagnostic reliability and to decrease the degree of personal interpretation. The task of classifying a patient's personality is a difficult one. The history of this effort is fraught with disagreements and questions regarding the meaning of diagnoses, clinical validity, inconsistent usage, and divergent theoretical foundations. All of these problems are suggestive of the conceptual challenge involved in summarizing the cogent features of an individual's personality with a single term. Review of the different diagnostic manuals used in the past reflect the waxing and waning of the popularity of certain diagnoses, schools of thought, and therapeutic frameworks. The DSM-III includes deletions from the last manual, the inadequate personality disorder; additions to the manual, the narcissistic and schizotypal personality disorders; and the revival of a diagnosis dismissed in the preceding manual, the dependent personality disorder. These changes are not arbitrary and represent a standardization of approach to the diagnostic labeling process.

The eleven personality disorders enumerated in DMS-III are categorized into three main groups.[2] The first group is comprised of the paranoid, schizoid, and schizotypal personality disorders. Patients with these disorders tend to be alienated from society and strange in their interactions with people. They seem to distance themselves from others. The second group includes the histrionic, narcissistic, antisocial, and borderline personality disorders. These types of individuals are emotionally expressive and reactive in interpersonal situations. They have the ability to get others actively involved in their personal affairs. The third group consists of the avoidant, compulsive, dependent, and passive-aggressive personality disorders. The major feature of these persons is a restrictiveness in their ability to express genuine, direct emotions, and a hypersensitivity to rejection in relationships. In addition there is a remaining group called the "Atypical, Mixed or Other Personality Disorder" for disorders that phenomenologically cannot be placed in one or the other categories. For the purpose of clarity, the three main groupings cited in the DSM-III will be utilized in this text to describe the personality disorders. The reader is referred to the DSM-III for the specific diagnostic criteria for each personality disorder.

EPIDEMIOLOGY

The impact of the DSM-III's goal to root the diagnostic process in observable phenomena is likely to have a positive influence on the availability and reliability of statistics reporting the prevalence and diagnosis of the personality disorders. Because these patients do not typically require hospitalization and many will never even seek treatment, there are many personality-disordered individuals who will never be counted as such. Many will never interact with a professional who would designate their personality adjustment as a psychiatric illness. Many statistical studies have focused on particular diagnostic subtypes, such as the antisocial personality disorder, because of their overrepresentation in prison populations. The paucity of comprehensive data reflects the need for precise diagnostic categories determined by precise diagnostic criteria.

A survey conducted by the U.S. Department of Health, Education, and Welfare[3] reviews the diagnostic distribution of admissions to state and city psychiatric hospitals and private psychiatric hospitals. There were approximately 385,200 admissions to state and city facilities in 1975, as compared to approximately 129,832 admissions to private psychiatric hospitals for the same year. Statistics for state and city hospitals report that 6.8% of this population was classified as personality disordered. Of the 18 to 24 age-group, 13% of all patients were diagnosed with personality disorders. Of the 25 to 34 year age-group, the largest age-group represented in the total population, 9.4% received a primary diagnosis of personality disorder. The incidence of this diagnosis decreased with older age-groups in this population. These statistics can now be compared to the incidence of the diagnosis of personality disorders in private psychiatric hospital for 1975[5]; 5.1% of this population was classified as personality disordered, a slightly smaller percentage than reported in public facilities. Of the 18 to 24 year age-group, 8.1% of all patients were diagosed with personality disorder, a significantly lower percentage than the 13% of public facility patients. Of the 25 to 34 year age-group, again the largest age-group represented, 5.7% had a diagnosis of personality disorder, a smaller percentage compared to public facilities. Statistics from private facilities report a higher incidence in older age-groups than reports from public hospitals, but this is a general trend downward, nonetheless.

CAUSATIVE FACTORS

The exact source of the psychological disturbances that are referred to as personality disorders is an area of contention. There are many theories seeking to explain the roots of these dysfunctions and although the etiological formulations that exist are varying, there appears to be general agreement that the roots are in childhood. The theories acknowledge the tenacity of a person's personality style by dating the onset to the early years of life.

The theories developed that address the factors contributing to the development of a personality disorder are distinguished from one another by the amount of emphasis placed on internal vs. external determinants. While it is impossible to enumerate every theory that offers an etiological explanation, the three major categories of theories will be reviewed. The three types of categories found are the biological, social, and psychodynamic theories.

Biological theory

Biological theories attribute personality disturbance to constitutional abnormalities. The subscribers of these theories suggest that there is a biological base to behavioral and emotional deviations. Their research seeks a scientific demonstration of the chromosomal and neuronal abnormalities in this category of patients. There are many scientists working to demonstrate a correlation between a person's behavior and the biological makeup of the person.

For many years researchers have studied twins raised together, as well as twins separated at birth and adopted, in order to track social and psychological development. The importance of hereditary factors has been investigated in the etiology of antisocial behavior by Slater and Cowie[5] and by Christiansen[6] in Denmark. Their research has demonstrated a high concordance between monozygotic twins and a significant concordance between dizygotic twins. Crowe[7] has followed the development of children born to parents demonstrating antisocial trends. Crowe's study compared the incidence of antisocial trends in two adopted populations: those born to antisocial parents and those born to control group parents. Both groups of children had been separated from their parents during infancy. The study found a higher rate of antisocial personality trends in the adoptees born to antisocial parents. This study as well as the studies of twins supports the role of heredity in the development of antisocial personality disorder.

Genetic research studying abnormal sex chromosomes has been investigating the correlation between XYY karyotypes and psychopathology. Forssman[8] and Hope[9] have found a higher incidence of XYY sex chromosome complements among the mentally ill. Other studies have correlated XYY complements to the characteristics of emotional lability and immaturity. Zeuthen et al.[10] found these traits to be more common in the XYY population than in a normal population. There is debate as to whether the higher incidence of violence found among this group is directly attributable to genetic variations or whether the aggressiveness is a secondary result of the common presence of unusual physical characteristics in this group. It is questioned whether the intimidating physical presence of these individuals is responsible for the higher incidence of violence.[11,12]

The correlation between violence and seizure disorders has been studied. Kanaka et al.[13] and Betts[14] have reported a higher incidence of pyschiatric symptoms in patients suffering seizure disorders. These investigations have been further clarified by authors who have found a higher incidence of psychopathology in patients with temporal lobe epilepsy vs. those with grand mal epilepsy.[15-17] Neuroses, schizophrenias, and personality disorders were found to occur more often in patients with temporal lobe abnormalities than in a group with grand mal epilepsy in a study completed by Shukla[17] in 1979. Animal studies completed by Goldstein[18] have also supported the correlations made between violence and brain function.

Social theory

Social theories attribute the acquisition of personality styles to the process of learning. These approaches do not readily designate behavior as good or bad, favorable or unfavorable. Instead, they view any behavior as the result of learned experience and determine the value of the behavior from a sociological perspective.

There are many patients who are considered to be suffering from a personality disorder because their behavior seems aversive to others and counterproductive. And yet these patients do not view themselves as having any problems and the "offensive" behavior is consistent with values with which they were raised. The social norms, mores, and customs of their subculture have supported the development of behaviors that run contrary to the standards of other subcultures or to the larger culture. They are not labeled as being disordered until their behavioral norms clash with the norms of the larger society. Social theorists believe that these "patients" are only as troubled as their behavior is troubling to society. In this frame of reference, the designation of personality disorder is a social diagnosis—that of deviance—rather than a psychiatric diagnosis.[19,20]

Alan Blum[21] advances this line of reasoning to the subject of psychiatric illness. He asserts that mental illness is not definable along any consistent, reliable criteria and that a given social organization or milieu defines a wide and varied range of behaviors as mentally ill. This designation is based on the societal response to the behavior, not on the basis of the behavior itself. From this point of view the social response is more important than the behavior evoking the response.

Hilgard and Marquis[22] and Meyer and Liddell,[23] as well as others, regard all behavior, including dysfunctional behavior, to be the result of learning. Dysfunctional behavior originates with the situation that first elicits the response. The response may be elicited by the social modeling of behaviors or attitudes, or it may be stimulated by an aversive situation. The emotional, verbal, or behavioral response to the stimulus is sustained by positive reinforcement and is integrated with other behaviors. All behavior is regarded from this framework with the critical determinant being the stimulus-response connection.

Psychodynamic theory

Psychodynamic theories of the etiology of personality disorders explain these disturbances as being the result of deficiencies in the patient's ego and superego development. The development of the ego occurs in early childhood and is influenced by environmental and constitutional factors as well as by the critical mother-child relationship. This relationship must be both gratifying and challenging to the extent that the child is neither overly indulged nor overly frustrated. Theorists suggest that this balance determines whether there is healthy or faulty development of conscience, frustration tolerance, impulse control, empathy, sense of self, and appropriate defense mechanisms. Personality-disordered adjustments are viewed as evidence of poorly developed ego strengths.

Whereas the everyday manifestations of these poorly developed internal resources result in tension and discomfort for the anxiety-disordered patient, the personality-disordered patient does not experience anxiety in response to their adaptation. The personality-disordered patient's psychological apparatus is not flexible enough to deviate from an established pattern of feelings or behaviors even if it is counterproductive. They experience the source of their difficulties to be outside of them and not a result of internal processes for which they are ultimately responsible.

Psychodynamic theories differ from one another in the amount of emphasis placed on various psychological structures in explaining the causes of personality disorders. Freud's constructs of id, ego, and superego provide the model for personality organization. The superego, according to Freud,[24] develops through the child's relationships with parents and results in the internalization of values belonging to the parents, the family, and society. In this model, the healthy superego's regulatory function inhibits behavior and attitudes that do not adhere to personal and social values. Personality disorders develop because of abnormal superego development. The process of internalization is disturbed in the mother-child relationship, or because the family, the unit of socialization, failed to supply appropriate rules and regulations for internalization.

In the first few months of life an infant gradually develops a relationship with the world outside of itself through the nurturing interactions with the mother. Mahler[25] has studied this developmental process and documented the maternal interactions that coax the infant's relationship with the world. This process of stimulation, responsiveness, and interaction lays the groundwork for the infant's capacity to differentiate between internal and external stimuli and eventually results in a differentiation between self and others. When this process is disturbed as a result of physical or emotional deprivation or as a result of an out-of-tune or unresponsive mother, the faulty development of trust, empathy, and a sense of self may result. It is speculated that these ego deficits may also result in the development of many psychiatric disturbances, including the personality disorders.

Wishnie[26] proposes that people with personality disorders suffer a disturbance of impulse control. He traces this deficit to a child's early relationships. In his work with personality-disordered people who were also substance abusers, he developed a theory to explain their style of life adjustment. It was his understanding that the majority of personality-disordered people experienced the loss of the primary nurturing person between the ages of 3 and 7, which resulted in a developmental disturbance. This traumatic loss leads to the inability to tolerate painful emotions. The resulting personality disorder is centered on the patient's impulsive reaction to stress, a manifestation of the individual's developmental disturbance, stemming from the inability to modulate the re-stimulated panic of the original traumatic loss.

CLINICAL PRESENTATION

Many patients whom the clinician would consider to have a personality disorder never come to the professional's attention. Although their individual difficulties are discernible, their life situations do not demand that their personality style be altered. Many potential "patients" are able to function and fulfill responsibilities without considering that their professional or personal relationships and activities might be less turbulent with psychiatric intervention. The nurse is likely to encounter many patients in a variety of medical settings who are unaware of their self-defeating or self-limiting personality trends. These trends must always be taken into consideration, regardless of the individual's awareness of them. A greater understanding of the total patient leads to a more comprehensive plan of nursing care.

Category I

The first category of personality disorders includes the diagnoses of paranoid personality disorder, schizoid personality disorder, and schizotypal personality disorder. At first glance, the most striking characteristic common to these three diagnoses is the patients' strangeness and aloofness in social interaction. They frequently appear to be misfits, socially uncomfortable, and unusual.

This group of patients does not typically seek psychiatric help. Because of their difficulties in maintaining relationships, they have discomfort continuing with treatment if it has been initiated. They are much more likely to seek assistance in an emergency when their internal stability has been disturbed. Their inability to tolerate closeness and the anxiety generated by self-disclosure typically reinforces their aloofness except in crisis situations. These patients will not draw attention to themselves on medical services and will not present with unnecessary complaints. They will typically avoid contact with medical professionals in the same manner in which they avoid contact with others.

Behavioral manifestations. The patients in this category are typically ill at ease with other people and aloof in their behavior. This social coolness may range from the overtly suspicious behavior of the paranoid personality, whose activities include precaution-taking (for example, checking to make sure no one is listening at the door or varying travel routes to make sure no one is following) to the socially withdrawn and isolative behavior of the schizoid personality disorder (for example, refusing to answer the door for a mail carrier or insisting on sitting apart and alone in a classroom). Schizotypal personality-disordered patients typically demonstrate the reclusive behavior of the schizoid personality disorder but also show additional bizarre or odd disturbances of cognition. Nurses may directly inquire about the patient's amount of social contact and ask whether the patient prefers being with people or being alone. Observing whether or not the patient remains consistently isolated on an inpatient unit may also be informative.

Emotional manifestations. The "coldness" of these patients is differentially expressed in the manifestation of common moods and affects. As a rule, affect is generally constricted with little range for all three diagnostic categories. There is a rigidity of emotional expression that belies their social vulnerability. The paranoid personality-disordered patient is the most likely of this category to appear hostile in mood and argumentative in manner. Their hypervigilant need to take precautions rules out an ability to relax. Their careful guardedness can only result in overcritical fault finding. They become very angry about small errors or inconsistencies and view these as demonstrations of the untrustworthiness of people and situations.

The schizoid and schizotypal personality-disordered patients are also unable to relax, but their expressions of tension are less likely to be angry. Instead these patients manifest a flat or depressed affect and no emotional reactivity. They appear emotionally unreachable and detached with an inability to experience pain or pleasure. There is a general "washing out" and muting of moods and affects that gives the impression of cold passivity. Nurses interacting with these patient may feel a strange sense of alienation that may sometimes cause anxiety for the clinician.

Social manifestations. Interpersonal relationships and social behavior are severely strained for these patients. Patients in these three diagnostic categories find the development of friendships difficult and the self-disclosure and trust necessary for intimate relationships untenable. Their relationships lack warmth and they are insensitive and unaware of the needs and feelings of others. The suspicious manner of paranoid personality-disordered patients does not facilitate closeness and their perfectionistic criticism and overconcern for trustworthiness can only result in disappointment, jealousy, or social isolation. The hypervigilance and meticulous concern for detail may be assets in certain careers (for example, private investigators or accountants) but these patients will not be successful in work situations requiring cooperation and collaboration. The nurse should inquire about the patient's line of work. A discussion regarding the work environment, the presence of team-work, and the patient's experiences with collaboration can reveal many relevant feelings and trends.

Although patients with a paranoid personality disorder do not favor close interpersonal relationships, these patients are the most likely of the three diagnoses in this category to desire personal contact, albeit on their own demanding terms. Schizoid and schizotypal personality-disordered people are more likely to completely avoid interpersonal contact and seek out life-styles and occupations that preserve solitary independence (for example, night watch guards or creative artists). They experience even superficial relationships as intruding and attempt to remain at arm's length from everyone. When enduring relationships are found they are likely to be overly dependent or symbiotic and with a family member or childhood acquaintance.[27]

> CASE EXAMPLE: A 39-year-old single male views himself and is considered by others to be a loner. He maintains no social contacts beyond those required at his job as a computer programmer. His only friend is a boyhood friend with whom he was very close and inseparable through-out school. His attachment to this friend is intense and the patient feels unable to make decisions without his friend's involvement. The patient will forego any opportunities for other personal contact and views him-self as fiercely self-sufficient and independent. He views other people's social activities as unnecessary complications. He was referred for psy-chiatric treatment by his medical doctor after seeking help for symptoms of severe anxiety, sleepless nights, and weight loss after his only friend was transferred to another state for employment reasons.

Paranoid personality-disordered patients' relationships with the world are likely to be antagonistic because of the presumption of mal-evolence and a self-imposed expectation that they must outsmart the world or perish. The schizoid and schizotypal personality-disordered patients may be viewed as much more passively antagonistic; they will meet social conventions with the hope that they will be lost in the shuffle and unnoticed and their personal sphere unintruded. Schizotypal personality-disordered patients are more likely to explain their avoidant behavior with magical thinking or bizarre fantasies. A patient's explanation that he doesn't talk to people and answer their morning greetings because he is working on a mathematical formula for world peace is an example of this feature.

Cognitive manifestations. The suspiciousness and carefulness of the paranoid personality disorder are behavioral expressions of a cognitive style. These patients' attitudes and perceptions of the world and of themselves provides the foundation for their behavior. The speech content of these patients is distinctive and diagnostic. Nurses should pay close attention to major or recurrent themes mentioned spontaneously by the patient. Typical trends of thought for the paranoid personality-disordered patient will reveal concerns for their own well-being, an overconcern for other people's interest in them, and a preoccupation with being in control and not having others influence them, make their decisions, or threaten their autonomy. Consequently, many of these patients report chronic conflicts with authority and cannot tolerate being in subordinate positions.

> CASE EXAMPLE: A 42-year-old businessman had worked in a company where he was responsible for supervising the daily activities of a small group of employees. His successful management style was related to his keen awareness for detail, his highly organized approach, and his cool ability to enforce departmental regulations and achieve employee compliance. These qualities led to his being offered a similar position in a larger company where many people worked in comparable supervisory positions and cooperation was required for the preparation of monthly reports from all of the supervisors. The patient was perceived as stubborn and hostile and could not lend his participation without struggling for a position of superiority among his peers. He was disparaging to others and would, on occasion, accuse peers unjustly of trying to get him fired. He could not trust others to fulfill their share of the obligations.

The schizotypal personality-disordered patient's speech productions will demonstrate the hallmark cognitive disturbances of this disorder. They may show more spontaneous speech production because of an overall loosening of cognitive functions but without loose associations. The content is more disturbed and more difficult to understand but not psychotic or schizophrenic. They may have difficulty in completing sentences because of tendencies toward elaborately detailed or overly vague speech. They may rely on metaphorical expressions or develop a personalized use of words, but they remain broadly understandable. Common themes may include ideas of reference, superstitions, experiences of telepathy or communication with the dead, and experiences of feeling depersonalized or in a dreamlike state.

A prevailing sense of uneasiness typifies the paranoid personality disordered individual's self-experience. The amount of attention devoted to details and to the nuances of other people is reflective of the self-absorption these patients enforce. They are especially careful not to appear weak, emotional, or out of control and are wary of these traits in other people. Patients may perceive the nurse's questions as attempts to make them appear weak and they may resist the interviewing process. This watchfulness and intolerance for ambiguity is indicative of this type of patient's unstable and extremely vulnerable self-image. It requires an enormous amount of energy to constantly monitor oneself and one's surroundings to guard against the slights and offenses that diminish self-esteem. The resulting sense of self is always battling to recoup from perceived attacks or struggling to maintain a feeling of safety and superiority. Other people's discomfort in reaction to this patient's style tends to reinforce the patient's experience of the world as unsafe and hostile. The nurse must maintain a calm neutrality and control feelings of frustration or irritation often felt in response to these patients' angry guardedness.

The primary disturbance of the schizoid personality-disordered patient is the inability to engage in normal interpersonal relationships. Relationships with others test the stability of a person's self-image and the integrity of the person's sense of self. The schizoid and schizotypal personality-disordered patients demonstrate extreme fragility in their sense of self. Simple interactions with the world are undesirable, unnecessary, and superfluous. These patients can be quite stubborn in their efforts to preserve this sense of autonomy. The primary disturbances of cognition in the schizotypal personality disorders are often evident in situations where the patient feels stressed by the threat of interpersonal closeness. These patients can be difficult to interview because the nurse's inquiry about personal matters may be experienced as an intrusion by the patient. Efforts to calmly reinforce potential benefits to the patient can facilitate the patient's cooperation. Reminders to the patient of confidentiality and trustworthiness can also assist in soothing a patient's anxieties.

Category II

The second category of personality disorders includes the diagnoses of histrionic, narcissistic, borderline, and antisocial personality disorders. These four disorders are reviewed as a group because patients with these diagnoses characteristically appear very emotionally expressive and reactive. These patients tend to be difficult to work with because the emotional manifestations often generate intense reactions in the nurse.

Patients with diagnoses of histrionic, narcissistic, and borderline personality disorders tend to experience strong discomfort and disquietude in their day-to-day lives and they are frequently in emotional crisis. Their erratic decisions and inconsistencies may realistically generate many external struggles; however, these patients feel themselves regularly to be experiencing an internal emergency regardless of the external situation. As a result, nurses may have frequent opportunities for routine, urgent, and emergent contact with these patients. They attend clinics and are usually well known to the staff in outpatient settings. They will be seen on virtually every kind of inpatient service, including medicine, surgery, and psychiatry. They frequent emergency rooms with numerous and dramatic physical complaints and with accompanied emotional distress. Their physical complaints may represent their internal disorder and they can be very demanding patients, insisting on prolonged one-to-one contact with the nurse.

It is very important for the nurse to be aware of the emotions triggered by these patients. An awareness of countertransference of feelings is necessary for the control of these reactions. The nurse's personal response to these patients can also serve as a diagnostic tool. It is not uncommon to feel discounted, inadequate, and never quite good enough to satisfy and comfort the seemingly insatiable demands of these patients.

Typically, although not exclusively, the clinician's contact with the antisocial personality-disordered patient is initiated by a third party, not by the patient. These patients tend to be distressed by the consequences of their actions, for example, arrest, bankruptcy, or dismissal, and not by the action itself. It is also not uncommon for social agencies and institutions to mandate the antisocial personality-disordered patient's contact with the psychiatric clinician. Courts, probation officers, and personnel directors may order evaluation or treatment as a condition to the patient. The involvement of such a third party must be established early on in the nurse's contact with the patient.

Behavioral manifestations. The lives of the patients in this category are usually quite populated with people and social interactions. Patients in this category tend to prefer contact and interaction despite the fact that interpersonal relationships are a source of major difficulties. Histrionic, narcissistic, borderline, and antisocial personality-disordered patients prefer stimulation to isolation and have little tolerance for being alone. Their desire for affiliation is striking in contrast to the isolative trends of the patients in Category I. The nurse may directly inquire about the patient's feelings about being alone in order to understand the need for social stimulation.

The histrionic patient's high degree of emotionality and intense expressions frequently serve as a means for engaging other people and involving them in their personal situation. These patients tend to be women who seem to be mimicking a flirtatious, seductive, and helpless female stereotype. Their emotional manner may be charming and beguiling or obnoxious and overstated. The behavior demonstrated is lively and exciting and usually successful in attracting attention. These patients may be very adept at generating conflicts among the medical staff, for example, pitting doctors and nurses against each other with antagonistic struggles.

The narcissistic and borderline personality-disordered patients also seek other people's attention and prefer being the focus of admiration. While their presentations may seem emotional and intense, the appearance of the emotionality will differ. Whereas the histrionic personality-disordered patient's expressions have a stereotypically "feminine" quality, the narcissistic and borderline personality-disordered patients' will not. The narcissistic personality-disordered patient will frequently appear confident and arrogant to the public, projecting an "image" rather than becoming genuinely involved with the nurse. They will project an air of self-importance and self-aggrandizement. They behaviorally communicate that their needs and concerns take priority over other people's and can be ruthless in their self-centeredness. Other patients may need to complete registration forms, but these patients need not comply with procedures because they are unlike other patients and need not waste their time with preliminary routines. These patients may tell the nurse that their problems are much more important than any paperwork. They may seem disapproving of people around them and scorn those who are "below standard." They may insist that only the chief of the department can listen to their complaints and attempt to dismiss the nurse.

The borderline personality-disordered patient's appearance can only be described in terms of its intense emotionality. These patients frequently appear to be emotionally upset and intensely caught up in their emotional experience, and they demonstrate rapid, unpredictable, and strong mood swings. They can become extremely angry, often inexplicably.

CASE EXAMPLE: A 24-year-old college student came to the infirmary insisting that she had an ulcer and demanding immediate treatment. Preliminary reports were all negative and as the nurse was explaining that no treatment could begin until further test results were available, the patient began to cry and beseech the nurse for help. The nurse attempted to explain the significance of further laboratory results when the patient became hostile, berating, and verbally abusive to the nurse and stormed out of the room maintaining that everyone was always trying to tell her what to do and stating that she would never follow any medical recommendations.

The behavioral manifestations of the antisocial personality-disordered patient are typically less tumultuous but not necessarily less intense. Their emotional display, which is also central to their behavioral presentation, tends to have a focal, consistent theme, using the other person for their personal gain. These patients are chameleon-like in their superficial adaptiveness. They can appear very charming, contrite, or intensely angry depending on which expression seems most appropriate to meet their intended goals. Nurses may obtain an understanding of the patient's sincerity by asking the patient questions about their plans if their request is not granted; antisocial personality-disordered patients react with anger to the frustration of their hopes and often try to bully the nurse into compliance.

Emotional manifestations. As indicated, intense emotions are hallmarks of the histrionic, narcissistic, borderline, and antisocial personality disorders. The emotional reactions of the patients in this group are erratic, extreme, and usually more appropriate to internal experience than to external reality.

People with histrionic personality disorder may appear ingenuous and dramatic in their emotional experiences. Their moods fluctuate widely and the affects expressed will often seem to be an exaggerated overreaction. Other people provide a kind of audience for their emotional demonstrations. Nurses describe these individuals as being helpless and needy, always wanting more and more assistance. They also feel helpless and in need of an immediate solution for their feelings of depression, emptiness, or loneliness. When stimulated and interacting with another they appear to feel less depressed and involved in the interaction. When the excitement and gratification of attention stops, their depression returns. Their mood fluctuations tend to be less chaotic than the borderline personality-disordered patient's. Borderline personality-disordered patients may feel reactive and emotional but their tremendous mood changes are more a response to internal shifts and less predicated on external changes. That is to say, borderline patients also experience more cognitive distortions than histrionic patients. The borderline personality-disordered patient's emotional experience can be as much of a result of the patient's distortion of reality as a reaction to external reality. Nurses must be mindful of these internal shifts in order to remember that the patient's response to the nurse is not necessarily appropriate or reality bound. An awareness of the patient's severe difficulties can assist in maintaining a therapeutic attitude.

The narcissistic personality-disordered patient frequently feels depressed, embarrassed, or humiliated. Their efforts to draw attention to themselves and be admired are sometimes disappointingly insufficient or result in exposing an imperfection. Narcissistic personality-disordered patients will exaggerate their self-importance and expect people's compliance and attention. Their sense of entitlement may also result in disappointment, anger, and ultimately alienation from others. The nurse can inquire about the patient's interpersonal relationships and investigate the kinds of complaints that patients offer to explain their dissatisfaction with people. Does the nurse sense that the patient expects to reciprocate meeting another person's needs or is the patient viewing personal relationships as a one-way proposition? The nurse can inquire about the presence or absence of satisfaction experienced by the patient in gratifying others.

The antisocial personality-disordered patient typically feels contempt for society, rules, and social order and expresses feelings of entitlement that are less related to grandiosity than to the absence of concern for other people. Whereas narcissistic personality-disordered patients may expect preferential treatment because their rights and needs are more important than the rights and needs of others, the antisocial personality-disordered patient reacts as if other people's rights did not exist. Characteristically they will not identify feeling more important than others, rather their behavior will suggest this attitude.

The narcissistic and borderline personality-disordered patients' affect will appear more genuine and less "acted" than the histrionic personality-disordered patient's, but it will not necessarily be more appropriate to the situation. For example, histrionic personality-disordered patients may react to having made a mistake in a profusely apologetic, self-effacing manner that exaggerates their helplessness and begs for rescue. The narcissistic personality-disordered patient may respond to the same situation with tremendous embarrassment and humiliation for the public lowering of self-esteem. The borderline personality-disordered patient's reaction is less predictable except in its intensity and probable inappropriateness.

Social manifestations. Interpersonal and social relationships are a source of chronic problems for patients comprising this category. Atlhough the antisocial personality-disordered patient's relationships reveal fundamental disturbances, these patients are much less likely to experience internal distress about these difficulties. People are experienced as replaceable and the antisocial personality-disordered person will typically have a history including serial relationships that suffer from the consequences of the patient's occupational instability, financial unreliability, and personal irresponsibility. The antisocial personality-disordered patient's disregard for the truth and inability to make a reliable commitment weighs against stable personal relationships.

The interpersonal relationships of the histrionic and narcissistic personality-disordered patients are characteristically disturbed by the qualities of self-centeredness and need for attention. Although the histrionic personality is likely to have a capacity for empathy, these patients cannot forego the frustration of placing another person's needs before their own and end up being inconsiderate and helpless. The nurse can ask patients to imagine placing themselves in another person's position. Do patients grasp the other person's feelings in the situation and reconsider their own behavior? Do patients empathize with another's feelings and decide that their own needs are more desperate and deserving?

The narcissistic personality-disordered patient's capacity for reciprocal, mutually satisfying relationships is more hampered. These patients are not truly able to step outside of themselves and empathize with another person. Their relationships focus on their unrelenting need for admiration. Their responses to people in their lives are predicated on whether or not the other person satisfactorily maintains their sense of specialness. As might be expected, it is impossible for another person to consistently interact in a manner that is so unrealistically gratifying. The partner's value to the patient will be determined by the ability to mirror such unrealistic self-esteem. It is not unusual for these patients to complain of their specialness going unappreciated and unaccommodated by the people in their lives.

The most consistent feature of the borderline personality-disordered patient's interpersonal relationships is marked inconsistency and instability. The presence of impulsivity, emotional reactivity and intensity, and propensity for anger add up to tumultuous and chaotic relationships. These patients seem to rely on others to determine their personal sense of goodness or badness and experience tremendous anxiety and depression when alone. Their capacity to neutrally interact with others is impaired by their emotional reactivity and their inability to reflect upon themselves. They are subject to feel depressed and rejected very easily and they respond with tremendous rage and despondency. It is not unusual for these patients to mutilate themselves or attempt suicide at the anticipation of disappointment or to a misinterpreted rejection. The key features are a prevailing instability of experience, emotion, and identity.

Cognitive manifestations. The borderline personality-disordered patient's internal experience is a painful and difficult one. Cognitive functions may be interfered with and flooded with intense affect that impairs judgement and rational thought. Although these patients are typically in touch with reality and not psychotic, it is not uncommon for their poorly functioning defense mechanisms to break down under situations of extreme stress or with the use of drugs or alcohol. These patients may develop transient psychotic symptoms during these experiences.

Common themes and concerns for these patients pertain to their internal confusion, their chronic anxiety regarding who they are and what they want and their profound depression related to their disappointment with themselves and others. They may ask the nurse to make their decisions and overvalue the nurse's opinions and feelings. Many patients in this group appear genuinely confused and uncertain about their identity. Other people, situations, and occupations serve to prescribe a definition that affords these patients the boundaries for their behavior. There will seem to be no internal certainty regarding their personal preferences, tastes, hopes, or values. They often grope for whatever external cues and structure are available to retain integrity. It is not unusual for these patients to report periods of stable functioning in their history that coincide with their participation in highly structured life-styles, for example, the armed services. The inconsistency that might be expected from such an externally determined self-definition contributes to the instability of personal relationships. These patients may recontact the nurse many times after the initial contact in order to maintain stability and a sense of security.

The histrionic patient's reliance on emotion, drama, and attention in order to charm other people is an attempt to gain approval, affection, and someone to take care of them. The patient's superficial attachment to other people and life experiences are all utilized to maintain a flurry of internal excitement. These patients frequently feel depressed and dissatisfied and suffer physical complaints precipitated by external disappointments.

For the narcissistic personality-disordered patient the characteristic diagnostic attitudes pervade the patient's cognitive style. Their feelings of self-importance affect their view of other people and their expectations of what experiences their lives should provide. They frequently entertain grandiose fantasies of success and relate to the world as if their fantasies were appropriate. They may express ideas that view the nurse as helping them fulfill their destiny and flatter the clinician for the wisdom of their support.

The potential for disappointment and depression is extreme for these patients. They are bound to experience disappointment. Common themes are their personal worth, their expectations for extreme success and admiration, their jealousy for others whom they view as receiving the reception that the patient deserves, and grandiose plans that will demonstrate their superiority. Such externally determined value results in self-esteem that is fragile and very tentative.

Because of the complexity of personality organization, it is difficult to assess all of these features without lengthy evaluation. Although preliminary diagnostic impressions might be made after the nurse's single contact with a patient, none of the personality disorders can be diagnosed firmly on the basis of one contact.

Category III

The third category of personality disorders includes the diagnoses of avoidant, dependent, compulsive, and passive-aggressive personality disorders. Although each diagnostic subtype has characteristic manifestations, anxiety, apprehension, and a constricted manner are typical of this category of patients. Their anxiety is especially observable in the area of interpersonal relationships, yet each group's demonstrations are distinctive.

Nurses will encounter the patients in this category in virtually every kind of setting. Many medical patients will demonstrate hallmark personality styles in their interactions with nurses on inpatient services. It is not unusual for these patients to seek psychiatric services when confronted with an interpersonal crisis. For example, avoidance and dependent personality-disordered patients will feel emotionally devastated by the loss of a close relationship. These patients, along with the passive-aggressive personality-disordered patient, will frequently somatize their psychological difficulties and may request unnecessary medical care. The hard-driving compulsive personality-disordered patient will frequently develop physical problems secondary to internalized stress, strain, and overwork. All of these patients demonstrate symptoms that when taken out of context represent everyday, common behavior traits. Their "symptoms" in isolation, and without regard for frequency and persistence, do not appear pathological. It is the constellation of personality manifestations and the tenacity of their expression and inflexibility that adds up to a pattern of adaptation that is socially and occupationally counterproductive.

Behavioral manifestations. The designation "avoidant" personality disorder is diagnostically descriptive. These patients actively avoid social interactions and interpersonal relationships despite the fact that they would like to be emotionally close and accepted by others. These patients are frightened of other people's reactions to them because they assume that others will criticize them and ultimately reject them. Their tension and apprehension for being rejected results in behavior that is anxious and shy. They interact with others from the perimeter, ready to disappear at the slightest suggestion, real or imagined, of criticism. Their anxiety is apparent and tends to make others uncomfortable. These patients never seem to "warm up" because of their mistrustfulness and unrelenting fear of rejection, which they experience to be a shameful humiliation. The avoidant personality-disordered person may develop a few relationships if an unqualified acceptance is constantly reflected to the patient. Without such a reception, the patient cannot tolerate simple interactions. These patients differ from the schizoid and schizotypal personality-disordered patients in their explanations for their avoidant behaviors. The nurse can inquire about the patient's reasons for withdrawing from other people. Whereas the schizoid and schizotypal personality disordered patients prefer isolation, the avoidant personality-disordered patient will complain of the loneliness that comes from isolation, and explain a preference for human contact that is overriden by a fear of criticism and rejection.

The dependent personality-disordered patient's anxiety is not manifested in avoidant social behavior. These patients typically prefer and seek out human contact and they are solicitous and deferring to people around them. They will comply with people and situations and follow the leader, avoiding any demonstration of initiative or independence. Their anxiety is demonstrated in their attention to social cues or the nurse's "lead" and they seem overly careful to avoid any disapproval.

> CASE EXAMPLE: A patient comes to the clinic waiting room for a scheduled appointment. She is observed to inquire at the desk about whether or not she is in the proper area despite the fact that she has been seen in the same clinic several times in the past. She comments to the receptionist that she is never sure she's in the right place and that she has a terrible memory and cannot trust herself to find where she belongs. She requests permission to hang her coat in the patient's closet and sheepishly and self-consciously picks a seat being careful to adjust herself to sit like other patients in the waiting room. Although her appointment is scheduled for 2:00 PM, she sits and passively waits until 4:00 PM before timidly inquiring about her appointment. The receptionist had misplaced the patient's chart and forgotten about her. When casually chided for not speaking up earlier, the patient stated that she doesn't like to make waves and was afraid the doctor's time was too valuable for her, and she didn't want to make him angry if he was too busy to see her.

These patients seem capable of warmth and they develop friendships but their anxiety about maintaining the relationship makes them seem clinging and helpless. Nurses will need to utilize their understanding and awareness of interpersonal process to tune into these dynamics.

The passive-aggressive and compulsive personality-disordered patients appear much more at ease and confident than the avoidant and dependent personality-disordered patients. Their difficulties are also demonstrated in interpersonal relationships but initial observation will typically not reveal social anxiety. The compulsive personality-disordered patient will seem rigid, stiff, and cold. Their presenting problems in psychiatric services frequently pertain to these superficial behavioral qualities. Families and friends frequently exert pressure on the compulsive personality-disordered patient to seek psychiatric care because of their coldness and difficulty expressing affectionate feelings. Their behavioral rigidity will often be noticed in their grooming, clothing, and body language, all of which reflect stiff perfectionism.

The behavioral manifestations of the passive-aggressive personality-disordered patient are diverse and not easily typified. Their hallmark diagnostic feature is demonstrated in the process of interacting with other people and less observable without direct contact. The "passive-aggressive" designation describes their mode for expressing hostility, resentment, or exerting authority. These emotions are indirectly expressed; they demonstrate resistant behavior that passively results in evoking frustration in the other person or in the frustration of another person's goals. Their resistance can be manifested in dawdling, stalling, feigned deafness, stubbornness, ineptness, unproductiveness, or any variation of these behaviors.

> CASE EXAMPLE: A couple is out for dinner in a restaurant and while waiting for a table, the wife notices an old college boyfriend across the lobby. She comments to her husband and goes over to talk to her old acquaintance. Her husband ignores his wife's calls to join her for an introduction, pretending to be completely absorbed in reading the menu. Their later interactions reveal the husband's jealousy and anger about having never been told about this old romantic relationship.

Emotional manifestations. As already suggested the emotional presentation of the avoidant personality-disordered patient is anxious, constricted, and uncomfortable. The degree of emotional and affective constriction of these patients is similar to the rigidity and limited expressiveness of the compulsive personality disorder. However, the avoidant person's decreased range and depth of affect appears to be the result of overriding fear. The compulsive person's emotional manifestations are not dominated by apprehension. Avoidant personality-disordered patients will be unable to relax because of their prevailing fearfulness, whereas compulsive personality-disordered people present a rigid formality that excludes a relaxed and easy manner. Compulsive personality-disordered patients will not express soft, affectionate feelings and will maintain a seriousness of mood and affect. The nurse's own response to the avoidant personality-disordered person will more likely be to want to offer soothing reassurance, while the compulsive person evokes a more businesslike, cool reaction to the nurse. The skittish fearfulness of avoidant personality-disordered patients makes them seem more emotionally inaccessible. The compulsive personality-disordered patient's interpersonal distance and stiffness creates a barrier to emotional accessability.

Although all of the personality disorders included in this section are likely to appear anxious, depression is also a common manifestation. It is easy to imagine depressive features in the pictures of both the avoidant and compulsive personality disorders. Depression is likely to be noted in the dependent personality disorder as well. These patients frequently complain of dysphoria related to their feelings of inadequacy and may present a mournful demonstration of their need for protection and guidance. Their fear of disapproval and abandonment by others is more actively demonstrated as compared to the avoidant behavior of the avoidant personality-disordered patient. Their range of affect will typically be less constricted than the avoidant and compulsive personality-disordered patients' and they will utilize emotional displays to evoke affection, reassurance, and decision making by others. Their helplessness may seem akin to the histrionic personality-disordered patient's but will not include the flirtatiousness or provocativeness of the latter diagnostic category. These patients will seem to be very emotionally accessible as a means for maintaining a subordinate position.

The passive-aggressive personality-disordered patient's emotional manifestations typically consist of anxiety and depression regarding their low self-esteem and feelings of inadequacy. The passivity of their angry expressions may concurrently be displayed in an unspoken resentment that is represented in the patient's affect. They may appear to sulk or pout but superficially cooperate and conform to the nurse's questions or requests. An important diagnostic indicator will be the subtle emotional cues emanated by the patient to the nurse that suggest a stubborn, hostile tone to the interaction. They may express feelings of hopelessness but not avail themselves in an open and participatory manner that reveals a genuine emotional accessability. The nurse may notice a persisting discrepancy in the assessment of what the patient's words are saying and what message is communicated in the patient's emotional expression.

Social manifestations. The interpersonal relationships of all four diagnoses within this category are strongly influenced by their personality styles. The loneliness and isolation of avoidant personality-disordered patients results from their social withdrawal. Their fear of rejection permeates every kind of human interaction. The inhibited, aversive social behavior is confirmation of their unyielding belief that other people will reject them. Their search for an unconditional acceptance is solitary and typically frustrating, yet these are the only kinds of relationships the avoidant personality-disordered person can tolerate risking. Their occupational choices will also reflect their fear of risking the criticism they believe is forthcoming, and these patients will typically seek jobs that allow them privacy and a minimum amount of contact with other people.

The dependent personality-disordered patient's interpersonal relationships are characterized by strong dependency. These patients will seek out relationships with people who are willing to make their decisions. They will subvert their own interests, needs, and feelings for the provision of a sense of security that hinges on complete dependency. They will often cling to these relationships regardless of the physical or emotional damage incurred. It is more comfortable, for example, to tolerate a physically abusive husband than to expose oneself to autonomy. Even casual friendships will manifest the dependent features of this personality disorder. Their unwillingness to risk making an independent decision can range from the minor situation of choosing the kind of candy preferred at a concession stand to a major life decision, such as choosing one's employment or spouse. These patients will not imperil their relationships by making any independent decisions or demands.

The compulsive personality-disordered patient tends to prefer work over relationships, business over pleasure, and facts over feelings. Their emotional impairment limits the experience and expression of affection. This in turn inhibits camaraderie and friendship, let alone intimacy. These patients deal with their fear of disapproval with their overconcern for order, efficiency, and rules. As a result their interpersonal relationships are stilted and anxious.

In their personal lives, these patients often have difficulty trusting people and relaxing. Their fear of rejection results in self-protective and rigid behavior. They need to feel in charge of their emotions and emotional expressions and they may demand conformity as a means for maintaining a sense of control. They have difficulty sharing themselves and may seem unyielding in their self-control.

These attributes may be very successful in the working world, especially if the patient's job does not require cooperation with other workers and also if the patient is not in a decision-making position. The compulsive personality-disordered patient demonstrates tremendous difficulty making decisions because of a preoccupation for perfection and detail. Decisions may be made more easily if exact and specific guidelines exist for decision-making criteria.

The passive-aggressive personality-disordered patient's characteristic pattern for the expression of conflict or anger can be very frustrating to other people. These patients try other people's patience and exasperate friends, spouses, and work associates. Their interpersonal relationships become tension ridden as a result of the patient's passive-aggressive behavior. These behaviors can be very difficult to confront, often because of their seeming innocence or randomness.

Whereas these patients prefer affiliation and social contact, their passive-aggressive behavior frequently drives people away from them because of the frustration engendered in others. These patients may express confusion, depression, and guilt in response to the unpleasant frustration other people in their lives experience, yet they seem unable to modify their behavior. They have little awareness of their stereotypic behavior patterns and feel unable to make sense of their interpersonal experiences.

Cognitive manifestations. Avoidant personality-disordered patients' chronic anxiety about other people's acceptance of them creates an internal tension that affects their cognitive processes. These patients are constantly monitoring their environment for signs of disapproval and they do not prioritize their perceptions. Every detail of their environment, as well as every person in their environment, is scanned for potential rejection and they may read into the significance of small events, such as another person's break in eye contact or a slamming door. Their preoccupation with all of these minor events results in a kind of sensory overload. Their efficiency and coping ability is decreased by their attention to detail as well as by the fear and anxiety experienced in response to the disapproval read into all of these details.

The avoidant personality-disordered person's self-esteem suffers from their experiences of loneliness and isolation. They may come to feel tremendous anger about their inability to relax and develop appropriate social relations. The internal conflict between wanting to be with people and feeling afraid of people because they will be rejected does not promote healthy feelings of self-worth.

Because these patients maintain a desire for social relationships and because they experience their isolation as painful, they frequently develop rich fantasies of successful relationships to compensate for their loneliness. Their fantasies will reflect their desire for completely unconditional acceptance, as well as their distortions about the devastation risked interacting with other people. Nurses can request that the patient use imagination and share a fantasy of what the patient's life would be like under ideal circumstances. If a basic trust can be attempted by patients, they might confide fantasies revealing these typical concerns.

The dependent personality-disordered patient's internal life is also dominated by the need for approval. These patients define themselves as much as possible in accordance to another person's instructions, specifications, or demands. They tend to monitor other people and their environment for direction and approval.

The speech of these patients may sound childish and immature or inappropriate. Their language can be another vehicle for invoking a protective, parental response from another and eluding adult individual responsibilities. These patients commonly express themes focusing on their fears of abandonment. Their inner lives are absorbed by this fear and as a result, their self-esteem is frequently determined by the amount of safety and reassurance offered them in a particular relationship. Unfortunately, no amount of safety and reassurance is ever truly enough, and these patients vacillate between trying to please another person and fearing that they have displeased the other person.

The cognitive manifestations of the compulsive personality-disordered patient provide valuable diagnostic material. As noted, these patients appear rigid, cold, and perfectionistic. Their speech and thought processes reflect these characteristics in the production of highly detailed, formal comments. Their overconcern for minor, petty, unnecessary details is similar to that of the avoidant personality-disordered patient's but its focus is more related to the maintenance of a sense of order and control. These patients also seek to avoid disapproval like the avoidant person. The disapproval that the compulsive personality-disordered person feels compelled to avoid stems from the fear of making an error. They think about mistakes as being avoidable and the result of an oversight, a miscalculation, or insufficient information. Their attention is attracted to every detail and they often have difficulty grasping the general context or main meaning in a situation. It is this lack of understanding that typically leads to mistakes. Internally they are constantly weighing alternatives, determining priorities, and judging themselves and others against a perfectionistic (and unattainable) standard. They consciously value efficiency, order, and decisiveness, but their severe perfectionism rules out attainment of these goals and results in meaningless busy work, ambivalence, and indecisiveness. The compulsive personality-disordered patient is likely to recognize these shortcomings and experience depression in response.

The passive-aggressive personality-disordered patient tends to think about the world in negativistic terms. These patients are rarely aware of their characteristic behavior patterns and they are unable to determine the connection between their behavior and other people's reactions to them. These individuals often feel confused, mistreated, and resentful of other people. They may experience other people to be reacting to them unjustly because of their unawareness of interpersonal processes. Other people frequently seem to have more control, more authority, and more power, and these patients fail to evaluate themselves as they search to understand their inability to get ahead and succeed. The patient's resentment of others and poor self-esteem may precipitate the passive-aggressive strategy that only serves to confirm their experience of the world as a hostile and unfair environment.

ASSESSMENT TOOLS

The following tools have been developed as beginning guides for the assessment of personality-disordered patients. Nurses may find them useful in the process of collecting and organizing information gathered about the patient. The reader is referred to the DSM-III for specific diagnostic criteria that may be utilized in conjunction with this text.

Tool 7:1 describes the cogent indicators of a personality disorder. Any yes response on this tool should direct the nurse to further clarify whether the patient is experiencing an anxiety disorder vs. a personality disorder.

Tools 7:2, 7:3, and 7:4 operationalize the key signs and symptoms of the three major categories of personality disorders. A yes response should direct the nurse's attention to a more detailed investigation and evaluation of specific personality disorders.

TOOL 7:1	Brief assessment for distinguishing personality disorders from anxiety disorders

Does the patient:	Yes	No
1. Identify the problem as being strictly the result of other people or forces outside of himself/herself?	___	___
2. Deny experiencing any anxiety in conjunction with the behavior pattern?	___	___
3. Avoid taking responsibility for behavior?	___	___
4. Describe behavior patterns that are longstanding?	___	___
5. Trace back the problematic behavior trend or pattern of emotional response to adolescence?	___	___
6. Describe life experiences that suggest that the problematic behavioral trend or pattern of emotional response is inflexible and consistently repeated?	___	___
7. Describe specific behavioral patterns being demonstrated in a variety of relationships and life situations?	___	___
8. Describe feeling unable to change and give a history of unsuccessful attempts at modifying behavior patterns?	___	___

TOOL 7:2	Brief assessment for paranoid, schizoid, and schizotypal personality disorders

Does the patient:	Yes	No
1. Appear to be detached, unreachable, interpersonally cold?	___	___
2. Appear to be rigid, serious, and maintain a "strictly business" manner?	___	___
3. Steer away from describing any affectionate or sensitive feelings?	___	___
4. Speak in a manner that sounds severely logical and factual?	___	___
5. Easily take offense to casual remarks?	___	___
6. Readily read into the nurse's comments and hear criticism?	___	___
7. Seem to be on the defensive and react antagonistically to neutral nonjudgmental comments?	___	___
8. Appear unable to loosen up and feel at ease?	___	___
9. Seem overconcerned with protecting themselves from harm?	___	___
10. Question the nurse's intentions repeatedly?	___	___
11. Question the use or meaning of words?	___	___
12. Refuse to answer questions?	___	___
13. Take unnecessary provisions to guard against self-disclosure?	___	___
14. Inquire repeatedly about confidentiality?	___	___
15. Complain of not every being able to trust anyone?	___	___
16. Seem gratified when another's faults or vulnerability or untrustworthiness is proven?	___	___
17. Avoid expressing any warm feelings?	___	___
18. Deny feeling close to any other person?	___	___
19. Describe friendship as being unnecessary or a waste of time?	___	___
20. Scorn other people's personal relationships?	___	___
21. Genuinely seem to prefer being alone?	___	___
22. Disclaim a preference for social contact?	___	___
23. Seem to be unmoved by other people's interest in them?	___	___
24. Have bizarre, illogical ideas, yet not appear psychotic?	___	___
25. Speak coherently but idiosyncratically?	___	___
26. Describe anxiety in response to having to be around people?	___	___
27. Avoid simple interactions with people if possible?	___	___
28. Speak in overly vague terms?	___	___
29. Actively avoid people who seek their company?	___	___
30. Experience perceptual disturbances but not appear psychotic?	___	___

TOOL 7:3   Brief assessment for histrionic, narcissistic, borderline, and antisocial personality disorders

Does the patient:	Yes	No
1. Appear overly dramatic?	___	___
2. Exaggerate his/her emotional state?	___	___
3. Seem preoccupied with own interests to the exclusion of an interest in others?	___	___
4. Seem to be acting a role?	___	___
5. Exaggerate the significance of common, day-to-day events?	___	___
6. Seek to attract the attention of others?	___	___
7. Avoid being alone?	___	___
8. Appear to be immature, ingenuous, superficial?	___	___
9. Seem self-centered?	___	___
10. Act childishly helpless?	___	___
11. Repeatedly ask questions about his/her value?	___	___
12. Invoke the nurse's support and guidance?	___	___
13. Speak of himself/herself as being better than others?	___	___
14. Describe himself/herself as being special?	___	___
15. Seem to boast about achievements?	___	___
16. Avoid seeing himself/herself as being like others?	___	___
17. Seek other people's admiration?	___	___
18. Expect others to automatically meet his/her needs?	___	___
19. Have difficulty understanding why others do not comply with his/her demands, expectations?	___	___
20. Seem unable to put himself/herself in another person's shoes?	___	___
21. Seem to lack an ability to understand another person's feelings?	___	___
22. Have a history of frequent job changes?	___	___
23. Have a history of impulsive behavior?	___	___
24. Consistently demonstrate behavior that violates basic social norms?	___	___
25. Have a history of conflicts with the law?	___	___
26. Deny feeling any remorse for criminal acts?	___	___
27. Deny feeling any guilt for taking advantage of other people?	___	___
28. Have a history of transient relationships?	___	___
29. Admit to lying freely?	___	___
30. Have a history of barroom brawls?	___	___
31. Repeatedly end up in physical fights?	___	___
32. Try to intimidate the nurse?	___	___
33. Refuse to pay child support?	___	___
34. Renege on financial agreements?	___	___
35. Engage in potentially dangerous behavior?	___	___
36. Abuse drugs or alcohol?	___	___
37. Demonstrate abrupt, intense mood swings?	___	___
38. Seem unreasonably or inappropriately angry?	___	___
39. Feel genuinely confused about his/her identity?	___	___
40. Have difficulty identifying his/her values?	___	___
41. Avoid being alone at all costs?	___	___
42. Complain of frequent, inexplicable depression?	___	___
43. Have a history of suicide attempt, gestures?	___	___

TOOL 7:4 Brief assessment for avoidant, dependent, compulsive, and passive-aggressive personality disorders

Does the patient:	Yes	No
1. Avoid talking to the nurse?	____	____
2. Appear to cut short interactions with routine staff?	____	____
3. Stay isolated from others?	____	____
4. Appear anxious and uncomfortable?	____	____
5. Express a belief that others will criticize him/her?	____	____
6. Expect to be rejected?	____	____
7. Feel lonely a majority of the time?	____	____
8. Feel uncomfortably self-conscious around others?	____	____
9. Feel depressed about lack of social relationships?	____	____
10. Envy others' success with people?	____	____
11. Get angry at himself/herself for being so shy?	____	____
12. Work independently of others?	____	____
13. Get anxious in a group of people?	____	____
14. Feel that people will make fun of him/her?	____	____
15. Feel badly about himself/herself?	____	____
16. Minimize abilities?	____	____
17. Ask the nurse to make decisions?	____	____
18. Tolerate poor treatment in order to have another person make the decisions?	____	____
19. Avoid being alone?	____	____
20. Give a history of never functioning independently?	____	____
21. Appear helpless?	____	____
22. Lack self-confidence?	____	____
23. Appear passive or submissive?	____	____
24. Minimize own needs?	____	____
25. Speak about himself/herself very negatively?	____	____
26. Seem overly concerned with details?	____	____
27. Seem very cold and stern?	____	____
28. Try to be perfect?	____	____
29. Prefer work to recreation?	____	____
30. Have difficulty making decisions?	____	____
31. Seem overly concerned with order, rules, or procedures?	____	____
32. Complain about other people's inefficiency?	____	____
33. Have difficulty cooperating with others?	____	____
34. Try to take charge of the interview?	____	____
35. Feel uncomfortable when not in control?	____	____
36. Procrastinate?	____	____
37. Seem overconcerned with making a mistake?	____	____
38. Have difficulty expressing affection?	____	____
39. Express anger passively?	____	____
40. Appear stubborn?	____	____
41. Resent people in authority?	____	____
42. Excuse mistake on the basis of forgetfulness?	____	____
43. Frustrate the nurse repeatedly?	____	____

DIAGNOSIS
Nursing diagnosis of personality disorders

Personality-disordered patients experience a variety of maladjustments in life-style and response to their surrounding environment. In general, the observed symptoms delineate impaired abilities to adapt to society's norms, solve problems effectively, or respond in a health-promoting manner to internal and external stresses. A major, notable feature is the patient's lack of insight and concern about the specific maladaptive behaviors. The individuals do not perceive themselves as having difficulty adjusting or, if they do, consider it to be the result of external forces.

The nursing diagnosis most applicable in describing the mental health status of personality-disordered patients is ineffective individual coping. The box below lists a taxonomy for this nursing diagnosis. When the patient with a personality disorder experiences superimposed psychiatric or physical symptoms, additional nursing diagnoses reflective of those behavioral and physical states would be identified.

TAXONOMY OF NURSING DIAGNOSES FOR PERSONALITY DISORDERS

Ineffective individual coping

1.10 Impaired social functioning
    1.11 Violation of social rules and norms
    1.12 Lack of participation in organizations, activities
    1.13 Relinquishment of social/role responsibilities
1.20 Impaired relationships with significant others
    1.21 Suspicious, aloof, mistrustful of others
    1.22 Inability to develop or maintain close relationships
    1.23 Demanding, dependent in relationships
1.30 Impaired occupational functioning
    1.31 Inability to maintain employment
    1.32 Difficulties in employment setting
1.40 Impaired cognitive abilities
    1.41 Impaired problem solving
    1.42 Impaired judgment and insight
1.50 Impaired emotional responses
    1.51 Lack of emotional responses
    1.52 Impaired control of anger, temper
    1.53 Demanding, overreacting responses
    1.54 Hypersensitivity

Psychiatric diagnosis of personality disorders

The psychiatric diagnoses for the personality disorders are listed as follows:

1. Paranoid personality disorder
2. Schizoid personality disorder
3. Schizotypal personality disorder
4. Histrionic personality disorder
5. Narcissistic personality disorder
6. Antisocial personality disorder
7. Borderline personality disorder
8. Avoidant personality disorder
9. Dependent personality disorder
10. Compulsive personality disorder
11. Passive-aggressive personality disorder
12. Atypical, mixed or other personality disorder

The DMS-III presents criteria necessary for a proper diagnosis.[2] The refinement of the diagnostic criteria available for the personality disorders varies in the degree of specificity and precision. In order to appreciate the complexity of the task of diagnosing personality-disordered patients, the nurse is encouraged to become familiar with the criteria and to avoid the hasty assignment of a diagnosis. Proper diagnosis of the personality disorders requires observation over time. The patients manifesting personality disorders require evaluation on more than one occasion. Quite frequently patients will manifest personality trends that meet the diagnostic criteria for more than one personality disorder. In those cases, all appropriate diagnoses should be indicated. In those situations where long-standing maladjustments are noted that do not meet the criteria for any personality disorder, a diagnosis of "Atypical, Mixed or Other Personality Disorder" should be made.

CASE EXAMPLE: Assessment of Ms. Barton

Identifying information. Ms. Barton is a 31-year-old student studying journalism at a local university. She is a patient on a medical unit after transfer from the Intensive Care Unit and has been referred for a psychiatric consultation.

Presenting problem. Ms. Barton is admitted to the ICU after overdosing on a combination of alcohol and barbiturates. She states that she was depressed about her boyfriend leaving her behind while he went off on a business trip 2 days ago. She felt overwhelmed with fears that he would never return and angry that his going without her was proof of his lack of love for her.

Brief recent history. Ms. Barton complains of always feeling depressed and empty. She lives with her boyfriend of 4 months and her 6-year-old daughter from a previous marriage. She describes chronic difficulties in both of these relationships. She doesn't understand why her boyfriend is cruel to her by going away and leaving her behind and becomes outraged at these separations. These separations are especially infuriating to her because she feels her boyfriend is perfect for her in every other respect. Approximately 2 weeks ago, Ms. Barton's daughter began attending nursery school in the morning. She had looked forward to having some time to herself without her daughter but instead feels panicked by being alone. On the day of the overdose, Ms. Barton had a nasty, intensely angry argument with her boyfriend about his leaving and then prepared her daughter for nursery school. After her daughter left, Ms. Barton began to feel extremely hungry and consumed large amounts of food. She induced vomiting to relieve her physical discomfort, then began drinking wine and taking sleeping pills because she felt so unhappy.

Family history. Ms. Barton is the second of three siblings. Her mother was described as a depressed woman who was subject to fits of rage that included physical abuse to the patient. Her father was described as an alcoholic who was passive and uninvolved with his wife and children. The patient married at the age of 20 during her sophomore year of college in an effort to eliminate a feeling of "floating around." She felt that her husband helped her feel that she knew who she was; however, this marriage ended in divorce after Mr. Barton was incarcerated on a charge of breaking and entering.

Personal history. Ms. Barton grew up in a small, rural city with a strong fundamentalist religious community. Her childhood is characterized by memories of physical abuse and terror. The patient recalls her mother as being very unpredictable and explosive. Her mother would indiscriminately blame the patient for disappointments and punish her by leaving her in the backyard, alone in the dark. Ms. Barton's father was a kind of ghost in the household and avoided dealing with his wife because of her intense anger. The only time that family members related to each other as a unit was on Sundays when they attended Bible service. The patient recalls being forced to attend these services even when physically sick and feverish so that everyone in the community would know that they were a close-knit family. She has not had previous psychiatric help.

Mental status. Ms. Barton was sitting in a chair in her hospital room and stared out of the window when interviewed. She was a large and morbidly obese woman who appeared slightly older than her stated age. She fiercely picked at her cuticles throughout the interview and avoided eye contact with the nurse. Her voice was low and frequently quivered during intervals of tearfulness. Her mood was intermittently hostile and depressed, and her affect was very reactive and intense. Her speech was spontaneous, goal directed, and coherent. Major themes were her feelings of depression and emptiness, her anger about her boyfriend's desertion, and her self-doubts about not knowing how to be a good mother to her daughter. There was no evidence of hallucinations or delusions. The patient denied homicidal ideation but admits to chronic suicidal ideation and a history of self-mutilation. There is no history of drug abuse and a history of alcoholic binges during times of stress. The patient was oriented in four spheres. Her memory functions were intact. Her cognitive functions were unimpaired. Her concentration was decreased. Her personal and impersonal judgment was poor.

Summary. Ms. Barton is experiencing a personal crisis that is typified by depression, internal confusion, chaotic interpersonal relationships, suicidal ideation, and fears of abandonment. Her present difficulties are reflective of long-term social and interpersonal dysfunction. She has no history of ongoing psychiatric treatment.

Psychiatric diagnosis. 301.83 Borderline Personality Disorder

Nursing diagnosis. Ineffective individual coping with impaired social functioning, impaired relationships with others, and impaired emotional responses, including high-risk suicidal potential.

Plan. Transfer Ms. Barton to the psychiatric inpatient unit to further assess suicidal state and observe closely.

REFERENCES

1. McNeil, E. *Neuroses and personality disorders.* Englewood Cliffs, N.J.: Prentice Hall, Inc., 1970, p. 87.
2. American Psychiatric Association. *Diagnostic and Statistical Manual of Mental Disorders* (3rd ed.). Washington, D.C.: American Psychiatric Association, 1980.
3. United States Department of Health, Education, and Welfare. Public Health Service, Alcohol, Drug Abuse and Mental Health Administration. Statistical Note #138, Table 1b, August 1977.
4. Distribution of admissions to private mental hospital inpatient units by primary diagnosis and age, U.S., Table 5c. National Institute of Mental Health, 1975.
5. Slater, E., & Cowie, V. The genetics of mental disorders. London: Oxford University Press, 1971, p. 114.
6. Christiansen, K.O. Crime in a Danish twin population. *Geneticae Medicae et Gemellologiae* (Rome), 1970, *19*, 323.
7. Crowe, R. An adoption study of antisocial personality. *Archives of General Psychiatry*, 1974, *31*, 785.
8. Forssman, H. The mental implications of sex chromosome aberration. *British Journal of Psychiatry*, 1970, *117*, 353.
9. Hope, K. Psychological characteristics associated with XYY sex chromosome complement in a state mental hospital. *British Journal of Psychiatry*, 1967, *113*, 495.
10. Zeuthen, E., et al. A psychiatric—psychological study of XYY males found in a general male population. Acta Psychiatrica Scandinavica, 1975, *51*, 3.
11. Sandberg, A., et al. An XYY human male. *Lancet*, 1961, *48*, 488.
12. Jacobs, D.A., Bronton, M., & Melville, M.M. Aggressive behavior, mental subnormality and the XYY male. *Nature*, 1965, *208*, 1351.
13. Kanaka, T.S., Balasuhramaniam, V., & Ramamurthi, B. Mental changes in epilepsy. *Neurology India*, 1967, *15*, 116.
14. Betts, T.A. Psychosomatic aspects of epilepsy. *Practitioner*, 1972, *209*, 574.
15. Gibbs, E.L., Gibbs, F.A., & Fuster, B.: Psychomotor epilepsy. *Archives of Neurology and Psychiatry*, 1948, *60*, 331.

16. Flor-Henry, P. Psychosis, neurosis, and epilepsy. *British Journal of Psychiatry*, 1974, *124*, 144.
17. Shukla, G.D., et al. Psychiatric manifestations in temporal lobe epilepsy: A controlled study. *British Journal of Psychiatry* 1979, *135*, 411.
18. Goldstein, M.: Brain research and violent behavior. *Archives of Neurology*, 1974, *30*, 1.
19. Cloward, R., & Ohlin, L. The differentiation of delinquent subcultures. In D. Cressey, & D. Ward, Eds. *Delinquency, crime and social process.* New York: Harper & Row, Publishers, Inc., 1969.
20. Cohen, A. The sociology of the deviant act: Anomie theory and behind. In D. Cressey, & D. Ward, Eds. *Delinquency, crime and social process.* New York: Harper & Row, Publishers, Inc., 1969.
21. Blum, A.F. The sociology of mental illness. In J. Douglass, Ed. *Deviance and respectability: The social construction of moral meanings.* New York: Basic Books, Inc., Publishers, 1970, p. 38.
22. Hilgard, E.R., & Marquis, D.G. *Conditioning and learning.* New York: Appleton Co., 1940.
23. Meyer, V., & Liddell, A. Behavior therapy. In D. Bannister, Ed. *Issues and approaches in the psychological theories.* London: John Wiley & Son, 1975, p. 224.
24. Freud, S.: The ego and the id, standard ed., Vol. 19. London: Hogarth Press, 1961.
25. Mahler, M.S. On human symbiosis and the vicissitudes of individuation. In M.S. Mahler. *The selected papers of Margaret S. Mahler, M.D.,* Vol. 2. New York: Jason Aronson, Inc., 1979.
26. Wishnie, H. *The impulsive personality.* New York: Plenum Press, 1977.
27. Siever, L.J. Schizoid and schizotypal personality disorder. In J. Lion, Ed. Personality disorders, diagnosis and management, rev. for DSM-III, 2nd ed. Baltimore: Williams & Wilkins, 1981.

ADDITIONAL READINGS

Bischoff, L. *Interpreting personality theories.* New York: Harper & Row, Publishers, Inc., 1964.
Cadoret, R.J. Psychopathology in adopted away offspring of biologic parents with anti-social personality. *Archives of General Psychiatry,* 1978, *35*, 176.
Hoffman, B.F. Two new cases of XYY chromosome complement and a review of the literature. *Canadian Psychiatric Association Journal,* 1977, *22*, 447.
Hook, E.B. Behavioral implications of the human XYY genotype. *Science,* 1973, *179*, 139.
Jenkins, R.C. Psychiatric syndromes in children and their relations to family background. *American Journal of Orthopsychiatry,* 1966, *36*, 450.
Kyes, J., & Hofling, C. *Basic psychiatric concepts in nursing,* 3rd ed. Philadelphia: J.B. Lippincott Co., 1974.
Menuch, M., & Voineskos, G. The etiology of violent behavior: An overview. *General Hospital Psychiatry,* 1981, *3*, 37.
Rutter, M. Maternal deprivation reassessed. London: Books Limited, 1972.
Whybrow, P., Kane, F., & Lipton, M. Regional ileitis and psychiatric disorders. *Psychosomatic Medicine,* 1968, *30*, 209.
Witkind, H.A., Mednick, S.A., & Schulsinger, F. Criminality in XYY and XXY men. *Science,* 1976, *193*, 547.

CHAPTER 8

ASSESSING SUICIDAL POTENTIAL

It is both fascinating and abhorring to entertain the concept of suicide. Throughout history the very idea of self-murder has called forth such emotions as anger, admiration, patriotic pride, disgust, sympathy, curiosity, and fear. Many of these responses are determined by the social factors and norms operating in the specific culture in which the suicide is accomplished. A society such as twentieth century America, for example, places high value on wellness and life and tends to view suicide with horror, shame, and antagonism. On the other hand, Japanese culture has historically viewed some suicides as honor-saving acts or patriotic feats.

Traditionally, health care personnel have had a difficult time reviewing and discussing suicide. After all, the very act of self-destruction is antithetical to the health-care mission to save lives and promote health. It was only in the 1960s, with the advent of the community mental health movement, that a more intense effort was made to understand, diagnose, and treat the suicidal individual. Suicidology became a popular psychiatric subspecialty and prevention, intervention, and postvention with the suicidal person became more common topics in research and the literature. Suicide prevention centers began to spring up throughout the country. Professional education encouraged open discussion regarding attitudes toward suicide and suicidal patients. Yet in spite of a surge of understanding and open expression, the concept of suicide continues to provoke feelings of anger, anxiety, disbelief, and helplessness for many individuals. Several years ago in Vermont, for example, a distraught person was perched atop a high bridge over the railroad tracks, threatening to jump. A crowd had gathered to observe the incident. Before long, the 20 or so spectators were cheering the young man on, "Jump, jump. . . we dare you to jump!" The man did jump and subsequently died as a result of multiple injuries.

Why did a group of fellow human beings dare this individual to take his own life? The answer lies in the emotional response of each person in that crowd to the threat of suicide. It angers, frightens, dares, and fascinates. And, in spite of the surge of study in the past two decades, suicide ultimately remains an elusive force controlled by the unique matrix of motivations of each suicidal individual.

Unlike the spectators at the bridge, health care professionals must begin their study of suicide by acknowledging their own attitudes and beliefs about this phenomenon. Negative or discounting attitudes toward suicide and suicidal patients will interfere with the prompt and accurate assessment of suicidal potential and resultant intervention. Since suicide is not unique to psychiatric patients, nurses from every clinical orientation need to entertain the possibility that their patients in the community, medicine, surgery, and elsewhere may be potentially suicidal. Again, this requires an openness in acknowledging biases toward suicide and an adequate knowledge base in suicide assessment and intervention.

As we move toward understanding suicide as an act of frustration, desperation, and relief, we can begin to communicate the necessary messages of help and hope to those persons locked into a perceived life or death forced-choice situation. As Alvarez so sensitively writes, "A suicidal depression is a kind of spiritual winter, frozen, sterile, unmoving. The richer, softer and more delectable nature becomes, the deeper that internal winter seems, and the wider and more tolerable the abyss which separates the inner world from the outer."[1] Nurses have the responsibility not to prevent all suicides but to identify those individuals who are in an abyss of despair and assist them in formulating alternative choices within a hopeful perspective.

DEFINITION

Suicide is a broad term that is often used to describe the ideation, attempt, and completion of self-inflicted cessation. Shneidman describes suicide as

. . . involving an individual's tortured and tunneled logic in a state of innerfelt, intolerable emotion. In addition, this mixture of constricted thinking and unbearable anguish is infused with that individual's conscious and unconscious psychodynamics. . . . playing themselves out within a social and cultural context which itself imposes various degrees of restraint on, or facilitation of, the suicidal act.[2]

In essence, suicide can be viewed as aggression directed inward. The basis for this aggressive action toward the self is constructed from a constellation of psychosocial-cultural variables that impact on the individual.

The term suicide is frequently used to describe an ideation, threat, gesture, attempt, or completed act. *Suicidal ideations* are thoughts about killing oneself. Many people entertain ideas about suicide at some point in a lifetime without ever verbally or behaviorally expressing those thoughts. A *suicide threat* is a verbal or behavioral indication from the person that denotes a self-destructive intent. Not every suicide threat is eventually acted upon by the individual. However, the nurse must be able to determine the degree of seriousness of all suicidal threats. A *suicidal gesture* is an act of self-harm that is not a serious risk to the person's life. For example, a teenage girl threatening suicide took a nail file and made a one-inch cut on her arm that barely broke the skin. This suicidal gesture was not considered serious. However, clinicians often discount the potential seriousness of a suicidal gesture by failure to heed the cries for help that are usually inherent in most gestures. A *suicide attempt* may follow a suicide gesture. An attempt occurs when individuals initiate behavior they believe will cause death. These patients usually live because of circumstances beyond their control, such as unexpected rescue. A suicide attempt is very serious and involves risk to the person's health and life. *Completed suicide* results when patients take their own lives with conscious intent.

Self-destructive behavior is another term that encompasses a range of acts that are detrimental to a person's well-being. Noncompliance with treatment regimes, excessive smoking, alcohol and drug abuse, reckless driving, self-inflicted wounds, or completed suicide fall under the auspices of self-destructive behavior. Any self-initiated activity that damages the individual emotionally, socially, or physically can be called self-destructive.

Clinicians occasionally describe a patient's suicidal status as active or passive. Actively suicidal persons are considering purposeful, self-initiated action for the purpose of self-harm. Patients who are passively suicidal wish to die, but rather than inflict self-harm, they hope for circumstances that will promote death. One young man, for example, lay in his bed day after day wishing he would have a heart attack.

The nurse who interviews a patient to determine whether or not the person is suicidal will be assessing suicide potential. Suicide potential is the degree of probability that the patient will attempt self-harm. Suicidology is the broad scientific study of suicide that includes the analysis of such potential.

Suicide is not only a clinical term but also one with legal implications. In the United States, suicide is one particular mode of death. Other legal types of death are natural causes, accidents, and homicides. Until recently, the act of suicide was considered illegal and those who were unsuccessful could be arrested for attempted self-murder. Fortunately, this judgment is changing as our society begins to recognize suicide as a phenomenon to be understood with intellect, compassion, and concern.

CLASSIFICATION

Suicide is a specific behavioral phenomenon rather than a diagnostic category. Researchers involved in the study of suicide have categorized types of suicide and suicidal potential.

Shneidman delineates three types of suicidal acts: egotic, dyadic, and ageneratic.[3] Egotic suicide occurs as the result of an intrapsychic debate. The suicidal person is absorbed in an internal world that seemingly dictates self-harm. These individuals may be psychotic, delusional, or existential. People who attempt or commit suicide in relation to an interpersonal event typify dyadic suicide. The wish for death pertains to unfulfilled wishes and needs involving a significant other. The suicidal act represents withdrawal, revenge, punishment, or a plea for unmet needs. Ageneratic suicide results from a loss of involvement in the social institutions with which one is connected. The individual no longer feels a sense of belonging to the family, culture, or socioeconomic-political environment.

Wekstein has also identified types of suicidal behaviors.[4] Chronic suicide is accomplished when a person engages in self-destructive actions that, over time, threaten life. Substance abusers and excessive cigarette smokers may, at some psychological level, be committing suicide. Neglect is another type of suicide in which the individual refuses to care for physical-psychosocial needs or is noncompliant with prescribed health care regimens. Medical-surgical patients such as those with cardiac disturbances and diabetes mellitus who refuse to take medications or adhere to altered life-styles may be neglectfully suicidal. Surcease suicide results when an individual desires relief from pain or a physical malady and logically chooses self-cessation as freedom from the affliction. Terminal cancer patients who kill themselves commit sur-

TABLE 8:1   Classification of suicidal behavior

Type I	Type II	Type III
Verbal threats	Verbal threats	Verbal threats
No specific plan	Specific plan	Specific plan
Gesture with no threat to life	Lethal plan	Lethal plan
	Attempts where rescue is possible	Attempt with highly possible fatal outcome
Immediate risk: low	Immediate risk: moderate	Immediate risk: high

Adapted from Hoff, L.A. *People in crisis: Understanding and helping*. Menlo Park, Calif.: Addison-Wesley Publishing Co., Inc., 1978.

cease suicide. Paleological suicide constitutes those individuals who kill themselves during a psychotic state. Accidental suicide is unintended. It occurs when a person makes a suicidal gesture or attempt but circumstances prevent the expected rescue. For example, one young woman swallowed a bottle of barbiturates minutes before her husband usually arrived home from work. That evening, however, her husband decided to dine with a client and did not return until 5 hours later. Existential suicide results from an internal philosophical debate on the meaning of life. The individual concludes that life is essentially meaningless and chooses death as the final act of control.

Suicide risk potential has been classified by Hoff into three categories listed in Table 8-1. These categories qualitatively describe the amount of suicidal risk inherent at each level of suicidal behavior. Although the risk is presented in a hierarchical order, self-destructive behavior at any level should be considered serious.

EPIDEMIOLOGY

Suicide is the tenth leading cause of death in the United States. In 1979 a total of 27,206 people took their own lives. This figure does not reflect the number of suicides that were labeled as accidents, such as drug or alcohol ingestion and automobile accidents. Of this number, 20,256 were males and 6,950 were females.[6] As depicted in these figures, males are three times more likely to commit suicide than females. However, females attempt suicide more than males at a rate of 3:1. Men use more lethal means to commit suicide, such as firearms or hanging, whereas women tend to attempt suicide by overdosing, poisoning, or cutting. Table 8:2 lists the leading methods used to commit suicide in 1979.

TABLE 8:2   Deaths by methods of suicide, 1979

Cause of death	Number of deaths	Male	Female
1. Firearms and explosives	15,558	12,919	2,639
2. Hanging, strangulation, suffocation	3,525	2,758	742
3. Poisoning, overdose	3,344	1,384	1,960
4. Gases	2,384	1,590	794
5. Jumping	888	587	301
6. Drowning	583	329	254
7. Cutting, piercing	416	311	105
8. Others	495	347	148

Adapted from National Center for Health Statistics. Unpublished data. Hyattsville, Md.: U.S. Department of Health and Human Services, 1979.

Wekstein estimates that there are 2 to 5 million suicide attempts each year.[4] Approximately one suicide occurs for every eight to ten attempts. Of the people who complete suicide, 80% have had at least one previous suicide attempt. Of those individuals who attempt suicide, 12% will succeed in killing themselves within 2 years. Most suicides and attempts occur during the winter months. The least number of suicides are attempted and completed in the summer and fall.[7]

Suicidal thoughts tend to be common in the general population. Beck, Resnik, and Lettieri postulate that suicidal ideations and attempts can be depicted on a bell curve as shown below*:

No suicidal wishes	Ideations	Attempts

General population

Suicidal ideation may be passing thoughts or repetitive and intense serious considerations of suicide. Research by Beck has indicated that at any given time, 12% of the general population has suicidal wishes whereas at least 74% of depressed patients consider suicide.[9]

Persons at high risk for suicide include elderly, white, Protestant males; adolescents; college students; alcoholics; drug abusers; depressed individuals; those downwardly mobile in socioeconomic status; and people who have experienced interpersonal loss. Suicide generally increases with age; however, the number of suicides in the 15 to 24-year-old age-group has been steadily increasing. Table 8:3 identifies the number of suicides in 1979 and the ranking of suicide as a cause of death for each age-group.

---

*This material has been reprinted from *The Prediction of Suicide,* edited by Beck, Resnik and Lettieri, with the permission from the Charles Press Publishers, Philadelphia, Pa.

TABLE 8:3	Suicide as a cause of death per age-group, 1979	
Ranked cause of death	*Ages*	*Number of suicides*
7th	5-14 years	152
3rd	15-24 years	5,246
5th	25-44 years	9,733
8th	45-64 years	7,357
—	65-74 years	2,730
—	75-84 years	1,577

Adapted from National Center for Health Statistics. Unpublished data. Hyattsville, Md.: U.S. Department of Health and Human Services, 1979.

Variables such as marriage, religion, and race seem to influence suicide. Married persons over the age of 23 have a lower suicide rate than nonmarried people. However, below age 23, married individuals have a higher rate of suicide. Jews have a low rate of suicide, usually attributed to cultural and religious emphasis on family. In the United States, Protestants have a high rate of suicide whereas Catholics exhibit low rates. American whites have a much higher suicide rate than blacks, although black suicide is increasing. White suicides are more pronounced in the older age-groups whereas blacks between the ages of 20 and 35 have a higher rate of suicide. American Indians exhibit a very high rate of suicide.

Suicides tend to occur more in industrialized, urban societies and areas in which there is governmental unrest or intense individual performance expectations. This is in contrast to societies that are developing, nurturing, and family oriented. Suicide increases during times of economic recessions for all socioeconomic groups.[10]

The rates of suicide in the populations of various diagnosed psychiatric disorders have been studied by Pokorny. He found that depressed patients have the highest suicide rate per 100,000 per year. The second highest rate, by diagnosis, was schizophrenia, followed in descending order by alcohol abuse, personality disorders, neuroses, and organic mental disturbances.[11] As indicated in these studies, depressed patients are serious risks for suicide. However, Choron states that although at least one half of all completed suicides were depressed, only 5% to 15% of depressed persons actually commit suicide.[12]

Suicide in hospitals far exceeds that of the general population. Farberow found that psychotic patients were most likely to kill themselves during hospitalization.[13] Psychiatric patients were 30 times more likely to commit suicide in the hospital than persons in the general population, with 65% occurring while on pass or unauthorized absence and 35% in the hospital. Patients hospitalized for depression are at greatest risk for suicide within the first several months following discharge. Medical-surgical patients constituted 18% of the hospital suicides with 72% killing themselves while in the hospital. For hospitalized patients, suicidal risk is greatest during the first month of admission. Many medical-surgical patients kill themselves during the first several months following discharge. These data suggest the importance of nurses being aware of the potential for suicide among hospitalized and recently discharged patients and skilled in assessing suicidal risk in all patient populations.

CAUSATIVE FACTORS

It is a monumental task to dissect the unique elements of human nature that propel an individual to commit suicide. Despite the analysis of multiple variables that influence the commission of suicide, ultimately, whole people are more than the sum of their parts and live or die based on that gestalt of internal and external factors. Generally, three major etiological factors contribute to suicide: individual psychodynamics, sociocultural influences, and specific external stressors.

Psychodynamic factors

Sigmund Freud postulates that suicide is the result of intrapsychic variables. He identifies thanatos as the aggressive death drive inherent in all persons. Thanatos operates opposite eros, the life instinct. Both forces exert a pulling effect on the individual and life becomes a constant struggle between the will to live and the wish to die.[14] Freud ultimately contributed the concept of suicide as aggression turned inward on the self. According to this premise, people identify with those they love and internalize these relationships into their own egos. When frustration or loss occurs in the relationship, the person is unable to vent the anger onto the lost love and subsequently directs it inward on that part of the ego that identified with the love object. Childhood experiences that weaken the ego and contribute to a negative self-concept promote suicidal behavior. In fact, the loss of a parent before age 5 has been found to be a significant factor in suicidal profiles. Psychodynamically, suicide is a means to punish the self, punish the lost love, or exert final control over one's destiny.

Menninger presents a tripartite view of suicide, the wish to kill turned inward on self, the wish to be killed as a punishment for aggressive forces, and the wish to die as an emotional release.[15] From this perspective, suicide is seen as expression of emotions resulting from intrapsychic forces. The scenario of rage turned inward and released through the act of suicide highlights the psychodynamic tenets of suicide.

A major concept that stems from the psychodynamic view of suicide is that of ambivalence. Various theorists ascribe ambivalence to the struggle between thanatos and eros, the submission to the superego's demand for punishment, and the dualities existing in a defended psychological state. The individual who makes plans for suicide also entertains fantasies of rescue. The amount of ambivalence will vary depending on the psychological matrix of each suicidal person as unconscious rage is placed in opposition to a punitive superego.

Sociocultural influences

In 1897 Emile Durkheim proposed a major sociological theory of suicide.[16] According to Durkheim's theory, suicide results from the amount of control exerted over the individual by society. Suicide becomes the failure of the individual to find a niche in the society that balances rejection, isolation, and integration. Durkheim describes three types of suicide that result from the influences of society—altruistic, egoistic, and anomic suicide. Altruistic suicide occurs when the person has become intensely attached to the ideals of the society and is preoccupied with commitment and duty. An individual who commits egoistic suicide has been rejected by society and feels alienated from family, friends, or organizations. The anomic suicide results from weak control by society over the individual who experiences self-isolation and poor adjustment to social change.

There seems to be a relationship between socioeconomic conditions and the incidence of suicide. Any condition that interferes with the stable maintenance of socioeconomic status can influence the commission of suicide. Suicide is then viewed as an aggressive consequence of frustration in climates of unrest, pessimism, and poor economic conditions.

Farberow describes two components of suicide—personal and social. Personal suicide serves as a protest against hurts or transgressions whereas social suicide is self-destruction dictated by the influence of social variables on the individual.[17] Farberow urges us to understand the cultural influences on suicide, including the religious, legal, and philosophical tenets that define the meaning and patterns of suicide in society. Indeed, it is not possible to study suicide or intervene with a suicidal patient without comprehending the impact of socioeconomic-cultural conditions and attitudes that affect the suicidal individual.

External stressors

The desire to commit suicide is often precipitated by stressors impacting on the individual at a given point in time. Most significant among these stressors are losses and disturbances in relationships. Although these crisis situations are not the foundations that predispose a person to suicide, they do create situational stress that the person with diminished coping ability may not handle well.

A real or perceived loss triggers suicide attempts. The loss can be a person, object, social status, income, or physical health. When loss is experienced, usual coping mechanisms fail and suicidal individuals choose to withdraw, punish themselves for failure, or seek retribution toward others involved in the loss. Frequently, the loss is viewed in terms of a dichotomy: "Either I get it back or there is no future." Suicide precipitated by loss occurs with unemployment, unfavorable publicity, failure in a job, school, or social situation, or physical illness or injury. The loss may be recent or remote. In fact anniversary dates of losses such as the death of a significant other are times of increased suicidal risk.

Suicide also results from the disruption of interpersonal relationships. Events such as death, divorce, separation, imprisonment, or major conflict are potent precipitants of suicide. These phenomena sever or weaken interpersonal bonds and lead to feelings of loneliness, isolation, hopelessness, and helplessness. Those persons considered high suicidal risks frequently live alone, feel isolated, have experienced recent social or family disorganization, or have been recently rejected by significant others. These people feel sad, angry, and hopeless and usually desire a way to escape their intolerable state, punish significant others they believe are promoting their situation, or seek a better afterlife, possibly with a deceased loved one. Suicide attempts and gestures may be used as a way to communicate anger, frustration, and despair to significant others.

CLINICAL PRESENTATION

Assessing the potential for suicide includes observing and analyzing a variety of clinical and demographic variables that are associated with suicide attempts and completions. Suicide is not a singular, sudden event but rather the climax of a process of interlocking occurrences that can be interrupted at any time. The nurse's goal is to assess individuals' potential for self-harm, identify those persons who are at risk, and intervene promptly.

The suicidal individual can be found anywhere in the community or health care system. Whereas some people are overtly depressed and verbal about their intentions, others are quietly planning self-harm in response to life stress, physical illness, or broken relationships. Impulsive suicides occur during drug or alcohol abuse, during psychotic episodes, or following perceived loss or failure for individuals who are usually reactive. Some patients with a high degree of ambivalence realize the seriousness of their intentions and seek help from family, friends, or professionals. Others are brought into contact with the health care system by concerned family or friends. Sometimes, suicidal patients obtain assistance following an actual attempt during which they were rescued by others or by seeking help themselves for their physical injuries. People who consider or implement self-injury are often frightened by their thoughts and actions and are open to help from others.

Suicidal individuals demonstrate a multitude of presenting problems. They may enter the health care system seeking help for depression or anxiety. The nurse needs to query every patient with depression as to suicidal intentions, since depressive diagnoses are highly correlated with suicide attempts.[18] Many people who commit suicide have been physically ill, seeking assistance from family physicians, surgeons, neurologists, and internists. The nurse should be particularly attentive to those persons who are psychotic, alcoholic, and impulsive since many suicides occur in these patient populations. Emergency situations involving poisoning, auto accidents, falls, and gunshot wounds indicate potential suicidal attempts. It is crucial to assess these individuals and ascertain the nature of the injury. A list of common presenting problems of suicidal persons is found below:

Suicidal ideation

"I wish I could sleep forever . . ."

"Nothing matters anymore . . ."

"They'll be sorry when I'm gone . . ."

"I want to die . . ."

"I'm afraid I'll drive the car off the road . . ."

"Yes, my father is dead. . . . I need to be with him now . . ."

"There has to be a better place than this world . . ."

"Take all my clothes. I won't need them anymore . . ."

"The seasons come and go. . . . and so do I . . ."

Suicide attempt

"I took some pills . . ."

"Yes, I cut my wrists. My mother will feel bad now . . ."

'The angels were calling me to be in heaven . . ."

"Just let me die . . ."

Before conducting a suicide assessment, nurses must be cognizant of their own feelings and values that can prevent or interfere with identifying and assisting a potentially suicidal person. Since the very act of self-murder is in direct opposition to nursing's mission to support life, nurses often find it difficult to acknowledge the presence of a suicidal clue or the emotional turmoil of the suicidal patient. The clinician needs to assess the anxiety associated with evaluation of suicidal patients and control anxiety-laden, angry, or bewildered responses. It is difficult to ask, "Have you ever had thoughts of hurting or killing yourself?" Yet this is the most important question of the suicide assessment. Once a patient has admitted to having suicidal thoughts, the nurse explores this further by inquiring as to suicide plans, methods, past suicide attempts, and the availability of means to carry out the self-injury. Most patients will be relieved that someone has acknowledged their distress and will respond in a truthful manner. Contrary to myth, asking patients about their suicidal thoughts and intentions will *not* prompt a suicide attempt.

The ability to establish a rapport with the suicidal patient is essential. A positive, organized, and decisive approach will facilitate the assessment and allow the patient to engage in frank discussion. When questioning a patient about suicidal intentions, the nurse assumes a caring and concerned posture. It is important to convey an attitude of hope and optimism without an effervescent or "pollyanna" demeanor. The patient needs to know that the clinician understands the pain and distress yet is able to envision a time when life will seem better. A major objective of the assessment is not only to ascertain suicide potential but to illuminate possible hopeful action alternatives for the individual.

Behavioral manifestations

Suicidal patients display a variety of behaviors that are indicative of potential suicide risk. Frequently, the nurse, friend, or family member will notice a recent change in the patient's usual behavior. An outgoing individual may suddenly become reclusive. A spendthrift may go on a shopping spree or donate large sums of money to a local charity. The nurse should particularly note any patient who has been depressed but then demonstrates sudden animation and improvement. This can signal the patient's relief for having made the decision to commit suicide and resolve the inner torment. Patients who are taking antidepressant medications are particularly prone to suicidal risk when the drugs have begun to improve outward behavior and energy levels but have not altered suicidal thoughts or feelings of hopelessness.

Individuals considering suicide often attend to final business and personal affairs. Finances may be put in order and a will composed. The person may give away possessions such as sentimental mementos or automobiles. One patient, for example, wrote a letter to his mother offering reconciliation after 5 years of estrangement. Whenever the nurse observes behaviors that are suggestive of putting final affairs in order, a thorough suicide risk assessment should be conducted.

The initial assessment question asked is "Have you had thoughts of hurting (harming or killing) yourself?" If the patient responds affirmatively, the nurse needs to assess the suicide plans by asking "What are you thinking of doing to yourself?" Occasionally, patients will deny suicidal ideations in spite of the nurse's suspicion that they are truly considering self-harm. In this instance, it is often fruitful to pursue the questioning with "If you were thinking of harming yourself, how would you do it?"

Suicide plans provide important information about the patient's suicide risk potential. Each plan is analyzed for its specificity, lethality, and availability of means. A very specific, detailed plan for suicide indicates an organized, thought-out process suggestive of high suicide risk. A plan with high lethality of the proposed method poses a serious threat. Persons who attempt suicide with guns, hanging, or jumping have a higher rate of success than those who overdose or cut their wrists. The nurse needs to find out if the patient has access to the proposed suicidal means. "You say you would shoot yourself. Do you have a gun?" By asking the patient to describe the envisioned suicidal scene, the nurse is able to ascertain the seriousness of the patient's intentions.

> CASE EXAMPLE: Mrs. Reed is recovering from depression. She suddenly appears bright and energetic. She calls her brother in Alaska whom she has not seen in 8 years. The nurse, concerned about this sudden change in behavior, asks Mrs. Reed if she is thinking of hurting herself. Mrs. Reed glances at the floor and admits to suicidal thoughts. She states she plans to drive her car off an embankment. At the hospital Mrs. Reed has her own car that she is intending to drive home. The nurse decides that Mrs. Reed's suicide potential is very high.

A history of past suicide attempts is a major variable that requires assessment. In a study conducted by Kaplan, Kottler, and Frances, the highest reliable indicator of suicide potential was the seriousness of a patient's past attempt.[19] A patient who has used a highly lethal method of self-harm is at great risk for eventual suicide. Any history of past suicide attempts should be noted and discussed with the patient' "Have you ever tried to kill yourself before?" "You said you jumped off a five-story building but hedges broke your fall. Are you thinking of doing that again?" The more frequent the past attempts, the higher the potential risk. Generally, more recent attempts indicate current greater risk.

Obtaining information about a patient's life-style provides insight about coping abilities, relationships, and general functoning over time. A person with a chaotic life-style is more vulnerable to stress and subsequently, suicide. It is helpful to identify recent events that have precipitated current suicidal ideations as well as past events that have triggered difficulty in coping. Individuals who are impulsive tend to be higher suicidal risks. They engage in behavior that is reactive to momentary emotional upsets. They suddenly feel badly, find an immediate available means of self-harm, and attempt suicide. Later, they regret their impulsive actions and admit that emotion overcame logic.

Alcohol abuse is closely associated with suicide. Alcohol impairs the senses and clouds judgment, predisposing one to impulsive suicide. Impairment from alcohol also masks inhibitions and allows people who have planned suicide the opportunity to initiate the act. Depressed individuals, who have higher suicide rates, also consume alcohol in an attempt to soothe their inner turmoil. In addition, people who do not normally use alcohol tend to drink just before attempting suicide. Miller estimates that 20% of the people who commit suicide are alcoholic and another 20% are heavy drinkers.[20] A thorough suicide assessment includes observations about the patient's current alcohol intake and past drinking behavior. The patient who appears intoxicated is a higher immediate suicidal risk. A history of using alcohol as a coping device predisposes the individual to a higher suicidal potential.

Emotional manifestations

There is a strong relationship between a diagnosis of depression and suicide.[13] A high suicidal risk is indicated when the patient exhibits feelings of worthlessness, helplessness, and hopelessness, all feelings associated with depressed states. In fact, the feeling most frequently observed in suicidal individuals is depression. The suicidal person is unable to see a future or meaning for living. The nurse may ask patients, "How depressed are you?" or "What do you think you'll be doing 2 years from now?" or ascertain feelings about their current state and perceptions of the future. Often, patients may cry as they discuss their situation.

An individual who is extremely depressed, exhibiting psychomotor retardation, is a candidate for potential suicide. The risk, however, becomes more immediate when the depression is accompanied by agitation and restlessness. In this instance, the depressed patient has more energy to plan and implement the suicide.

Suicidal persons are often anxious and fearful. They are frightened by overwhelming feelings of isolation and hopelessness. They are anxious about their inner pain and the plans they are making to resolve it. The feeling of ambivalence—wanting desperately to die yet hoping just as desperately to live—creates anxiety and panic. Patients often admit "I don't know what to do—these feelings and my life are intolerable." Suicide is seen as a means for escaping intensively frightening situations or as relief from constant, overwhelming anxiety.

Anger is frequently expressed by suicidal persons. The anger may be directed inward, "I hate myself for what I did. . . . I deserve to die," or onto another individual or situation, "She'll be sorry when I'm dead." The nurse needs to assess for angry feelings and assist the patient to direct the anger into channels more appropriate than self-harm. Excessive guilt, self-blame, and severe frustration may also be evident.

Patients considering suicide can also exhibit tranquility and an emotional calmness. This often is evident just before the suicide attempt. When a decision has been made to commit suicide, the patient experiences relief from emotional struggles and unrelenting emotional (or physical) pain. Patients who plan suicide from the posture that they are going to a better world or rejoining a deceased loved one may be quite relaxed and calm. Persons who seem to suddenly recover from depression or anxiety in actuality may have made the decision to kill themselves. The nurse must be alert to sudden changes in mood and discuss these changes with the patient. When the patient's mood seems remarkably calm in view of recent stresses and events, the nurse can ask, "You seem so relaxed with all these things that have happened to you. How is that?" The clinician who notes a mood change should ask the patient, "Two days ago you were very upset. Now, you seem so cheerful. What has happened to cause that change?"

Patients who are extremely upset are more prone to suicide. Shneidman uses the word perturbation to describe the state of being emotionally upset and distressed.[3] The nurse needs to gain understanding of the patient's inner turmoil, the degree of emotional upset. This upset can take the form of anxiety, anger, aggression, depression, or even mute withdrawal. The patient's words, expressions, and behaviors provide insight into the intensity of the patient's emotional state.

Cognitive manifestations

A mental status examination of the suicidal patient reveals destructive thought content themes. The patient is preoccupied with thoughts of self-harm. These thoughts may range from self-mutilation with minimal actual suicide intent to meticulous planning of a final suicidal act. Some individuals express suicidal ideation in terms of wanting to die, but they have not yet considered the destructive means to accomplish this. In many instances of attempted suicide, the patient has not fully considered death as a desired state but rather views suicide as a way out of an unbearable situation.

Shneidman discusses three types of suicidal logic: logical, paleological, and catalogical suicide.[3] Logical suicides are committed by people in physical pain. They desire relief from the pain and deduce that suicide is the most attractive alternative. This type of thinking is often most difficult for health care personnel when interacting with the suicidal patient. It is reasonable and logical, and the nurse finds it difficult to convey hope or optimism when the pain and illness are chronic or terminal. However, the clinician needs to point out the treatments, such as medications or surgery, that are available to help alleviate the patient's condition.

Paleological suicide is accomplished by persons who are delusional, hallucinatory, or disorganized. Many suicides are completed by individuals who are psychotic. Pokorny found that by diagnosis, the second highest number of suicides following depression suicides are committed by schizophrenic individuals.[11] In the hospital schizophrenic patients commit suicide 13.3% more than any other group.[21] Thus psychotic individuals are high suicidal risks. During the mental status examination, psychotic suicidal individuals may describe hallucinations in which voices or visions tell them to jump out of windows, shoot themselves, or walk in front of moving vehicles. The nurse should always ascertain what voices or visions are saying to the psychotic person. Delusions should also be assessed for their content and meaning. A patient who believes he is Superman and can fly, for example, may very well attempt to jump off a building.

> CASE EXAMPLE: Mary states she is hearing her dead father speak to her. The nurse asks, "What is your father saying to you?" Mary is hesitant but then says, "He is calling me. I hear him calling me." Since Mary's father is dead, the nurse suspects that Mary is contemplating suicide to be with her father.

Psychotic patients may appear to attempt suicide when actually they perform the suicidal act for reasons other than self-harm. A patient may consume an entire bottle of pills thinking if one pill makes you feel better, then 100 pills should make you feel 100 times better. This type of logic, a deductive fallacy, is apparent with disorganized, illogical thinking.

Since the risk of suicide is great for psychotic individuals, nurses need to be particularly attuned to the thought content, the lack of judgment, and the potential impulsivity of the psychotic patient. Suicidal behavior of psychotic people tends to be more unpredictable and fatal than suicidal behavior of others. A thorough mental status examination will usually provide some indication of possible risk. Observation will elicit clues, such as the patient pretending to be at a funeral or wearing black clothes. Peaks of suicidal risk for the psychotic patient occur with sudden onset of psychosis, remission of psychotic symptoms, and fear of recurrence of mental illness.[22]

The third type of suicide is catalogical. The thinking exhibited by this type of individual contains dichotomous thinking and semantic fallacies. This type of thought creates double bind situations for the patient. The choices become dichotomous phenomena, that is, A or B, black or white: "If I can't be married to John, then I can't be married to anyone"; "If I don't get an A +, then I am a bad student." These individuals tend not to see alternatives or use problem solving as a mechanism for coping with the stress. Insight and judgment are impaired. They may say, "If nothing gets better, I will have to kill myself," where the vagueness of the terms "nothing" and "better" are left open to semantic questioning. During the interview, the nurse should note this particular type of thinking and point out to the patient the polarity and lack of attention to alternatives and ambiguities.

Physical manifestations

Physical illness and injury is strongly associated with suicide attempts. In fact nearly 75% of people who successfully commit suicide visit a physician within 4 months prior to their deaths.[23] Physical illness can reduce a person's ability to cope with stress. Severe pain or the perception of continuing chronic disease may precipitate suicidal ideations. High rates of suicide are reported for patients with cancer, spinal cord injuries, and chronic obstructive pulmonary disease (COPD).[24]

Suicidal people contact physicians for a variety of somatic complaints. Many describe headaches, chest pain, insomnia, anorexia, general malaise, gastrointestinal upsets, and backaches. These physical symptoms are also indicative of depression and anxiety, two significant emotional states of suicidal individuals. These patients may be admitted to medical units for diagnostic evaluation. All too often, they are dismissed by doctors, nurses, and other health care providers as being "complainers" or "hypochondriacs." When this occurs, there has been no assessment of the patient's mental state, life stresses, or past coping abilities. It is indeed a tragedy when suicidal people, using physical symptoms as a means to access help in the health care system, do not have their cries for help noticed. Yet, one study suggests that 18% of all hospital suicides are on medical-surgical units.[13]

Utilizing a holistic approach to health care, nurses are in opportune positions to suspect emotional turmoil behind a patient's stated physical complaints. Whenever a patient describes symptoms indicative of depression such as insomnia or anorexia, the nurse should investigate the nature of these maladies. This may occur in the community, in the general hospital, in clinics, or in physician's offices.

> CASE EXAMPLE: Mr. Abraham arrived in the Emergency Department complaining of chest pain. An ECG, physical examination, and laboratory tests were negative. The physician had ordered an additional blood test. As the nurse was drawing blood, the man sighed and said, "You know, my blood is blue, blue, blue." The nurse thought this was a strange comment and asked Mr. Abraham what he meant. He again sighed and explained that his daughter had blue eyes. The nurse continued questioning Mr. Abraham and discovered that his only daughter had recently died following neurosurgery for a brain tumor. His wife had died in an auto accident several years ago. Mr. Abraham explained he had not been sleeping and had been pacing the floor the past 24 hours. He admitted to having suicidal thoughts when directly questioned by the nurse.

Social manifestations

Most people who kill themselves feel isolated. Many have experienced upheaval in interpersonal relationships or from significant losses. When stress increases, these individuals feel they have no one to turn to for support. Suicidal persons often withdraw from social activities, resign from clubs, and eliminate contact with friends or family. This state of isolation may result from the suicidal feelings or precipitate these feelings.

Women are most prone to suicide when there is a loss of a significant relationship. Widows and widowers have a suicide rate five times higher than married persons. Single men and women have a rate that is twice as high.[25] A review of the patient's support network is an important component of every suicide assessment. It is not sufficient to note the existence of friends and family. Rather, the nurse needs to explore the nature of the patient's relationships and their perceptions of support. A person can be surrounded by a loving family but still feel totally alone. In addition, anger toward significant others may be a precipitant of the suicidal ideations. An assessment of the patient's actual living situation and environment will enhance the nurse's understanding of the patient's social situation.

The nurse should also explore the patient's religious affiliation, work history, and school history. Prostestants in the United States tend to have a higher rate of suicide than Catholics or Jews. This does not preclude the fact, however, that many Catholics and Jews do commit suicide. Unemployment and occupational stress contribute to suicidal potential. A history of failure at school, or the patient's perceived failure, increases the risk potential.

A family history of successful suicide and attempted suicide predisposes an individual to suicidal risk. Many people who complete suicide have had a parent commit suicide before they were a teenager. About 25% of the people who attempt suicide have had a family member also attempt suicide.[25] The nurse needs to ask, "Has anyone in your family ever attempted suicide?"

> CASE EXAMPLE: Mr. Krone requested a psychiatric evaluation at the local community mental health center. He had been retired for 2 years when he wife suddenly died 6 months ago. He states he has two daughters who live in the area with their families. He has stopped attending his senior citizens' activities and spends his day sitting at home watching television. Mr. Krone feels very alone and isolated and admits to having suicidal thoughts.

ASSESSMENT TOOLS

The nurse, assessing a patient's potential for suicide, examines a host of demographic and clinical elements that indicate suicidal risk. Suicidological research has attempted to develop tools that assist in the prediction of suicide. Yet each individual is unique, and a multidimen-

TOOL 8:1   Brief assessment for potential suicide

Signs and symptoms	Yes	No

1. Behavioral clues

a. Sudden change in usual behavior ____ ____
b. Giving away possessions ____ ____
c. Arranging personal affairs ____ ____
d. Contacting family or friends ____ ____
e. Composing a will ____ ____

2. Emotional clues

a. Depression ____ ____
b. Anxiety, fear ____ ____
c. Agitation ____ ____
d. Hopelessness, helplessness ____ ____
e. Anger, revenge, hostility ____ ____
f. Tranquility, calmness ____ ____
g. Emotional upset ____ ____
h. Crying ____ ____
i. Sudden change in emotional state ____ ____

3. Cognitive clues

a. Suicidal thought content ____ ____
b. Thoughts of death, violence ____ ____
c. Desired relief from pain, illness ____ ____
d. Desired relief from unbearable situation ____ ____
e. Psychosis ____ ____
f. Dichotomous thinking ____ ____
g. Unable to envision a future ____ ____

4. Physical clues

a. Physical illness/injury in past 6 months ____ ____
b. Chronic illness, pain ____ ____
c. Physical complaints ____ ____
   Insomnia ____ ____
   Headache ____ ____
   Gastrointestinal upset ____ ____
   Anorexia ____ ____
   Malaise ____ ____

5. Social clues

a. Social isolation ____ ____
b. Perceived lack of support ____ ____
c. Relationship loss ____ ____
d. Disturbance in relationships ____ ____
e. Lives alone ____ ____
f. Unemployment ____ ____
g. School failure ____ ____
h. Family history of suicide ____ ____
i. Withdrawal from social activities ____ ____

sional assessment of variables that suggest a potential still does not yield totally valid prediction data. However, the knowledgeable clinician does assess identified elements of suicidal risk that contribute to the diagnosis of suicidal potential.

Tool 8:1 lists symptomatology that should alert the nurse to the patient's potential for self-harm. Tool 8:2 identifies components of the suicide plan that are assessed for specificity, lethality, and availability. The score on this tool can range from 3, the lowest immediate risk potential, to 11, the highest risk potential. The intensity of suicidal risk based on behavioral symptoms is depicted in Tool 8:3, adapted from Hatton, Valente, and Rink.[26] Weisman and Worden devised a suicide assessment tool, Tool 8:4, based on risk and rescue factors relating to the patient's most recent suicide attempt.[27] This helps to classify patients who have made previous attempts. Tool 8:5 assists the nurse in assessing suicidal potentiality by deriving a numerical risk score.[20]

Text continued on p. 231.

TOOL 8:2   **Suicide plan assessment**

PLAN (Describe):

I. Specificity

    a. None (1 point)
    b. Vague plan, no specific plans (2 points)
    c. General idea for plan and method (3 points)
    d. Very specific plans, including details (4 points)

II. Lethality

    a. No method chosen (1 point)
    b. Low danger to life (2 points)
    c. Danger to life if not rescued (3 points)
    d. Immediate high danger to life (4 points)

III. Availability of means

    a. Not available (1 point)
    b. Available within short time (2 points)
    c. Very available (3 points)

Scoring: (range of 3-11 points)

No immediate risk   *High immediate risk*

3   11

TOOL 8:3   Assessing the degree of suicide risk

Behavior or symptom	Intensity of risk		
	Low	*Moderate*	*High*
Anxiety	Mild	Moderate	High, or panic state
Depression	Mild	Moderate	Severe
Isolation/withdrawal	Vague feelings of depression, no withdrawal	Some feelings of helplessness, hopelessness and withdrawal	Hopeless, helpless, withdrawn, and self-deprecating
Daily functioning	Fairly good in most activities	Moderately good in some activities	Not good in any activities
Resources	Several	Some	Few or none
Coping strategies/devices being utilized	Generally constructive	Some that are constructive	Predominantly destructive
Perception of significant others' support	Several who are available	Few or only one available	Only one, or none available
Psychiatric help in past	None, or positive attitude toward	Yes, and moderately satisfied with	Negative view of help received
Life-style	Stable	Moderately stable or unstable	Unstable
Alcohol/drug use	Infrequently to excess	Frequently to excess	Continual abuse
Previous suicide attempt	None, or of low lethality	None to one or more of moderate lethality	None to multiple attempts of high lethality
Disorientation/disorganization	None	Some	Marked
Suicidal plan	Vague, fleeting thoughts but no plan	Frequent thoughts, occasional ideas about a plan	Frequent or constant thought with a specific plan

From Hatton, C.L., Valente, S.M., & Rink, A. *Suicide: Assessment and intervention.* New York: Appletone-Century-Crofts, p. 56.

TOOL 8:4   Risk-rescue rating

Risk factors	*Rescue factors*
Agent used	Location
Ingestion, cutting, stabbing 1	Familiar 3
Drowning, asphyxiation, strangu- lation 2	Nonfamiliar, nonremote 2
Jumping, shooting 3	Remote 1
Impaired consciousness	Person initiating rescue
None in evidence 1	Key person 3
Confusion, semicoma 2	Professional 2
Coma, deep coma 3	Passerby 1
Lesions, toxicity	Probability of discovery by a
Mild 1	rescuer
Moderate 2	High, almost certain 3
Severe 3	Uncertain discovery 2
Reversibility	Accidental discovery 1
Good, complete recovery ex- pected 1	Accessibility to rescue
Fair, recovery expected with time 2	Asks for help 3
Poor, residuals expected, if recov- ery 3	Drops clues 2
Treatment required	Does not ask for help 1
First aid, emergency ward care 1	Delay until discovery
House admission, routine treat- ment 2	Immediate, within one hour 3
Intensive care, special treatment 3	Less than four hours 2
	Greater than four hours 1

Degree of risk, by risk score		Degree of risk, by rescue score*	
High risk:	13-15 points	Least rescuable:	5-7 points
High moderate:	11-12	Low moderate:	8-9
Moderate:	9-10	Moderate:	10-11
Low moderate:	7-8	High moderate:	12-13
Low risk:	5-6	Most rescuable:	14-15

*If there is undue delay in obtaining treatment, the final rescue score should be reduced by
one point.
From Weisman, A.D., & Worden, A.J. Risk-rescue rating in suicide assessment. *Archives of
General Psychiatry*, 1972, 26(6), 553-560.

TOOL 8:5   Assessment of suicidal potentiality

This instrument may be useful to you in the evaluation of suicidal risk, but it is only meant to be suggestive and not conclusive. The numbers in parentheses provide a range of numerical values based on a scale of one through nine—nine indicates the greatest suicidal risk. Within each category rate every item that applies to the person you are evaluating and place a numerical value on the line to the left of each applicable item. If any item is not relevant, simply disregard it completely. Next, indicate the overall evaluation for that category by averaging the numerical values (using arithmetic mean) and placing the average in the box at the end of the category. The suicidal potentiality rating is found by averaging all of the averages (i.e., the numbers in the boxes at the end of each category). The average of the averages, rounded to the nearest whole number, will give you an indication of suicidal potentiality.

Category one: AGE and SEX

_____ (7-9) male 50 or older   _____ (5-7) female 50 or older
_____ (4-6) male 35 to 49   _____ (3-5) female 35 to 49
_____ (1-3) male 15-34   _____ (1-3) female 15 to 35
    Place the average rating for this category in this box ☐

Category two: SYMPTOMS

_____ (7-9) severe depression (in the form of sleep disorders, anorexia, weight loss, withdrawal, despondence, loss of zest, apathy)
_____ (7-9) feelings of hopelessness, helplessness, or exhaustion
_____ (6-8) delusions, hallucinations, loss of contact with reality, disorientation
_____ (6-8) compulsive gambler
_____ (5-7) disorganization, confusion, chaos
_____ (4-7) alcoholism, drug addiction, homosexuality
_____ (4-6) agitation, tension, anxiety
_____ (4-6) guilt, shame, embarrassment
_____ (4-6) feelings of rage, anger, hostility, revenge
_____ (4-6) frustrated dependency
_____   other (describe) _____
    Place the average rating for this category in this box ☐

Category three: STRESS

_____ (5-9) loss of loved ones by death, divorce, or separation
_____ (4-8) loss of job, money, prestige, status
_____ (3-7) sickness, serious illness, surgery, accident, loss of limb
_____ (4-6) threat of prosecution, criminal involvement, exposure
_____ (4-6) change(s) in life, environment, setting
_____ (2-5) success, increased responsibilities
_____ (1-3) no significant stress
_____   other (describe)_____
    Place the average rating for this category in this box ☐

TOOL 8:5   Assessment of suicidal potentiality—cont'd

Category four: SUICIDAL PLAN

_____ (1-9) lethality of proposed method (e.g., gun, jumping, hanging, drowning, stabbing, poisoning, ingesting drugs or aspirin)
_____ (1-9) availability of the proposed method
_____ (1-9) specific details in the "plan of action"
_____ (1-9) specific time planned for the suicide
_____ (4-6) bizarre plans
_____ (1-9) rating of previous suicide attempt(s)
_____ (1-3) has no "plan of attack"
_____   other describe _____

Place the average rating for this category in this box ☐

Category five: ACUTE vs. CHRONIC

_____ (1-9) sudden onset of specific symptoms
_____ (4-9) recurrent outbreak of similar symptoms
_____ (4-7) long-standing traits became more pronounced lately
_____ (1-4) no specific recent change
_____   other (describe) _____

Place the average rating for this category in this box ☐

Category six: RESOURCES

_____ (7-9) no sources of support (e.g., employment, family, friends, agencies, etc.)
_____ (4-7) family and friends are available, but won't help
_____ (4-7) financial problems
_____ (2-4) available professional help
_____ (1-3) family and/or friends are willing to help
_____ (1-3) employed
_____ (1-3) finances not a problem
_____   other (describe) _____

Place the average rating for this category in this box ☐

Category seven: PRIOR SUICIDAL BEHAVIOR

_____ (6-7) one or more prior attempts of high lethality
_____ (4-6) one or more prior attempts of low lethality
_____ (3-5) history of repeated threats and depression
_____ (1-3) no prior suicidal or depressed history
_____   other (describe) _____

Place the average rating for this category in this box ☐

Continued.

TOOL 8:5   Assessment of suicidal potentiality—cont'd

Category eight: HEALTH STATUS

_____ (5-7) chronic debilitating illness
_____ (4-6) pattern of failure in previous therapy
_____ (4-6) unsuccessful experiences with physicians
_____ (2-4) psychosomatic illness (e.g., asthma, ulcer, etc.)
_____ (1-3) chronic complaints of illness or hypochondria
_____ (1-2) no medical problem
        Place the average rating for this category in this box ☐

Category nine: COMMUNICATION ASPECTS

_____ (5-7) communications were broken and efforts to reestablish com-
        munication by patient and others have met with rejection
_____ (2-4) communications have an internalized goal (e.g., to cause guilt
        in others, to force behavior, etc.)
_____ (3-5) communications directed toward the world and people in gen-
        eral
_____ (1-3) communications directed toward one or more specific people
_____   other (describe) _____
        Place the average rating for this category in this box ☐

Category ten: SIGNIFICANT OTHER

_____ (5-7) defensive, paranoid, rejected, or punishing reactions
_____ (5-7) denial of own suicidal person's need for help
_____ (4-6) no feelings of concern for the suicidal person; does not under-
        stand the suicidal person
_____ (3-5) indecisiveness, feelings of helplessness
_____ (2-4) alternates between feelings of anger and rejection and feelings
        of responsibility and a desire to help
_____ (1-3) sympathy and concern plus admission of the need for help
_____   other (describe) _____
        Place the average rating for this category in this box ☐

☐ In the box to the left, place the total of all of the average ratings for the
  ten categories. Now divide that number by 10, round off the result to
  the nearest whole number, and circle that number on the assessment
  scale below to indicate your assessment of risk.

                          1 2 3   4 5 6   7 8 9
assessment scale   _low risk_   _medium risk_   _high risk_

This scale is for _estimating_ suicidal potential was developed at the Los Angeles Suicide Prevention
Center. It is only one of many such scales and is therefore not meant to be definitive.

DIAGNOSIS

The observation of any clue suggestive of suicide calls for an immediate assessment. Suicide assessment is not a one time occurrence but rather an ongoing process that should be conducted as frequently as needed to ascertain the patient's suicidal risk. The suicide assessments can be formal or informal. During formal assessments, a thorough risk assessment is completed. An informal assessment involves observation of the patient's behaviors as preludes to suicidal ideation and planning. With the completion of each formal assessment, the nurse should elicit a commitment from the patient to contact appropriate staff, family, or friends if the suicidal feelings are imminent. Patients who are diagnosed as high suicidal risks should be observed frequently or continuously by qualified personnel.

The potential for suicide is not a specific diagnostic disorder, illness, or syndrome. It is a description of a range of behaviors that lead to self-murder. The span of behaviors as influenced by internal and external variables is depicted as follows:

INTERNAL STRESS FACTORS

No suicidal ideation	Self-destructive behavior	Suicidal ideation	Suicidal planning	Suicide attempt	Suicide completion

EXTERNAL STRESS FACTORS

Therefore the all-encompassing term "suicidal" is not a sufficient diagnosis since this does not specify the patient's location on the continuum of suicidal behavior. The box on the next page provides a taxonomy of nursing diagnoses for suicidal behavior, showing the potential for self-directed violence. These descriptive terms convey the relative risk of self-harm as elicited from an assessment interview.

CASE EXAMPLE: Assessment of Mr. Ravich

Identifying information. Mr. Ravich is a 59-year-old married male, father of two grown children. He has come to the outpatient clinic psychiatric evaluation at the request of his wife.

Presenting problem. Mr. Ravich states that he feels "depressed" and has "no interest in things anymore." He sits around the house day after day and watches television. Mr. Ravich agreed to seek help after his wife contacted their family physician.

Brief recent history. Mr. Ravich states that he was feeling fine until 6 months ago, at which time he was laid off from his job as an auto worker. He has searched for work since that time but has been unable to find a job because of his age. Over the past 2 months, Mr. Ravich has had trouble sleeping and has been eating only one meal a day. He stopped attending his Thursday poker games and rarely leaves the

---

TAXONOMY OF NURSING DIAGNOSES FOR SUICIDAL BEHAVIOR

1.10 Self-destructive behavior
    1.11 No conscious intention of death
    1.12 Awareness death may result from behavior
1.20 Suicidal ideation
    1.21 Vague, passive ideas about death being welcome
    1.22 Fleeting thoughts of active suicide, no plans
    1.23 Persistent thoughts of active suicide, no plans
1.30 Suicide planning
    1.31 Thoughts of a general plan, no specifics
    1.32 Thoughts of a plan; specific, nonlethal method
    1.33 Thoughts of a plan; specific, lethal method
    1.34 Thoughts of a detailed plan; very lethal, available means
1.40 Suicide attempt
    1.40 Nonlethal attempt, minimal medical treatment required
    1.41 Potentially lethal attempt, treatment required
    1.42 Dangerous, life-threatening attempt
1.50 Completed suicide: determination of suicide as a cause of death.

---

house. He denies any current physical illness but states he feels "tired" most of the time. He denies use of alcohol, drugs, and cigarettes. Mr. Ravich says he doesn't sleep well and paces frequently. Mr. Ravich's wife has not worked outside the home in the past but found a job 3 weeks ago as a cashier to supplement their income. Mr. Ravich has complained of insomnia and headaches for 2 months and has seen his family physician. The physician ordered diazepam (Valium) 2 mg h.s. for the insomnia.

Family history. Mr. Ravich's mother died when he was 6 years old. His father died 2 years ago at age 79. Mr. Ravich has two younger sisters, one who attempted suicide 7 years ago by driving her car off a bridge. She was paralyzed but survived. Mr. Ravich has two children who live 2000 miles away and rarely visit. He was sole supporter of his family until he lost his job. Mr. Ravich states he has a "good" relationship with his wife but feels badly that she now has to work.

Personal history. Mr. Ravich was born October 12, 1920. His mother died when he was 6 years old. After this, he spent weeks at a time with aunts and uncles while his father traveled. Mr. Ravich moved three times during his school years. He states he had "few friends." He graduated from high school and married Mrs. Ravich 2 years later. Mr. Ravich worked as a carpenter until he entered World War II as a Navy enlistee. After the war Mr. Ravich got a job as an auto worker. The Ravich's have two daughters. Their only son died shortly after birth in 1948. Mr. Ravich became despondent at this time and was suspended from his job for several weeks because of absences and tardiness. He returned to work and seemed to be functioning better. Mr. Ravich states he has had episodes in which he questions "his lot in life." He has minimal social activities, citing, "I'm a homebody." Mr. Ravich states he has considered suicide several times in his life but has only gotten to the point of sitting on his bed, gun in hand. He says he never pulled the trigger because his wife "needed" him. He says it is against his religion (Catholicism) to commit suicide. Mr. Ravich does not attend church.

Mental status examination. Mr. Ravich is a 59-year-old man who is tall and of average weight. He appears somewhat disheveled and has a beginning beard. He sat and tapped his foot throughout the interview. He maintained minimal eye contact. His mood was depressed and his affect was flat. He was alert and oriented. His speech was slow at times. His statements were organized and clear. He denied any hallucinations. He was self-condemning throughout the interview. Upon questioning, he admitted to suicidal ideation and planning. Mr. Ravich stated he isn't needed by anyone anymore. He would kill himself either with his rifle or by gassing himself in the garage. He has a rifle at home. Mr. Ravich stated he has put his personal affairs in order and has composed a will.

Summary. Mr. Ravich is a 59-year-old unemployed man who is currently a high suicidal risk. He exhibits depressed mood and flat affect. He has a definite suicide plan of high lethality and very available means. He has put his personal affairs in order. He has a history of suicidal ideation but no previous attempt. His mother died when he was six. His sister attempted suicide and is paralyzed. He is experiencing insomnia and restless agitation.

Nursing diagnosis. Mr. Ravich is a high-risk potential for suicide as a 59-year-old unemployed male with perceived social isolation, role change, history of suicidal ideation, family history of suicide, early death of mother, specific plan with lethal means and availability. Nursing diagnosis: 1.34.

Plan. Voluntary admission to the psychiatric unit. Place Mr. Ravich on 15 minute checks by staff. Mr. Ravich has agreed to this. Evaluate further for depression.

REFERENCES

1. Alvarez, A. *The savage God,* New York: Random House, Inc., 1971, p. 79.
2. Shneidman, E.S. Suicide. *Suicide and Life-Threatening Behavior,* 1981, 2(4), 198, 223, 282-285.
3. Shneidman, E.S., Ed. *On the nature of suicide.* San Francisco: Jossey-Bass, Inc., Publishers, 1969, pp. 11-16.
4. Wekstein, L. *Handbook of suicidology.* New York: Brunner/Mazel, Inc., 1979, pp. 27, 40.
5. Hoff, L.A. *People in crisis: Understanding and helping,* Menlo Park, Calif.: Addison-Wesley Publishing Co., Inc., 1978, pp. 126-130.
6. National Center for Health Statistics. Unpublished data. Hyattsville, Md.: U.S. Department of Health and Human Services, 1979.

7. Wenz, F. Effects of seasons and sociological variables on suicidal behavior. *Public Health Reports*, 1977, *92*(3), 327.
8. Beck, A.T., Resnik, H.L.P., & Lettieri, D.J. *The prediction of suicide.* Bowie, Md.: The Charles Press Publishers, Inc., 1974, p. 18.
9. Beck, A.T. *The diagnosis and management of depression.* Philadelphia: The University of Pennsylvania Press, 1973, p. 20.
10. Greyson, B. *Suicide.* Unpublished paper, The University of Michigan, 1980.
11. Pokorny, A.D. Suicide rates in various diagnostic disorders. *Journal of Nervous and Mental Disease*, 1964, *139*, 499-506.
12. Choron, J. *Suicide.* New York: Charles Scribner's Sons, 1972, p. 76.
13. Farberow, N.L. Suicide prevention in the hospital, *Hospital and Community Psychiatry*, 1981, 32(2), 99-103.
14. Freud, S. Mourning and melancholia (1917). In *Collected papers.* New York: Basic Books, Inc., Publishers, 1959.
15. Menninger, K. *Man against himself.* New York: Harcourt, Brace, 1938.
16. Durkheim, E. *Suicide: A study in sociology,* Glencoe, Ill.: Free Press, 1951.
17. Farberow, N.L., Ed. *Suicide in different cultures.* Baltimore: University Park Press, 1975.
18. Avery, D., & Winokur, G. Suicide, attempted suicide, and relapse rates in depression. *Archives of General Psychiatry*, 1978, *35*(6), 749.
19. Kaplan, R.D., Kottler, D.B., & Frances, A.J. Reliability and rationality in the prediction of suicide. *Hospital and Community Psychiatry*, 1982, *33*(3), 212.
20. Miller, M. *Suicide intervention.* Unpublished paper, The Center for Information on Suicide, San Diego, 1980.
21. Farberow, N. *Suicide inside and out.* Berkeley, Calif.: The University of California Press, 1976.
22. Anderson, N.P. Suicide in schizophrenia. *Perspectives in Psychiatric Care*, 1973, *11*(3), 111.
23. Reubin, R. Spotting and stopping the suicide patient. *Nursing '79*, 1979, *9*(4), 84.
24. Soreff, S.M. *Management of the pyschiatric emergency.* New York: John Wiley & Sons, Inc., 1981, p. 154.
25. Margolin, C.B. Evaluating suicide potential in the emergency department. Journal of Emergency Nursing, 1977, *3*, 21, 23.
26. Hatton, C.L., Valente, S.M., & Rink, A. *Suicide: Assessment and intervention.* New York: Appleton-Century-Crofts, 1977, p. 56.
27. Weisman, A.D., & Worden, A.J. Risk-rescue rating in suicide assessment. *Archives of General Psychiatry*, 1972, *26*(6), 553-560.

CHAPTER 9

ASSESSING ORGANIC
MENTAL DISTURBANCES

Our mental functioning is a major element that differentiates us from lower life forms. Our cognitive abilities allow us to store pieces of information in our memories, interpret our environment, communicate, solve problems, and make decisions about our survival needs and daily functioning. The mind is our greatest asset in promoting and maintaining a high quality of life. The organic integrity of the brain is necessary for successful human adaptation.[1]

An individual's loss of ability to think clearly, understand input from the environment, or recall information is a serious interruption in daily living. Persons experiencing organic mental disturbances have difficulty relating to their environment, expressing their needs, and, in many instances, caring for themselves. Sadly, however, medical and mental health professionals have historically paid little attention to the difficulties and needs of organically impaired patients. Often, the abnormal behavior of organically disturbed patients is seen as difficult and irritating. Although there may be a minimal awareness as to the rationale for the patient's behavior, the affliction is viewed as a lower class of medical problem. The patient who demonstrates psychiatric symptoms continues to be stigmatized by society at large and by many health care personnel. And although organically ill patients are abundant in medical-surgical facilities and in the community, their difficulties are given little credence. The end result has been a paucity of research and education regarding the etiology, clinical presentations, treatments, and even mutually agreed upon terminology.

Fortunately, mental health professionals are becoming increasingly sensitive to the existence and needs of organically impaired patients. Psychiatric symptoms caused by organic brain dysfunction have received more attention in the literature and in clinical practice over the past several years. There has been a greater emphasis on the recognition and differentiation of psychological and behavioral problems caused by organic brain involvement from psychiatric disturbances of a functional nature.

The recent surge in research and accurate diagnosis of organic mental impairment has been influenced by a variety of factors. Perhaps foremost are the technological advances in diagnostic medicine including electroencephalography, computerized tomography, electrophoresis, and hematological analysis. In addition, the changing focus of health care from an illness orientation to a promotion of well-being has caused health care professionals to take note of disturbances that interfere with cognitive, social, and personal functioning. Social factors such as the increased percentage of elderly in our population and the recognition of the prevalence of substance abuse have also contributed to the awareness of organic mental impairment.

We cannot afford to mitigate our efforts to recognize, understand, and diagnose organic mental disturbances. There is no reason for these patients and their families to needlessly suffer when curative, palliative, and comfort interventions exist. We should remember, as Pitt so vividly reminds us, that "The disoriented patient travels in a once familiar world as a stranger, at sea where once was land. Muddled, the person attempts to comprehend and cope with a changing internal universe."[2]

DEFINITION

Organic mental disturbances are temporary or permanent alterations in brain functioning that result in psychological and behavioral impairments.[3] Much confusion exists over the terminology used to describe the various organic mental disturbances. Common terms found in the literature and clinical practice include organic mental disorder, organic brain syndrome, delirium, dementia, and confusion.

The DSM-III distinguishes between the terms organic brain syndrome and organic mental disorder. Organic brain syndrome, according to the DSM-III, is a nonspecific term describing a constellation of psychological and behavioral signs and symptoms without references to etiology.[3] Clinical presentations of organic brain syndrome are manifested by impairment in memory, orientation, affect, state of consciousness, judgment, problem solving, and abstract thinking. Organic brain syndrome is not a specific neurological diagnosis, though it is a diagnostic category.[4] Organic mental disorder refers to a specific organic brain syndrome in which there is a known cause.[3] Hence organic mental disorders relate to identified medical diagnoses whereas organic brain syndromes are descriptive of clinical manifestations.

Delirium is an organic brain syndrome that features a clouded state of consciousness and reduced levels of cognitive clarity. Delirium is usually a short-term state that diminishes within several days to several weeks. Although the literature describes delirium as a reversible state, Murray postulates three possible outcomes of delirium: complete recovery, progression to dementia, or progression to coma and death.[5] Therefore reversibility is not a distinguishing characteristic between delirium and dementia. Delirium may have an insidious or acute onset, depending on the underlying cause. The mental state of delirium fluctuates, with the patient often experiencing increased clouding of consciousness at night. Synonymous terms used to describe delirium include acute organic brain syndrome, acute organic psychosis, and metabolic encephalopathy.

Dementia is a broad spectrum of brain dysfunctions evidenced by loss of intellectual abilities and personality changes. This organic brain syndrome usually persists over time; however, it can be reversed if the cause is related to trauma or a metabolic disturbance that can be effectively treated. Terms that are commonly used interchangeably with dementia include chronic organic brain syndrome and senility. Dementia may have an acute or insidious onset, depending on the causative medical condition.

The term confusion has a history of vague and imprecise clinical usage. Nurses have used the word to describe memory loss, clouding of consciousness, and disorientation. Confusion describes a variety of behaviors that include inattention, memory deficits, inappropriate verbiage, disruptive behavior, noncompliance, and failure to perform activities of daily living.[6] Wolanin describes confusion as behavior manifesting cognitive inaccessibility, in which the patient has difficulty interacting with the environment, and social unacceptability or disruptive social behaviors. Dodd has attempted to define confusion in behavioral terms related to the patient's orientation and memory, ability to communicate pain, and visual recognition of stimuli.[7] There continues to be, however, a lack of mutual understanding among nurses as to the precise definition and use of the term. Currently, confusion can mean anything that deviates from a normal mental status examination. More research is needed on this important concept.

CLASSIFICATION

Throughout the years there has been considerable confusion regarding the description and classification of organic mental disturbances. Seltzer and Frazier acknowledge that these disorders straddle a borderland between psychiatry and neurology, with each specialty viewing them from different perspectives.[8] Neurological literature discusses organic disturbances under the auspices of the individual medical diagnosis. Psychiatric literature, on the other hand, has tended to be more descriptive of the clinical syndromes. The DSM-II classified organic mental disturbances as organic brain syndromes grouped into psychotic or nonpsychotic disorders. Each psychotic or nonpsychotic disorder was further identified by cause; for example, 291.1: alcoholic psychosis, Korsakoff's psychosis.[9] Seltzer and Frazier followed the trend of previous authors by discussing organic mental disorders as acute confusional states or progressive dementias.[8]

The DSM-III attempts to refine the classification of organic mental disturbances by differentiating between organic brain syndromes and organic mental disorders. These have been defined in the previous section. The diagnostic categories for organic brain syndromes describe groupings of clinical signs and symptoms without reference to cause. These identified syndromes are heterogeneous, depicting a variety of psychiatric symptoms that represent organic disturbances. The categories discussed in this text include delirium, dementia, organic hallucinosis, organic delusional syndrome, organic affective syndrome, and organic personality syndrome. Alcohol and drug intoxication and withdrawal are presented in Chapter 10.

Delirium and dementia are syndromes that feature global impairment of cognitive abilities. The delirious or demented patient has difficulty thinking, concentrating, memorizing, and problem solving. With organic hallucinosis, the patient experiences hallucinations with no loss of intellectual functioning. In organic delusional syndrome, delusions occur in a normal state of consciousness with no cognitive impairment. The primary feature of organic affective syndrome is a major mood disturbance not attributed to a functional disorder. The patient exhibiting organic personality syndrome demonstrates a notable change in personality without evidence of a clouded sensorium or cognitive dysfunction.

The classifications of organic mental disorders are more specific to etiological considerations. The DSM-III describes two major types of disorders—dementias and substance abuse organic mental disorders. The dementias are classified as a primary degenerative dementia in which there is a global loss of intellectual abilities with progressive deteriorations and multi-infarct dementia in which there is a patchy deterioration of cognitive abilities with evident neurological signs and symptoms. Substance abuse organic mental disorders are discussed in Chapter 10.

Controversy continues to exist regarding the nosology of organic mental disorders. Continued research and clinical scrutiny are necessary in order to perfect diagnostic terminology and classification of these disturbances.

EPIDEMIOLOGY

Studies regarding the prevalence and diagnosis of organic mental disturbances have been tentative at best. Most surveys have been conducted on specific populations, usually in hospital environments. As a result, it has been difficult to extrapolate and estimate prevalence rates in the general population. Many organically impaired patients are functioning in the community or have episodes of acute organic brain syndrome during hospitalizations for medical, surgical, and obstetrical care. The occurrence of dementia has been most frequently examined, probably because of its chronicity, which facilitates study. Many deliriums, however, are the result of a variety of etiological factors that result in singular, episodic, or reversible confused states.

The elderly are most prone to dementia and delirium. Katzman postulates that 3 million or one-tenth of all persons over age 65 have some cognitive impairment.[10] Adolfsson et al. studied institutionalized patients over 65 years of age in Sweden.[11] They found that approximately one-third were experiencing some form of dementia. These researchers hypothesize that 3.7% of the population of the county in which the survey was conducted suffer from dementia.

A survey conducted by the U.S. Department of Health and Human Services in 1978 cites data regarding the diagnoses of resident patients in state and county mental hospitals.[12] For all age-groups, organic brain

---

TABLE 9:1   Diagnoses for 100 outpatients with complaints of organic mental disorder

Diagnosis	Number of patients
Primary degenerative dementia (presenile and senile onset)	43
Multi-infarct dementia	10
Dementia associated with alcoholism	7
Dementia associated with specific neurologic disorders	6
Huntington's chorea (2)	—
Pseudobulbar palsy (1)	—
Seizure disorder (2)	—
Normal-pressure hydrocephalus	1
Dementia associated with metastatic cancer	1
Dementia associated with chronic arsenic ingestion	1
Dementia associated with hypothyroidism	1
Delirium	2
Paget's disease (1)	—
Metabolic disorder (insulinoma) (1)	—
Major depressive disorder (with or without melancholia)	24
Schizophrenia	4
Memory problems of unknown etiology	1

From Maletta, G.J., et al. Organic mental disorders in a geriatric outpatient population. *American Journal of Psychiatry*, 1982, 139(4), 522.

syndrome accounted for 25,230 or 17.1% of that population nationally. The statistics demonstrate wide variability among age-groups with 4.3% of organically impaired patients under age 18 and 37.5% of the patients over age 65. A 1975 survey by the Department of Health and Human Services reports the percentage of patients diagnosed with organic brain syndrome upon discharge from nonfederal general hospital psychiatric inpatient units.[13] For both sexes, 18,981 or 3.7% of the discharge diagnoses involved organic mental disorders.

Maletta et al. describe the diagnosis of 100 outpatients at a Veterans' Administration Medical Center who were referred for complaints of organic mental disturbance. Table 9:1 shows data obtained in that study.[14] Notable results include the high number of patients ultimately diagnosed as suffering from primary degenerative dementia and the large number of patients who were actually experiencing depression and schizophrenia. The latter result exemplifies the problem in making differential diagnoses between organic mental impairments and functional disorders. This concern is of particular importance since proper diagnosis leads to effective interventions by health care professionals.

CAUSATIVE FACTORS

Organic brain syndrome and organic mental disorder are terms describing clinical manifestations of pyschiatric symptoms caused by an organic insult to the brain or central nervous system. The behavioral and psychological symptoms are the result of a multitude of anatomical and physiological disruptions that interfere with neural transmissions in critical brain pathways. The neurological insult can be caused by circulatory impairment, infectious processes, metabolic alterations, hormonal disturbances, trauma, toxic influences, including drug and alcohol intoxication and withdrawal, and degenerative disturbances.

As with any organic illness or injury, manifestations of organic mental disturbances are influenced by environmental, emotional, and personality elements. Certain factors predispose patients to develop organic mental disturbances. People over age 65 are most apt to develop dementia from degenerative processes and delirium from metabolic alterations. Young children, whose brains are still immature, are most susceptible to delirium from infections, high fevers, fluid and electrolyte imbalances, and any type of poisoning. Individuals who are markedly frightened, anxious, or depressed tend to develop organic disturbances more readily than persons who have similar medical illnesses.[15] Patients taking prescribed medications, drugs, or alcohol are also more likely to exhibit organic mental dysfunction.

The actual clinical presentation of the organic disturbance is affected by the patient's personality characteristics. The symptoms result from the interplay between an organically noxious stimulus and the immunity of the patient to withstand the insult, the major considerations of which are the personality coping mechanisms.[15] Often, the psychiatric symptoms will represent an exaggeration of the individual's usual personality. For example, a usually moody person may demonstrate wide lability of mood and affect. An obsessive individual may become more obsessed in an attempt to compensate for memory impairment. The interdependence between the organic insult and the standing personality will determine, to a large extent, the way in which the patient reacts to the mental changes.

The physiological disturbances that provoke the mental and behavioral symptoms can be caused by a variety of etiological factors. Purdie et al. reviewed 100 admissions to a large, metropolitan hospital with the diagnosis of acute organic brain syndrome to determine the common causative factors.[16] Their findings indicated that 44% of the patients were actually suffering from an exacerbation of chronic organic brain syndrome caused by dehydration or stressful environmental changes. The patients with acute organic brain syndrome were experiencing more severe systematic or cerebral insults. The leading cause of confusion was poisoning resulting from accidents, suicide, and recreation. Infections, primarily urinary tract infections, were the next major cause of the organic brain syndrome, followed by fluid and electrolyte imbalances. Table 9:2 lists the discharge diagnoses for the 100 patients participating in this study. As Purdie's study indicates, drug ingestion is a major

TABLE 9:2   **Discharge diagnoses for 100 patients with complaints of organic brain disorder**

Diagnosis	%
Systemic (toxic, metabolic, infectious)	63
Toxic	28
Infection	13
Fluid and electrolytes	12
Alcohol withdrawal	6
Endocrine	2
Hepatic encephalopathy	1
Congestive heart failure	1
CNS	22
Seizure disorder	12
Cerebrovascular disorder	4
Head injury	4
Wernicke-Korsakoff syndrome	1
Complex migraine	1
Functional	15

From Purdie, F.R., Honigman, B., & Rosen, P. Acute organic brain syndrome: A review of 100 cases. *Annals of Emergency Medicine*, 1981, *10*(9), p. 458.

cause of organic brain syndrome. These may be taken for recreational or self-destructive purposes or may be prescribed by physicians. Steroids, sedatives, barbiturates, and anesthesias in normal or above average dosages are particularly potent stimuli for organic impairment. Over-the-counter medication such as sleeping pills contain bromides and other chemicals that may trigger psychiatric symptoms.

The actual cause of the organic mental disorder must be determined so that prompt, appropriate treatment can begin. Tables 9:3 and 9:4 depict medical conditions that were found to be definitely or probably causative of the psychiatric symptoms of 9.1% of a total of 658 psychiatric outpatients reviewed by Hall et al.[17] In this study, cardiovascular, endocrine, infectious, and pulmonary disorders were the most frequent medical causes of the psychiatric symptoms.

TABLE 9:3	Medical conditions considered definitely causative of psychiatric symptoms
Psychiatric diagnosis	*Medical diagnosis*
Neurosis	
Depression	Hypothyroidism
	Pneumonia
	Infectious viral hepatitis
	Hyperthyroidism
	Hyperparathyroidism
	Hepatic insufficiency
	Mononucleosis
	Bundle branch block
	Arteriosclerotic cardiovascular disease
	Hypertension (essential)
	Metastatic carcinoma of the uterus
	Hypochromic anemia
	Peptic ulcer
Anxiety	Hyperthyroidism
	Pneumonia
	Hyperparathyroidism
	Ulcerative colitis
	Bundle branch block
	Arteriosclerotic cardiovascular disease
	Hypothyroidism
	Paroxysmal atrial tachycardia
	Hypochromic anemia
	Scabies

From Hall, R.C.W., et al. Physical illness presenting as psychiatric disease. *Archives of General Psychiatry*, 1978, 35(11), 1316.

TABLE 9:3   Medical conditions considered definitely causative of psychiatric symptoms—cont'd

Psychiatric diagnosis	*Medical diagnosis*
Reactive, unspecified	Hypertension
	Arteriosclerotic cardiovascular disease
	Neurosyphilis
	Cirrhosis
	Incipient delirium tremens
	Diabetes mellitus
	Congestive heart failure
	Chronic bronchitis
	Sphenoidal ridge meningioma
	Viral upper respiratory infection
	Cerebral insufficiency
	Hypothyroidism
Major affective	Viral pneumonia
	Rheumatoid arthritis
	Aortic stenosis
	Cerebral anoxia
	Hypothyroidism
	Erythremia
	Pernicious anemia
	Black lung
	Congestive heart failure
Schizophrenia	Diabetes mellitus
	Alzheimer's disease
	Hypoglycemia
Organic brain syndrome	Pneumonia
	Bronchogenic carcinoma
	Cirrhosis
	Pancreatitis
	Hepatoma
	Hypochromic microcytic anemia
	Emphysema
	Congestive heart failure
	Metastatic carcinoma of the uterus
	Hepatic insufficiency
Personality disorder	
Unspecified	Cerebrovascular accident
	Hypertension
	Viral pneumonia
	Rheumatoid arthritis
	Anemia
Alcoholism	Cirrhosis
	Pancreatitis
	Hepatoma
Behavior disorder of childhood	Pinworm

TABLE 9:4   **Medical conditions considered probably causative of psychiatric symptoms**

Psychiatric diagnosis	Medical diagnosis
Neurosis	
Depression	Pulmonary infarction
	Pulmonary emboli
	Hypothyroidism
	Diabetes mellitus
Anxiety	Hyperthyroidism
	Hypothyroidism
Obsessive compulsive	Diabetes mellitus
Psychosis	
Reactive, unspecified	Diabetes mellitus
	Hepatitis
	Bronchitis
	Hypochromic microcytic anemia
	Rheumatoid arthritis
	Viral pneumonia
	Mitral stenosis
	Congestive heart disease
Major affective disorder	Hyperthyroidism
	Pulmonary infarction
	Pulmonary emboli
	Congestive heart failure
	Hypertension
	Chronic bronchitis
	Pulmonary insufficiency
	Emphysema
Schizophrenia	Neurosyphilis
	Diabetes mellitus
	Pyelonephritis
	Congestive heart failure
	Infectious hepatitis
Organic brain syndrome	Congestive heart failure
	Neurosyphilis
	Hypertension
	Diabetes mellitus
	Bronchitis
	Pyelonephritis
	Infectious hepatitis
Personality disorder	
Unspecified	Sickle cell anemia
	Mitral stenosis
	Congestive heart failure
	Rheumatic heart disease
Hysterical	Juvenile diabetes mellitus
Sociopathic	Viral pneumonia
Alcoholism	Hepatitis
	Bronchitis
	Hypochromic microcytic anemia
	Rheumatoid arthritis
Drug dependence	Hyperthyroidism

From Hall, R.C.W. et al. Physical illness presenting as psychiatric disease. *Archives of General Psychiatry*, 1978, 35(11), 1316.

TABLE 9:5   Diagnoses in 222 patients evaluated for dementia

Diagnosis	Number	Percent
Atrophy of unknown cause	113	51
Vascular disease	17	8
Normal pressure hydrocephalus	14	6
Dementia in alcoholics	13	6
Intracranial masses	12	5
Huntington's chorea	10	5
Depression	9	6
Drug toxicity	7	3
Dementia (uncertain)	7	3
Other	20	9

From Wells, C.E. Chronic brain disease: An overview. *American Journal of Psychiatry,* 1978, *135*(1), 3.

Delirium can be caused by a host of physiological occurrences that are time limited. Dementia, however, is often the result of a more permanent or progressive brain disturbance. Dementia involves the atrophy of brain structures, including loss of nerve cells, changes in the vascular system, alterations in neurons, and the development of senile plaques. Dementia can also result from vascular disease, normal pressure hydrocephalus, brain tumors, subarachnoid hemorrhage, and vitamin B-12 deficiency. Table 9:5 lists the diagnoses of 222 patients evaluated for dementia.[18] The DSM-III describes two major dementias, primary degenerative and multi-infarct dementia. Studies indicate that degenerative diseases such as Alzheimer's disease account for over 50% of dementia, whereas brain infarction and ischemia contribute to less than 10% of the diagnoses of dementia.[18]

CLINICAL PRESENTATION

Organic mental disturbances appear as a heterogenous grouping of psychiatric symptoms that can be difficult to differentiate from functional illness. Although superficially the symptoms of organic and functional disorders appear similar, closer scrutiny reveals subtle differences that will be discussed in the following pages. Table 9:6 depicts some of these differences.

Patients experiencing organic mental disorders may or may not be aware of their impairments. For those who are, an open acknowledgment or request for assistance may provoke feelings of embarrassment and vulnerability. Many people lack insight into their problem because

TABLE 9:6	Symptoms of organic mental disorders as compared to functional mental disorders

Organic mental disorders	Functional mental disorders
Has an identifiable organic base	Does not have an identifiable organic base
Emotional blunted affect or wide range of affect, including sudden or insidious personality changes	Wide range of affect; rarely do personality changes occur outside the context of explainable stress
Memory loss begins with recent events and progresses to remote events	Memory loss relates to emotionally significant material, either recent or remote
Thinking is concrete	Thinking may be concrete or very abstract in a bizarre manner
Time disorientation is usually within the patient's lifetime	Time disorientation may be years off, with symbolic meaning
Patients exhibiting place disorientation believe they are in a familiar place or somewhere they could actually be. Patients tend to lose their way back to homes, rooms, etc.	Patients believe they are in some symbolic place that relates to their emotional state and delusions
Patients disoriented to person identify others as people close to them	Patients identify others or self as symbolic people
Difficulty problem-solving because of cognitive deficits is evident	Difficulty problem-solving because of emotional state
Sensory-perceptual disturbances are usually illusions and visual hallucinations	Sensory-perceptual disturbances are usually auditory hallucinations
Delusion and bizarre thought content are delusional and seek to explain reality	Delusions and thought content can be very bizarre and symbolic with emotional meaning
Symptoms tend to fluctuate over the day, generally worsening at night	Symptoms tend to remain stable

of the cognitive deficits. Others tend to deny their difficulties with thinking and functioning and make attempts to mask the problem through
rationalization or overcompensation. Since the symptoms of organic
mental disturbances can be mild and subtle, the patient's attempts may
be successful and the nurse or family fails to notice the actual symptom
onset. Initially, patients may begin to repeat their own statements and
questions. Signs of mild forgetfulness are often discounted with remarks
such as, "Gee, I must be getting old!" Sometimes, patients become
unable to carry out instructions for care and make errors in completing
tasks. Agitation and irritability become more pronounced.

The onset of these symptoms can be acute or insidious, depending
on the cause of the organic problem. The intensity of organic mental
disorders can range from mild to severe. As the severity progresses, the
patient becomes increasingly incapacitated by confusion, loss of cognitive abilities, and disturbances in behavior, affect, and social and occupational functioning.

Any patient with an organic problem is a potential candidate for
organic brain syndrome. Likewise, the behavioral, emotional, and cognitive symptoms of an identified psychiatric patient could result from
organicity. Occasionally, the psychiatric symptoms will become evident
before the development of physical symptoms. The severity of these
symptoms generally progresses as the physical condition worsens. Studies on dementia, for example, have demonstrated a high correlation
between degrees of intellectual impairment and the amount of cerebral
atrophy.[19] Early detection of symptoms can provide clues as to the nature
of the underlying organic insult.

Assessment of the organically impaired patient usually occurs following a request by a family member, friend, employer, or other health
care professional who has become concerned about the patient's behavior. Hospitalized patients on medical-surgical units or in the emergency
department are observed by the nurse to be agitated, disoriented, confused, and unable to follow instructions and to exhibit clouded senso-
riums. Nurses in the community, physicians' offices, and clinics are
likely to encounter demented patients who have been brought in by
family or friends who are distraught over the patient's memory impairment, personality changes, cognitive deficits, and diminished functioning. It is worthwhile to note that any individual in the community or in
a health care setting can develop an organic mental disturbance, particularly elderly persons or those with physical illness or injury.

Cognitive manifestations

Impairments in cognition are the most striking features of organic
mental disturbances. Major areas of deficit include memory, orientation,

attention and arousal, judgment, intellect, perception, and thought processes. Although these abnormalities exhibit wide ranges of variability and acuity, the nurse is able to elicit a reliable indication of the patient's cognitive deficits by conducting a thorough psychiatric interview and mental status examination. It is often helpful to begin the interview by asking several open-ended questions, such as "What brought you to the clinic today?" and "Tell me what has been going on." Persons with cognitive impairment may have difficulty responding to these open-ended statements because of memory loss, attention deficits, or problems with abstract thinking. If the patient is unable to answer or responds with a concrete statement, such as "A car brought me here" or "The lights go on," the nurse should ask short, simple, direct questions that the patient is able to answer.

Memory loss is a major component of dementia and delirium. This can be the result of neurological impairment in information storage, information processing, and information recall. The loss can be mild or severe depending on the nature of the structural or physiological insult. Recent memory is usually affected first. The nurse may initially notice a hospitalized patient asking questions such as "When will I get my bath?" shortly after receiving the morning bath. Simple forgetfulness may be apparent to family members who describe the patient as "constantly losing things" or "not following through with tasks such as mailing a letter." Forgetfulness is evident during a mental status examination when the patient is unable to recall or reproduce material within several minutes. The individual often cannot recall the names of three objects given at the beginning of the mental status examination or the name of the current president. As the memory impairment becomes more severe, long-term or remote memory loss becomes apparent. The patient is unable to recall personal experiences in chronological order, gives erroneous dates for a birthday or anniversary, or fails to provide names of significant others in the past. In organic mental disorders, memory impairment progresses from recent to remote with no discrimination as to the type of data that becomes part of the memory loss. Patients with functional disorders, however, usually do not demonstrate consistent recent or remote memory loss but rather utilize the loss as a protective mechanism to forget particular disturbing events or feelings.

CASE EXAMPLE: Mary, age 38, and Tom, age 40, are patients on a mental health unit undergoing psychiatric assessment for recent behavioral problems. Both exhibit memory loss during mental status testing. Mary has excellent recent memory recall but is unable to describe her life during her early teenage years. The nurse knows from Mary's family that her mother and father were killed in an automobile accident when Mary was 13. Tom, however, is able to describe his past in vivid detail but cannot remember current day-to-day events, names of current political and sports figures, and three objects given him to remember at the beginning of the mental status examination. The nurse begins to suspect that Tom may have an organic mental impairment resulting from the nature of his memory loss.

Memory loss and disorientation are often interconnected symptoms observed in organically impaired patients. Orientation involves the individual's ability to grasp the environment and make sense out of the surroundings. The patient with organic brain syndrome struggles to interpret the environment and, in doing so, attempts to explain and manage daily living activities by relating them to concrete, previous experiences. Disorientation occurs when the patient is unable to integrate and recall multiple environmental stimuli. The disorientation can relate to time, place and situation, or persons. There may be deficits in all or one of these areas. The nurse assesses these components by asking very specific questions during the mental status examination such as "What is today's date?" or "Where are you now?" A response such as "It's July 18th" or "I'm in the hospital" needs to be investigated further since patients frequently have only part of the information correct. More detailed questioning such as "July 18th, what year?" or "Which hospital are you in?" reveals the actual orientation of the patient.

Orientation to time is the most common impairment evidenced by patients with organic mental disorders. Occasionally time disorientation results from lack of amount or variety of sensory stimulation. Organically impaired patients may not know the hour, date, or year, but they usually give the interviewer a date that is close to the actual one or a date within their lifetimes. A person with functional impairment, however, often gives a date many years away or one that is symbolic in some way.

An organic disorientation to place involves a lack of situational awareness. Patients believe they are at home or in another hospital, places where they could realistically be. In addition, these individuals may lose their way when they leave their homes or rooms and not know where they are or how to get to their desired location. Persons with functional disorders think that they are in symbolic places such as heaven, hell, or jail. Their disorientation to place is recognized as part of their delusional and abnormal thinking.

Disorientation to person is often considered the most severe orientation impairment. This occurs when the patient mistakes unfamiliar persons for familiar ones. In its most acute form, disorientation to person involves patients' inability to identify themselves. Organically impaired patients usually know their own names and retain a sense of identity but identify strangers as those close to them. An elderly gentleman, for example, may call the nurse by his granddaughter's name. Functionally impaired patients, however, may discount their current identities or assume new ones. They also identify others as strangers, enemies, or allies, composing a delusional thought system.

Confusion occurs as the patient experiences disorientation and memory loss and becomes mentally scattered. In delirium a clouding of consciousness occurs in which the patient is unable to shift, focus, and sustain attention to environmental stimuli.[3] Patients are usually awake and able to respond to others, although their mental arousal state may be dulled or hypervigilant. They are easily distracted by multiple incoming stimuli. Patients experiencing dementia usually do not exhibit a clouding of consciousness as part of their confusion.

Confusion becomes more pronounced when the patient encounters decreased sensory stimulation. This phenomenon often occurs at night and is popularly referred to as "sundowner's syndrome." This explains why day nurses frequently insist a patient is clear and coherent whereas the evening or night nurses describe the same patient as confused, disoriented, or agitated. An organic confusion is inconsistent with the patient exhibiting clear periods between scattered confused episodes. This feature of organic confusion differs from a functional confusion that is consistent and does not worsen at night.

A primary feature of organic brain syndrome is a global loss of intellectual functioning. The patient begins to have difficulty with problem solving, following simple instructions, and abstract thinking. Demented patients suffer a loss of intellectual ability so severe that it begins to interfere with social and employment functioning.[3] During a mental status examination, the patient experiencing dementia will demonstrate concrete interpretation of proverbs and the inability to describe similarities and differences between objects. Impaired concentration and judgment may also be evident. A hospitalized patient, for example, may pull out the IV apparatus or a patient at home may take a letter from the mailbox and throw it in the trash. Although functionally disturbed individuals may also exhibit impaired abstraction, problem-solving, concentration, and judgment, the deficits relate to the emotional state of the patient. In addition, patients with functional disorders can be extremely abstract in a bizarre or symbolic fashion, for example, a pyschotic woman who describes the differences between an orange and an apple as "God's own preference for particular tastes."

Sensory-perceptual disturbances are common in delirium. Patients may experience illusions and hallucinations. Illusions occur when the delirious person misinterprets environmental stimuli. Visual illusions, in which the patient mistakenly identifies an object as something else, are most predominant. Hallucinations that result from organic impairment are primarily visual. This is in contrast with functional hallucinations that tend to be auditory. One exception is alcohol hallucinosis in which auditory hallucinations are most common. Any patient exhibiting visual hallucinations should be suspected of being delirious. Visual hallucinations and illusions are the symptoms most discriminative of organic psychiatric disorders.[17] Hallucinations that occur in the absence of clouding of consciousness and loss of intellectual abilities are suggestive of organic hallucinosis.

Thought process and content are usually disrupted with organic mental disturbances. The delirious patient exhibits a clouded sensorium that impedes clear, rational, and logical thinking ability. The patient's flow of thoughts may be loose, rambling, or disconnected. Thought content can become bizarre and delusional. Many of the delusions are transient and serve to reinforce the reality of the sensory-perceptual experiences. They may seem almost believable to the interviewer. The delusions experienced by the patient with a functional disorder, however, are usually more bizarre and exude persecutory, religious, and other symbolic themes. Organic delusional syndrome is one organic mental disorder in which delusions are the predominant feature in the absence of any clouding of consciousness or hallucinations. These delusions may be bizarre and persecutory in nature. Demented patients are delusional usually only to the extent of reinforcing their disorientation. Confabulation is used by persons with dementia as a means of filling in the gaps created by loss of memory. A patient can create an entire imagery of events and experiences, all of which are developed to explain the past.

High cortical functions such as language, spatial conceptualization, writing, and constructional ability are often impaired with dementia. Patients have difficulty following simple instructions that involve such motor-perceptual skills as drawing a picture or arranging blocks. There may be inability to correctly identify objects (agnosia) or to carry out motor activities despite complete comprehension of the instruction (apraxia).[3]

CASE EXAMPLE: Mr. Bissonette, age 68, was admitted to a general medical unit for a thorough diagnostic workup. He has not "felt well" for several months and has been sleeping longer hours. Mr. Bissonette has continued to work and is currently vice president of a management consulting firm. His colleagues have noted progressive "forgetfulness" to the point where business has been lost because of the failure of Mr. Bissonette to follow through on client issues. During the initial assessment interview, Mr. Bissonette is hesitant in answering questions. He gives the nurse an incorrect date and is unable to quickly name the hospital. The patient provides concrete interpretations of proverbs: "I wouldn't cry over spilled milk because I would be busy cleaning it up." Mr. Bissonette does not believe that anything is wrong with him; he just needs some rest. He is unable to place shaped blocks in matching inserts. The nurse suspects that Mr. Bissonette may be experiencing the organic brain syndrome of dementia.

Emotional and behavioral manifestations

The first symptoms of delirium are often restlessness and irritability. In fact, clinicians warn that any nighttime agitation is a probable indication of the onset of delirium.[15] Concomitantly, the patient may describe vivid nightmares and disturbed sleep patterns. As the delirium progresses, the individual has difficulty distinguishing between dream activity and reality.

Delirious patients are frightened, anxious, and apprehensive. As the irritability increases, they may become uncooperative with care, combative, angry, suspicious, and prone to rages. At some level, patients have insight into their predicament and may experience depression.

Demented and delirious patients can experience labile, intense affect. People may alternatively laugh and cry irrespective of the environmental circumstances. In organic affective syndrome, the patient exhibits a disturbance in mood of the magnitude of mania or major depressive disorder. This occurs without a clouding of consciousness or loss of cognitive abilities. This disorder is differentiated from functional mood disturbances by evidence of organic abnormality as a causative factor.

Many organically impaired patients exhibit a flat, dull, or unresponsive affect. The nurse who observes such a blunted affect will find its quality uniquely stark as contrasted to the apathetic mood and dulled affect that accompany many functional disorders. This type of affect is most notable with demented patients.

Personality changes are common features of organic brain disorders. The patient has difficulty with activities of daily living, including dress and hygiene. Persons may ignore grooming habits and become disheveled and slovenly. Any change in usual functioning such as changes of routine or location can confuse and upset the organically impaired patient. A mellow, good-natured individual may start to exhibit self-destructive qualities. Impulse control becomes diminished and socially unacceptable behavior, such as coarse language, sexual provocation, recklessness, and disregard for rules, is evident. One specific disturbance, organic personality syndrome, occurs when there is a major change in personality or behavior. Primary symptoms include emotional ability, impaired impulse control, apathy, or suspiciousness. There is no clouded sensorium or loss of cognitive abilities.

The specific changes in personality reflect more pronounced characteristics of the patient's usual personality or an alteration of the premorbid traits. The manner in which individuals react to the organic insult depends on the location and severity of the impairments and their past life experiences and personality structures. For example, a usually obsessive-compulsive person experiencing dementia may become even more rigid and inflexible in routine in an attempt to compensate for the deficits or may neglect personal hygiene and become untidy and careless.

Motor activity may also be altered in organic mental disorders. In delirium psychomotor activity can be accelerated, in which patients are agitated and restless, or diminished, in which they become apathetic and listless. The nurse frequently observes delirious patients picking at their bedcovers or groping at bedrails. This can abruptly shift to sluggish withdrawal. Demented patients exhibit a variety of changes in motor activity. They may pace or wander aimlessly. Perseveration, repetitive movements such as constant tapping or chewing, often becomes evident as the dementia progresses. Patients may also demonstrate ataxia or peculiar wide gaits.

Social manifestations

The organically impaired patient has difficulty continuing to function in home, social, educational, and work environments. Many of these persons are unaware that they have a physical problem that is provoking the psychiatric symptomatology. As patients' behavior changes and usual tasks become complex challenges, they deny the problem or use an array of coping strategies in attempt to preserve normal functioning.

The delirious patient with a clouded state of consciousness is unable to focus on job, family, friends, or routine tasks. The delirium, if self-induced by drug or alcohol abuse, can be a mechanism that distances the patient from current pressures or unhappiness by fogging reality. Fortunately, most causes of delirium are short-lived, if treated properly, and the patient is able to resume usual functioning.

Social behaviors most apparent with the insidious onset of dementia are lack of initiative and loss of interest in usual activities. The patient may stop attending social events and seemingly withdraw from significant others. As a result of the cognitive deficits such as memory loss and impaired problem-solving ability, the patient's occupational performance begins to erode. Assignments are not completed, creativity and conceptual abilities become nonexistent, and routine tasks become time consuming and difficult. Spouses or significant others note these same problems at home.

As the symptoms progress, employers, colleagues, friends, and family members tend to become upset and angry. It may become quite difficult to live with patients who are irritable and combative and who demonstrate poor impulse control. Relationships among family members become strained and unpleasant. The family becomes confused by the variance in the patient's behavior and functioning. These feelings may be intensified when there is an absence of any previous medical or psychiatric history. Significant others occasionally deny the initial clues and rationalize the patient's unexplained behavior: "He's working too hard" or "We all have bad days." Some families become quite protective of the impaired member and resent comments by others noting the changes in the patient's behavior. In time, family and friends describe fear, depression, and feelings of being overwhelmed. This is particularly apparent when a diagnosis of irreversible organic brain syndrome has been made.

COMMON PHYSICAL SYMPTOMS SEEN WITH ORGANIC MENTAL DISORDERS

Symptom

Sleep disorder	Lymphadenopathy
Severe weakness	Severe anorexia
Extreme fatigue	Dyspnea
Inability to concentrate	Arrhythmia (perceived by patient)
Memory loss	Paroxysmal nocturnal dyspnea
Change in speech	Costal vertebral angle pain
Auditory hallucinations	Chest pain
Chest pain	Wheezing
Intermittent tachycardia	Diminished coordination
Recent nocturia	Skin has recently become dry
Recent-onset confusion	Lost all desire to eat
Tremulousness	Recent fragility of hair
Productive sputum	Ankle and/or pretibial edema
Urinary frequency	Diminished sense of touch
Dyspnea on exertion	New and different headache
Recent personality change	Neck pain
Paresthesias	Difficulty with mastication
New cough	Two-pillow orthopnea
Polyuria	Recent change in menstrual periods
Pleuritic pain	Recent muscular weakness
Visual hallucinations	Dysuria

From Hall, R.C.W., et al. Physical illness presenting as psychiatric disease. *Archives of General Psychiatry*, 1978, *35*(11), 1318.

Physical manifestations

Organic mental disturbances are the result of physiological and structural abnormalities that impair normal brain functioning. Specific physical disorders that cause psychiatric symptoms have been discussed earlier. The nurse should be alert to the types of patients most susceptible to organic mental disorders, including elderly, young children, substance abusers, and any patient in whom a physical ailment has been diagnosed. A list of physical symptoms that have been found to be correlated with organic mental disturbances is depicted in the material on the opposite page.

ASSESSMENT TOOLS

A meaningful number of patients exhibiting psychiatric symptoms are actually suffering from physical illness.[17] Therefore the most significant diagnostic indicators of organic mental disturbances are phsyical examinations and laboratory screening. Purdie et al. recommend a complete physical examination, a complete blood count, BUN, glucose, calcium, electrolytes, toxicology screen, and urinalysis as routine procedures for any patient suspected of having an organic mental disorder.[16] Research, however, demonstrates that certain hallucinogens such as PCP and LSD may not be detected in toxicology screens because of their close relationship to neurotransmitters.[16] In addition, an electroencephalogram (EEG), computed tomography (CT) scan, and lumbar puncture should be conducted for definitive diagnosis of probable brain dysfunction.

A physical examination should include a thorough health history. Often, patients are reticent to describe seemingly inconsequential symptoms, stresses, or changes in habits and behaviors. However, it is extremely important to understand not only the presenting problems but any physical ailments, medication ingestion, and stresses the patient may have experienced in the recent or remote past. A comprehensive drug history should include prescription and over-the-counter medications. Many nonprescription drugs such as sleeping aids, diet pills, and cold remedies contain chemicals that can cause delirium.

Nurses can be instrumental in advocating that the patient receive adequate diagnostic screening. Frequently, nurses are in the most opportune positions to observe the patient's symptomatology on a short-term or longitudinal basis. Any unexplained cognitive, behavioral, and emotional changes, particularly when there is no previous psychiatric history, should be assessed for organic mental disorder. Nurses also need to be cognizant of the results of completed diagnostic tests to assure that appropriate health care intervention is initiated.

The conjoint use of physical assessment and diagnostic testing, mental status examinations, and behavioral checklists provides a comprehensive battery of assessment tools to assist in identifying the accurate nursing and psychiatric diagnoses of organic mental disorders. Behavioral descriptions of a patient's mental status are imperative for assessing organic mental disturbances. Tools 9:1 and 9:2 will assist the nurse with data collection and classification regarding delirium and dementia. The symptoms listed are not definitive diagnostic criteria. The reader is referred to the DSM-III for specific criteria.

Tool 9:3 was devised by Folstein, Folstein, and McHugh as a method

---

TOOL 9:1   Brief assessment for delirium

Does the patient exhibit:	Yes	No
1. Clouding of consciousness*	___	___
2. Decreased attention span	___	___
3. Decreased concentration	___	___
4. Disorientation to:		
a. Time	___	___
b. Place	___	___
c. Person	___	___
5. Memory impairment		
a. Recent	___	___
b. Remote	___	___
6. Inability to follow instructions	___	___
7. Visual hallucinations*	___	___
8. Illusions*	___	___
9. Impaired problem solving	___	___
10. Concrete thinking	___	___
11. Impaired judgment	___	___
12. Bizarre, delusional thinkings	___	___
13. Confused, rambling speech	___	___
14. Irritability, agitation, restlessness*	___	___
15. Nighttime agitation*	___	___
16. Listlessness	___	___
17. Anxious, fearful affect	___	___
18. Personality changes	___	___
19. Waxing and waning of symptoms*	___	___
20. Evidence of organic abnormality*	___	___

*Strongly suggestive of delirium.

of assessing the cognitive status of patients.[20] This test provides the clinician with baseline data about the patient's cognitive abilities that can be used as a reference for assessing deterioration and improvement.

The Set Test, developed by Isaacs and Kennie, can assist the nurse in assessing dementia.[21] The patient is asked to name as many items as possible in any four general categories such as countries, states, trees, and colors. For each item named, the patient is given one point. The goal is to achieve ten items in each category. A score of fifteen or less is indicative of dementia and a score of 15 to 24 is suggestive of dementia.

There are several simple tests the nurse can administer to assess cognitive impairment. The patient can be asked to perform commands such as touching right hand to left shoulder or left hand to right knee.

TOOL 9:2   Brief assessment for dementia

Does the patient exhibit:	Yes	No
1. Memory loss*		
a. Recent	——	——
b. Remote	——	——
2. Concrete thinking*	——	——
3. Decreased concentration	——	——
4. Decreased attention span	——	——
5. Impaired judgment	——	——
6. Inability to follow instructions*	——	——
7. Failure to complete tasks*	——	——
8. Impaired problem solving	——	——
9. Clear state of consciousness	——	——
10. Impaired drawing, writing*	——	——
11. Inability to assemble blocks, sticks*	——	——
12. Personality changes	——	——
13. Diminished impulse control	——	——
14. Blunted, dulled affect*	——	——
15. Euphoric, labile effect	——	——
16. Irritable, depressed mood	——	——
17. Impaired social functioning	——	——
18. Impaired occupational functioning	——	——
19. Consistency of symptoms	——	——
20. Evidence of organic abnormality*	——	——

*Strongly suggestive of dementia.

TOOL 9:3	**"Mini-mental state"**	

Patient _____

Examiner _____

Date _____

"MINI-MENTAL STATE"

Maximum score	Score	Orientation
5	( )	What is the (year) (season) (date) (day) (month)?
5	( )	Where are we: (state) (county) (town) (hospital) (floor)?

		Registration
3	( )	Name 3 objects: 1 second to say each. Then ask the patient all 3 after you have said them. Give 1 point for each correct answer. Then repeat them until he learns all 3. Count trials and record.
		Trials_____

		Attention and calculation
5	( )	Serial 7's. 1 point for each correct. Stop after 5 answers. Alternatively spell "world" backwards.

		Recall
3	( )	Ask for the 3 objects repeated above. Give 1 point for each correct.

		Language
9	( )	Name a pencil, and watch (2 points)
		Repeat the following "No ifs, ands or buts." (1 point)
		Follow a 3-stage command:
		"Take a paper in your right hand, fold it in half, and put it on the floor" (3 points)
		Read and obey the following:
		Close your eyes (1 point)
		Write a sentence (1 point)
		Copy design (1 point)
		Total score
		ASSESS level of consciousness along a continuum

Alert	Drowsy	Stupor	Coma

INSTRUCTIONS FOR ADMINISTRATION OF "MINI-MENTAL STATE" EXAMINATION

Orientation

(1) Ask for the date. Then ask specifically for part omitted, e.g., "Can you also tell me what seaon it is?" One point for each correct.

(2) Ask in turn "Can you tell me the name of this hospital?" (town, county, etc.). One point for each correct.

Registration

Ask the patient if you may test his memory. Then say the names of 3 unrelated objects, clearly and slowly, about one second for each. After have said all 3, ask him to repeat them. This first repetition determines his score (0-3) but keep saying them until he can repeat all 3, up to 6 trials. If he does not eventually learn all 3, recall cannot be meaningfully tested.

Attention and calculation

Ask the patient to begin with 100 and count backwards by 7. Stop after 5 subtractions (93, 86, 79, 72, 65). Score the total number of correct answers.

If the patient cannot or will not perform this task, ask him to spell the word "world" backwards. The score is the number of letters in correct order, e.g., dlrow = 5, dlorw = 3.

Recall

Ask the patient if he can recall the 3 words you previously asked him to remember. Score 0-3.

Language

Naming: Show the patient a wrist watch and ask him what it is. Repeat for pencil. Score 0-2.

Repetition. Ask the patient to repeat the sentence after you. Allow only one trial. Score 0 or 1.

3-Stage command: Give the patient a piece of plain blank paper and repeat the command. Score 1 point for each part correctly executed.

Reading: On a blank piece of paper print the sentence "Close your eyes," in letters large enough for the patient to see clearly. Ask him to read it and do what it says. Score 1 point only if he actually closes his eyes.

Writing: Give the patient a blank piece of paper and ask him to write a sentence for you. Do not dictate a sentence, it is to be written spontaneously. It must contain a subject and verb and be sensible. Correct grammar and punctuation are not necessary.

Copying: On A clean piece of paper, draw intersecting pentagons, each side about 1 in., and ask him to copy it exactly as it is. All 10 angles must be present and 2 must intersect to score 1 point. Tremor and rotation are ignored.

Estimate the patient's level of sensorium along a continuum, from alert on the left to coma on the right.

Reprinted with permission from *Journal of Psychiatric Research*, vol. 123, Folstein, M.F., Folstein S.E., & McHugh, P.R., "Mini-mental state": A practical method for grading the cognitive state of patients for the clinician, Copyright 1975, Pergamon Press, Ltd.

The nurse can have the patient draw simple pictures such as a man, a tree, and a house or arrange sticks in a specified shape. If the patient is hesitant or unable to carry out any of the above tasks, organic mental disturbance should be suspected.

The mental status examination is an excellent indication of cognitive impairment. All components should be thoroughly assessed and documented. When conducting the examination, the nurse needs to be sensitive to the patient's ability to respond to the questions. If it becomes apparent that the patient is having difficulty answering questions and performing tasks, the nurse should avoid promoting patient frustrations and not pursue those particular aspects.

DIAGNOSIS
Nursing diagnosis of organic mental disturbances

Organically impaired patients are individuals who unexpectedly experience mild to severe behavioral, emotional, physical, and social disturbances. The physical ailment creates havoc with the individual's usual routine, life-style, and psychological functioning. Nurses collect data as to the patient's specific symptoms, problems, needs, and strengths and analyze that data to diagnose health care problems amenable to nursing intervention.

The box on the facing page identifies nursing diagnoses most applicable to organically impaired patients. These classifications of nursing inferences can assist the nurse in planning appropriate care with the patient. Additional nursing diagnoses relating to specific physical alterations may serve as useful adjuncts in conceptualizing patients' needs and planning relevant care. The reader is referred to the Kim and Moritz text on *Classification of Nursing Diagnoses* for supplemental diagnoses relating to physiological functioning.[22]

Psychiatric diagnoses of organic mental disturbances

Theoretically, the signs and symptoms of organic mental disturbances appear to be rather clear-cut. The novice clinician, however, soon learns that these symptoms can be elusive and misleading. Differentiating organic and functional illnesses requires fine discrimination abilities in tandem with astute clinical observation and assessment skills. Patients with physically induced psychiatric symptoms are frequently misdiagnosed as having functional illness. On the other hand, elderly patients are often misdiagnosed as suffering from organic brain syndrome when in actuality they are depressed.

Delirium and dementia are the two psychiatric diagnoses of organic brain syndrome most difficult to differentiate. Delirium involves a clouded sensorsium whereas in dementia the patient is clear but cognitively impaired. Patients may exhibit both syndromes. Depression is charac-

TAXONOMY OF NURSING DIAGNOSES FOR ORGANIC MENTAL DISORDERS

1. Sensory-perceptual alterations
   1.10 Hallucinations
       1.11 Visual
       1.12 Auditory
   1.20 Illusions
   1.30 Agitation and restlessness
   1.40 Change in usual response to stimuli
2. Alterations in thought processes
   2.10 Impaired memory
       2.11 Recent
       2.12 Remote
   2.20 Disorientation
       2.21 Time
       2.22 Place
       2.23 Person
   2.30 Altered levels of consciousness
   2.40 Impaired problem-solving
   2.50 Impaired abstraction ability
   2.60 Impaired attention and concentration
   2.70 Inability to follow verbal commands
   2.80 Inappropriate, unrealistic thought content
   2.90 Impaired judgment and insight
3. Impaired verbal communication
   3.10 Inability to speak logically and coherently
   3.20 Inability to express thoughts and feelings
   3.30 Inappropriate verbalizations
4. Ineffective individual coping
   4.10 Impaired social functioning
   4.20 Impaired relationships with significant others
   4.30 Impaired occupational functioning
   4.40 Impaired cognitive abilities
   4.50 Impaired ability to carry out daily activities
5. Self-care deficit
   5.10 Impaired ability to maintain personal hygiene
   5.20 Impaired ability to maintain adequate grooming
   5.30 Impaired ability to feed self
   5.40 Impaired ability to toilet self
   5.50 Impaired ability to adapt in environment

terized by a major disturbance in mood that secondarily affects cognitive functioning, whereas dementia and delirium involve loss of intellectual abilities as a primary feature.

The following outline lists primary psychiatric diagnoses applicable to organic mental disturbances that have been discussed in this chapter.

The reader is referred to the DSM-III for additional diagnoses and specific diagnostic criteria.[3]

I. Organic brain syndromes
   A. Delirium
   B. Dementia
   C. Organic hallucinosis
   D. Organic delusional syndrome
   E. Organic affective syndrome
   F. Organic personality syndrome
II. Organic mental disorders
   A. Dementia
      1. Primary degenerative dementia
      2. Multi-infarct dementia

CASE EXAMPLE: Assessment of Mrs. Dillow.

Identifying information: Mrs. Dillow is a 56-year-old housewife, mother of two children. She is admitted to the mental health unit from the Emergency Department.

Presenting problem: Mrs. Dillow states she feels "scared all the time." She was brought to the Emergency Department by her husband after being found hiding in the bathroom and rambling incoherently. Her tentative E.R. diagnosis is paranoid schizophrenia.

Brief recent history. According to her husband, Mrs. Dillow has been mildly depressed since the marriage of her youngest child 3 months ago. She has had difficulty sleeping but has maintained her normal activities until 2 weeks ago when she stopped going to work. Mrs. Dillow is a secretary in a local bank. Mr. Dillow reports that during the past 2 weeks, the patient has become agitated, suspicious, and withdrawn. Mrs. Dillow has no current physical illnesses. She denies use of alcohol and cigarettes. She has taken a nonprescription sleeping medication for 2 months to help her fall asleep.

Family history. Mrs. Dillow had an unremarkable childhood and her mother and father are currently living. The patient's family states there is no history of family discord. Mrs. Dillow has two brothers in the area, both very concerned about her. Mr. Dillow is a chemical engineer and the family is financially stable.

Personal history. Mrs. Dillow's childhood was unremarkable. She graduated from a secretarial college and has been employed throughout her life. She was married at age 23. Mr. Dillow describes his wife as being "very close to all of us" and as having a difficult time since the youngest daughter married and moved out of state. Mrs. Dillow is involved in church activities, the Women's League, and the American Red Cross. She has stopped participating in these affairs over the past 2 weeks. There is no known psychiatric history.

Mental status examination. Mrs. Dillow is a thin woman who appears disheveled and pale. She paced the room during most of the interview.

Her speech was rapid and, at times, incoherent. She was suspicious of the interviewer's motives and stated she couldn't understand why she was "put away." Her mood was suspicious and depressed. Her affect was blunted but hostile at times. Her thoughts were intermittently loose and tangential. Mrs. Dillow was disoriented to time and place. She was confused and repeated several statements. She refused to cooperate with specific cognitive testing such as serial sevens. She did respond to one proverb: "People who live in glass houses break windows with stones." She was unable to respond to a request to turn off the radio. She denies any hallucinations.

Summary. Mrs. Dillow is exhibiting impaired cognitive abilities, including disorientation, lack of insight, impaired thought processes, concrete thinking, and inability to respond to commands. Her mood is suspicious and depressed with a blunted and periodically hostile affect. She exhibits psychomotor agitation. She is unable to function socially or in her job. She has no apparent physical illness but takes nonprescription sleeping pills, 100 mg. h.s., two times the usual dose. Family is concerned and supportive. There is no known psychiatric history for this previously well-functioning woman. Nurses report that Mrs. Dillow's symptoms seem inconsistent and fluctuate in intensity over the course.

Psychiatric diagnosis. Possible delirium.

Nursing diagnosis. 1. Alterations in thought processes; disorientation, level of consciousness, problem-solving, abstraction, attention, concentration, and thought content
2. Ineffective individual coping with impaired social, occupational, and cognitive functioning, and inability to carry out daily activities.

Plan. Immediate toxicology screen to determine substance intoxication, particularly bromide level in sleeping pills. Nursing staff needs to document Mrs. Dillow's mental status several times throughout the day. Contact Dr. Williams for a thorough physical examination and history. Orient Mrs. Dillow during interactions and keep statements simple and brief. Discuss plans with family and offer support services.

CASE EXAMPLE: Assessment of Mr. Barnes.

Identifying information. Mr. Barnes is a 65-year-old male, father of four children. Mr. Barnes is Vice-President of the company where he has been employed for 30 years.

Presenting problem. Mr. Barnes was seen in the mental health clinic as the result of an appointment arranged by his wife. Mr. Barnes' supervisor had contacted Mrs. Barnes with concerns that the patient was not "functioning well" at work. Mrs. Barnes states that her husband has been forgetful and irritable at home. He agreed to the psychiatric evaluation after an argument with his wife.

Brief recent history. Mr. Barnes states that nothing unusual has happened over the past year. He denies any work difficulties and believes he is just "slower" now that he's older. According to Mrs. Barnes, her husband has been increasingly "forgetful" over the past 6 months and has done things such as leave the stove on and the water running in the bathtub. She states he makes frequent mistakes in the family finances and has been "disagreeable" and more listless than usual. Mr. Barnes' employer states that the patient is unable to complete projects and follow through on company matters. He has made numerous errors in his written work and no longer contributes helpful information at meetings. There is no significant medical history or physical complaints. The patient denies any history of alcohol and drug use.

Family history. The patient's four children are married and live in the area. He denies any marital discord. The family is financially well off.

Personal history. Mr. Barnes is an only child. His parents were divorced when he was 16 and he lived with his mother. The patient earned his own way through college and graduate business school. He has been a financially successful executive for 35 years. Mr. Barnes is active in the Kiwanis and the United Way. Mrs. Barnes states he has missed recent meetings because of his "forgetfulness." Mr. Barnes did consult a psychiatrist 20 years ago after having chest pain that was diagnosed as an anxiety attack. He remained in therapy only 6 months. He believes he is a "tense" person but has been able to master relaxation skills.

Mental status examination. Mr. Barnes is a robust, gray-haired man who appears somewhat unkempt with an unshaven face and wrinkled shirt. He sat quietly, tapping his fingers during the interview. His speech was normal, hesitant at times. He expressed concern that he had come for the interview. His mood was slightly depressed and his affect was flat and sporadically irritable. Mr. Barnes was oriented except to date, giving the wrong day but correct year and month. He was unable to remember the names of three objects given at the start of the interview. He did recall past events in correct chronological order. He responded concretely to proverbs and hesitated in describing similarities and differences between objects but eventually did so in a concrete manner. He was able to get to 86 on serial sevens and with great difficulty got to 79. His drawings of figures were not identical to the ones requested. He denies hallucinations. There was no evidence of suicidal ideation. Mr. Barnes believes he is just "getting old" and denies any problems functioning. He believes his employer is just trying to get him to retire early.

Summary. Mr. Barnes is exhibiting impaired cognitive abilities, including memory, orientation, insight, problem solving, and mathematical ability. His mood is slightly depressed and his affect is irritable and flat. He is having difficulty functioning at his job and at home. The family is concerned and upset. There is a psychiatric history of 6 months of therapy 20 years ago for anxiety. The symptoms have appeared gradually over the past 6 months. Mr. Barnes denies he is having difficulty.

Psychiatric diagnosis. Dementia.

Nursing diagnosis. 1. Alterations in thought processes; impaired recent memory; disorientation to time; impaired abstraction, problem solving, and insight
2. Ineffective individual coping with impaired social, occupational, and cognitive abilities

Plan. Referral to family history for complete physical examination and diagnostic testing for degenerative or multi-infarct dementia. Discuss with Mr. Barnes and family possible options for maintaining employment or taking a medical leave. Recommend psychotherapy to Mr. Barnes and family for assistance in this crisis period and to help the patient utilize his strengths in dealing with this problem.

REFERENCES

1. Wells, C.E. Chronic brain disease: An overview. *American Journal of Psychiatry,* 1978, *135*(1), 1.
2. Pitt, B. The muddled patient. *Practitioner,* 1978, *220,* 199-202.
3. American Psychiatric Association. *Diagnostic and statistical manual of mental disorders,* 3rd ed. Washington, D.C.: American Psychiatric Association, 1980, pp 101, 107, 109, 111.
4. Seltzer, B., & Sherwin, I. "Organic brain syndromes:" An empirical study and critical review. *American Journal of Psychiatry,* 1978, *135*(1), 13.
5. Murray, G.B. Confusion, delirium, and dementia. In T. Hackett and N. Cassem, Eds. *Massachusetts General Hospital handbook of general hospital psychiatry.* St. Louis: The C.V. Mosby Co., 1978, p. 96.
6. Wolanin, M.O., & Phillips, L.F. *Confusion: prevention and care.* St. Louis: The C.V. Mosby Co., 1981, p. 2.
7. Dodd, M.J. Assessing mental status. *American Journal of Nursing,* 1978, *78*(9), 1502-1503.
8. Seltzer, B., & Frazier, S.H. Organic mental disorders. In A.M. Nicholi, Jr., Ed. *Harvard guide to modern psychiatry.* Cambridge, Mass.: The Belknap Press, 1978, pp. 297, 299-312.
9. American Psychiatric Association. *Diagnostic and statistical manual of mental disorders,* 2nd ed. Washington, D.C.: American Psychiatric Association, 1968.
10. Katzman, R. The prevalence and malignancy of Alzheimer's disease. *Archives of Neurology,* 1976, *33,* 217-218.
11. Adolfsson, R., et al. Prevalence of dementia disorders in institutionalized Swedish old people. *Acta Psychiatrica Scandinavica,* 1981, *63*(3), 225-244.
12. Additions and resident patients at end of year state and county mental hospitals by age and diagnosis, by state, United States, 1978. National Institute of Mental Health, p. 48.
13. Primary diagnosis of discharges from non-federal general hospital psychiatric inpatient united. National Institute of Mental Health, 1978, p. 14
14. Maletta, G.J., et al. Organic mental disorders in a geriatric outpatient population. *American Journal of Psychiatry,* 1982, *139*(4), 522.
15. Davidhizar, R., Gurden, E., & Wehlage, D. Recognizing and caring for the delirious patient. *Journal of Psychiatric Nursing and Mental Health Services,* 1978, *16*(5), 38, 39.
16. Purdie, F.R., Honigman, B., & Rosen, P. Acute organic brain syndrome: A review of 100 cases. *Annals of Emergency Medicine,* 1981, *10*(9), 455-460.
17. Hall, R.C.W., et al. Physical illness presenting as psychiatric disease. *Archives of General Psychiatry,* 1978, *35*(11), 1315-1320.
18. Wells, C.E. Chronic brain disease: An overview. *American Journal of Psychiatry,* 1978, *135*(1), 3.
19. Gutzmann, H., & Avdaloff, W. Mental impairment (dementia) and cerebral atrophy in geriatric patients. *Mechanisms of Ageing and Development,* 1980, *14,* 459.

20. Folstein, M.F., Folstein, S.E., & McHugh, P.R. "Mini-mental state," a practical method for grading the cognitive state of patients for the clinician. *Journal of Psychiatric Research*, 1975, *12*, 189-198.
21. Isaacs, B., & Kennie, A.T. The set test as an aid to the detection of dementia in old people. *British Journal of Psychiatry*, 1973, *123*, 467-470.
22. Kim, M., & Moritz, D.A. *Classification of nursing diagnoses*. New York: McGraw Hill Book Co., 1982.

CHAPTER 10

ASSESSING SUBSTANCE ABUSE

The use and abuse of drugs and alcohol is an extremely controversial and problematic area, both in contemporary U.S. society in general and in clinical practice in particular. With the possible exception of religion and politics, it is difficult to imagine a topic more guaranteed to produce hotly contested differences of opinion among most adults and adolescents. The use of alcohol and other drugs is extremely pervasive and culturally sanctioned in a variety of ways, some clear and straightforward and others indirect and obscure. As opposed to most of the other mental disorders discussed in this book, a myriad of legal, social, and historical factors are extremely important in understanding the phenomenon of substance abuse or chemical dependence. The latter is a new term coined to emphasize the dependence part of this problematic behavior. In addition, the word chemical, as well as the word substance, underscores the fundamental similarity of the use, misuse, and abuse of both alcohol and other drugs.

An in-depth investigation of most of these factors is beyond the scope of this chapter, and the interested reader is referred to other sources included in the bibliography for more information. It must be remembered, however, that much of the complexity of this phenomenon results from the large variation of individual and cultural attitudes that exist concerning this topic. Furthermore, various subcultures have complex, varied, and sometimes contradictory attitudes about many of the individual aspects of substance use and substance abuse, not to mention differential feelings toward specific drugs in specific amounts in specific situations. In short, the variation and complexity of peoples' feelings and attitudes are extremely great and tend to motivate behavior in ways not often recognized.

Additionally, further controversy is added by the intercultural and intergenerational aspects of substance abuse and chemical dependence, not to mention the influence of various groups that have a financial and personal stake in the social use of various substances, such as the liquor industry, the tobacco lobby, and the pharmaceutical industry.

This chapter will be limited to an investigation of the clinical aspects of substance abuse—in particular, the differential assessment of various drug- and alcohol-induced states. As we will see, the effects of drugs and alcohol can mimic many other mental disorders.

Specifically, we will investigate the following substances:

1. Alcohol
2. Barbiturates and similarly acting sedatives and hypnotics
3. Cannabis
4. Cocaine and amphetamines and similarly acting sympathomimetics
5. Hallucinogens and PCP and similarly acting arylcyclohexylamines
6. Opioids

These are the same substances categorized in DSM-III.

We will investigate the use and abuse of these substances from the point of view of the following phenomena:

1. Intoxication
2. Withdrawal (in applicable cases)
3. Abuse (in applicable cases)
4. Dependence (in applicable cases)

DEFINITIONS

Intoxication is a physiological effect produced by a substance, such that the individual's mental condition (affect, level of consciousness, thought process, cognitive functions, central nervous system manifestations) is altered in some recognizable way. Clearly, a state of intoxication resulting from alcohol is quite different than that produced by amphetamines—the intoxication phenomenon is substance specific.

Withdrawal is a physiological effect produced by the cessation of use of a substance that was previously regularly used. This phenomenon is also substance specific. In a very general way the withdrawal from a substance can be thought of as the opposite of its intoxication effect. In some cases, simply a substantial decrease in the amount of use can cause a withdrawal reaction; complete cessation is not necessary. Resumption of use of the substance or another substance in the same class stops the symptoms.

Tolerance is a manifestation of repeated use. With many, but not all, classes of substances, more and more is needed to produce the same effect. Over a period of time an individual may need to increase the dosage by a factor of 2, 5, or even 10 for an equivalent effect. On the other hand, if the dosage is not increased, the effect produced may decrease substantially or may even be difficult to detect at all.

Abuse is a very controversial and subjective phenomenon. Over the years a large number of different definitions of substance abuse have been suggested. These have varied a great deal depending upon the general point of view of the author (medical, psychological, sociological, political, legal, anthropological) and have varied for each substance in question. We will use the definitions of DSM-III, which state that:

Three criteria distinguish nonpathological substance use from substance abuse:

A pattern of pathological use. Depending upon the substance, this may be manifested by: intoxication throughout the day, inability to cut down or stop use, repeated efforts to control use . . . and episodes of a complication of the substance intoxication (e.g., alcoholic blackouts, opioid overdose).

Impairment in social or occupational functioning caused by the pattern of pathological use. Social relations can be disturbed by the individual's failure to meet important obligations to friends and family, by display or erratic and impulsive behavior, and by inappropriate expression of aggressive feelings. . . .

[Substance abuse can interfere with occupational functioning in a variety of ways, including simply causing the individual to miss work.]

Duration (of) . . . at least *one month.* Signs of the disturbance need not be present throughout the month, but should be sufficiently frequent for a *pattern* of pathological use . . . to be apparent . . .[1]

Dependence is also a concept that has a large variety of definitions. In the past, distinctions have been made between psychological, emotional, physical, physiological, and mental dependence, and the term habituating has also clouded the picture. In DSM-III, dependence corresponds to physical or physiological dependence. Again, to quote:

The diagnosis of all the substance dependence categories requires only evidence of tolerance or withdrawal, except for alcohol and cannabis dependence, which in addition require evidence of social or occupational impairment from use of the substance or a pattern of pathological substance use.[1]

ALCOHOL ABUSE AND DEPENDENCE
Epidemiology

Most authorities agree that alcoholism and alcohol-related problems are the number one drug problem in the United States. Estimates vary, but there appear to be approximately 5 million alcoholics in the United States at present. In addition, 25% to 50% of all medical and psychiatric hospital admissions are alcohol related.[2]

More men than women are dependent upon alcohol, although this gap has become smaller. In addition, the patterns of drinking and associated features of alcoholism may often be different between men and women.[3]

Obviously alcohol dependence is an extremely widespread and prevalent problem with many personal and social consequences.

Causative factors

The various theories of the etiology of alcohol abuse follow the general pattern of many of the other disorders discussed in this book. There have been psychodynamic theories, learning theories, and bio-logical/physiological ones. However, for alcoholism perhaps it is important to add that *moral* theories of etiology have long existed and still exist in certain forms.[4] There are many people who still believe that alcoholics or heroin "addicts" suffer from a "lack of willpower" and are to be judged negatively for their failure to control themselves. Professionals rarely consciously subscribe to such conceptions, but perhaps it is in part an unconscious resonance to this viewpoint that explains the highly negative attitudes many health professionals have toward individuals who are dependent upon alcohol or other drugs.

Other than popular "moral" theories about the etiology of alcoholism, the most prevalent theoretical position has been a psychodynamic one. In other words, since clinicians have observed a range of common personality characteristics in many alcoholics, early developmental conflicts have been postulated as responsible for a later development of alcoholism. For example, alcoholism has been thought to be a manifestation of depression, of oral dependent personality, or of covert hostility and aggressiveness. In more general terms, alcoholics have been thought to be more insecure, have lower self-esteem, and to be less generally psychologically healthy than the normal population.[5,6] In a recent study, based on the Minnesota Multiphasic Personality Inventory (MMPI) and other tests, alcoholics were found to be significantly lower in a measure of ego strength than nonalcoholics. Several other personality variables were studied (field dependence, state anxiety, and stimulus augmentation), and tentative differences appeared between the two groups, although such differences were postulated as being closely related to or dependent upon ego strength. However, this study was retrospective and thus it was impossible to determine whether any of these characteristics predated or appeared later than the alcoholism.[7]

Although genetic and biological theories of the etiology of alcoholism have existed in various forms for some years, it is only in the past 15 years that they have again been generally discussed. Hereditary factors in human illnesses have been studied in three ways: (1) twin studies, (2) genetic marker studies, and (3) adoption studies. All three of these methods have been applied to alcohol research.[5,8] Some of the more compelling evidence of a genetic factor in at least some types of alcoholism comes from a series of studies sponsored by the National Institute of Alcohol Abuse and Alcoholism on adoption in Denmark, where there is a central register of such cases. These studies have found that:

. . . sons of alcoholics were about four times more likely to be alcoholic than were the sons of nonalcoholics, whether raised by nonalcoholic foster parents or raised by their own biological parents.[5]

The findings with regard to female alcoholics were less clear-cut. One other interesting hypothesis to come out of these studies, which was not new, is that alcoholism and "problem drinking" may *not* be on a continuum but may represent two distinctly different disorders.

Other studies have cast doubt on some of the psychodynamic beliefs noted above. For example, a prospective, 33-year study of 456 individuals[5] found that:

. . . if one controls for antisocial childhood, cultural attitudes toward alcohol use and abuse, for alcoholic heredity, and most especially for the *effects* of alcohol abuse then many of the childhood and adult personality variables to which adult alcoholism has traditionally been attributed will appear as carts and not horses.[6]

This study has been criticized on methodological grounds, however, and its results remain highly controversial.

Another recent study found no correlation between alcoholism and "oral-dependent" behavior in males.[9]

One of the most "common sense" linkages has been between alcoholism and depression. More specifically, it has been suggested that alcoholics drink because they are depressed. The newest empirical data available seem to indicate that, at least in men, alcoholism causes depression more often than vice-versa.[10] Exactly how this happens is unclear, but it is possible that it is a physiological relationship.[11]

Social learning and "sociopsychological" formulations of alcoholism have also been articulated. This is in many ways a straightforward approach, in that alcohol and drug-taking behavior is for many individuals intrinsically rewarding and reinforcing:

. . . the drinking response becomes habitual because it leads to a reduction in drive (anxiety). To the extent that alcohol reduces tensions, worry, and "anxiety," it serves as a source of reward to the individual.[12]

A clear outgrowth of these theories is the study of cultural variations in the prevalence of alcoholism.[5,10] The amount of problem drinking and alcoholism varies tremendously from country to country, and the nuances of this variation are complex. However, it appears that the culture's attitudes toward drinking in children, along with those toward drunkenness in adults, are major factors. That cultural factors can so strongly affect the prevalence of alcoholism, of course, is a strong argument for psychological and perhaps social-learning etiological theories.

No discussion of the etiological theories of alcoholism and alcohol abuse would be complete without some mention of the central contribution of E. M. Jellinek. More than any other authority he is responsible for the general acceptance of the "disease model" of alcoholism—that the alcoholic is sick and deserving of compassion, understanding, and treatment as opposed to being evil and deserving of moral censure and punishment.[13,14] This belief has been a central tenet of many, if not most, treatment and rehabilitation programs of the past generation, including Alcoholics Anonymous. Even Jellinek, however, viewed alcoholism as a result of other, more general psychopathology:

> The "loss of control" is a disease condition per se which results from a process that superimposes itself upon those abnormal psychological conditions of which excessive drinking is a symptom.[14]

Ultimately, of course, the etiology of alcoholism and alcohol abuse may be a staggeringly complex intermixture of all of the above explanatory theories. In addition, it may be that there are not only two or three different "types" of alcoholics but perhaps many syndromes differing in the relative "weight" for which the various causative factors are responsible.

Clinical presentation

As noted above, alcoholism and alcohol problems are highly prevalent in contemporary U.S. society, and the clinician must maintain a high degree of diagnostic suspicion in a large variety of contexts. Perhaps one of the easiest situations in which to identify the individual with an alcohol problem is the rare occurrence of such an individual directly requesting help for the drinking. Unfortunately, such an occurrence is rare. When it does take place, the individual often directly contacts one of the many agencies identified as assisting substance abusers, such as the National Council on Alcoholism or Alcoholics Anonymous. In some parts of the country it is still commonplace to treat indigent alcoholics in state psychiatric hospitals, but this practice is decreasing.

Individuals with alcohol problems are very prevalent on medical and surgical units. They may be hospitalized for a large variety of reasons, many of which may be secondary to alcoholism. These same individuals are also often seen in outpatient medical clinics. Examples are discussed in the physical manifestation section.

Persons with alcohol problems often present themselves for treatment at mental health or psychiatric clinics, although rarely straightforwardly admitting their dependence upon alcohol. Often the presenting complaint is some other difficulty such as depression or memory loss.

Behavioral manifestations. The most common clinical context in which intoxicated persons are seen by the nurse is the medical/surgical emergency room or mental health emergency clinic. The clinician must not assume that intoxication necessarily indicates abuse or dependence. There is no substitute for a careful history and mental status examination. A seemingly intoxicated individual—manifested by staggering gait, impulsivity, slurred speech, general loss of coordination, talkativeness, euphoria and/or irritability, and the smell of alcohol—must be examined for possible injuries, especially head injuries. Clearly, if such injuries are found, medical treatment becomes the first priority.

When an individual is highly intoxicated, an accurate history and mental status examination are difficult to obtain, and the individual must simply be observed until sober enough for evaluation. This observation may be done by family or friends, if available.

It is also important to remember that an apparently intoxicated individual may not be intoxicated on alcohol at all, but rather use other sedative drugs. Such intoxication, including that caused by benzodiazepines, exactly mimics alcohol intoxication. It is not sufficient merely to detect the odor of alcohol on a person's breath; the person may have had one drink and a large number of sleeping pills. Conversely, some forms of alcohol leave very little mouth odor.

Diabetic coma—insufficient insulin in a diabetic person—can also appear similar to alcohol intoxication, including the odor of acetone, a sweet, fruity smell similar to some types of alcohol. Infrequently, insulin shock—excessive insulin or insufficient food in a diabetic person—also produces the acetone smell, along with a confused mental state that may mimic alcohol intoxication.[15]

Although repeated instances of significant intoxication are suggestive of an alcohol problem, the diagnosis of alcohol dependence is not made on the basis of the amount or frequency of alcohol consumption. In other words, we have not answered the question "How much or how often does someone have to drink in order to be alcoholic?" The diagnosis of alcohol dependence is made on the basis of the behavioral and social consequences of alcohol consumption, not on the amount consumed. Recall the diagnostic criteria: (1) a pattern of pathological use; (2) impairment in social or occupational functioning; (3) duration of at least one month; and (4) tolerance or withdrawal.

It is these factors that define alcohol dependence, not the amount consumed. This realization should help clinicians refrain from comparing the amount drunk by a patient with one's own intake, with the all too common outcome of diagnosing an alcohol problem only if the patient drinks more than the clinician.[16]

Much has been written about alcoholics' inability to control their drinking. However, this is still a controversial area. It is not exactly clear what "lack of control" means, and experimental evidence for the existence of this phenomenon is mixed. The idea is, however, that the normal drinker "automatically" or "naturally" stops drinking after a reasonable time, presumably through some physiological or psychological feedback mechanism. Individuals with alcohol abuse or dependence, however, invariably drink more than they intend. That is, once they begin drinking, they "lose control" and drink until some external factor interrupts the drinking episode. Such individuals are, presumably, "unable" to stop. The mechanism of this "inability" is a bit unclear, however. It is especially unclear given the self-report of a number of alcohol-dependent patients, who state that once they begin drinking they do not *want* to stop. It is only later, upon reflection, that they seem to have been *unable* to stop.

The nurse may observe patients attempting to bring alcohol into the hospital, drinking mouthwash with alcohol content, or searching for other items that contain some type of alcohol, One patient, for example, stole other patients' perfumes and drank them.

Much of what the clinician learns about an individual's drinking behavior is learned through the interview. However, since the hallmark dynamic of alcohol dependence is denial, the clinician must be aware of the pattern of the patient's responses, not just the content of the answers. Routine questioning about substance use, abuse, and dependence should be included in all clinical interviews. When the pattern of responses indicates possible alcohol abuse and/or dependence, further questions should be included. The most common pattern of responses is one that seeks to convince the clinician that there is no problem, along with a rigidity or vagueness or other pattern of answering that is different from the remainder of the interview.

When evaluating a patient for a chief complaint of depression, anxiety, or marital problems, it is helpful to introduce the topic of substance use with a short introduction such as "Now I'd like to ask you a few questions about alcohol or drugs" or "Now I have some questions about a different area, drugs and alcohol."

Below are some examples of routine inquiries that could be used by the nurse in any evaluative interview:

"How much do you drink?"

"What prescription medications or other drugs do you use?"

"How often do you drink?"

"Let's take a typical day—let's say yesterday. How much did you drink yesterday?"

"Has the use of alcohol or drugs ever caused you any family problems?"

"Has the use of alcohol or drugs ever caused you any work problems?"

"Have you ever considered cutting down on your use of alcohol?"

"Have you ever had a blackout—a period during which you were
drinking but later could not remember what happened?"

As noted above, the key in these questions is not the specific answer
given by the patient but the pattern of responses indicative of minimization, denial, or evasion. An individual in the early stages of alcoholism
may be able to admit some difficulty in one or more of the above areas,
but a person with a more advanced problem will almost invariably give
answers designed to cause the interviewer to believe that no problem
exists. The experienced clinician can often easily identify this pattern—
a cooperative patient suddenly becomes vaguely distant and defensive,
a rather serious one abruptly begins to tell jokes, a patient who gave
clear and concise answers to earlier questions begins to give vague and
oblique replies, or the patient becomes rigidly defensive in general.

NURSE: How often do you drink?
PATIENT: Five days a week at most, and I only drink at night.
NURSE: Typical day . . . how much did you drink?
PATIENT: I had only two or three beers while watching TV, I'm sure,
that's all.
NURSE: Use . . . caused family problems?
PATIENT: No, except my wife sometimes complains, but she complains
about everything. You should hear her talk about her cousin; he drinks
a lot.

For the individual with at least the beginnings of an alcohol problem,
the interviewer must assume that many of the answers given will be
denials, minimizations, or evasions of the truth. As noted above, the
clinician does not place much faith in the details of the answers but
looks at the patterns of responses, the change in affect accompanying
the answers, and the shift in tone of the interview. In addition, chemically dependent patients often given away their dependence by being
acutely aware of days, times, amounts, circumstances, and patterns of
both drinking and attempts to control the drinking. For example, most
people have to stop and think how many aspirin they take in a week
and in what circumstances, and even then their answers are only educated guesses. However, alcoholic people are often quite specific but
not accurate about the amount of alcohol consumed, revealing an unusual awareness of their own drinking patterns.

It goes without saying that when answers seem defensive, vague,
or evasive, the clinician should not assume they are accurate. Admission
of amounts consumed, for example, must routinely be considered inaccurate. Decisions regarding the necessity of inpatient detoxification,
for example, must not be based on patients' own estimates of their
consumption. Moreover, even if the patient were able to give an accurate

estimate, such information is not an accurate predictor of who will or will not have a physiologically difficult withdrawal.

Physical manifestations. Direct measurement of the amount of alcohol in the blood is often helpful to obtain, when this is possible. By far the simplest and most practical method of measurement of the blood alcohol level (BAL) is by Breathalizer. Measurements of BAL by Breathalyzer should not be taken within 15 minutes of the last drink, or a falsely elevated reading may be obtained.[6] In the United States, two different ways of measuring BAL are used, and it is helpful to understand the difference and the relationship between the two:[17]

$$G/dl = mg/dl$$
$$\text{or} \qquad \text{or}$$
$$\% = mg/dl$$
$$\text{or}$$
$$mg\%$$
$$0.1 = 100$$

BAL measured in "%" is used by police and other legal agencies, whereas "MG%" is used in many medical settings. Thus a general hospital emergency department will report a BAL of 190, whereas the police officer who brought in the intoxicated driver will record this level as 0.19. In most states, a level of 0.10 is legal evidence of intoxication.

However, it must be remembered that different individuals absorb and metabolize alcohol at different rates. Body weight is also an important factor. An individual weighing 100 lb will have a BAL of about 0.22 after drinking five drinks in an hour, whereas one weighing 200 lb will register about 0.11.[17]

The most significant variable is tolerance. Individuals who are tolerant to alcohol will have, at all levels of BAL, a reduced level of other symptoms of intoxication, such as loss of coordination, slurred speech, talkativeness, and disinhibition. An individual with a high tolerance to alcohol may not even appear intoxicated at a level of 0.15 or even 0.20, whereas a casual drinker may have already passed out at these blood levels.

Simply being intoxicated does not necessarily imply the existence of an alcohol problem, but the level of intoxication is significant. The National Council on Alcoholism states that a BAL of 0.3 at any time is suggestive of alcoholism, and a level of 0.15 without obvious signs of significant intoxication should be interpreted in the same way. Both of these situations indicate substantial tolerance to alcohol, one of the major indicators of alcohol dependence.[17]

Other than intoxication itself, there may often be no obvious physical manifestations of alcohol abuse or dependence. Except for alcohol-related traffic accidents, most health issues only become of concern rather late in the cycle of alcohol dependence. A patient may attempt to point out that he or she cannot have a drug or alcohol problem because the family physician just found the individual to be "in perfect health." In the early stages, most health issues are irrelevant.

Withdrawal from alcohol after chronic use may produce physical manifestations. "Morning shakes," which is a tremor primarily of the upper body and upper extremities, is a mild and common form of withdrawal. Patients who are seen in clinics before noon may exhibit this phenomenon, whereas by afternoon such individuals may have already had a few drinks and are therefore no longer tremulous.

More significant withdrawal phenomena begin to occur approximately 24 hours after cessation of drinking, when, in addition to tremor, the individual may display sweating, weakness, nausea, and have a mildly elevated pulse and blood pressure. The nurse should be especially alert to these symptoms in individuals suspected of alcohol use. In a small proportion of serious drinkers the withdrawal will progress to uncontrollable bodily shaking, total insomnia, extreme restlessness, vomiting, confusion, profuse sweating, and visual hallucinations. Auditory hallucinations occur but are less common. Tactile hallucinations are also experienced, the sensation that insects are crawling under one's skin is typical. Mild withdrawal is diagnosed as alcohol withdrawal; the disorder characterized primarily by hallucinations is diagnosed as alcohol hallucinosis; the severe delirium state is diagnosed as alcohol withdrawal delirium. This last disorder is commonly called "delirium tremens" or "DTs" and represents a serious medical disorder.[18,19]

As noted above, many persons with alcohol abuse and dependence do not exhibit significant physical manifestations of the illness until their disorder is fairly well advanced. Later a number of physical disorders and symptoms may appear. These are listed in the box on p. 278. The nurse needs to be alert to patients who first appear with physical problems that are potentially indicative of alcohol use and abuse.

One of the major diagnostic confusions common in alcoholic persons is that of seizures. Patients may be routinely hospitalized for one of the disorders in the boxes on pp. 279 and 280 or for any other unrelated disorder and unexpectedly have grand mal seizures 3 or 4 days after admission. Often the cause of the seizures—alcohol withdrawal—is overlooked, and anticonvulsants are prescribed. The alert nurse will pay special attention to this possibility; often careful history-taking will uncover the connection between the abrupt cessation of drinking and the onset of seizures.

Cognitive and emotional aspects. It is difficult and sometimes impossible to evaluate an individual who is intoxicated or having significant withdrawal distress. At these times, if an evaluation must be done, it

PHYSICAL MANIFESTATIONS OF ALCOHOL DEPENDENCE[18,20]

Liver disease: fatty liver, hepatitis, cirrhosis, hepatocellular carcinoma
Chronic gastritis
Hematological disorders: anemia, clotting disorders
Peripheral neuropathy
Toxic amblyopia
Alcohol myopathy
Alcohol cardiomyopathy
Beriberi
Esophagitis
Mallory-Weiss syndrome
Boorhaave syndrome
Colitis
Esophageal varices
Pancreatitis
Sleep disturbance
Cerebellar degeneration
Degeneration of the corpus callosum (Marchiafava-Bignami disease)
Central pontine myelinolysis
Hypokalemia
Hypomagnesemia
Chronic obstructive pulmonary disease
Osteonecrosis of the hip
Fetal alcohol syndrome

Based on data from Shaw, G. K., Alcohol dependence and withdrawal. *British Medical Bulletin,* 1982, *38* (1), 99, 102, and Estes, N. J., Smith-DiJulio, K., & Heinemann, M. E. *Nursing diagnosis of the alcoholic person.* St. Louis: The C. V. Mosby Co., 1980, 14-18, 29-38.

will only be of the degree of physiological disorder present and must be based mostly on physical signs and symptoms. In certain cases, such as when violent or suicidal behavior has taken place, an intoxicated individual must not be left alone to "sleep it off." Often family or friends can be utilized to monitor the individuals until they are sober enough to be evaluated.

When a formerly intoxicated person is interviewed at some later time, the person may have no memory of the previous period. This loss of memory—a "blackout"—is of controversial clinical significance. Many authorities in the field of alcoholism, beginning with Jellinek, believe that frequent blackouts are an early diagnostic sign of alcoholism, especially blackouts that occur when the individual is not highly intoxicated.[13] Others, however, feel that an alcoholic and a nonalcoholic person, equally intoxicated, will exhibit an equal frequency of blackouts. In any case, frequent blackouts are certainly indicative of frequent episodes

ALCOHOL-RELATED DISORDERS[45]

Gastrointestinal
  Esophagitis + acid reflux
  Esophageal carcinoma
  Gastritis
  Malabsorption (amino acids,
    thiamine, minerals)
  Chronic diarrhea
  Pancreatitis/pancreatic
    insufficiency
  Fatty liver
  Alcoholic hepatitis
  Cirrhosis (may lead to liver
    cancer)
  Peptic ulcers

Cardiovascular
  Alcoholic cardiomyopathy
  Coronary heart disease
  Hypertension
  Stroke
  Holiday heart arrhythmias
  Fetal Alcohol Syndrome (FAS)
    Tetralogy of Fallot
    Patent ductus
    Septal defects

Skin and face
  Rosacea
  Rhinophyma
  Cutaneous ulcers
  Nummular eczema
  Psoriasis
  Fetal Alcohol Syndrome (FAS)
    Altered palmar creases
    Epicanthal folds
    Micrognathia
    Cleft lip/palate
    Micropthalmia
  Premature wrinkles (smoking)

Hematologic
  Megaloblastic anemia (folate or
    B-12 deficiency)
  Iron deficiency
  Hemolytic anemia (spur cell)

Acquired stomatocytosis
Thrombocytopenia + bleeding
  diathesis
Leukopenia + impaired
  chemotaxis

Metabolic and Nutritional
  Alcoholic hypoglycemia
  Alcoholic hyperlipemia (type
    IV & V)
  Beriberi
  Pellagra

Respiratory
  Tuberculosis
  Lung abscess (aspiration)
  Pneumonia
  Asthma
  Bronchitis (smoking)
  Head and neck cancer
    (smoking)

Genitourinary
  Impotence/dyspareunia
  Testicular atrophy
  Aseptic (toxic) cystitis
  Fetal Alcohol Syndrome
    Hydronephrosis
    Genital anomalies

Peripheral Nervous System
  Peripheral neuropathy-Sensory
  Crush neuropathy ("Saturday
    Night" palsy)

Central Nervous System
  Tremor (withdrawal)
  Delirium (withdrawal)
  Convulsions (withdrawal)
  Hallucinations/sensory
    distortions (withdrawal)
  Paranoia (withdrawal)
  Alcoholic hallucinosis
  Wernicke-Korsakoff syndrome
  Coma
  FAS-Microcephaly

From Liepman, M.P. Unpublished document, Ann Arbor: The University of Michigan
Hospitals. Another version of this box can be found in Liepman, M.P. Chemical dependence
in the family. In J. Seeley & Y. Talbot (Eds.) *Working with the family in primary care*. New
York: Praeger Press, 1982.

Continued.

ALCOHOL-RELATED DISORDERS—cont'd	

Central Nervous System—cont'd
  Cerebral cortical atrophy
  Cerebellar degeneration
  Subdural hematomas
  Marchiafava-Bignami disease
  Central pontine myelinolysis
  Ataxia
 	
Mental
  Amnesic (blackout) spells
  Phobias
  Family problems
  Arrested grief reactions
  Violence
  Depression and suicide
  Sexual abuse (e.g., rape,
    incest)
  Pathological intoxication
  Accidents
	Risk-taking
	  Fetal Alcohol Syndrome (FAS)
	  Hemachromatosis
	    Dilutional hyponatremia
	    FAS-failure to thrive
	    Alcoholic ketoacidosis
	
	Musculoskeletal
	  Fractures and sprains (trauma)
	  Gouty arthritis
	  Myopathy
	  Aseptic necrosis of femoral
	    head
	  Fetal Alcohol Syndrome (FAS)
	    Digital anomalies
	    Dwarfism
	    Hyperactivity
	    Mental retardation
	    Motor incoordination

of at least moderate intoxication and as such are suggestive of alcoholism. Loss of memory—amnesia—is a troublesome clinical phenomenon.

> CASE EXAMPLE: A 57-year-old divorced, umemployed man was arrested and placed in a holding cell after walking out on his front porch one evening, taking out a handgun, and proceeding to play "Russian roulette." A horrified neighbor called police, and the man was taken into custody without injury. He was found to be highly intoxicated. When the local mental health emergency services unit interviewed him 6 hours later, he was virtually sober and had no memory of the earlier incident with the gun. In fact, he denied being suicidal at all, denied that he would ever do such a foolhardy thing, and denied that he had a problem with alcohol.

Obviously, evaluating this patient's suicide potential was essentially impossible, even though it was quite clear that he could become suicidal again the next time he became intoxicated. The only possible course of action was to aggressively pursue treatment for the patient's alcoholism. In any case, when a formerly intoxicated individual is sober, the usual evaluation can be performed—history, mental status examination, and the gathering of collateral data from family and friends.

The hallmark of chemical dependence is denial, a nonpsychotic, psychological defense mechanism by which individuals attempt to "hide" from some painful truth. Ultimately, alcoholic people are attempting to hide the truth of their own disorders from themselves and only secondarily from other people. For this reason, it is the rare individual who, *before treatment*, is able to admit to alcoholism. Much more often the individual will request help for some other primary problem, and it is only through skillful interviewing that the nurse will be able to uncover the substance abuse and/or dependence. In all evaluations, no matter what the presenting problem, a routine assessment of the possible contributions of alcohol and drug problems should be included.

One common presenting problem is depression. Such an individual will first appear in a variety of different settings, mental health clinics, general outpatient clinics, medical clinics, and hospital emergency rooms complaining of depression. Depression is an extremely common concomitant of alcohol dependence. It is also a serious disorder in its own right. The chief complaint may be of chronic sadness, difficulty in carrying out daily activities, lack of energy, or sleep disturbance, for example. Many of these individuals may not connect their feelings of depression, or the other somatic symptoms, to their drinking. In fact, it is a common observation that a few drinks make a depressed person feel better. Unfortunately, it is not true that a few more drinks make the person feel better. The outcome is usually the opposite.

The evidence is becoming increasingly convincing that most of the time, depression does not cause alcoholism but that alcoholism causes depression. Although it is not clear whether the alcoholic person's inability to control drinking or the inevitable problems in social, family, and/or occupational functioning that the drinking produces are responsible for the depression, the end result is the same. It is possible that the depression resulting from chronic intoxication is physiologically caused. In any case, the answer is not to try to treat the depression, either with psychotherapy or somatic therapies, but to treat the alcoholism. In a number of studies abstinence from alcohol also relieved the depression.[11] For example, a 36-year-old married woman came to a mental health clinic complaining of depression. Although she admitted to drinking regularly throughout the afternoon and evening on a daily basis, she claimed that her drinking helped her cope, and she was convinced that her depression was related to her marriage and children. She reluctantly and skeptically agreed to alcoholism treatment. Two months later she sent a short note to the clinic, stating that now that she was no longer drinking, she still had marital and family difficulties, but she was less depressed and felt much more able to cope with these difficulties.

Only by developing a number of routine inquiries regarding substance use, abuse, and dependence and then following up with detailed questioning when the initial results are positive, can the nurse elicit the actual alcohol dependence underlying the depression. In most cases the patient will not volunteer the information, or may actively attempt to conceal or minimize it.

The person who comes to a hospital or clinic with what usually appears to be generalized anxiety disorder may also have a primary disorder of alcoholism. Often the "morning shakes," insomnia, and a general feeling of nervousness is one effect of chronic drinking, and in some cases the patient may not be aware of this connection. Unfortunately, many physicians in internal medicine and family practice may also overlook or choose not to acknowledge an individual's problem with alcohol and sometimes compound the problem by prescribing benzodiazepines for tranquilization.

Individuals with panic disorders, including agoraphobia with panic attacks, do not usually have a primary diagnosis of alcohol dependence. In these cases the individual often increases drinking in an attempt to allay the panic, usually unsuccessfully. A careful clarification and differentiation between generalized anxiety and discrete panic attacks and between the onset of the panic and the onset of the increased drinking will usually sort out this diagnostic difficulty.

Patients may come to medical facilities complaining of memory loss, or it may be uncovered in the course of a routine history that the individual apparently has adult-onset seizures. The individual may be taking anticonvulsant medication. Despite the clear connection between alcohol use and alcohol-caused amnestic episodes—"blackouts"—many people are not aware of this connection. The nurse must be careful to define "blackouts" when questioning a patient; many people think "blackouts" refer to alcohol-caused loss of consciousness. The actual diagnosis of the cause of memory loss can be a complex neurological problem, but a clear temporal relationship between drinking episodes and periods of amnesia yield a probable diagnosis of alcohol blackouts. In this differential diagnostic problem the nurse must not overlook the rare disorder psychogenic amnesia. In this disorder the memory loss almost always follows a severe emotional trauma, such as the sudden death of a friend or family member.

As noted earlier, the nurse must pay special attention to the pattern of the patient's responses and notice any increased defensiveness, vagueness, and/or alterations in affect that may occur while discussing chemical dependence or related issues. If any of these questions raise the clinician's suspicions, or if any physical manifestations raise the possibility of substance abuse or dependence, or if the patient's family beings up the issue, then further questioning must be done.

This sort of interviewing can become difficult and uncomfortable. It is important for nurses to monitor their own reactions and attitudes for signs of moralizing and judging. Taking a drug and alcohol history must be done nonjudgmentally, with persistence, directness, sensitivity, and good humor. This is, or course, no different than interviewing any individual with any other kind of psychological or medical problem, but many otherwise competent clinicians have significant difficulty interviewing and interacting with chemically dependent persons.

When patients do have a substance abuse or dependence problem, their answers will become increasingly "hedged" with vagueness, denial, avoidance, and even attempts to change the subject. Clinicians are often unsure about how much to "press the issue." Too forceful or too relentless an inquiry can result in the patient becoming overtly hostile and terminating the interview and perhaps the relationship. Too deferential an approach can result in missing important cues and misdiagnosing the problem. Obviously, some combination or persistence and deference—a "middle ground"—is the solution, but sometimes this is a difficult compromise to achieve. An important consideration is the context in which the interview is being conducted and whether the clinician and patient have an ongoing relationship. If the context is an ongoing relationship, the nurse should take care not to provoke the patient past the point of losing the working alliance. If the patient's hostility begins to become overt, or the anxiety becomes excessive, the issue should be dropped temporarily and taken up again at some other time. In other words, the inquiry can proceed relatively slowly. The clinician must not expect to avoid the patient's inevitable denial or minimization; such responses are an intrinsic part of the disorder. However, a skillful, slow set of questions, perhaps spread over several weeks, can detect the hidden substance abuse problem, without breaking the trust and losing the alliance previously built up. The relationship can then be the basis for a nonjudgmental confrontation about the individual's alcohol or drug dependence and perhaps the beginning of accepting treatment.

On the other hand, in a setting where there is no ongoing relationship between the nurse and patient, the clinician must assume that there is only one opportunity to assess the problem and take some action. Without a previous relationship to build upon, many invitations to return for a second visit to an emergency clinic, mental health clinic, or medical practitioner's office result in cancelled appointments and "no shows." In this context the clinician must confront the patients' denials and urge that they accept treatment, all in the first (and usually only) interview. To avoid this confrontation is to accomplish nothing. In some cases, a small part of the denial may have been penetrated, making it easier for the next clinician to progress even further.[16]

At this point a brief discussion of the word "alcoholic" may be in order. In some treatment models it is essential that individuals admit that they are "alcoholics." In fact, this is the basis without which no real treatment can take place. On the other hand, the term has such strong connotations that patients will often admit to anything and everything except to being an alcoholic. For example, a patient may very well state that he cannot control his drinking, that he is ruining his life and that of his family as well, or any number of other things, but not to being an alcoholic. If this is the case, it is not so crucial what word is used. If a patient admits to having a problem, perhaps that is enough. With this in mind, it is often more helpful, when a patient asks if the nurse thinks that the person is an alcoholic, to reply, "Well, there are so many different definitions of that. I would say you have a drinking problem." Or, the clinician might reply, "Well, I think you have a problem with alcohol; I don't know if you should be called an alcoholic or not; there's no clear definition of what that is." Note that even this much should only take place late in the interview or interviews, after the evaluation is essentially complete. Only at this point is it appropriate to review the findings and begin planning for treatment, if the patient will accept treatment.

In most situations the assessment of alcohol dependence will be based on the above interview findings, along with any physical findings that may be exhibited. In these cases the patient will have essentially a normal mental status examination. Manifestations of anxiety, or depression, or of previous alcohol blackouts may be present, but there will be no abnormalities of perception, of the form or content of thought, or of cognitive functions. Occasionally, however, the nurse might uncover some specific intellectual abnormalities, such as memory deficits, inability to perform tasks requiring concentration, or disorientation to time or place. This is the clinical picture of dementia, and when it occurs in an individual with long-term alcoholism and no other ascertainable etiological factor, the diagnosis is dementia associated with alcoholism. This dementia is rarely severe.[1]

More commonly, a related form of organic brain syndrome may be observed, in which primarily memory is impaired, as opposed to the more global impairment found in dementia. Often both short-term and long-term memory are impaired, although usually short-term is more affected. This disorder is only found in individuals who have used alcohol quite heavily for many years and has been termed Korsakoff's disease or Korsakoff's psychosis. This disorder frequently follows and is thought to be closely connected to the neurological disorder called Wernicke's encephalopathy. Wernicke's disease is caused by thiamine deficiency, commonly found in chronic alcoholics.[19]

Social manifestations. Impairment in social and/or occupational functioning is one of the core components of alcohol dependence. Normally this impairment is assessed by questioning both the patient and the collateral contacts—family, co-workers, and friends. Below are examples of the types of impairment that commonly occur, phrased in question form:

Family

Has your wife (husband) ever complained about your drinking? In what context? How often?

Have you ever had an actual physical fight with your wife (husband)? Was alcohol involved?

Have other family members ever complained about your drinking, such as son or daughter, parents, in-laws, others? Who, and in what circumstances? What did they say?

Have you ever had a problem controlling your anger at your children? Have you ever hit them harder than you intended to? Was alcohol involved?

Have you ever felt you were not spending enough time with your family because of your drinking? Has anyone else ever said this?

Have you ever spent household, rent, mortgage, utility, or grocery money on alcohol? How often?

Occupation

Have you gotten into any difficulty on your job because of drinking? What kind of difficulty?

Has your boss or supervisor ever expressed concern about your drinking?

Have you missed work because of either being intoxicated or too "hung over" to go in?

Have you ever lost a job because of drinking?

Has it ever been necessary for your co-workers to "cover" for you because of your drinking?

(The clinician should also be aware that certain jobs make drinking while working much easier, such as being a traveling salesman or a real estate agent.)

Social

Have any of your friends ever expressed concern about your drinking? What did they say?

Have you lost or seen less of your nondrinking friends?

Do you plan social activities primarily around whether they offer an opportunity for drinking or not? Have you decreased the activities that do not permit drinking, such as movies, plays, or outings with children?

Are you the person who drives everyone else home after a party?

Do you ever feel awkward or ill at ease in social situations in which no alcohol is involved?

Legal

Have you ever been arrested for an alcohol-related traffic offense? How many times?

Have you ever lost your license? Points on your license? Had to attend "alcohol education" classes?

Have you ever been arrested for any other sort of alcohol-related incident, such as fighting, urinating in public, being "drunk and disorderly," or public intoxication?

Have you ever spent time in jail for an alcohol-related offense? Details?

Drinking itself

How often do you drink? Under what circumstances? With whom?

How much do you drink on a typical day, such as yesterday? Last Friday or Saturday night? How intoxicated were you when you finished drinking that amount?

Are you the kind of person who can drink a great deal and not appear intoxicated? Are you more able to "hold your liquor" than most people you know?

What is the most you ever drank at one time? In what condition were you when you finished?

What is the longest period of time of continuous drinking you have ever done?

Have you ever felt embarrassed or ashamed about things you did while intoxicated?

Have you ever felt you should cut down on your drinking?

Have you ever made rules for yourself about drinking, such as time, place, amount?

Do you ever have a few drinks before going to a party or social event to get a "head start?"

Do you usually want to continue to "party" when most others are ready to go home?

Have you ever felt you lost control of your drinking—that you drank more on a given occasion than you planned to?

Obviously, there is an extremely large number of questions the nurse might ask in order to assess alcohol dependence. The experienced clinician will not only heed the guidelines already listed but also select the questions most appropriate to each patient's particular situation. By matching the areas of inquiry to that which appears most fruitful, a tentative decision about possible alcohol abuse and dependence can be made in 15 to 20 minutes and sometimes less. Not surprisingly, the extreme cases are the easiest to diagnose.

Assessment tools

Many interview schedules and questionnaires have been developed to aid the clinician in making the diagnosis of chemical dependence in general and alcohol dependence in particular. One of the most well-known in the alcohol field is the Michigan Alcoholism Screening Test (MAST), reproduced below and on p. 288.

MICHIGAN ALCOHOLISM SCREENING TEST (MAST) (Revised 5-24-76)[21,22]

Points			Yes	No
	0.	Do you enjoy a drink now and then?	☐	☐
(2)	*1.	Do you feel you are a normal drinker? (By normal we mean you drink less than or as much as most other people.)	☐	☐
(2)	2.	Have you ever awakened the morning after some drinking the night before and found that you could not remember a part of the evening?	☐	☐
(1)	3.	Does your wife, husband, a parent, or other near relative ever worry or complain about your drinking?	☐	☐
(2)	*4.	Can you stop drinking without a struggle after one or two drinks?	☐	☐
(1)	5.	Do you ever feel guilty about your drinking?	☐	☐
(2)	*6.	Do friends or relatives think you are a normal drinker?	☐	☐
(2)	*7.	Are you able to stop drinking when you want to?	☐	☐
(5)	8.	Have you ever attended a meeting of Alcoholics Anonymous (AA)?	☐	☐
(1)	9.	Have you gotten into physical fights when drinking?	☐	☐

From Selzer, M.L. The Michigan Alcoholism Screening Test (MAST): The quest for a new diagnostic instrument. *The American Journal of Psychiatry,* vol. 128, pp. 176-181, 1971. Copyright 1971, the American Psychiatric Association. Reprinted by permission.
*Alcoholic response is negative.
**5 points for Delirium Tremens
***2 points for *each* arrest
SCORING SYSTEM: In general, five points or more would place the subject in an "alcoholic category". Four points would be suggestive of alcoholism, three points or less would indicate that the subject was not alcoholic. Programs using the above scoring system find it very sensitive at the five point level and there is a tendency to find more people alcoholic than anticipated. However, it is a *screening* test only, and should be sensitive.

Continued.

MICHIGAN ALCOHOLISM SCREENING TEST (MAST)—cont'd

Points			Yes	No
(2)	10.	Has drinking ever created problems between you and your wife, husband, a parent, or other near relative?	☐	☐
(2)	11.	Has your wife, husband (or other family members) ever gone to anyone for help about your drinking?	☐	☐
(2)	12.	Have you ever lost friends because of your drinking?	☐	☐
(2)	13.	Have you ever gotten into trouble at work because of drinking?	☐	☐
(2)	14.	Have you ever lost a job because of drinking?	☐	☐
(2)	15.	Have you ever neglected your obligations, your family, or your work for two or more days in a row because you were drinking?	☐	☐
(1)	16.	Do you drink before noon fairly often?	☐	☐
(2)	17.	Have you ever been told you have liver trouble?	☐	☐
		Cirrhosis?	☐	☐
(2)	**18.	After heavy drinking have you ever had Delirium Tremens (DTs) or severe shaking, or heard voices or seen things that really weren't there?	☐	☐
(5)	19.	Have you ever gone to anyone for help about your drinking?	☐	☐
(5)	20.	Have you ever been in a hospital because of drinking?	☐	☐
(2)	21.	Have you ever been a patient in a psychiatric hospital or on a psychiatric ward of a general hospital where drinking was part of the problem that resulted in hospitalization?	☐	☐
(2)	22.	Have you ever been seen at a psychiatric or mental health clinic or gone to any doctor, social worker, or clergyman for help with any emotional problem, where drinking was part of the problem?	☐	☐
(2)	23.	Have you ever been arrested for drunk driving, driving while intoxicated, or driving under the influence of alcoholic beverages? (If YES, How many times? _____)	☐	☐
(2)	***24.	Have you ever been arrested, or taken into custody, even for a few hours, because of other drunk behavior? (If YES, How many times? _____)	☐	☐

Collateral information

It is extremely important for the nurse to obtain collateral information from family or friends. In fact, it is usually through information obtained from these other sources that the correct diagnosis of alcohol dependence is made. In a setting where the patient and clinician have an ongoing relationship, patients can be requested to have their spouse, son or daughter, or mother or father attend the next session. This request must be made in a matter-of-fact manner, emphasizing that such adjunctive interviewing is a routine part of assessment and is done with almost all patients. In a setting where no further contact is likely, family or friends must be contacted immediately. Often they will have accompanied the patient or they can be contacted by phone.

Of course, the patient's permission should be sought before such a step is taken. All possible measures must be taken to try to enlist the patient's trust and cooperation, and so contacting the family without permission is not advisable. However, if the family member or friend has accompanied the patient to the appointment, and you simply gather additional data, without revealing any information obtained in the interview, then you have not behaved illegally. But it is always advisable to try to obtain permission first.

Interviewing a spouse or other family member can be extremely helpful—in some cases essential—in correctly diagnosing the alcoholic patient. Although spouses are also often defensive and protective of the patient, in most cases they are so desperate for help that they offer reliable information. Many of the questions listed above should also be asked of the spouse or family member, but in this case the answers can usually be trusted. The major exception is when the spouse is also an alcoholic or drug dependent. In this case the clinician will be met with the same rigidity of denial, the same vague generalizations, and the same covert attempts to convince others that there is no problem. However, although specific figures are not available, in the majority of cases only one member of a couple is chemically dependent. Thus the situation of encountering a couple in which both members are dependent will be rare.

The fact that the spouse of an alcoholic person is not also alcoholic does not mean that the spouse has no role in the problem. In fact, newer models of treatment are stressing that alcoholism is a "family disease," not simply an individual problem. This does not mean that the middle-aged male alcoholic's wife "caused" his drinking—no matter how much he insists this is true!—but rather that a reciprocal role usually develops, which paradoxically often aids in the continuation of the problem. This reciprocal role has been termed the "enabler" and the "co-alcoholic" by various theoreticians.

The crux of this role is that the same behavior that is supportive and helpful to a family member with problems becomes its opposite—a part of the continuation of the problem. If a man or woman is feeling ill, it is not uncommon for his or her spouse to call the supervisor or employer and explain the spouse's planned absence from work. However, when this same behavior is carried out to "cover" for a person's inability to go to work because of a "hang-over," then such behavior makes it easier for the alcoholic person to go on drinking and to not face the obvious problem. The central point is that it is love and caring that motivate family members to help protect each other, and yet it is these same emotions that, in the case of the alcoholic person, make things worse.

"Enablers" or "co-alcoholics" also exhibit other behaviors. Commonly they beg, plead, blackmail, bargain, and try every other tactic imaginable to try to force the alcoholic person to control the drinking, including pouring liquor down the sink when a new cache is found. None of it does much good, or course, because the alcohol-dependent person is unable to control the drinking. These attempts to help the alcoholic person are intermixed with behavior that "enables" the person to continue drinking, and thus there is no consistency. In many cases the "covering up" may be necessary for the spouse as well; it is embarrassing to be married to someone who cannot control drinking, and the alcoholic's paycheck may be the family's sole support. Often the spouse feels very trapped.

BARBITURATE AND SIMILARLY ACTING SEDATIVE OR HYPNOTIC SUBSTANCE ABUSE AND DEPENDENCE
Classification

Substances included in this category are:

Barbiturates, such as secobarbital (Seconal), phenobarbital, amobarbital (Amytal), and combination of secobarbital and amobarbital (Tuinal)

Glutethimide (Doriden)

Methaqualone (Quaalude, Sopor)

Meprobamate (Miltown, Equanil)

Ethchlorvynol (Placidyl)

Chloral hydrate

Methyprylon (Nodular)

Paraldehyde

Benzodiazepines, such as diazepam (Valium), chlordiazepoxide (Librium), flurazepam (Dalmane), lorazepam (Ativan), oxazepam (Serax), and alprazolam (Xanax)

Epidemiology

All of the named substances have multiple pharmaceutical uses and enjoy widespread popularity as prescribed drugs, especially the benzodiazepines. Beginning in the 1960s, the benzodiazepines have become the most widely prescribed drugs in the United States; in one year in the early 1970s, prescriptions for Valium and Librium together totaled about 75 million.[24] With this much use, significant abuse is inevitable.

Although exact figures are unavailable, individuals who abuse or become dependent upon these substances tend to fall into two categories, as noted in DSM-III. One pattern is the individual who originally obtained the drug for legitimate medical need and then began to use the drug for other purposes, such as general tranquilization, as an antianxiety agent, or (sometimes in conjunction with alcohol) for its disinhibitory effects. The second pattern is the individual who primarily obtains the drug through illegal channels and uses the drug in relatively large amounts as a euphoriant, to "get high." This second group more often is male and is often younger than the first group.

Causative factors

The abuse of and dependence upon substances other than alcohol has not been studied sufficiently to clearly identify causative agents. However, it is clear that here too the behavior is multidetermined. The use of illicit drugs by adolescents, for example, is highly dependent upon availability. A desire for altered states of consciousness has been postulated as an innate need of human beings in all cultures. [23] Depending upon the substance, culture, general availability, and other factors, various theorists have suggested that a certain percentage of users will become abusers. If this is true, it implies that efforts to reduce the overall use of a drug in a given culture will reduce the incidence of drug abuse and dependence as well. Of course, no one is as yet able to uncover the idiosyncratic factors that determine who uses a drug or drugs safely or constructively or who becomes dependent and destructive.

As previously noted, psychological, learning theory, psychodynamic, and biological/physiological factors have been suggested as causative factors in substance abuse and dependence.

Aside from the fact that substance abuse of all types is associated with antisocial personality disorder,[5,6] no personality type or style has been shown to "cause" drug abuse or dependence. Substance abuse of all types exists in all diagnostic categories.

Clinical presentation

Physical manifestations. Intoxication with any of these substances, either alone or in combination with each other or with alcohol, produces a state similar to alcohol intoxication. The symptoms are the same: staggering gait, loss of coordination, slurred speech, disinhibition, impaired judgment, and usually some affective change. It is common for an individual to mix several sedatives with each other, often with alcohol added as well. Thus the clinician should always suspect the possibility of a mixed intoxication whenever an apparently "drunk" individual is encountered.

Although one or two incidents of intoxication are not necessarily indicative of abuse or dependence, significant tolerance does indicate frequent use and thus is an indirect clue to abuse or dependence. There is a high degree of cross-tolerance within the general category of central nervous system depressants, including alcohol, and so tolerance to one will produce tolerance to the others. The nurse may particularly note this phenomenon when a patient requires an unusually high dosage of sedatives, anesthetics, or analgesics. This is often indicative of substance abuse and a high drug tolerance.

It is impossible to easily quantify the degree of intoxication with sedatives and tranquilizers. No easy measure, such as blood alcohol level, is available. Vital signs are not usually affected until the individual is already stuporous or comatose and thus cannot be used as a measure. Intoxication that progresses to unconsciousness from which arousal is difficult should be considered a medical emergency. Once dependence has occurred, withdrawal produces physical manifestations much the same as alcohol. In its mildest form or in the early stages of a more difficult withdrawal, vital signs are slightly elevated and the individual feels tremulous and "shaky" and may also have headaches, a sense of restlessness, nausea and vomiting, orthostatic hypotension, and a general feeling of anxiety; this is barbiturate or similarly acting sedative or hypnotic withdrawal.

Just as with alcohol, a more severe withdrawal produces a delirium, which is virtually the same as alcohol withdrawal delirium. In this case, the diagnosis is barbiturate or similarly acting sedative or hypnotic withdrawal delirium. In both of these instances, if the particular substance is known, it should be substituted in the statement of diagnosis, for example, Valium withdrawal or Seconal withdrawal delirium.

As with alcohol, an amnestic disorder following prolonged heavy use of these substances can take place. Often this disorder will follow a withdrawal delirium.

There is an extremely wide variability in the duration and extent of the withdrawal syndrome. Many individuals use fairly large amounts of certain sedatives and tranquilizers for significant periods of time and are able to stop abruptly without experiencing serious physiological withdrawal symptoms. Others, however, are not so fortunate. One report suggests that for secobarbital and pentobarbital, 0.80 to 2.20 gm/ day for 35 to 37 days was sufficient to produce dependence.[19] However, no clear, agreed-upon guidelines exist. Benzodiazepines were originally thought not to cause a withdrawal reaction at all, but a number of recent reports have clearly demonstrated mild to severe withdrawal reactions, depending upon dosage and length of time taken.[24,25] Withdrawal reactions have been described even with therapeutic dosages, such as one case of a 32-year-old-man who took 15 mg of Valium daily for 6 years.[25]

The onset and duration of the abstinence syndrome is extremely difficult to predict. The half-life of the substance in question is one major factor. Amobarbital, a rapid-acting barbiturate, has a withdrawal similar in onset and duration to that of alcohol. On the other hand, phenobarbital withdrawal often does not begin for some days after discontinuing the drug.[19] However, mixing these drugs is very common; it is relatively unusual to find an individual who has been dependent upon only one sedative or tranquilizer. The benzodiazepines are also extremely variable with withdrawal reactions occurring as rapidly as 48 hours after the last dosage but often much later.[25]

One special problem sometimes presents itself with benzodiazepine withdrawal. In many cases individuals have been maintained on these medications for years, often beginning with some stressful life circumstances. For a variety of reasons, with or without medical supervision, such an individual may abruptly discontinue use of these tranquilizers. When people experience a mild withdrawal syndrome, they often interpret this syndrome as a return of the supposed "underlying" anxiety and begin taking benzodiazepines again. This is unfortunate in that it is difficult to justify the long-term use of any of these medications for antianxiety purposes.

Differentiating the withdrawal from functional anxiety, such as in generalized anxiety disorder, can usually be done by noting the pattern of "anxiety symptoms." Withdrawal is characterized by an initial increase, followed by a slow decrease in these symptoms, following discontinuation of the drug. If the symptoms do not decrease in the subsequent 6 to 8 weeks, an underlying functional anxiety disorder may be present.[25] This judgment must be made very cautiously, however, for there are a few reports of vague but persistent withdrawal symptoms, primarily consisting of sleep disturbance, nightmares, and mild depersonalization, continuing for up to 6 months following cessation of benzodiazepine use.[26]

Significant physical damage from the chronic use of these substances, such as is found in alcohol dependence, is quite rare.

Behavioral manifestations. As noted above, there are two types of abusers of these drugs, quite distinct from one another. The young, predominantly male type of patient may appear in a variety of settings in a state of intoxication, requesting or demanding a further supply of the drug. These individuals can often be quite insistent and may threaten violence.

Sometimes these individuals come to a medical facility requesting treatment when their supply of drugs is interrupted. Beginning signs of withdrawal may be present. Often these individuals are poor treatment candidates and are usually easily recognized. The patient is usually uninterested in an inpatient detoxification program but requests a prescription to assist in coping with the impending withdrawal. The person will, in short, be primarily interested in obtaining a substitute supply of the drug and only secondarily in real treatment issues. If the clinician responds with any other offers or suggestions, these individuals usually respond angrily that they need help *now.*

The second subpopulation of sedative abusers are those who were introduced to the drugs by way of a legitimate medical need. Once such an individual has begun to increase the dose, further supplies of the drug are needed. In contrast to the first group, this individual will usually make multiple contacts of primarily medical agencies, as opposed to psychiatric or mental health agencies. Such an individual may visit several neighborhood medical clinics with complaints of nervousness, insomnia, and various mild somatic disorders. Nurses in such agencies and clinics must be aware of this pattern and not neglect to conduct a substance abuse evaluation in all cases.

Cognitive and emotional manifestations. Cognitive manifestations of intoxication and withdrawal are substantially similar to that of alcohol.

In situations in which the patient is neither intoxicated or in withdrawal, the "euphoria-seeking" abuser will often be more open about the drug or drugs used. In many situations, some drug users are not nearly so psychologically defensive and denying of their dependence as those with alcohol dependence. It is unclear why this is the case. To some extent, any problematic behavior that is inherently reinforcing but that produces negative consequences, such as alcohol or drug use, gambling, or indiscriminate sexual behavior, produces denial. On the other hand, in many drug-using subcultures there is little or no stigma attached to illicit drug use. In fact, there is often a kind of superior, "in-group" attitude, a feeling that people who use that drug are somehow rising above the ordinary drudgery of everyday life—a romanticized, overvalued view. This view is often further reinforced by the criminal underworld that such drug users encounter in obtaining their drugs.

The drug user who began by taking the medication for a legitimate medical purpose will often continue in this manner. That is, the person will deny using "drugs" but will admit to taking "medication" and will (if pressed) ignore the increase in dosage and continue to insist that the use is "strictly doctor's orders."

Occasionally individuals with a more serious mental disorder may illicitly use sedatives or tranquilizers in an attempt to medicate their condition themselves. This phenomenon commonly takes place with individuals with panic disorders and manic episodes. The use of sedating drugs, often combined with alcohol, can become a problem in its own right. If the underlying mental disorder is of significant proportions, it must be diagnosed and treated first before the extent of the alcohol and drug problem can be accurately evaluated. Most individuals who try to control their panic attacks or manic episodes with alcohol and tranquilizers will significantly reduce their intake once the primary disorder is adequately treated. However, abrupt discontinuation of the alcohol and tranquilizers can still precipitate a withdrawal reaction, and this possibility must not be neglected.

Individuals who come to a medical facility with any complaint but who are unusually familiar with the names and dosages of this class of drugs should be suspected of possible drug abuse and/or dependence. For example, a 31-year-old married man came to a hospital emergency room complaining of anxiety and insomnia, apparently a result of being laid off from work. His family had significant financial problems. He was offered Dalmane 30 mg as a sleeping medication but insisted on Seconal, because "5 or 10 mg of Valium, 10 or 25 of Librium, and 500 mg of Placidyl don't even touch me."

Social manifestations. Many of the social manifestations of the abuse and dependence of these drugs are similar to that of alcohol. However, there are a few differences, primarily resulting from problems of availability. Alcohol is legal and readily obtainable by almost anyone, even minors. The barbiturates, benzodiazepines, and other sedatives and tranquilizers discussed in this section, however, are available by physician's prescription only. These two distinct subtypes of abusers described earlier each have their characteristic methods of obtaining the drugs. The younger, "euphoria-seeking" users typically obtain theirs through illicit channels, whereas the older, "medical patients" often seek out a number of medical clinics, complaining of various minor maladies, many of which are often treated with sedatives and tranquilizers.

CANNABIS ABUSE AND DEPENDENCE
Classification

Drugs in this group are those in which delta-9-tetrahydrocannabinol (THC) is the psychoactive agent:

Marijuana
Hashish
Hash oil

Disorders that exist relative to these substances include cannabis intoxication, cannabis delusional disorder, cannabis abuse, and cannabis dependence.

Cannabis abuse, following the pattern for other substances, is diagnosed when the individual manifests (1) a pattern of pathological use, (2) impairment in social or occupational functioning resulting from cannabis use, and (3) duration of disturbance of at least 1 month. Cannabis dependence is diagnosed when the individual exhibits either a pattern of pathological use *or* impairment in social or occupational functioning *and* tolerance to the substance, the need for increased amounts to achieve the desired effect. There is no demonstrated abstinence syndrome.

Epidemiology

Marijuana use is very widespread in the United States. In 1976 it was estimated that over 36 million U.S. citizens had at least tried the drug and that at least 15 million had used it within the preceding month. A Gallup poll in 1977 reported that 25% of Americans over the age of 18 had tried marijuana.[4]

It appears there has been some moderate decrease in usage over the past few years, however. The percentage of high school seniors in 1981 who used marijuana in the month preceding a national survey was 31.6, down from 37.1 in a survey taken 3 years before.[39] Annual prevalence decreased from 50.2 to 46.1 in the same period.

Causative factors

There is little known about the causes of cannabis abuse or dependence. Since the use of the drug is so widespread in U.S. society, it is clear that some users are bound to become abusers. However, it is unknown if biological or physiological factors have a role to play in this disorder or if it is strictly an interaction between cultural, social factors on the one hand and individual psychological factors on the other.

Clinical presentation

Physical manifestations. There are subtle but clear physical manifestations of cannabis intoxication. A substantial increase in pulse rate is perhaps the most consistent and clear, an increase in 24 beats per minute in one study.[4] Other signs are conjunctival infection—red eyes—and dryness of mouth. Increased appetite is a subjectively reported symptom. Intoxicated individuals tend to become passive, quiet, and contemplative. Since the most usual route of administration is smoking, the distinctive smell of the drug may cling to clothes and hair.

In rare cases individuals may develop panic or extreme anxiety reactions while intoxicated, similar to the "bad trip" of hallucinogens. Most acute adverse reactions are of this type, while a toxic psychosis or precipitated psychotic episode, while not unheard of, is extremely rare.

Most controversial is the issue of physical damage from chronic use. While the so-called "amotivational syndrome" will be discussed below in the section on behavioral manifestations, there is some evidence that marijuana smoke is as toxic to the lungs as cigarette smoke and that chronic use lowers hormone levels in some cases. These findings are still tentative, and research is continuing.[42] There is no abstinence syndrome.

Behavioral manifestations. As noted above, individuals who are intoxicated on marijuana tend to become passive, withdrawn, and contemplative. Many become lethargic and sleepy, while others report feeling "energized" and hyperactive. In some cases evidence of increased anxiety may be noticeable, with pacing and hypervigilance. Rarely does outright panic occur.

Much has been written about the so-called "amotivational syndrome" of individuals with cannabis dependence. Individuals who chronically use high amounts of cannabis (such as two, three, or more "joints" every day) seem to develop a syndrome of chronic passivity, introversion, loss of interest in school, work, or interpersonal relationships, and apathy. Cross-cultural studies of the phenomenon have been inconclusive, and in the United States the picture is complicated by the lack of clear-cut experimental evidence. Although much anecdotal evidence exists about the reality of this clinical picture, it is unclear if marijuana causes the syndrome or if marijuana is simply more often used by individuals who would be "dropouts" from society anyway.[43,44]

As noted above with hallucinogens, some observers think the amotivational syndrome is a mild dementia resulting from a toxic effect of the drug itself. Others think it is a depression, with the lack of motivation and apathy being symptoms of and secondary to the affective disorder.[35] Some clinicians report a return to premorbid level of functioning when chronic cannabis use is discontinued. Thus if it is a dementia, it appears to be a reversible one, at least in some cases.

Cognitive and emotional manifestations. When intoxicated on cannabis an individual may experience a variety of subjective changes, including the sense that time has slowed down, a general moderate sense of pleasure, which may progress to euphoria, subjective intensification of perceptions (sounds are heard more keenly, colors appear brighter, patterns appear to be more intricate and interesting), and a general feeling of apathy and of being removed from one's surroundings. Sometimes the individual will become anxious, which may progress to panic on rare occasions. Occasionally a cannabis user will feel suspicious or paranoid, although rarely with delusional certainty.

Intoxication usually causes mild short-term memory impairment, although the experienced user could probably compensate for this impairment with increased concentration such that it would not be noticeable in a standard mental status examination.

Social manifestations. Chronic use of cannabis can easily impair social or occupational functioning, although many users report being able to use low doses on a daily basis without a decrease in functioning. There is some speculation that chronic intoxication may not affect boring, repetitive tasks but may strongly decrease performance on tasks requiring concentration and creativity.[44] To the extent that the amotivational syndrome is a real clinical entity and is caused by cannabis abuse, severe impairment results.

Driving is impaired by cannabis intoxication; the widespread use of marijuana has no doubt already contributed to some traffic accidents. Impairment seems to be less severe than that caused by alcohol, however.

Since marijuana is readily available and not exceedingly expensive, little interference in daily living is produced by the tasks of funding and obtaining the drug.

COCAINE AND AMPHETAMINE OR SIMILARLY ACTING SYMPATHOMIMETIC ABUSE AND DEPENDENCE
Classification

Although there are some differences, much similarity exists between cocaine and amphetamines and similarly acting sympathomimetics. Chief among the latter is methylphenidate (Ritalin). The most significant commonality between all of these drugs is that they are central nervous system (CNS) stimulants. CNS stimulant effects include increased pulse, blood pressure and respiration, suppression of appetite, and enhanced wakefulness.

Amphetamines and other sympathomimetics are used intravenously and orally. Cocaine, on the other hand, is distinctive in its route of administration—intranasally, called "snorting." In addition, cocaine is a local anesthetic as well as a CNS stimulant. It too can be administered intravenously.

Epidemiology

Abuse and dependence of these substances is common. Cocaine has become increasingly popular in the past few years, so that in some areas it is the most common drug of abuse. The use of amphetamines has declined somewhat in recent years, probably because of its inclusion in

Schedule II of the Controlled Substances Act of 1970.[4] Since then there has been a dramatic increase in the prevalence of illicit "look-alike" drugs. "Look-alikes" are illicitly packaged or prepared drugs that are made to resemble pharmaceutically manufactured preparations. For example, caffeine is placed in black capsules, which resemble a legally manufactured amphetamine-dextroamphetamine combination. Caffeine, or a caffeine and phenylpropranolamine combination, is used to simulate the CNS stimulant effect of amphetamine, and the seller can make a large profit on these counterfeit stimulants.

Causative factors

Little is known about the causes of cocaine and amphetamine abuse and dependence. However, it seems clear that at least part of the explanation is simply the subjectively pleasurable experience provided by moderate dosages of all of these drugs. In addition, many people become amphetamine users through dieting. Physicians prescribe amphetamines as a method for weight loss.

Clinical presentation

Physical manifestations. In small doses, amphetamines and cocaine tend to have very mild physical symptoms. There is a small increase in pulse rate and blood pressure, dilation of the pupils, and sometimes perspiration and/or chills. Needle marks may be present since these drugs can be taken intravenously. Chronic cocaine users often have a perpetual "runny nose," resulting from the continual irritation caused by "snorting" the drug. Individuals often have a great deal of energy, may walk or pace about, and may be hyperactive in general. The use of amphetamines and cocaine can mimic hypomania or mania, depending upon the dosage.

In larger doses amphetamines and similarly acting sympathomimetics can cause a delirium, with confusion, waxing and waning alertness, and generalized impairment of intellectual abilities. Pulse and blood pressure are elevated, and the individual will be perspiring heavily and may experience nausea or vomiting. The individual may be aggressive or violent, and tactile or olfactory hallucinations may occur. In addition, amphetamines and similarly acting sympathomimetics can also produce a delusional disorder, which cocaine rarely does. In this instance, the disorder mostly follows a period of chronic or almost continuous use, such as over a period of 1 to 2 weeks. In this case the physical symptoms are not so pronounced, but mental aberrations are most evident.

The regular user of amphetamines or cocaine, when appearing at a medical or psychiatric setting, will often have no physical manifestation of drug use. Sometimes needle marks may be evident, or the cocaine user's constant "sniffles" may be present. But often there will be no indications.

After regular and prolonged use of amphetamines or similarly acting sympathomimetics, abrupt cessation will produce a withdrawal reaction. The withdrawal, as usual, is roughly the opposite of the drug effect. Physical manifestations include lethargy, increased and disturbed sleep, increased dreaming, and often increased hunger. The existence of a withdrawal reaction from regular use of cocaine is controversial—DSM-III states that there is "apparently no withdrawal syndrome" whereas others suggest that the "crash" following a period of continual use is a legitimate withdrawal reaction.[19] "Crashing" essentially includes the above symptoms—lethargy and increased sleep, along with the depression to be discussed below.

Withdrawal from amphetamines, similarly acting sympathomimetics, and cocaine is not physiologically hazardous and so use of these substances can be stopped abruptly; a taper is not necessary. However, the "craving" is so powerful that often an inpatient rehabilitation program is necessary to assist the dependent individual to remain abstinent.

Behavioral manifestations. As noted above, use of these substances can mimic a hypomanic or manic episode. Thus the individual may be hyperactive, pacing, talkative, hypersexual, aggressive, violent, and "high energy," depending upon the dosage taken and duration of use. Individuals experiencing an amphetamine delusional disorder may be extremely paranoid and may act on fearful, paranoid beliefs, perhaps taking violent action against those whom they fear. Such individuals may not be hyperactive, as is the individual who is experiencing an amphetamine intoxication, and so their violence may be unexpected. The nurse must always be aware of this possibility.

Cognitive and emotional manifestations. As noted above, intoxication with any of these substances produces a number of CNS stimulant effects. In addition, there are several characteristic emotional reactions. The individual who is intoxicated will usually feel extremely confident, even euphoric, with an exaggerated sense of competence and self-worth. The person may be hypervigilant, grandiose, elated, and agitated. In higher doses hallucinations may occur, often tactile and olfactory.[29]

Delirium may also occur. As with all delirium, the mental status examination will reveal an individual with a variable level of consciousness, who has a general, pervasive loss of intellectual abilities. The person will often be disoriented and have a severe short-term memory loss and will be unable to perform other simple mental tasks.

In the amphetamine delusional disorder, a moderately elaborate set of paranoid delusions is produced rather quickly, almost always after a period of chronic and continual use. The individual will often be agitated, anxious, aggressive, and hostile and may act on fixed, false beliefs. Ideas of reference, such as strangers on the street plotting or special references on the television or radio, may occur. This disorder resembles paranoia, as well as paranoid schizophrenia. However, sometimes amphetamine delusional disorder is accompanied by tactile hallucinations of "bugs" crawling under the skin, which is rare in other disorders. Very abrupt onset of a delusional system is suggestive of a drug-induced disorder. Of course, nothing is as helpful as the admission by the patient or the patient's family that an amphetamine or cocaine has recently been used.

CASE STUDY: A 28-year-old married woman was brought by her husband to a psychiatric emergency clinic for "paranoia." They both readily admitted that she had been using "diet pills" on a regular basis and over the past 2 weeks had increased her daily dosage from 10 to 12 30-mg capsules. For the past week or so she had believed that her husband was "bugging" the house with microphones and listening devices, that the television was "two-way," and that other people could watch her through it. Her husband had suspected that her drug was responsible and had talked her into stopping 2 days previously. On the day she was seen she was beginning to understand the delusional nature of her ideas and said, "I had the crazy idea that a light bulb in a certain lamp was somehow a microphone and a light bulb at the same time." However, the patient still felt vaguely uneasy and was not totally intact in her thinking. She had not come in sooner because of some delusional fears. She agreed to an admission to a substance abuse unit in the hospital.

In the individual who abuses or who is dependent upon amphetamines, similarly acting sympathomimetics, or cocaine, denial is often pervasive. This denial is no different than that found with the other substances discussed so far in this chapter. However, if anything, it is even more pervasive. Especially powerful is the denial and rationalization produced by the regular use of cocaine. Perhaps part of the reason is the "high status" in which the drug is held in certain segments of the population.

It is especially difficult if the individual is interviewed while under the influence of cocaine—if the person is mildly intoxicated. Since the effect of the drug is to produce overconfidence, euphoria, grandiosity, and inflated self-esteem, it is almost impossible to break through this array of defensive symptoms.

Social manifestations. The continual use of amphetamines and similarly acting sympathomimetics, as well as cocaine, can be quite similar to that of alcohol. With cocaine in particular, individuals have been known to go on "binges" almost identical to that of the alcoholic individual. Since cocaine is extremely expensive, individuals dependent upon it steal money from their family or friends, are extremely manipulative and deceitful in their relationships, and often spend household money on the drug. The cycle is as difficult to break as that of alcohol, and it can be argued that cocaine is even more reinforcing than alcohol, perhaps more so than any other drug, which makes interruption of the cycle extremely problematic.

> CASE STUDY: A substance abuse program received a call from the father of a 32-year-old married man who was the owner of a popular bar in a college town. He stated that his son was "hooked" on cocaine and was ruining his business and his marriage. The patient went on regular "binges," using up thousands of dollars of cocaine in a 3- to 4-day period, not sleeping, wandering all over town, and would become very belligerent and even violent if his wife or father attempted to intervene in any way. After the binge was over he would sleep for 1 to 2 days and then beg forgiveness from his wife and promise never to do it again. Then the entire cycle would repeat itself a few weeks later. His business was floundering, both because of his inattention and because he was spending all the profits on drugs. His wife was ready to file for divorce. A number of suggestions were given to the father to help him try again to intervene with the patient, but the patient never contacted the clinic.

HALLUCINOGEN ABUSE AND DEPENDENCE
Classification

In this section a number of drugs are discussed together, even though their effects are quite varied and unpredictable. The traditional hallucinogens are the following:

LSD (lysergic acid diethylamide)
Psilocybin
Peyote
Mescaline
STP (dimethoxymethylamphetamine [DOM])
DMT (dimethyltryptamine)

In addition, two other drugs have somewhat different effects, but are sufficiently similar, especially in clinical presentation, to warrant their discussion here:

PCP (phencyclidine)
Ketamine

One of the difficult aspects of evaluating and treating individuals who use any of these drugs is the uncertainty as to what the substance actually is. All of these substances are illegal and have no accepted medical usage, and thus virtually all are manufactured illicitly in clandestine laboratories. Needless to say, "quality control" and "truth in advertising" does not apply to illegally manufactured drugs, with the result that poorly synthesized substances are sold for as much money as possible and under whatever name consumers seem to favor at that time. In drug analysis after drug analysis, in city after city in the United States, over the past 10 years LSD and PCP tend to be the actual active ingredients in most hallucinogens, no matter what they are sold as. There is very little actual mescaline or psilocybin or any of the other more "esoteric" hallucinogens in use today, and there is no "THC." THC, or tetrahydrocannabinol, the psychoactive material in marijuana, is a very popular "street drug," and yet virtually all samples analyzed in the past 10 years have actually been LSD or PCP.[30-33]

Epidemiology

Use of these substances appears to have decreased somewhat over the past 10 years. One survey of high school students, for example, shows a modest decrease in lifetime prevalence for use of hallucinogens from 16.3% to 13.3% from 1975 to 1981.[34]

Although it appears that abuse of hallucinogens and of PCP is relatively uncommon, PCP is perhaps the most common illicit substance sold, excluding marijuana. Not only is PCP sold as "THC" and as many other hallucinogens (mescaline, psilocybin, "magic mushrooms," peyote), but it is also sold as cocaine. Other "street names" for PCP include "angel dust," "the Peace Pill," "hog," and "crystal T."

Causative factors

As noted in DSM-III, hallucinogen and PCP (and similarly acting arylcyclohexylamine) abuse occurs and is defined much the same as with other drugs. In other words there must be (1) a pattern of pathological use, (2) impairment in social or occupational functioning, and (3) a duration of at least 1 month. However, because no clear withdrawal reaction has been demonstrated for these drugs, and because the existence of tolerance is controversial, no diagnostic category for dependence has been included in DSM-III.

Hallucinogen and PCP use has been tied to a great extent to the "hippie" and "countercultural" movements of the late 1960s and early 1970s. Thus specific subcultural factors appear to play some role in the use of these drugs, but it is unclear to what extent such factors are responsible for *abuse*. Similarly, it is unknown why one individual will have an adverse psychological reaction to a hallucinogen ("a bad trip" or a "hallucinogen affective disorder," for example) whereas another one will not. It has become relatively clear, however, that in individuals with a vulnerability to psychosis, such as an individual with schizophrenia, use of these substances may precipitate a reemergence of the thought disorder.

Clinical presentation

Physical and behavioral manifestations. Individuals intoxicated on hallucinogens such as LSD may have few physical signs and symptoms of this intoxication. Often pupils are dilated, pulse and blood pressure are mildly elevated, and there may be some sweating and tremors. All of these signs may be easily overlooked; the individual intoxicated on a hallucinogen is not always particularly noteworthy. With PCP and ketamine, often there is horizontal or vertical nystagmus, obvious ataxia, dysarthric or garbled speech, and significant hypertension.[35] Perhaps because of the anesthetic-like effect of the drug, individuals often walk with an extremely peculiar and characteristic high-stepping gait, termed "moon walking."

DSM-III defines hallucinogen intoxication not as an intoxication but as a hallucinosis. However, at least in low doses, true hallucinations are relatively rare. Much more often the sensory distortions and perceptual alterations are intensifications in all of the senses, synesthesias, and illusions.

LSD-type hallucinogens are almost always ingested orally. PCP and ketamine may also be smoked or "snorted." These latter substances may also be injected, but such use is relatively rare. Needle marks are therefore rare.[36]

Both hallucinogen hallucinosis and PCP intoxication can often produce adverse emotional and behavioral reactions. With the former, the most common negative reaction is the so-called bad trip. This phenomenon is not an organic mental disorder in its own right but a panic reaction to the other symptoms of the hallucinosis. Individuals may become extremely anxious or panicked, may fear losing their minds, and are extremely distractible, hypervigilant, and sometimes paranoid. Lessening of stimuli and the verbal "talk-down" technique are often quite effective.

In contrast, PCP and ketamine intoxication can sometimes produce a superficially similar response but with important differences. Because of the anesthetic-like effects of these drugs, individuals often report an inability to feel parts of their body or that part of them is "dead." They often become belligerent, impulsive, aggressive, and combative. Sometimes catatonic excitement or catatonic withdrawal are the result. Perceptual changes are so profound that many individuals are unable to comprehend language and are also often unable to talk intelligibly. "Talk-downs" are seldom effective.[35,37,38]

In higher doses, PCP and ketamine can cause convulsions and coma.[35] Such reactions are extremely rare with hallucinogens, and when they do occur they are often caused by adulterants rather than by the hallucinogen itself. However, the use of strychnine as an adulterant is quite uncommon, despite "street mythology" to the contrary.[38]

In most cases, hallucinogen hallucinosis or PCP/ketamine intoxication lasts from about 6 hours to perhaps 1 to 2 days. However, some other reactions may last much longer, especially with PCP. In addition to an intoxication, PCP can produce a toxic psychosis, termed a delirium in DSM-III. This delirium, with waxing and waning level of consciousness, disorientation, short-term memory impairment, increased psychomotor activity, perceptual disturbance, and confused speech, can last for up to a week and occasionally even longer.[35] PCP can still be found in the patient's urine during such an episode, although blood tests will be negative.[35]

PCP can also produce one "mixed" organic mental disorder, in which the symptoms fluctuate from one kind of disorder to another. For example, the episode may begin with a delirium, progress to a delusional disorder, and then become an organic affective syndrome. These episodes can also last up to one week and occasionally several weeks.

Several other types of organic mental disorders can occur with LSD-type hallucinogens as well. A hallucinogen delusional disorder and a hallucinogen affective disorder can occur, producing systematic delusions with no other signs of impairment or an affective disorder without a concomitant thought disorder. Each of these occurs 24 hours after the cessation of hallucinogen use and may follow an episode of hallucinogen hallucinosis. The longer any of these disorders persists, the more question exists as to whether they may actually be a percipitated functional disorder, such as an affective disorder brought on by the use of LSD. There are no clear guidelines available to assist the clinician in making this diagnostic decision.

When individuals who abuse LSD or PCP are seen while they are not intoxicated, there are few or no physical manifestations. while various reports of chromosome damage, blindness resulting from staring at the sun while "tripping," and other bizarre happenings were reported in the popular press and magazines in the past, most of these reports turned out to be exaggerations. There is no clearly demonstrated evidence of chromosome breakage.[4] There have been occasional reports of violence linked to hallucinogen use, especially with regard to PCP.

Since there is no demonstrated withdrawal syndrome, individuals do not become dependent on these substances. There is no physiological abstinence syndrome.

Cognitive and emotional manifestations. As noted above, intoxication on these drugs produces a variety of physical and emotional effects. The latter include euphoria, anxiety, emotional lability, grandiosity, a sensation of slowed time, synesthesias, belligerence, impulsivity, and unpredictability in PCP and ketamine use.

With LSD-type hallucinogens some of these same emotional or psychological reactions can occur, although the belligerence and impulsivity are much rarer occurrences. Much more commonly, the individual feels elated, anxious, and often very preoccupied by the perceptual changes, illusions, and (more rarely) hallucinations. Individuals may experience ideas of reference of a particular kind—that the user has an intimate and special connection with the world, accompanied by elation or euphoria—termed "cosmic consciousness." In less pleasant episodes individuals may feel afraid of becoming insane, paranoid, and markedly anxious or depressed. With these substances the user's expectations and surroundings have great effect on the outcome of the experience.

Individuals experiencing any of the LSD or PCP/ketamine mental disorders may be brought to emergency rooms and medical clinics for treatment. Laboratory analysis of blood and urine is often very useful in making a correct diagnosis, and in differentiating between a drug-induced mental disorder and a functional one. In these situations often the central difficulty is panic or anxiety, as opposed to the actual mental disorder itself.

In any of these disorders there may be loss of cognitive abilities, with disorientation, inability to perform simple tasks, and poor performance on questions regarding fund of knowledge, such as presidents or well-known current events.

Social manifestations. It is rare for the social manifestations of the abuse of these substances to be as severe as that of alcohol, barbiturates and sedatives, or cocaine and amphetamines. It is rare for individuals to use these substances on a daily basis, and in many cases the period of most severe abuse is relatively short. Individuals may abuse these substances for a few months or perhaps a year and then return to their previous life-style. In unusual cases severe abuse does take place, many timea among individuals with antisocial personality disorder. Occasionally individuals report years of hallucinogen and/or PCP abuse, usually in the context of polydrug abuse. Some of these individuals are described by their friends as "burned out," referring to a poorly-defined syndrome of low motivation, aimlessness and goallessness, with subjectively reported short-term memory impairment, difficulty concentrating, and vague depression. It is unclear if this is a mild dementia brought on by severe and continuous poly-drug abuse or a depression with so-called pseudo-dementia.[33]

Some of these individuals experience "flashbacks." Flashbacks are spontaneous recurrences of a hallucinogen intoxication or hallucinosis, which take place weeks or months after the last incidence of drug use. The emotional manifestations are usually exactly the same as the drug experience itself. The cause of flashbacks is unknown, but it is clearly not the drug remaining in the body for long periods of time. There is some evidence that the probability of flashbacks is higher for individuals who have had "bad trips," panic or anxiety during PCP intoxication, or LSD or other hallucinogen hallucinosis, and that the flashback often mimics the "bad trip." Often flashbacks are precipitated by environmental stimuli that remind the individual of the circumstances surrounding the adverse hallucinogen experience.[40,41]

OPIOID ABUSE AND DEPENDENCE
Classification

Substances included in this category include heroin, morphine, opium, and methadone, as well as the synthetic analgesics pentazocine (Talwin), meperidine (Demerol), oxycodone (Percodan), hydromorphone (Dilaudid), and codeine.

Epidemiology

Although heroin abuse had been highly publicized, the total number of "addicts" in the United States was only about 300,000 in the early 1970s,[27] and about half of these live in New York City.

The incidence of abuse and dependence on the synthetic analgesics is unknown but may be many times higher than the number of heroin abusers.

Causative factors

Little is known about the factors that cause an individual to use, abuse, or become dependent upon opioids. Since individuals from backgrounds of poverty and social deprivation are known to make up a large proportion of all heroin abusers, social factors have been postulated as playing a large role in causing heroin use.

Clinical presentation

Physical manifestations. Opioid intoxication, since it is a central nervous system depressant like alcohol and the sedatives, is somewhat similar to these other drugs. The individual is often slow-moving, with loss of coordination, slurred speech, and passivity. There are, however, two distinctive features of opioid intoxication, pupillary constriction and "nodding." Pupils are reduced to pinpoint size, and the individual often demonstrates a characteristic series of brief periods of light sleep alternating with brief periods of wakefulness. This cycle is referred to as being "on the nod." Individuals may "nod off" abruptly while sitting, talking, or engaging in other passive activities, sleep briefly and lightly, and awaken again spontaneously. This cycle may be repeated for the duration of the intoxication, a period of several hours with heroin. Since heroin is used primarily intravenously, its effects are short-lived.

In overdoses individuals are stuporous and have severely impaired respiration, as well as the above symptoms. A practically foolproof diagnostic test for opioid intoxication exists and is also a treatment for overdoses. Narcotic antagonists are drugs that reverse the "agonist" effects of opioid substances. In the past, only "partial" antagonists were available, in that these substances had some "agonist" effects of their own. In practice this means that if an individual were in respiratory distress because of an unknown overdose, and the antagonist were administered, the outcome was a gamble. If the overdose were caused by an opioid, its effect would promptly be reversed. But if the overdose were caused by barbiturates or other central nervous system depressants, the partial antagonist would worsen the respiratory problem. But for the past few years a "pure" narcotic antagonist, naloxone (Narcan) has been widely available. Narcan has no effect on an overdose of sedatives or tranquilizers but reverses an opioid overdose.[28]

Many so-called heroin overdoses, however, may not really be overdoses at all. Experimental studies have shown that individuals can tolerate large amounts of morphine without suffering significant respiratory distress, and many of the deaths in question take place within seconds or minutes of injection. "Addicts" are found dead with needles still in their arms. The best evidence so far is that these deaths are not overdoses but allergic reactions, either to the heroin itself or to any of the various adulterants that are commonly mixed with the heroin in order to dilute the drug.[27]

Withdrawal from opioids is uncomfortable but rarely serious or life threatening, despite being portrayed as such in movies and on television. The withdrawal reaction produces no significant mental symptoms and no delirium or amnestic syndrome occurs. The physical manifestations of withdrawal include fever, abdominal aches and pains, diarrhea, yawning, lacrimation, sweating, and dilation of the pupils. It is a syndrome very similar to "the flu." Individuals in withdrawal may come to medical clinics and hospital emergency rooms, requesting or demanding medication to ease the withdrawal or feigning physical illness in order to receive analgesic drugs.

Users of heroin will usually have needle marks, bruises, and/or abscesses on various parts of their body, although some individuals are careful to use veins only in less obvious areas. Although the other opioid substances can be used intravenously as well, they are commonly taken orally.

Behavioral and social manifestations. Individuals who are dependent upon heroin often become engaged in various illegal activities in order to make the money necessary to support their habits, which may cost several hundred dollars per day. For males this commonly involves burglaries, breaking-and-entering, and petty theft. For females, prostitution is a common method of raising money. There may be brief periods of imprisonment during which drug use ceases followed by resumption of use after release.

Since the effects of a single administration of heroin last only 4 to 6 hours, dependent individuals must use the substance several times per day. In addition, obtaining the substance is often a time-consuming activity because of the illegal channels involved. For all of these reasons, regular use of heroin can easily become a full-time occupation. Users commonly neglect their families and other relationships, are often unable to hold regular jobs, and essentially build their entire life around raising money, obtaining and using heroin, and associated activities. Although individuals with antisocial personality disorders often become involved in drug use of various kinds, the use of heroin can produce a behavioral disorder essentially the same as sociopathy. However, after approximately 10 years or so many users stop using spontaneously and may become less deviant in their behavior once drug-free.

Cognitive and emotional manifestations. Once again, denial is a common concomitant of opioid use and dependence. Individuals are often severely impaired in their social and occupational functioning and yet will not admit that the drug use is a problem. When intoxicated, as noted earlier, individuals may appear to be "drunk," with reduced level of consciousness, slurred speech, and loss of coordination. However, such a person does not smell of alcohol, will "nod off" from time to time, and may have noticeable needle marks.

During withdrawal users will more often be seen by nurses at medical clinics and emergency rooms. There are no mental manifestations of withdrawal that will show up in a standard mental status examination. Orientation is not impaired, there are no hallucinations, and in general the individual will simply appear to be sick from the "flu."

Heroin users become very demanding, manipulative, and angry when frustrated in their demands for supplies of the drug. They can become so desperate that they may attempt to steal supplies from hospitals and emergency rooms and can become violent. It must be remembered, however, that this is not a drug effect but a result of withdrawal and the difficulty users sometimes experience in obtaining sufficient amounts of the drug.

NURSING DIAGNOSES OF SUBSTANCE ABUSE

As indicated by this chapter, there is a wide range of substance use, abuse, and withdrawal behaviors evidenced by users of a variety of chemicals. There are multiple complex psychosocial, behavioral, and physical ramifications of the use of drugs and alcohol. Nursing diagnoses of the substance abuser will span those behaviors apparent when the person seeks assistance for incapacitating psychosocial and physical problems. In the box below are selected nursing diagnoses for individuals who abuse drugs and alcohol.

TAXONOMY OF NURSING DIAGNOSES FOR SUBSTANCE ABUSE

1. Ineffective individual coping
   1.10 Impaired social functioning
   1.20 Impaired relationships with others
   1.30 Impaired occupational functioning
   1.40 Impaired cognitive abilities
   1.50 Impaired ability to carry out daily activities
2. Alteration in thought processes
   2.10 Impaired reality testing
   2.20 Impaired judgment and insight
   2.30 Impaired problem-solving
3. Sensory-perceptual alterations
   3.10 Hallucinations
   3.20 Agitation and restlessness
   3.30 Change in usual response to stimuli
   3.40 Disorientation

CASE EXAMPLE: Assessment of Mr. Coates

Identifying information. Mr. Coates is a 37-year-old married father of two children, ages 10 and 7. He is employed as a house painter by a small local firm.

Presenting problem. Mr. Coates was seen in the mental health clinic at his own request, although the original call came from his wife. He states he has been increasingly irritable at home, has been increasingly anxious, and has had difficulty in sleeping.

Recent history. Mr. Coates states that he and his wife of 12 years have always gotten along fairly well until recently. He has been employed at the same painting company for 8 years, but lately work has been slow, apparently because of the economy. Several other people with less seniority have been laid off, and lately the remaining men have only had 2 or 3 days work per week. Apparently because of his increased financial worries, Mr. Coates and his wife have been arguing more recently, and they both remark that the children seem timid and withdrawn lately.

Family history. The patient is one of five children; his parents live in a medium-sized city several hundred miles west of here and are retired.

His brothers and sisters live in various parts of the country; there is no history of emotional problems or mental illness in the family.

Personal history. Mr. Coates is the second oldest of five children, as noted above. He was raised in a city west of here and moved to this city soon after completing high school, at first taking a job at a local factory. Later he began to work as a house painter part-time with a friend whom he had met in the factory. Later still this friend left the factory and began his own house-painting firm, and within a year Mr. Coates had quit the factory to work with his friend. At about this time he met his current wife, and they were married several years later.

The patient has had no significant medical problems and states he has never had problems with anxiety and insomnia such as at present. His hobbies include bowling two nights per week and softball two nights per week in the summer; he engages in these activities with a group of men from work and friends whom he has known for many years.

He denies any marital problems until recently, admitting that he and his wife have been worried about possible financial problems, especially since layoffs took place within the past few months. He admits to possibly "taking out" his frustrations on his wife and feels at present that it is probably "75%" his fault that they have been arguing frequently lately. He denies ever being physically abusive to her or their children. He states he is a "social" drinker and denies other "street drugs."

Mental status examination. Mr. Coates is a moderately overweight man of medium height, dressed cleanly and neatly. He was markedly anxious with fidgety movements and mild tremor, and he seemed quite ill at ease throughout the interview. His mood was mildly depressed and anxious and his affect appropriate to the content of the interview. He has had initial insomnia for the past several months but is not anhedonic and has no appetite loss, weight loss, or any other vegetative signs of depression. There was no disorder of the form or content of his thinking, and he denied auditory or visual hallucinations at any time. Cognitively, he seemed entirely intact: he was oriented ×3, remembered presidents accurately, did serial sevens quite rapidly, and his interpretation of proverbs was abstract.

Interview with wife. Mrs. Coates was interviewed after Mr. Coates was seen. She admitted that times have been difficult financially for them and that they have been arguing more frequently lately, but she stated that their arguments usually revolve around his drinking. She reports that he has always drunk more than average and often drank when bowling or after softball games. However, she states, for the past several months his drinking has increased to the point that he now consumes at least 12 beers per night, plus several "shots" of whiskey. On the days when there is no work he often goes to a local bar with his laid-off friends, comes home intoxicated in the late afternoon, and sleeps throughout the evening. Occasionally he claims to not remember an argument between the two of them when she brings it up the next morning.

Mrs. Coates states clearly that she feels they could handle the financial problems, except that he is spending excessive amounts of money on alcohol, as well as functioning less well in all areas of his life. She has tried to discuss the matter with him, but he usually becomes angry quickly and refuses to consider that his drinking may be a problem.

She adds that two of his brothers have significant problems with alcohol and one of them has had several hospitalizations and detoxifications for his problem.

Summary. When confronted by the intake worker and his wife, Mr. Coates eventually agreed that his drinking "might" be a problem. It seems that his long-term use of alcohol has now become maladaptive, and he has reacted to job and financial stress by increasing his intake. He has occasional blackouts and impaired social and family functioning. Although it is not totally clear at present, it appears that his apparent anxiety and insomnia may be secondary to his alcohol abuse, rather than to his financial and job stress.

His depression appears to be reactive and he is not suicidal. He is not psychotic, nor does he demonstrate any cognitive impairment.

Psychiatric Diagnosis. 1. Alcohol abuse
2. Alcohol dependence
3. R/O Adjustment reaction with mixed disturbance of emotions and conduct

Plan. Mr. Coates agreed to enter the local alcohol detoxification and rehabilitation unit for their 21-day program. Mrs. Coates enthusiastically agreed to participate in the family aspect of the program.

REFERENCES

1. American Psychiatric Association. *Diagnostic and statistical manual of mental disorders,* 3rd ed., Washington, D.C.: American Psychiatric Association, 1980, pp. 164, 165.
2. Haglund, R.M.J., & Schuckit, M.A. The epidemiology of alcoholism. In N.J. Estes, & M.E. Heinemann. *Alcoholism: Development, consequences, and interventions,* 2nd ed. St. Louis: The C.V. Mosby Co., 1982.
3. Gomberg, E.S.L. Women with alcohol problems. In N.J. Estes and M.E. Heinemann. *Alcoholism: Development, consequences, and interventions,* 2nd ed. St. Louis: The C.V. Mosby Co., 1982.
4. Ray, O. *Drugs, society, and human behavior,* 2nd ed. St. Louis: The C.V. Mosby Co., 1978, pp. 131, 406, 410, 282, 366.
5. Goodwin, D.W. Alcoholism and heredity: A review and hypothesis. *Archives of General Psychiatry,* January 1979, *36,* 57-61.
6. Vaillant, G.E., & Milofsky, E.S. The etiology of alcoholism. *American Psychologist,* May 1982, *37*(5), 494-503.
7. Barnes, G.E. Characteristics of the clinical alcoholic personality. *Journal of Studies on Alcohol,* 1980, *41*(9), 894-910.
8. Mendelson, J.H., & Mello, N.K. Biologic concomitants of alcoholism. *New England Journal of Medicine,* October 25, 1979, *301*(17), 912-921.
9. Vaillant, G.E., Natural history of male psychological health: VIII. Antecedents of alcoholism and "orality". *American Journal of Psychiatry,* February 1980, *137*(2), 181-186.

10. Goodwin, D.W. Alcoholism and affective disorders: The basic questions. In J. Solomon, Ed. *Alcoholism and clinical psychiatry.* New York: Plenum Medical Book Co., 1982.
11. Mayfield, D.G., & Montgomery, D. Alcoholism, alcohol intoxication, and suicide attempts. *Archives of General Psychiatry,* September 1972, *27,* 349-353.
12. Ullmann, L.P., & Krasner, L. *A psychological approach to abnormal behavior,* 2nd ed. Englewood Cliffs, N.J.: Prentice-Hall, Inc., 1975, p. 450.
13. Jellinek, E.M. Phases of alcohol addiction. *Quarterly Journal of Studies on Alcohol,* December 1952, *13*(4), 673-684.
14. Jellinek, E.M. *The disease concept of alcoholism.* New Haven, Conn.: Hillhouse Press, 1960.
15. Committee on Injuries, American Academy of Orthopedic Surgeons. *Emergency care and transportation of the sick and injured.* Menasha, Wisc. George Banta, Inc., 1971, pp. 181-183.
16. Weinberg, J.R. *Interview techniques for diagnosing alcoholism.* Center City, Minn.: Hazeldon Literature, 1979.
17. Cohen, S. The blood alcohol concentration. *Drug Abuse and Alcoholism Newsletter,* July 1981, *10*(6), 1-4.
18. Shaw, G.K. Alcohol dependence and withdrawal. *British Medical Bulletin,* 1982, *38*(1), 99-102.
19. Shulte, H.J. Drug abuse: Diagnosis and treatment. In J.R. Novello, Ed. *A practical handbook of psychiatry.* Springfield, Ill.: Charles C Thomas, Publisher, 1974.
20. Estes, N.J., Smith-DiJulio, K., & Heinemann, M.E. *Nursing diagnosis of the alcoholic person.* St. Louis: The C.V. Mosby Co., 1980, 14-18, 29-38.
21. Selzer, M.L. The Michigan Alcohol Screening Test: The quest for a new diagnostic instrument. *American Journal of Psychiatry,* June 1971, *127*(12), 1653-1658.
22. Selzer, M.L., Vinokur, A., & van Rooijen, L. A self-administered short version of the Michigan Alcoholism Screening Test (SMAST). *Journal of Studies on Alcohol,* 1975, *36,* 117-126.
23. Weil, A. Man's innate need: Getting high. *Intellectual Digest,* August 1972, 69-71.
24. Preskorn, S.H., & Denner, L.J. Benzodiazepines and withdrawal psychosis: A report of three cases. JAMA, January 3, 1977, *237*(1), 36-38.
25. Winokur, A., et al. Withdrawal reaction from long-term, low-dosage administration of diazepam: A double-blind, placebo-controlled case study. *Archives of General Psychiatry,* January 1980, *37,* 101-105.
26. Kale, A., and Kale, J.D. Sleep disorders: Recent findings in diagnosis and treatment of disturbances. *New England Journal of Medicine,* 1974, *290,* 487-499.
27. Brecher, E.M., & the Editors of Consumer Reports. *Licit and illicit drugs.* Mt. Vernon, N.Y.: The Consumers Union, 1972, p. 62.
28. *Narcotic antagonists.* Report Series of the National Clearinghouse for Drug Abuse Information, Rockville, Md., Series 26, No. 1, October 1973.
29. Cocaine. Report Series of the National Clearinghouse for Drug Abuse Information, Rockville, Md., Series 11, No. 1, January 1972.
30. Phencyclidine (PCP). Report Series of the National Clearinghouse for Drug Abuse Information, Rockville, Md., Series 14, No. 1, April 1973.
31. Mescaline. Report Series of the National Clearinghouse for Drug Abuse Information, Rockville, Md., Series 15, No. 1, May 1973.

32. Psilocybin. Report Series of the National Clearinghouse for Drug Abuse Information, Rockville, Md., Series 16, No. 1, May 1973.

33. Goldfrank, L., & Osborn, H. Phencyclidine (angel dust). *Hospital Physician,* May 1978, *14*(5), 18-21.

34. Institute for Social Research, University of Michigan. *Highlights from student drug use in America, 1975-1981.* Rockville, Md.: National Institute on Drug Abuse, 1981.

35. Smith, D.E., et al. The diagnosis and treatment of the PCP abuse syndrome. In R.C. Peterson, & R.C. Stillman, Ed. *Phencyclidine (PCP) abuse: An appraisal* (NIDA Research Monograph 21). Washington, D.C.: U.S. Government Printing Office, August 1978, 229-240.

36. Cohen, S. Angel dust. JAMA, August 8, 1977, *238*(6), 515-516.

37. Done, A.K. The toxic emergency: More on PCP. *Emergency Medicine,* November 1976, 185-186.

38. Domino, E.F. From sernyl to angel dust: The return of PCP. *The Paeon,* Nos. 1 & 2, 1981, pp. 1-5.

39. Lampe, M. *Drugs: Information for crisis treatment.* Ann Arbor, Mich.: Free People's Clinic, 1970.

40. Schoener, G., Flashbacks or flashes. *STASH Capsules,* Student Association for the Study of Hallucinogens, Inc., August 1973, *5*(4).

41. Shick, J.F.E., & Smith, D.E. Analysis of the LSD flashback. *Journal of Psychedelic Drugs,* September 1970, *3*(1), 13-19.

42. Cohen, S. Marijuana and the public health: An analysis of four major reports. *Drug Abuse and Alcoholism Newsletter,* December 1982, *11*(10), 1-4.

43. Cohen, S. Cannabis: Impact on motivation, Part I. *Drug Abuse and Alcoholism Newsletter,* December 1980, *9*(10), 1-4.

44. Cohen, S. Cannabis: Impact on motivation, Part II. *Drug Abuse and Alcoholism Newsletter,* January 1981, *10*(1), 1-4.

45. Liepman, M. *Alcohol-related disorders.* Unpublished document, Ann Arbor: The University of Michigan Hospitals.

CHAPTER 11

ASSESSING CHILDREN AND ADOLESCENTS

Assessment of the child who has mental health problems involves two major components. First the nurse must possess and be adept at utilizing a knowledge base of normal growth and development to recognize deviation from the normal. An understanding of what to expect at the various levels of development will help in the process of identifying which behavioral manifestations of concern may be normal development and which represent true pathology. Once the foundation is laid the nurse can apply this knowledge in the second step of the assessment process, the collection and analysis of biopsychosocial data on the child and family.

The stages of developmental progression and their accompanying tasks are viewed uniquely by several developmental theorists. Table 11:1 illustrates a schematic comparison of the four most prominent theorists, their stages of development, and an approximate sequence of occurrence.[1] A discussion of theories representative of psychosexual, psychosocial, interpersonal, cognitive, and holistic schools offers the nurse an eclectic knowledge base from which to view the child. Further review of growth and development, including a normative approach to biopsychosocial maturation, supports and assists the nurse in compiling a framework to use in assessment.

This chapter presents the theories of Freud, Erikson, Sullivan, Piaget, and Rogers as a basis for child and adolescent psychiatric assessment. A narrative on normal growth and development, prenatal through adolescence, will suggest further information to assess development. The assessment process, including an outline for data collection, will offer the nurse an integration of theory and practice from which holistic assessment proceeds.

TABLE 11:1   A developmental stage comparison: Freud, Erikson, Sullivan, Piaget

	Freud	Erikson	Sullivan	Piaget
Old age		Integrity vs. despair		
Middle age		Generativity vs. self-absorption	Adulthood	
Early adulthood		Intimacy vs. isolation	Late adolescence	
18				
17				
16	Genital	Identity vs. role diffusion	Early adolescent era	Formal operations
15				
14				
13				
12				
11		Industry vs. inferiority	Preadolescent era	
10				Concrete operations
9	Latency		Juvenile era	
8				
7				
6				Preoperational
5		Initiative vs. guilt	Childhood era	
4	Phallic			
3				
2	Anal	Autonomy vs. shame-doubt		
18 mo.			Infancy	Sensorimotor
1	Oral	Trust vs. mistrust		

DEVELOPMENTAL THEORIES
Freudian theory

Freud's theory of psychosexual development suggests that development occurs in phases, each of which follows in predictable sequence.[2] Each has a task for completion in order for development to continue on an upward path. Freud believed that sexual energy or libido was the fuel for developing behavior. Maturation is his word for the ability of a growing individual to cathect or invest psychic energy in each of the progressive phases, oral, anal, and phallic.

Inherent in Freud's theory is the structural model of the mind. The id represents the drives and instincts of the mind. It is the entire psychic apparatus of the child at birth, operating independently to determine behavior until 6 months of age. The id is unneutralized drive energy and functions only to gratify needs. Though it functions in the unconscious, the effects of the id are felt as conscious perceptions of thought, desires, or feelings by the ego.

The ego is the psychic representation of the individual's interaction with the environment. Its purpose is to maximize the desires of the id in socially acceptable ways. The ego selects which stimuli are allowed into the mind. Five principal functions controlled by the ego are memory, thinking, perception, motor control, and affect. The body and its representation to the individual is an extremely important part of the developing ego.

A central concept known as object relations is the ability of the individual to consistently identify with a significant other in the environment. The acquisition of this psychic task forms the basis for all future interpersonal relationships. Another task of the ego is to effectively mediate between the desires of the id and the ethical standards of the superego. This is known as its reality functioning capacity.

The superego comprises the moral precepts of the mind as well as the ideal aspirations of the personality. It results from an interface with figures representing authority and enforces the ego defense mechanisms against the undesirable wants of the id.

The phases of psychosexual development comprise central tenets of this theory. They will be discussed sequentially along the developmental progression.

Oral stage. The stage of development from birth to 18 months Freud terms the oral stage. In this phase the mouth is the dynamic focus of energy. Through it the infant seeks both gratification from the environment and self-expression. During the early part of this phase the infant is passive and dependent on others and takes in to satisfy oral drives. As infants mature, they are more aggressive in active attempts at gratification, including biting and chewing. The overall task for completion at this stage is gratification of oral needs.

At first the object of gratification is incorporated as part of the self by the infant. Later the baby learns to differentiate between self and the object of the need gratifications, the result of selective delay in gratification. This is children's beginning attempts at personal mastery and meeting their own needs. The infant whose need gratifications are inconsistently satisfied on a regular basis experiences repeated tension and frustration, making identification with the mother difficult. In an attempt to secure the care required, the infant becomes demanding and establishes a cycle that encourages further parental rejection and lack of closeness needed for the child's development of object relations.

Several defense mechanisms are developed in this stage and utilized throughout life to reduce tension. These include sublimation, introjection, projection, and denial. The consistently ungratified infant becomes a narcissistic, pessimistic, overly dependent, envious individual who, according to Freud, is fixated at the oral stage of development. This seriously limits the amount of psychic energy available to the individual for forward developmental progression.

Anal stage. The anal stage encompasses the years from 1 to 3. The developmental task for mastery is control and the child struggles with retentive vs. eliminative drives. The libidinal energy focus shifts from an oral to anal mode for gratification. Toilet training becomes the arena in which the cathexis-anticathexis conflict is played out. The degree to which children can experience the process as one that they have control of and may offer for parental reward will influence their quest toward independence and self-control.

The anal stage has a major impact on continuing development of personality. An individual struggling with control issues is often aggressive and challenged by authority figures. Parental attempts to assume control by withholding love or criticizing the child who soils may result in an anxious, defiant, or overly compliant individual. The anal character is orderly and compulsive and attaches special significance to possessions. Major defense mechanisms utilized at this stage are sublimation, reaction formation, regression, and repression.

Phallic-oedipal stage. Freud identifies the phallic-oedipal stage as the phase of early childhood from 3 to 6 years. Psychic energy shifts to the genitals and begins the child's quest toward gender identity. Physiologically, the male begins to experience erections while both sexes engage in sexual play and exploration. Parental reaction to this explorative nature forms the basis for sexual and interpersonal attitudes the child carries throughout life. The major task of this stage is to experience the presence of the genital area in the process of developing sexual identity.

An important developmental event known as the castration complex occurs during this phase. The oedipal boy wishes to destroy his father to win his mother's attention. Castration anxiety develops when the male fears the father will castrate him in response to his desires. In the female counterpart, the electra complex, the father is the object of cathexis. The girl becomes hostile toward the mother and develops penis envy.

Successful resolution of the conflicts occurs as the children deny and repress their wishes in favor of same sex parent identification. Freud suggests this is essential for mature, sexually established behavior.

Latency stage. Freud's school-aged or latency-aged child turns the focus to solidifying goals in the social sphere. The child is curious, motivated, and involved with friends and group interests. The goal of this stage is skill mastery achieved by sublimating sexual energy. Children of this stage are typically interested in those peers of their own sex. Membership in same sex clubs and groups is common. The child tends to identify most closely with the parent of the same sex while increasing identification with individuals outside of the primary family unit. Social mastery and personal industry become important groundwork toward healthy adjustment in adulthood. Children who fail to master the latency tasks have difficulty identifying with peers.

Genital stage. During the genital stage years of adolescence, psychic energy is focused on a love object of the opposite sex. Freud discusses it as a time of identity crisis during which genital and hormonal systems reach sexual maturity. Increased sexual drive and activity is often threatening to adolescents struggling to define themselves in relationship to others. Conflicting desires for both independence and dependence make the adult role difficult to assume. Though largely egocentric in their view of life, adolescents struggle with altruistic, reality-based values they wish to respect. This confusion contributes to the erratic emotional picture presented by the adolescent.

Central to Freud's discussion is the reemergence of past conflicts during the genital stage. Unsuccessful resolution of the oedipal-electra complex surfaces in difficulty establishing further heterosexual relationships.

Table 11:2 illustrates Freud's five stages of psychosexual development and tasks in process during each. Suggestions for nursing assessment that address psychosexual developmental concepts are included.

Eriksonian theory

Erikson's theory of psychosocial development interfaces social and biological factors that combine to support development throughout the life cycle. The concept of epigenetics that Erikson adopted from embryology states that development evolves from physical and psychosocial abilities of the individual as well as the interactions the individual has with the environment.[3]

Erikson, a neofreudian, proposed that the psychological state of an individual reflects both the conflicts of the structures of the mind as well as the individual's relationship to society. Adaptation and psychological health are the result of the individual's ability to find a sense of belonging in the social environment. An interplay of the positive and negative social interactions forms the personality that emerges through succeeding developmental stages.

TABLE 11:2	Freud's psychosexual developmental stages		
Psychosexual stage	*Significant relationship focus*	*Experience vehicle*	*Personality need component*
Oral	Mothering object	Mouth-oral sensory experience Receives and takes into self	Trust
Anal	Parents	Anus-control exercised through retaining or letting go of musculature	Power; independence; personal control
Phallic	Opposite sex parent	Genitals exploration	Identification
Latency	Self and peer group	Peers Community	Competence Motivation Creativity
Genital	Love object of opposite sex	Genitals Society	Intimacy Self-worth

The dynamic interaction of individual and environment occurs on three levels.[4] Each person has an unconscious internal force or motivation that impacts on potential reactions of the environment. Second, the responses of others so crucial to self-perceptions are dependent on their interpretation of an individual's behavior. The most significant determinant of an individual's self-perception is the person's conscious experience in the world. Erikson states that all of these aspects combine to form the psychosocial picture of each person.

Like Freud, Erikson discusses stages or phases that pose both a conflict to approach and a task to accomplish in the process of development. A struggle for dominance of one or the other occurs at each developmental phase. Progression through the stages varies for each individual. In the process of maturation a person carries remnants of unresolved tasks into future stages. These uncompleted tasks are the result of biological and social threats to the individual.

Developmental focus	Defense mechanisms	Nursing assessment
Physical Biological	Sublimation Introjection Projection Denial	Prenatal and neonatal complications; feeding difficulties; sleeping patterns; growth record
Beginning social identity	Sublimation Reaction formation Regression Repression	Toilet training; early personality traits—temperament; developmental milestones; spontaneity
Beginning sexual identity	Identification Introjection Repression	Sexual exploration (activity reaction); relationships with family members; fears, dreams, regressions, anxiety level
Moral, growing social	Sublimation Identification Reaction formation Isolation	Interests in activities of community; activity level, school performance
Maturing Sexual	Regression Identification Displacement Rationalization Intellectualization Undoing	School performance (academic and social); pubertal changes; interest in opposite sex; dating patterns; sexual experiences and attitudes; peer group involvement

Erikson proposed that development throughout life is sequential and built on the success and struggles of past phases. As in biological development, psychosocial development has critical periods. During these periods specific task development should occur if the individual is to be equipped for later development. The impact of societal forces and the care of significant others contribute to the emerging being.

Development stretches into adulthood and continues until death. From this ongoing interchange individuals learn their positions with others and develop abilities of self-direction geared toward personal goal attainment.

Trust vs. mistrust. Erikson, in his oral sensory stage, discusses the first developmental task as establishment of a sense of trust in the primary caregiver. He terms this 18-month stage trust vs. mistrust. Children seek consistent, need-gratifying caretaking that provides the basis for their views of the world and future relationships. Children who experience this trust are less anxious and have more satisfied personalities because they have confidence that their needs will be met. The developmental thrust becomes greater since more energy is freed up to invest in further task achievement.

Failure to resolve basic trust issues of this stage is carried into later stages. The picture then becomes individuals lacking in self-esteem, uncertain of their own capabilities and of how much they should invest in other people. The mechanisms of defense utilized for coping may include fantasy, denial, and withdrawal.

Autonomy vs. shame and doubt. As children move into the second stage of development they are gaining mastery in muscular activities and seeking extended spheres of control. The critical task for mastery is establishing a personal sense of autonomy vs. shame and doubt. With a budding sense of trust and heightened muscular control the child seeks to explore the environment. Children begin to recognize that they are capable of impacting on the environment. The degree to which children attempt to feel success in new experiences is highly dependent on parental regard for them. Erikson suggests that a supportive, noncritical attitude encourages the child to take growth-promoting risks without fear of rejection from parents. This is at the base of beginning initiative that leads to autonomous behavior. Rejection of the child for failed attempts or unconscious parental attitudes of projected failure supports an attitude of self-doubt and shame in the child's ability to be in charge. This critical task, autonomy, like its predecessor trust, are foundations to the success of ongoing developmental growth.

Initiative vs. guilt. During the years in early childhood between 3 and 6 the child seeks to increase knowledge through experience in the world. Children begin to recognize that they are part of a complex network that both affects them and that they impact on.

As the personality grows the task becomes one of balancing initiative with guilt. Children begin to know themselves and gain pleasure in attacking tasks of the world. Increased energy promotes their repeated attempts, while jealousy and rivalry threaten their places with their mothers. If the mother is lost guilt ensues. Reduction of guilt is accomplished through eventual identification with the same sex parent.

The crisis posed by this representative conflict may be developmentally progressive if the child learns to legislate realistic participation with the strong demands of self-proof.

Industry vs. inferiority. The school-aged child is heavily embedded in social mastery outside of the home. During this time children strive for a sense of accomplishment that helps them define the quality of their self-appraisal. Erikson further discusses this stage of industry vs. inferiority as a time of systematic instruction during which children seek to prepare themselves with tools and skills needed for survival. The peer group becomes a proving ground to test and compare their skills with others. Children learn to exert cooperative effort while experiencing its addition to their growing sense of personal competence.

A conflict arises when for biological or psychosocial reasons children find acceptance and mastery lacking in their interpersonal environment. Parental support for the child's developmental progression demands realistic need-gratifying expectations geared toward the individual child. Family-supported successes equip the child with added tools to counter potential threats or inferiority.

Identity vs. role diffusion. Erikson's early adolescent era is a time of conflict between identity and role diffusion. This highly energized era is filled wtih changes in biologically and socially based tasks. Children experience a spurt in sexual maturation as they learn self-knowledge and their place in society. Anxiety centers around peer expectations, desires, and fears of failing.

In the early adolescent's fevered quest for adult identity the conflicts of previously unresolved tasks emerge. Erikson suggests that integration of past identifications with those of the present contribute to shape the emerging identity. Through their peer group participation and in choosing vocational pursuit adolescents seek this meaning. A balance of parental control and supportive independence encourages the child's integrating activities necessary for adult identity formation.

Intimacy vs. isolation. During this adolescent-young adult era individuals seek a sense of personal identity crucial to the development of interpersonal intimacy. Identity involves commitment to work and an acceptance of the social-interpersonal needs of the individual. Erikson discusses intimacy as involving mutuality and the ability to engage in friendships or sexual relationships without compromising the sense of self. Commitment and the ability to love another promote a new identity that supports developing intimacy. The inability to achieve intimacy presents itself in persons who seek distance or isolation to avoid interpersonal closeness and self-revelation.

Generativity vs. self-absorption. According to Erikson, the developmental task of middle age is to produce and teach the next generation. This production involves birthing children or other creative processes of life. Contributing to society in some way utilizes individual energy and accountabilities that counteract a tendency toward self-absorption. It frees the individual to engage further into the lives of others. An extension into the social world provides individuals with learning experiences that may refine their values toward personal growth.

Integrity vs. despair. The central issue in this developmental stage is a recognition of self-acceptance that allows personal integrity. An elderly individual who is able to view past successes while not feeling threatened by the advancing younger generation possesses an integrated personality. This objectivity illustrates heightened knowledge and acceptance of the universality of the human condition. Self-realization provides contentment that transcends current productivity and the grieving of despair.

Table 11:3 illustrates Erikson's eight stages of psychosocial devel-

TABLE 11:3	Erikson's psychosocial developmental stages	
Psychosocial crisis	*Significant relationship focus*	*Experience vehicle*
Trust vs. mistrust	Mothering individual	Oral-incorporative
Autonomy vs. shame and doubt	Primary significant others	Anal-retentive
Initiative vs. guilt	Nuclear family Beginning friends	Inclusive Intrusive Locomotion
Industry vs. inferiority	Peer groups (same sex); community and significant other adults	Socialization Experimentation
Identity vs. role diffusion	Role models; same sex peers; beginning opposite sex peer	Sexual and societal experimentation and integration of past and present experience
Intimacy vs. isolation	Opposite sex significant other	Personal conquests including competition, friendship, and cooperation
Generativity vs. self-absorption	Nuclear family	Community Spouse Family
Integrity vs. despair	Self and mate	Introspective self; community

opment and the tasks in process during each. Suggestions for nursing assessment of psychosocial development are also included.

Sullivanian theory

Sullivan's theory of interpersonal development suggests that individuals grow and mature as a function of their interpersonal interactions with the environment.[5] Each human being has two major goals: (1) the

Personality need component	Developmental threat	Nursing assessment
Trust; hope for need fulfillment	Loss of mother Abandonment	Maternal bonding Early separations
Independence; self-will	Parental disapproval; loss of love	Developmental milestones (walking, talking, etc.) Reaction to separations from mother
Confidence in willful maneuvers; purpose	Guilt; self-punishment Physical insult	Activity level; early personality traits; family relationships
Mastery Accomplishment	Failure to learn Absence of friends	Behavior problems; friendships (quality and quantity); hobbies; academic achievement; childhood illnesses or injury
Positive sense of self	Peer group rejection Role conflict	Academic performance patterns; friendships; community involvement
Interpersonal consistency, love	Absence of intimate relationship Absence of social involvement	Work status; social involvement; significant other; sexual activity
"Other centered" commitment, productivity	Lack of spouse Infertility Loss of job	Significant relationships (family); work; hobbies
Wisdom, contentment	Isolation Unresolved guilt	Support systems; physical health; social involvement

need for satisfaction represented by the biological needs and (2) the need for security and interpersonal relatedness. The individual's quest to reduce the tensions that result give rise to behavioral patterns called dynamisms. When a dynamism satisfies a need the crisis is resolved. Anxiety is present with unfulfilled needs and acts as a powerful force in personality development. Personality is the result of learning to handle anxiety in a way that gains approval from significant others in the environment.

The dynamism Sullivan terms the self-system is a composite of experiences that deter anxiety from taking hold, thus protecting the child from criticism by the real self. An individual uses this security measure by adopting a stance of "good-me," "bad-me," or "not-me." Good-me behavior is accepted by the parent and thus internalized by the child. Bad-me behavior is anxiety producing, rejected and defended against by the child. Sullivan states that the anxiety response cycle is determined by a look at the mothering one.

Modes of experience are a part of the Sullivanian developmental theory. As children grow they use certain vehicles that become increasingly more complex to accomplish their tasks. Individuals experience their environments through various modes. Through the earliest prototaxic mode the infant encounters raw data from the senses. The data is random, inconsistent, and without relatedness. The mouth and other apertures are the areas where individuals establish interpersonal contact. Personality development is significantly influenced by experiences of the oral aperture. As children progress to a parataxic mode they experience that there may be a perceived causal relationship between events that are not logically related.*

Infancy. Sullivan terms the first 18 months of life the infancy stage. Again the basic task to accomplish is trust. The child's experience of the world is sensual and perceived exclusively through the prototaxic mode. In the primary experience of feeding, the infant encounters anxiety, which motivates behavior, trust, and the beginning of the self-system. The degrees of satisfaction and comfort in the interpersonal experience of feeding are conveyed in Sullivan's concept of the nipple being good, unsatisfactory, wrong, or bad. Sullivan too vests the mouth with significance in experiencing and responding to the tensions of the world. Children learn the beginnings of need satisfaction by the self as they substitute their thumbs for feeding.

---

*The term parataxic distortion describes misinterpretations in judgement and attitudes of interpersonal relations based on previous encounters with significant others.[6] The syntaxic mode is logical, rational communication, a cognitive mode used to make sense of experiences in the environment.

Successful progression from this stage occurs when interpersonal intimacy is achieved between mother and child. The physiological benchmarks for phase termination is the appearance of articulate speech and a shift from prototaxic to parataxic form of experience.

Childhood era. Sullivan speaks of the period from 1½ years to 6 as the childhood era. During the transition from infancy to childhood, learning is accomplished with the mother's attention to the elements of frequency, consistency, and sanity in her child's interactional growth. The mother-child interpersonal relationship provides experience, reward, and anxiety, which contribute to a further developing self-system. The goal becomes acquisition of environmental approval through tempering satisfaction of needs. The child learns this in interpersonal experiences such as manipulation, autistic invention, identification, and experimentation. Responses including doubt, shame, guilt, and anger predicate increased knowledge of children's impact on their environments. Beginning use of language and the syntaxic mode of communication is a highly significant task of this phase of development.

Juvenile era. Sullivan's juvenile era extends through the grade school years. During this time the child seeks a group to satisfy needs of belonging. With an increase in socialization the child seeks experiences for identifying with authority figures outside of the home. The child learns to adapt and respond to the world by compromise and competition, a concept Sullivan terms sublimatory reformulations.

As a function of the socialization process and parental consensual validation the child experiences a growing need to distinguish between fantasy and reality. Through the ever-increasing power of the self-system geared to control the content of consciousness the child learns successful ways of performance and expression.

Interpersonal experiences of the juvenile era teach the child beginning concepts of gender identity and a cultural view of sex roles. Social judgments, social handicaps, and the learning of disparagement further influence the developing self-system.

Sullivan describes orientation in living as the ending point of the juvenile era. Individuals who attain beginning insight into the needs that characterize their relationships and their abilities to satisfy them begin an integration of character important in adult socialization.

Preadolescent era. The preadolescent years of 9 through 12 are an important stage in interpersonal growth. Sullivan describes this stage task as a need for interpersonal intimacy with a friend of the same sex. The presence of this chum encourages the preadolescent to share personal thoughts, feelings, and ability to love. Anxiety is reduced as the duo collaborate, experiment, and manipulate to experience achievements in the world.

Sullivan distinguishes between interpersonal intimacy of the pre-adolescent and sexual intimacy. Preadolescents strive for a nonsexual intimacy in which they and their chums may share information concerning their experience. This relationship serves as a support for emerging behaviors that address their desires and comforts. The preadolescent self-system that has not experienced interpersonal intimacy becomes a lonely, aggressive, or withdrawn individual.

Early adolescent era. In early adolescence the focus of interpersonal development turns to heterosexual interests. The mouth, hands, and genitals are zones of erotic exploration, the vehicles for experiencing the lust dynamism. A shift in the object of love turns to a heterophilic person, one who is dissimilar to the self. Intimacy may remain a part of same-sex relationships and not necessarily synonymous with erotic lust. Difficulties in interpersonal development begin to arise when security, freedom from anxiety, and the need for intimacy are not distinguished from a need for lustful satisfaction. Though the ultimate goal through adolescence remains an integration of these needs it is achieved only with a stable self-system.

Late adolescence. Late adolescence is described by Sullivan as the stabilizing of the self-system. It is difficult for the securest of self-systems since individuals are expected to take on adult career and social expectations often before they are ready to do so. Social and interpersonal focus is on functioning in society and on ensuring a place within it. Central to this stage is establishing a consistent, loving personal relationship.

Adulthood. Sullivan discusses adulthood as involving an acceptance of genital consistency and the assumption of adult roles in society. The individual who has achieved an established genital pattern of activity has less anxiety and a stronger base to invest in the world of interpersonal relationships. Maturity is distinguished from adulthood and achieved only when the individual meets interpersonal challenges with love, intimacy, and altruistic motivation.

Table 11:4 illustrates Sullivan's interpersonal stages of development and the tasks in process during each. Interpersonal data that reflect Sullivan's concept of development are included to assist the nurse in the assessment process.

Piagetian theory

Piaget's cognitive theory proposes that personality development occurs as the result of a series of cognitive processes.[7] These processes occur in stages with each stage requiring mastery before succeeding ones may be attempted. The personality develops as the result of inherent genetic forces and environmental determinants.

As children play they imitate and learn. Learning entails two components of adaptation, assimilation and accommodation. Children take in or assimilate new environmental data to fit their schema or structural framework. They then accommodate or modify themselves to that new object.

Intellectual functioning is the integration of previous cognitive schemata into more highly developed or operationlized behavior. This occurs with orderly progression of schemata through four periods of development: sensorimotor, preoperational, concrete operations, and formal operations.

In summary, Piaget believed that development occurred in an orderly fashion with the attainment of increasingly refined skills. These abilities proceed into succeeding phases and are redefined into more complex schemata and levels of behavior. The learning process is behavioral adaptation with the organism assimilating and accommodating to higher levels of function. The end result is an individual who has developed the complex structure needed to reason abstractly and to think in a logical manner. Piaget's stages are sequential. Developmental progression depends on successful ordered completion of each stage.

Sensorimotor. In discussing cognitive development Piaget termed the first 2 years of a child's life as the sensorimotor stage. Through sensations and motoric experiences children perceive and exert some control of their bodies in the environment. Piaget believed that thought begins with these experiences as the child passively observes and adaptively manipulates a response. Sucking, tasting, feeling, and seeing are early sensorimotor experiences that are organized by the infant.

At 8 months of age the infant acquires the ability to recognize that objects are permanent when out of sight. This is an important step in the process of movement toward logical thinking.

As the sensorimotor stage progresses the child begins to perceive a relationship between cause and effect. By 2 years of age children still perceive in a sensorimotor fashion but are able to exert primitive sequential, goal-directed activities in their growth toward true cognition.

Preoperational. When children move into the period between 2 and 7 years of age, they enter a phase of preoperational thought. They begin to use symbols such as language and memory to increase their experience of events. Preoperational thought is characterized by an inability to perceive relationships between objects.[4] The child sees the word "cup" as an object but is unable to recognize different characteristics as parts of the object.

Piaget states that preoperational children are egocentric and unable

TABLE 1:4	Sullivan's interpersonal developmental stages		
Developmental stage	Significant relationships	Experience mode	Tools for need satisfaction
Infancy	Mother	Sensory prototaxic mode (orifices)	Crying; ability to arouse tenderness
Childhood era	Parents Family	Prototaxic Parataxic Syntaxic	Demandingness; acculturation; willful activity
Juvenile era	Significant adult outside home	All modes— syntaxic	Cooperates Competes Compromises Sublimates
Preadolescent era	Same sex "chum" and peers	All modes	Mutual collaboration, friendship
Early adolescent era	Heterosexual object of love Friends	All modes— prototaxic, syntaxic	Sexuality; social and professional achievement
Late adolescence	Mate	All modes	Professional competency
Adulthood	Family	All modes	Love; realistic self-concept; family interactions

to recognize that others' thought and perceptions might be different from theirs. Children feel that their experience is universal and should be understood by all.

Children learn to play through imitation. Toys take on special powers and skills as the result of animistic thinking. Though symbolic representations are present they are unable to be organized to reflect their multiple dimensions.

Concrete operations. Concrete operational thinking emerges in the

Developmental focus	Interpersonal determinants	Nursing assessment
Trust; satisfaction; beginning self-system	Status of nipple determining anxiety	Mother-child anxiety level in interpersonal interactions (i.e., feeding, settling)
Language development; self-system begins concept of gender	Colored by distrust of others, cultural view of sex role, and extent of language capabilities	Reaction to others in environment, separations; ability to accommodate to societal expectations for personal control
Socialization Internal control of behavior Reality replaces fantasy	Quality of interpersonal experiences with authority outside of home	Experiences in society; performance anxiety; personality traits
Homosexuality intimacy and mutuality	Ability to share and become "other centered"	Quality and quantity of friendships; reactions to school performance
Heterosexual intimacy and eroticism	Strength of current self-system; physical-personal attractiveness	Involvement with opposite sex; societal successes; antisocial behavior; self-esteem level
Societal productivity	Personal and social potency	Job and community success and satisfactions
Sexual patterning established; adult role assumed	Intimacy; dependability	Ability to evidence a balance of dependence-independence toward mutual interpersonal satisfaction; quality and consistency of job and personal relationships

years between 7 and 11. Thinking becomes logical, utilizing reason and a sense of objectivity in determining relationships between objects. The concept of conversation in use at this stage describes the child's ability to recognize that things can take on different forms and still retain the original properties of the object.[7]

The child begins classifying and grouping objects with like properties. Thinking has advanced to an understanding of simple cause and effect relationships between objects. Egocentrism is replaced by an understanding that others' reasoning and the child's reasoning should correspond. Children seek socializing activities that provide opportunities to test out developing cognitive operations.

Formal operations. In formal operative thought the child is able to think and reason in abstract terms. This level of cognitive functioning is achieved between ages 11 and 15 and signifies an adult level of intellectual achievement.

No longer is thought content of primary concern to the child. Through the use of introspection the adolescent can conceptualize, hypothesize, and solve complex problems of logic. The scientific process and creative ventures spring from the freedom to consider structures in the cognitive mode as well as an end result.

Maturation of the cognitive processes supports and validates the emerging individual. The child is able to appraise past experiences and plant seeds for future growth.

TABLE 11:5	Piaget's cognitive developmental stages	
Cognitive stage	Origin of thought	Intellectual experience
Sensorimotor	Through experiences of sensation and movement in feeding	Observation and corresponding in adaptive manipulation of self to environment
Preoperational	Uses symbols (language, memory); conceptualizations begin but are without coordination of spatial and temporal qualities	Centering (attention to one feature of an object) common; egocentric thought
Concrete operations	Begins to understand cause and effect relatinships; deals with visible objects and their relationships	Able to classify multiple characteristics of objects; understands relationships of changing forms and shapes of objects
Formal operations	Introspectively thinks of own thoughts; no longer dependent on reality	Formulates and tests hypotheses; content of thought is less important than form

Table 11:5 illustrates Piaget's cognitive stages of development and the tasks in process during each. Important areas for the nurse to assess in determining cognitive development are also included.

Rogerian theory

Concept of unitary man. In discussing prominent developmental theorists Martha Rogers and her nursing conceptualization of unitary man must be considered. Riehle and Roy discuss nursing developmental models and suggest that they possess such common characteristics as identifiable states, direction, forces, form of progression, and potentiality.[8] Though the Rogers model is technically termed a systems rather than a developmental model its central concepts may be useful in approaching a developmental assessment of the child.

In this nursing model man is seen as a unified whole, a being who is uniquely different from the sum of his parts.[9] Man and his environ-

Focal tasks of learning	Skills for learning	Nursing assessment
Object constancy Object permanency Goal-directed actions	Experimentation; manipulation	Status of reflex activity; motor activity; alertness; exploration; recognition of mother, objects; goal-directed behavior
Growing understanding of past and present	Verbal exploration; observation	Language skills Memory skills
Masters reversibility and conservation	Observation Classification	Ability to recognize changing forms of objects; status of ability to classify
Able to abstract and solve problems	Able to deal with structure of thought sequence; logic; experimentation	Assess ability to abstract, solve problems and use logic

CHARACTERISTICS OF UNITARY MAN—ASSESSMENT FACTORS AND CRITERIA

Factor I: Interaction

Exchanging—interchange of matter and energy between man and environment.
> *Assessment factors:* eating, drinking, eliminating, breathing, giving-receiving, approval, advice

Communicating—interchange of information between man and environment
> *Assessment factors:* verbal, nonverbal

Relating—connecting with other persons or objects
> *Assessment factors:* spacing, touching, eye contact, belonging, referencing

Factor II: Action

Valuing—the assigning of worth
> *Assessment factors:* philosophical beliefs regarding health, spirituality, human interactions

Choosing—the selection of one or more alternatives
> *Assessment factors:* judgment—decision capacity regarding alternatives, consequences, commitments

> *Empirical indicators:* health choices and practices; perceived alternatives; perceived consequences; congruence of choice and value/belief patterns

Moving—activity within the environment
> *Assessment factors:* mobility rhythm/patterns (spatial, temporal, frequency of exercise and activity)

> *Empirical indicators:* locomotion characteristics (type, frequency, balance, equilibrium); control of intentional movement; joint flexibility; goal-directed movement (ADL, self-care practices); activity tolerance

Factor III: Awareness

Waking refers to levels of arousal

> *Assessment factors:* position and movement, verbal expression

> *Empirical indicators:* REM time, alterations in moving, alterations in speech

Feeling refers to quality of sensation and mood
> *Assessment factors:* position and movement, verbal expression

From Kim, M., & Moritz, D.A. *Classification of nursing diagnoses.* New York, 1982, McGraw-Hill Book Co., pp. 244-245. Used with permission.

CHARACTERISTICS OF UNITARY MAN—ASSESSMENT FACTORS AND CRITERIA—cont'd

Factor III: Awareness—cont'd

Empirical indicators: alterations in intake; alteration in movement (such as smiling, wringing of hands); alteration in mood (such as repetitive speech, laughing, crying)

Knowing refers to meaning associated with a world view
Assessment factors: position and movement, verbal expression

Empirical indicators: wrinkled brow, puzzled look, participation in planned regime, frequent questioning about phenomena, personal verification ("I don't know what's happening" or "I do know"), reports time, place, and person, for example, reports limited information, reports inaccurate information

---

ment are viewed as dynamic and changing and in constant interaction with each other. The life process of man evolves unidirectionally on a time continuum and is irreversible with its impact on the whole of man. Man is characterized by pattern and organization that reflect his innovative wholeness.

Man has the capacities of imagery, language, thought, sensation, and emotions. Development of the individual occurs with assistance in promoting an individual's rhythmic interactions with the environmental patterns. Rogers believes growing individuals have unlimited potential for development within their ever-changing environments. Growth occurs as a function of conscious choices designed to accomplish goals. This growth is orderly, predictable, and probable if the holistic, rhythmical pattern of evolving individuals and their environment is assessed.

Man is viewed as a process, an energy field that is open and extends into space. The pattern and organization of life as it evolves provides integrity, individuality, and wholeness reflecting a life process that is creative and formative. Man as an evolving energy field is highly dependent on and inseparable from the spiraling thrust of change and growth.

Assessment factors and criteria. Individuals assessing the child's development according to Rogers would choose the present to begin describing the extent to which the child is emerging toward maximum health potential. This would be done by observing the pattern and organization of the child's life processes, past and present, and determining the degree to which the child's current environment permits the achievement of potential. Through the work of an ongoing nurse theorist group, Rogers' conceptual schema has been redescribed in a three factor tool that reflects patterns of unitary man.[10] These factors address man's potential for dynamic change assessed by (1) interaction, (2) action, and (3) reaction. Further defined, the assessment criteria we might use in assessing the child's developmental pattern include the child's (1) exchanging, (2) communicating, (3) relating, (4) valuing; (5) choosing, (6) moving, (7) waking, (8) feeling, and (9) knowing. The boxed material on pp. 334-335 shows the factors, criteria, and further assessment data the nurse might seek in formulating a developmental assessment.

Our process of conceptualizing and adapting Rogers' theoretical constructs for use in child developmental assessment is in its infancy. However, we believe that nurses as eclectic practitioners must be exposed to and utilize a nursing theoretical base. Holistic assessment offers a perspective supportive of nursing's biopsychosocial approach to the individual.

NORMAL GROWTH AND DEVELOPMENT
Prenatal considerations

A psychological developmental assessment of the child begins with a look at events and conditions of the prenatal period. The impact that heredity and environment play in utero is sometimes underestimated when discussing psychological development of the child. Such obvious things as maternal health and trauma during the prenatal period impact on the physical and psychological development of the fetus. Equally as important is consideration of the mother's desire for the pregnancy, whether she was equipped emotionally and economically to care for a child, and the experience she has had as the recipient of mothering.[11] The reasons why a woman becomes pregnant, the amount of emotional and physical support she receives from the father, and her expectations of motherhood all contribute to the psychological investment she has in her child.

Infancy

When infants are born their primary tasks are to adjust to the physiological, psychological, and sociological world of which they are now a part. No longer is the safe, consistent insurance of an intrauterine life theirs for the taking. Many factors impact on their ability to respond to and thrive in their environments. At birth children exhibit random muscular movements indicative of their primitive neurological status.[12] The presence of several protective reflexes enhances the infant's thrust for survival. Though sight is not well-developed, the senses of touch, taste, and smell contribute to the child's growing fund of experiences. The child startles at sounds but is unable to connect a voice with its person.

As early as 1 month of age the infant begins to experience and establish relationships with significant others. This process of child-parent interaction is a major focus in the developing personality and forms the basis for all future relationships. Parental attitudes toward the child and their feelings about being parents contribute to the communication they establish with their infant.

Behavior of neonates is egocentric and revolves around their bodily needs. Because of their primitive cognition and perception the child perceives the world as self. All actions are geared toward attaining comfort. The child's state of satisfaction is dependent on the mother's consistent ability to meet the child's needs.[13] Mother and child develop a bond that forms the basis for trust and growing attitudes of life.

In the second month of life infants become more alert to the world around them. Their eyes still experience difficulty in focusing as they begin random smiling. Infants at this age are in great need of touching if they are to thrive. They begin anticipating a feeding schedule and have usually found their thumb as a substitute gratifier. As children grow into their third month they are able to turn their heads and reach out involuntarily. Children continue to cry when distressed and have low frustration tolerance. They begin cooing, babbling, and following an object within their sphere of vision. The neck muscles begin supporting an erect position and the child begins smiling.

By the fourth and fifth months infants are active in reaching for objects, holding them, transferring them, and attempting to take them into their mouths. Motor activity begins to be extended to purposeful rolling over and the infant is able to sit upright. During the fifth month the child begins teething and wanting to chew on objects. Children become increasingly more vocal, enjoy others' talking with them and show their reactions with frequent affectual changes. As they reach the sixth month the relationship of self–not self becomes evident to children as they recognize new and different stimuli around them. The mother is well-known to the 6-month-old child. The presence of strangers is threatening as the child seeks to have the mother near.

At 7 months strength and coordination develop to allow creeping and increased exploring with hands. The concept of space becomes increasingly more real as infants manipulate their bodies with growing skill. Teeth begin to erupt, and the child attempts self-feeding. Social games such as "peek-a-boo" and "patty-cake" become important socialization interactions. The 9-month-old begins to connect sounds to words, allowing comprehension of simple commands. As the child understands "no" parents begin to discipline and teach the child its meaning. Hand-eye coordination develops to allow the child increased fine motor activity and the pincer movement. Children are highly interested in their environments and require varied stimulation and encouragement to explore the environments. Gradual supportive weaning is in process at this time.

During the last 3 months of the first year the child begins standing beside chairs and sidestepping between them. One-year-old children say their first words, though often unintelligibly. "No" takes on increased meaning to infants as do their exercise of tantrumming. This is an important step toward independent action and ego development. An infant's lengthening attention span is indicative of growth in cognitive functioning.

In summary, primary developmental processes encountered during the birth to 18 month period are (1) an integration of sensory and motoric experiences to higher levels of functioning and (2) the development of a primary need-gratifying relationship, which directly impacts on all further development.

Toddler phase

The period of growth known as the toddler stage is a time of rapid physical, motoric, and social growth. Walking extends into multiple skilled fine motor movements. The child uses these skills in an ever-expanding quest to explore the environment. This thrust forward in learning assists the child in increasing attempts to differentiate self from the environment. In experimentation and manipulation the child gains heightened perceptual experience. Separation from mother becomes more acceptable yet ambivalently received. Children whose needs for love and security are adequately met separate more easily and will be more likely to try out their desires on the real world. A frequent accompaniment of the toddler is a favorite toy or rag known as a transition object.[14] Children use these objects to comfort themselves in times of stress and separation. The degree to which a child is able to accept separation from the mother is the result of (1) success of the previously established trust relationship; (2) current stresses impacting on the child's life; and (3) the successful resolution of past separations.

A toddler's emergence of personal control extends into an ability to master instinctual, emotional responses. As the child begins perceiving responses to situations as coming from the self, a struggle between accepting parental modeling or personal wish ensues. If parental actions are gratifying and offer approval the child will begin making choices to effect socially acceptable behaviors. The child learns quickly to manipulate with negative attention seeking if undesirable behavior is reinforced. Physiological control exhibited in toilet training is an important contribution to a child's emerging self-concept and self-control. A child's natural desire to self-realization is supported by reasonable expectations for performance. Rewards for achievement rather than punishment for failure are ego building. Behaviors representative of giving and withholding are generalized by the child into many contexts and relationships. They are often responsible for future resolution or failure of developmental issues.

An expanding ability to utilize verbal communication allows the toddler to express thoughts, feelings, and dimensions of an ever-expanding object and perceptual world. Increasing integration into the social world allows children to experience the effects of acting on their terms. Anger, jealousy, fear, and happiness occur in life experience and are adapted to in learning ways.

In summary, primary developmental tasks of the time between 18 months and 3 years are (1) maturation of physical capabilities and skills; (2) development of language for communication; and (3) the emergence of autonomy needed for future developmental challenges.

Early childhood

Between the ages of 3 and 5 the child gains skills and refinement in multiple activities of daily life. As growth and development progress the child practices rapidly emerging motor skills. Buttoning clothes, feeding, dressing, and brushing teeth are personal achievements for the child. The ability to stay dry at night supports the child's budding self-esteem. Maturation in perceptual motor activities is seen in the child's increasing ability to draw simple forms and geometric figures. As age 5 is reached drawings become more detailed with people taking on anatomical parts. Learning about numbers, counting, and color recognition are reinforced by the use of rapidly expanding language skills. The inquisitive, talkative child seeks out concrete answers to relationships of objects in the world.

Socially the child becomes more aware of people in the environment. What was previously individual play turns to parallel play and a growing ability to interact in peer group activities. Focus on the mother turns to a wish to identify more strongly with the parent of the opposite sex. Family members and the desire to have a position among them take on significance. The child learns to appreciate the feelings of others and experiences guilt when infringing on them.[15] Active pursuit of increasing powers is seen as the child charges into activities and brags of accomplishments. The child is possessive of belongings and rivals with siblings often result.

A full range of emotional responses, including fears exhibited in nightmares and aggression toward peers, are acted out. Imaginary companions are a part of the child's rich fantasy life. They are often used in dramatic, expressive, creative play characteristic of this age. Sexual curiosity increases with masturbation and attention to own sex issues. The child of this age is generally pleasing, helpful, and friendly. Occasional bouts of pouting and demanding behaviors are a result of stresses imposed by growing independence.

In summary, the primary developmental tasks of the early childhood phase involve (1) a shift in investment from mother to the opposite sex parent and (2) the need to exert personal potential while tempering it to internal and external demands.

School age phase

The school-age child is intensely involved in personal mastery of the world and its challenges. Rapid physical growth characteristic of previous stages is somewhat slowed, allowing the child to focus on social and intellectual maturational tasks. Past learning experiences are consolidated as the child struggles with the virtues of adulthood vs. childhood.

A major need for the child at this developmental phase is to experience a sense of achievement in work and play. Children are involved in multiple school and community activities, which serve to support or invalidate their growing sense of self-worth. Growing societal involvement teaches children about the world and assists them in skill development necessary for eventual emancipation from parents. Children at this stage grow through heightened development of peer relationships. Through them they learn the ability to compromise and cooperate and the value of fair play. Personal competence evokes peer acceptance and a sense of self-confidence that the child carries into further developmental tasks.

A spurt in intellectual growth is evidenced in the child's increasing ability to use memory and language skills in learning. Flexibility of thought promotes understanding relationships between objects and the ability to classify them in different forms.[16] The child brings eagerness, spontaneity, and personal experiences to aid them in the learning process. Children who experience learning disabilities at this stage suffer a major insult to their developing ego. Impulsive behavior problems are characteristic of the child and complicate intellectual and social growth.

Parents play an important role in the school-age child's life. Psychological guiding and societal interpretation replace the exclusive physical caretaking role prominent in past stages. The acquisition of sex role identity is achieved through observation of and identification with parental role models. Parents also promote the development of values and attitudes essential for societal functioning. The early school-age child experiences strict superego control. As sublimation becomes more successful the child becomes more adept at dealing with guilt and the demands of society.

In summary, the major developmental task of the school-age child is to gain a sense of mastery and personal identity within the social world.

Adolescence

The period of adolescence is a time of intense physical and psychosocial turmoil.[17] With the advent of puberty rapid physical maturation, including the development of secondary sex characteristics, becomes a focal concern. Variations in maturational timetables both between and within the sexes influences the individual's concept of sexual identity formation. The adolescent learns to cope with sexual feelings in light of overpowering psychosexual drives.

Cognitive development takes leaps during this phase. Increased ability to reason abstractly and to utilize insight is characteristic of the growing adolescent. Four major ego tasks in process include (1) defining one's individual self; (2) separating and coming to an understanding of one's family; (3) developing a love relationship; and (4) mastering personal impulses.[18]

During this identity crisis the adolescent adapts many behaviors to attempt resolution. Peer group conformity and struggles for personal uniqueness occur concurrently. Preoccupation with body image and idealized fantasy life plague the individual. Restless experimentation with drugs, alcohol, and sex are symptoms of the alienated identity. Suicidal behavior may be the reaction to overwhelming demands of development. Anxiety, guilt, aggression, and fear of losing personal identity promote its occurrence. Moodiness, uncommunicativeness, and impulsivity are actions the adolescent takes to individuate from parents. Ambivalence is seen in the acting out and authority challenges the adolescent does to retain parental involvement and love. Resolution of past developmental crises and the strength of previous primary relationships has much to do with successful resolution of adolescent identity.

The experience of love offers the adolescent a feeling of belonging and the ability to share. Through it personal experience and uniqueness are validated and self-esteem grows. As the adolescent matures this egocentric quest becomes a more genuine care for the other individual, needed for an adult love relationship.

Struggles for personal control and mastery over impulses invade all adolescent tasks. Adult roles are dutifully sought, while the comforts of childhood take preference. Instant gratification is gradually replaced by conscious decision making based on the result of an action.

In summary, consolidation of a mature identity is the central task of adolescence.

ASSESSMENT PROCESS WITH CHILDREN AND ADOLESCENTS

The first step in assessing a child or adolescent is the development of a knowledge base of normal child development. The nurse who has a sound working knowledge of the normal development of children and adolescents will be able to use such information to collect and critically analyze the data base. Comparing collected data to those norms that are theoretically expected for a child at a specific developmental stage assists the nurse to assess whether or not that child is within developmental norms. Data that do not fall within developmental limits give the nurse a clue that a "problem" may be present and a nursing diagnosis label may be utilized to describe such a problem, providing the patient problem is amenable to nursing interventions.[19]

After nurses have secured an understanding of normal developmental theories, they are in a position to draw conclusions about the data collected on children who have entered the treatment setting. If certain data appear as falling outside of what is developmentally expected for a child, the nurse develops hypotheses or "hunches" as to the meaning of the abnormal data. A data base describing a child as withdrawn and having frequent crying spells and temper tantrums over several months time after the father's death may cause a nurse to hypothesize that the child is having difficulty mourning the death of that parent. Testing the hypothesis by perceiving or gathering more data may validate the hunch.[19] Once a hypothesis is validated the nurse can identify the difficulty or problem as a nursing diagnosis, such as "Dysfunctional Grieving Process." Once a nursing diagnosis is determined and accepted the assessment process now leads to the initiation of planning interventions for treating the child.

PRELIMINARY CONSIDERATIONS FOR DATA COLLECTION

For nurses to be able to assess a child or adolescent and determine nursing diagnoses that will provide the direction for interventions, they must gather data about many different areas of the child's behaviors and life patterns. Even though psychiatric nurses are especially concerned about collecting psychosocial data about the patient, they need to assess the child in a holistic manner. The biological, psychological, social, cultural, and spiritual patterns of the child's life, as well as the characteristics of the environment, are inseparable and together constitute the entire field of the individual child with whom the nurse will interact.[9]

Ideally, the nurse will plan to spend time with both the child and the family. When a child is scheduled for admission in some psychiatric residential facilities the nurse who will be caring for that child makes a home visit before admission. In such a situation the nurse is able to observe and gather valuable data about how the child and parents function in their natural environment. In most cases, however, the assessment process begins in the facility to which the child is referred for treatment. This may be a psychiatric treatment setting or a pediatric unit or school setting. The nurse will want to spend time individually and conjointly with the child and family at admission or soon after so that the necessary nursing assessment data can be gathered in order to plan the appropriate nursing care specific to the child's individual needs.

PHASES OF THE NURSING ASSESSMENT INTERVIEW

During the assessment interview nurses structure their interactions with the child or adolescent according to the phases of the interviewing process. The four phases of the interviewing process are (1) the preinteraction phase, (2) the beginning phase, (3) the middle phase, and (4) the termination phase.[20]

Preinteraction phase

During the preinteraction phase the nurse makes preparations for the interview. This includes preparing the environment in which the interview will take place and developing an awareness of the variables that may influence the interview with the child. The location of the interview may be the child's home, a psychiatric unit, the school setting, a clinic, or a pediatric unit. While the setting may vary the nurse will need to ensure that the environment supports the privacy and comfort of the child as much as is feasible. Distractions within a busy hospital environment may detract from the interview. Interruptions should be avoided or kept to a minimum. Steps the nurse may take to make the environment more supporting of the interviewing process include moving to a private room, shutting the door, or pulling the bedside curtains.

Ideally, the interview may take place in a room that is oriented to the age of the child. Small chairs, a table, paper, crayons, and various toys may set the toddler or latency-aged child at ease and provide a natural medium in which to communicate with the nurse. Appropriate toys for the toddler may be puppets, dolls, drawing materials, clay, or building blocks. The latency-aged child may prefer board games, clay, or drawing materials. Adolescents may choose crafts or a board game, such as checkers, as activities in which to engage. While these supplies may be made available in the interviewing room, the nurse need not direct children into specific activities but allow them to just talk if they choose. Some children or adolescents may be very verbal and willing to engage in a conversation.

As nurses participate in an active role during the interview they need to be aware of how they may influence the quality of assessment data that they collect. The level of nurses' physical and emotional stress may affect their ability to conduct the interview and actively listen to the child. Their attitudes and values affect the interaction in that nurses may have preconceived opinions about the child or family. For instance, nurses may feel apprehensive or even somewhat hostile toward a child interviewed who was referred for treatment because of threatening a parent with a knife.

The socioeconomic background and value systems of nurses may lead them to form judgments about families or children who possess backgrounds and experiences that are very different from their own. Conversely, nurses who have similar backgrounds or experiences as some families or children may not objectively attune themselves to the family or child's problem or needs. Nurses need to be aware of their own attitudes and feelings and how these affect their perceptions of children and how this may affect the way they relate during the interview. Families of different socioeconomic levels and cultural and ethnic backgrounds may have different value systems, educational levels, language skills, and basic needs. An upper middle class family may be concerned with how their child's behavior interferes with their community status. A lower income family may be concerned about how they can find the gas money or transportation to visit their child in the hospital. Throughout the interview nurses need to be aware of these different family backgrounds and relate to children and families at the level appropriate to their personal reality.

Beginning phase

During the beginning phase of the interview the nurse makes introductions and states the purpose of the interview to the child and family. Nurses may simply state that they need to spend some time talking with the family and child to ascertain why they are seeking help and to be able to plan the type of care that will meet their needs. To provide structure and clarify expectations nurses may provide an estimate of how much time they will need to spend talking with them and the type of general topics they will be interested in exploring.

The beginning phase of the interview provides the nurse with the initial opportunity to develop a relationship with the child. Establishing trust and rapport early on promotes the flow of data collection and is an essential component of the therapeutic relationship. Nurses are initially strangers to children and their actions and behavior provide cues to children as to whether or not they are trustworthy. Nurses need to convey an attitude of acceptance, interest, and empathy. They wish to enter into children's frames of reference and awareness. They actively listen to children, making eye contact and speaking directly to them. Body language and noverbal communication should express openness and interest. Sitting at the eye level of children and giving them the comfortable space or distance that they need may also facilitate trust and rapport. Initially, general questions may be directed to children about interests, hobbies, or friends. For instance, the nurse may ask a toddler, "What do you like to play?" To an adolescent the nurse may ask, "What kind of activities do you like?"

Working phase

During the working phase the nurse collects data and analyzes the content and process of the interaction. The methods that nurses use to collect data will very much influence the quality of data they are able to gather for assessment purposes. Nurses must vary their methods of collecting data according to the age and developmental capacities of the child or adolescent.

Observational methods. The nurse may use verbal questioning, depending on the age of the child, or rely heavily on observations of behavior and nonverbal communication. With the infant, toddler, or nonverbal child, the nurse collects data primarily through observing the child's interactions, interests, skills, and hobbies. Additionally, children or adolescents who come for treatment may have difficulty in verbally expressing themselves. They may be withdrawn, uncooperative, resistive, or very apprehensive. Therefore observation of the child or adolescent plays a key role in the nursing assessment process. The nurse observes the child's appearance, motor movements, facial expressions, choice and use of play materials, and interactions with parents, peers, and the interviewer. Observational data often speaks more to what a child or adolescent is really communicating to the nurse than the words they use.

As play is a natural medium for children to communicate and express themselves, the nurse may choose to engage the child in a play activity if they show the interest, especially if they are very young or nonverbal. Through play the nurse can observe the child's wishes, areas of preoccupation, distractibility, self-perception, aggressive drive, and capacity to relate to others. Dolls, puppets, clay, board games, paints, crayons, and paper are tools the nurse can use to learn about the child's feelings and behaviors.[21] Children may use dolls to enact what their family relationships are like. A puppet may be used to express a secretive wish or fear. Children who use clay in a destructive rather than creative or constructive fashion may be expressing how angry they feel. Adolescents who attempt to control all the nurse's moves during a checker game may be expressing their need to be controlling in relationships.

> CASE EXAMPLE: Six-year-old Sherry was admitted on a pediatric unit for treatment of burns and bruises sustained during an incident of physical abuse by her mother. Sherry was quiet and nonverbal, except to frequently ask for her mother. When the nurse introduced a family of dolls for Sherry to play with, the child enacted a scene where the mother doll punished her children by keeping their dinner from them and locking them in closets for accidentally wetting their beds. The nurse was able to gether much assessment data about Sherry and her family by observing how the child used the doll family in play.

Verbal questioning. The sophistication of language and phrasing of questions by the nurse should parallel the cognitive level of the child. Children below 9 or 10 years of age have a concrete level of cognitive ability. Questions that are complicated or abstract may not be well understood by the younger child. Simple and straightforward questioning by the nurse with a young child will prove more successful in eliciting the necessary data. Adolescents, on the other hand, have developmentally reached the higher cognitive levels of formal operations.[7] Questions directed to them may take on a higher level of conceptual sophistication. In fact, the adolescent may feel indignant at questions that appear to be too childish or condescending. They may feel "grown up" in many ways and expect to be treated as such.

When talking with either child or adolescent the nurse must avoid relentless questioning and probing. Oftentimes the beginning practitioner, anxious to obtain factual data, will take on an interrogative role, asking question after question. As a result the response of the child or adolescent may be a defensive, mistrustful stance toward the nurse. While nurses need to obtain data, they must allow children to set the pace and present their interests.[15] Children should be permitted to tell their stories in the way that they choose to express them. They may pull out a storybook, bring in a teddy bear, or choose to paint pictures. The nurse needs to utilize the child's focus of interest from which to proceed. With a child who comes into the room tightly hugging a doll or stuffed animal, the nurse may comment, "Your teddy bear seems very important to you. What's his name?"

With older children, adolescents, and parents, the nurse may utilize a variety of techniques that encourage verbal expression. Asking open-ended questions is preferable to questions that require a simple "yes" or "no" response. The nurse wants to facilitate the expression and elaoration of information from the interviewee. The nurse may begin by asking open-ended questions, then gradually move into more direct questions. For instance, the nurse can ask the parents, "Tell me about the reasons you brought your child in for help." Parents may identify problems such as school difficulties, temper tantrums, lying, stealing, or fighting with other children. The nurse may then explore further and ask for more specific information about each of these areas. The nurse can ask, "What kinds of problems has your child had in school?" and "You've mentioned that your child has temper tantrums. How have you dealt with this problem?" The nurse needs to explore in more depth any areas that would provide data necessary to understanding the health needs of the child. To facilitate elaboration the nurse may at appropriate moments interject supportive comments such as, "And then what happened?" or "How did you feel when that happened?"

Some information that the nurse needs for assessment may require simple and direct questioning. Questions about the ages the child began walking and talking, how long the parents have been married, or the number and ages of the child's siblings are straightforward and to the point. Sometimes a child may not be willing or able to elaborate and respond to open-ended questions. In such a case the nurse may choose to present questions of a multiple choice nature. For instance, a child may respond to the question, "How did you feel when your dad moved away after he and your mom divorced?" with the answer, "I don't know." The nurse can facilitate further expression by asking, "Did you feel sad, angry, worried, or scared?"

During the interview nurses need to listen carefully to responses made by the child or parent. They note if there are any discrepancies between a child's and parents' responses. They need to listen to the meanings behind the words and behaviors of the child. For instance, children who have been moved in and out of numerous foster homes since infancy and who angrily relate to the nurse may be interacting in such a manner to avoid what they have learned to expect from adults— rejection.

To demonstrate supportive and active listening and to clarify and validate observations and responses, nurses may provide feedback about the information they receive from the child and family. For instance, the nurse may relate to a newly hospitalized child who is acutely homesick for the family by remarking, "It sounds as if you are really missing your family right now and feel very angry that you are here." To parents who have elaborated on their numerous attempts to help their adolescent who has been involved in theft and drug abuse, the nurse may comment, "It sounds as if you feel you have tried everything and feel very frustrated at this point."

Although nurses may be utilizing an established format for the areas of information they need to gather, they should remain flexible during the course of the interview. Because of interruptions or a change in the child's interest, the nurse may need to alter the order of the interview. Creativity and resourcefulness are indispensable assets in working with children and adolescents.

Ending phase

During the ending phase the nurse winds down the interview. The nurse may briefly summarize the interaction and ask the child and family if they have any questions. At this point nurses may also share how often they will be contacting the child and family and what the nurse's role will be in the child's care. The nurse may provide information about the facility, visiting hours, and expectations of them. It is important to allot time during the interview and at the end for questions the child or family may have. Frequently, they may have questions intermittently throughout the interview and the nurse needs to take the time to respond straightforwardly and with interest to their concerns and questions.

ROLE OF PARENTS

As mentioned, besides interviewing the child the nurse will need to gather information from the parents. Interviewing the parents augments historical data and provides information that the child is unaware of or unable to share. The child's early development and past physical and psychological stresses are areas for which the parents can supply data. Parents can provide facts and perceptions about themselves, the family, and the child's behaviors and activities that the child is unable to relate. While adolescents may be able to articulate data in more detail about their history, both children and adolescents may not remember of wish to reveal facts and experiences that may be essential for the nurse to include in the data base. They may feel hesitant or embarrassed to share their problems, limitations, or perceived weaknesses with the nurse and may choose to cover over pertinent material. Adolescents who have a drug or alcohol abuse problem may wish to play down or negate the seriousness of their actions.

Although parents can provide much factual data about their children's history and background, when nurses interview adolescents they need to consider the adolescent as a primary informant. It is important for the nurse to emphasize to adolescents that the information they share is confidential and will not be divulged to parents. Adolescents are in the throes of individuating from the family system and may wish to keep their sexual interests and activities, as well as other personal information, private.

ASSESSMENT OUTLINE

Through questioning, observations, play, and interviewing the parents, the nurse gathers data about the many different areas of the child's background and behavior. Following is a discussion of those specific areas the nurse will need to examine during the data collection.

Referral data

Before even meeting the child and family the nurse will want to know why treatment is being sought. The nurse may look through records or talk to coworkers to find out who made the referral and why the referral was made. The presenting problem and duration of symptoms should be included. For instance, "Seven-year-old Charlotte was referred to this hospital by a psychiatrist at the Family Services Clinic, who reports that over the past 8 months Charlotte has demonstrated increasingly aggressive and dangerous behavior toward peers and siblings and has been delayed a grade in school for poor academic performance."

To learn about the parents' preceptions about the child's need for intervention, the nurse may ask questions such as:

1. What are the concerns you have about your child?
2. What are the areas you would like to see your child change in?
3. What would you like us to do for your child?

During the nurse's interview with the child, information can be obtained about the child's perceptions regarding referral by asking questions such as:

1. Can you tell me why you've come here?
2. Have you had some worries or things on your mind?
3. How have things been going in school?

Oftentimes children will respond to such questions with "I don't know" or "Nothing's wrong." It is important for the nurse to be clear with the child about the purpose in being there. Nurses may state to the child, "You may feel that things are fine, but sometimes children have worries or feelings that cause them to have problems. You've been having some problem at school and your parents have brought you here to see if we can figure out how to help you."

Developmental data

The developmental history is obtained from the parents. The nurse will want to know at what ages the child reached developmental milestones. At what ages was the child able to sit up, stand up, and begin walking and talking? How did the child respond to the parents or caretakers during infancy? How did the parents or caretakers feel toward the child as an infant? At what age was the child toilet trained? How did the child respond to toilet training? What methods did the parents use to toilet train their child? With adolescents the nurse may address questions directly to them regarding the age pubertal changes began to occur. With females, when did menses begin? With males, when did they begin to shave?

CASE EXAMPLE: Developmental data is elicited from a 20-year-old mother whose 4-month-old male child was admitted to the pediatric unit for failure to thrive. The mother is tearful, appears very anxious about her caretaking role, and states, "I never planned to have this baby, because my husband and I are separated. When the baby cries and cries I have to walk out of the room because I can't handle it. When I pick him up he cries even more and won't let me cuddle or feed him." The nurse compared this data to developmental norms that had been theoretically and experientially learned. According to Sullivan,[5] the infant derives self-concepts through the interpersonal relationship with the significant caretaker. The child needs to develop a primarily "good-me" concept in relation to the caretaker. In this case the child may be developing a primarily "bad-me" concept and consequently anxiety because of the difficult time the mother is having in accepting and adjusting to her caretaking role. The mother and infant relationship falls outside of developmental norms and expectations.

Physical health

Much of the child's physical health history and current physical status can be elicited from parents during the interview. With adolescents direct questions can also be asked of them regarding their physical health status. Children and adolescents can be questioned about any somatic complaints they may be having, such as headaches or stomachaches.

To rule out any organic basis for the child's or adolescent's problems, a physical examination should be done or have recently been done. Sometimes a neurological examination or laboratory tests, such as an electroencephalogram (EEG), may be necessary to rule out any suspected neurological problems. For some emotional or behavioral problems children may be having, an organic dysfunction may play a significant role in the etiology and development of psychiatric symptoms. Although an organic dysfunction or abnormality may play a major role in the development of some behavioral problems, it is also thought that the parental reactions toward a child with organic problems may cause behavioral and emotional symptoms to develop. Children who have difficulty performing academically and who are having behavioral problems in school may have an underlying problem of retardation, a primarily emotional disorder, or a neurological dysfunction.[22] Children with a neurological dysfunction may show evidence of hyperactivity, distractibility, memory disability, gross or fine motor disability, or visual and auditory perceptual disability. Because of their neurological problems such children may often experience failure at task mastery and communication. They may feel frustrated and have a difficult time coping in the family, school, and neighborhood. Social and emotional problems may develop.

Brain injured or epileptic children tend to have psychiatric disturbances three times more often than children with physical disorders that do not involve the central nervous system.[23] A common parental reaction to epileptic children is to overprotect them and limit the range of their activities, reinforcing their view of themselves as being different. Such overprotectiveness may distort the child's psychological development by interfering with the processes of normal socialization. Further research needs to be done to differentiate the degree an organic dysfunction directly contributes to children's behavioral problems in contrast to how much the family and environment play a role.

Nurses need to be aware of any clues that a child's emotional problems may have an organic basis. They need to elicit information about the child from the parents regarding any history of hyperactivity, seizures, language problems, abnormal fine and gross motor movements, or learning difficulties. They need to ask questions about any prenatal, perinatal, or postnatal complications, because these may be associated with neurological dysfunctions. Through observation the nurse can note the child's neurological status. Is the child hyperactive or distractible? Does the child appear to have a difficult time understanding what the nurse is saying? Are fine and gross motor abilities intact? Or does the child appear clumsy, have muscle incoordination, or show unusual and repetitive movements and gestures? If children have had seizures, learning problems, or hyperactive behavior, what have the parents' reactions been toward them?

The nurse will want to know historical data regarding the usual childhood diseases, any major illnesses, hospitalization, allergies, and the child's general state of health. Other areas the nurse can ask questions about are the child's eating/drinking, elimination, and sleeping patterns. What is the child's weight and height?

Through observations the nurse can gather data about the child's physical status. By appearances does the child appear overweight or underweight? Are there any bruises, cuts, or other marks or scars on the body? Assessment of the child's neuromuscular skills and integration can be done by asking the child to throw a ball or to pick up a small object or toy.

Family and environment

The child or adolescent is a member of the family system and therefore data about the family is necessary to determine what precipitants, forces, or circumstances have played a role in the child's present maladaptive functioning.

Family composition. Who are the current family members? What are the ages of the parents? Is the family intact? What are the number and ages of siblings? Are all the children the biological progeny of the same parents?

Family history. How long have the parents been married? Are there previous marriages? If the child's parents are divorced, does the child have contact with both parents? Are extended members of the family involved with the nuclear family? Are maternal and paternal grandparents alive?

Family functioning. Are the parents employed? Where are they employed and for how long? Have there been financial problems for the family? Have there been any recent moves? Any recent deaths in the family? Have any of the family members been ill or hospitalized? Any family members receiving psychiatric treatment now or in the past? Have there been any marital difficulties?

Family interactions. What family dynamics does the nurse observe? How do family members communicate with each other? Do they interrupt one another or speak for each other, or do they listen when other family members talk? How do the parents set limits on the child's behavior? Do they treat their children differently from one another? Do family members appear disinterested in one another? Are there differences in how each parent relates to their children? Do they keep a wide emotional distance from each other or do they appear to be overinvolved and overprotective of certain family members? What activities do family members share together, such as picnics, vacations, or playing a video game?

Culture and community. What support network does the family have in the community? Does the family have friends in the neighborhood? Are family members involved in community activities, such as the PTA, neighborhood block club, civic affairs, or church groups? What is the neighborhood like? Is it safe or potentially a dangerous area? What is the socioeconomic level of the family? Does the family have an ethnic orientation? Do they have a religious affiliation that is important to them? What values are important to family members?

CASE EXAMPLE: Tim is a 16-year-old male admitted to an inpatient psychiatric unit with a history of alcohol abuse since age 12. During the interview he related that he is an only child and lives with his upper middle class family in a reputable community. He stated that he has never had a girlfriend or gone on any dates and mostly spends his time around the house watching television or building car models. Tim's mother discussed how she is in some ways overprotective of Tim and that after his older brother was killed in a motorcycle accident five years ago she became concerned that something harmful could happen to Tim also. She felt his school friends were "too wild" and not a good influence on her son. She wants him to help with chores around the house because her husband spends a great deal of time away on business trips. She related how lonely she feels with her husband away so much and stated that she has no church or community involvements. She often interrupted Tim during the joint part of the interview, answering questions for him, and making oversolicitous comments. The nurse who compared this family data to developmental norms reasons that average adolescents should be attempting to master the psychosocial task of identity vs. role diffusion.[3] They need to be separating from the parental system, associating with peers, and actualizing their own sense of self as independent persons. The nurse reasons that as an adolescent Tim's psychosocial development is not within developmental norms. Data about Tim's family reveals precipitants and circumstances related to his lack of psychosocial development.

Current functioning of the child or adolescent

The current functioning of the child or adolescent can be assessed through direct observation of the child during the interview. Additional data can be gathered from the parents about their perceptions of the child's school performance, recreational activities, peer relationships, family relationships, and any religious or cultural orientations.

Appearance. The first thing nurses notice when interviewing children is their appearance. How is the child dressed? Is the child appropriately groomed and cared for? What does posture and facial expression convey? Does the child appear physically healthy?

Affect. What is the child's predominant mood? Does the child exhibit happiness, anger, sadness, doubt, apprehension, or enthusiasm? When discussing a topic, does the mood or affect appear appropriate? For instance, if discussing problems at home, does the child look appropriately sad, or does the child smile? What range of emotions are demonstrated? How does mood fluctuate or change during the interview? What facial expressions does the child display?

Orientation. What is the child's awareness of time, person, and place? Do children seem to know what is happening environmentally or do they appear to be disoriented? The nurse can assess this by asking children what their age is, where they live, and whom they live with.

Perception. What is the child's ability to receive and interpret sensory information? Is there appropriate use of the senses of sight, smell, taste, touch, and hearing? Can the child differentiate fact from fantasy? By the ages of 6 or 7 years a child can make clear distinctions between a reality situation and fantasy life.

Speech and language. How do children express themselves through speech and language? Does the child speak clearly, stutter, or mumble? How verbal is the child? Is the rate of speech rapid or slow? Are verbal responses expressed spontaneously or in brief, monosyllabic statements? Is the child's vocabulary developmentally appropriate?

Thought processes and content. Is the child or adolescent preoccupied with certain thoughts? Do thoughts appear to be logical and flow sequentially? Does the child appear anxious or distractible? Are there disturbances in thought such as hallucinations, delusions, or illusions? Note whether children talk to themselves or appear to hear or see things that are not real. Has the child reached the appropriate developmental level of cognitive ability?

Motor activity. Is the child hyperactive? While younger children may be very curious about their surroundings and have shorter attention spans, the nurse needs to assess whether the child becomes overstimulated. Does the child stick to an activity or move from one thing to another? Does the child fidget or squirm in the chair or sit withdrawn and motionless? Are movements coordinated or are nervous, repetitive behaviors and gestures present?

Play and fantasy. What play activities do children get involved in? Do they play for a long period of time or briefly become involved in many activities? Are there certain toys or activities that the child especially prefers? Are any activities or toys avoided? Does the child become easily frustrated during play? Is fantasy expressed in play activities? Does the child treat toys or enter activities aggressively, timidly, or with a lack of enthusiasm? Does the child play alone or join with others in an activity? What types of figures and scenes are drawn or painted?

Object relations. The types of relationships the child has with other persons can be assessed through direct observations of how the child relates to the nurse, parents, and peers. Nurses may also question parents and children as to the status of the child's relationships with others.

Nurses will want to assess in what manner children relate to them. Is the child friendly, dependent, clinging, aggressive, mistrustful, hostile, placating, or demanding? Does the child relate similarly to the parents? How does the child separate from the parents? Does the child cling to them? Or does the child leave the parents easily and attach to other adults or activities?

How do children relate to peers? Do they have friends? Any best friends? What types of activities or recreation does the child share with peers or friends? Do they relate submissively, dominatingly, aggressively, provocatively, or appropriately with peers? Are they "leaders" or "followers?" Do children seek out peers or isolate? Do they become easily frustrated with others?

Does the child or adolescent have a history of difficulties with the law? Any drug or alcohol abuse problems? With adolescents, how do they interact with individuals of the opposite sex? Do they have a friend of the opposite sex? What kinds of activities do they enjoy together?

School. Is the child in the age-appropriate grade level or has the child been delayed in school? Has the child been disruptive, distractible, aggressive, overachieving, underachieving, or compliant in school? Does the child have any learning disabilities?

> CASE EXAMPLE: Two-year-old Lisa was admitted to the pediatric unit for pneumonia. The nurse noted that Lisa had a difficult time separating from her mother at admission and cried off and on for her mother all night. During the assessment interview Lisa's mother stated that sometimes Lisa was willful and stubborn. She described Lisa as liking to have things her own way and being occasionally very demanding. She related that at times Lisa wanted to be very independent of her mother, and at other times Lisa couldn't tolerate her mother being out of sight. She stated that Lisa plays well with other children and is especially fond of her 6-year-old sister. The nurse observed Lisa to be a friendly, outgoing child who showed her "dolly" to the nurse. Nurses comparing this data to developmental norms reason that Lisa's willfulness and ambivalent, independent behavior falls within expected developmental norms for her age. It is normal for a 2-year-old to struggle with issues over separation, individuation, and independence.[24]

FINAL STEPS IN THE ASSESSMENT PROCESS

Observations and collection of data are a continuous process beginning at admission and proceeding throughout the child's or adolescent's entire treatment. As a data base is collected the nurse analyzes the data and formulates an assessment. Based upon theory, research, and experience, nurses make judgments as to whether the child's health patterns are developmentally normal or whether there are deviations in the patterns. Data that are assessed as deviating from developmentally normal health patterns provide the nurse with clues that a nursing problem or patient need exists.

> CASE EXAMPLE: Paul, a 10-year-old Caucasian male, is admitted with the psychiatric diagnosis of depression. Paul attempted suicide by trying to hang himself with a belt. He was found semiconscious by his grandmother and taken to the emergency room. He was admitted to the pediatric unit and 3 days later transferred to the child psychiatric unit. Excerpts from his data base reveal that for the past 6 months he has

had a poor appetite and has had recurring nightmares. His affect is flat and he appears withdrawn. His expression is bland and he sits slumped, staring down at the floor. His personal appearance is disheveled. He has been living with his grandparents since his mother was killed in a car accident 6 months ago. Paul's father, who was divorced from his mother when Paul was 2, does not keep in contact with him. The grandmother expresses that although she cares about Paul she has her own financial and marital problems and doesn't have the time or money to care for Paul. Paul is doing poorly in school and avoids interacting with peers. He has no hobbies or interests and complains of feeling tired all the time. Paul responds to questions about his mother with statements such as, "She promised to take me to the zoo this summer. I wish I could go to heaven and be with her."

Analyzing the above data the nurse may hypothesize that one of the problems Paul is exhibiting is dysfunctional grieving. A nursing diagnosis that may be applied to the problem health pattern is "Dysfunctional Grieving related to the loss of his mother and stresses in the present family situation."

Several nursing diagnoses may be determined from the total data base. Development of nursing diagnoses are an integral part of the nursing assessment process. Once nursing diagnoses are identified, goals can be formulated and nursing interventions planned.

SUMMARY

The psychiatric nursing assessment of children and adolescents is heavily dependent on the nurse having a solid knowledge base of normal growth and developmental theories. As nurses collect data from the child and family they will be able to ascertain whether the child's health patterns deviate from what is developmentally expected by comparing what they actually observe in the child to what they have learned is normal for a child of that age. Furthermore, the nurse uses growth and development theories as guidelines to interview the child. The manner of questions and observations vary according to how old the child is. With younger children the nurse relies more prominently on observational skills and engagement in play activities. Questions and verbal comments are geared to a more concrete cognitive level. With older children and adolescents nurses may be able to use more verbal communication to engage a child. Adolescents should be able to demonstrate abstract reasoning and may be able to express some insight into what their difficulties are about.

During the assessment interview nurses need to make preparations for the interview (preinteraction phase), introduce themselves and establish trust and rapport (beginning phase), collect and analyze data (working phase), and finally summarize the interaction, provide significant information, and answer questions (ending phase). The assessment interview ideally includes both the child and parents. Children are dependent and integrally related to the family system and environment, and for nurses to gather a comprehensive and holistic data base, they need to include family and environmental patterns and characteristics. Parents can provide facts and perceptions about themselves, the family, and the child's behaviors and activities that the child is either unaware of or unwilling to share.

Nurses analyze and assess the biological, psychological, social, cultural, familial, and spiritual patterns of the child or adolescent and determine nursing diagnoses for those patterns which are validated as dysfunctional. Once nursing diagnoses are determined nurses can formulate goals and initiate interventions that aim to correct the identified dysfunctional health patterns.

REFERENCES

1. Eisenberg, L. Normal child development. In H.I. Kaplan, Ed. *Comprehensive textbook of psychiatry III.* Baltimore: Williams & Wilkins, 1980, p. 2433.
2. Freud, S. *The ego and the id.* J. Strachey, Ed., J. Riviere, Trans. New York: W.W. Norton & Co., Inc., 1962.
3. Erikson, E. *Childhood and society.* New York: W.W. Norton & Co., 1950, pp. 247-269.
4. Chess, S., & Hassibi, M. *Principles and practice of child psychiatry.* New York: Plenum Press, 1978, pp. 55, 63-64.
5. Sullivan, H.S. *The interpersonal theory of psychiatry.* New York: W.W. Norton & Co., Inc., 1953, pp. 49-297.
6. Kaplan, H., & Sadock, B.: Harry Stack Sullivan. In *Modern synopsis of psychiatry III,* Baltimore: Williams & Wilkins, 1981, p. 153.
7. Piaget, J. Piaget's theory. In P.H. Mussen, Ed.: *Carmicheals manual of child psychology,* 3rd Ed. New York: John Wiley & Sons, Inc., 1970.
8. Riehl, J., & Roy, C. Developmental models for nursing practice. In *Conceptual models for nursing practice,* 2nd Ed. New York: Appleton-Century-Crofts, 1980, pp. 30-33.
9. Rogers, M. *An introduction to the theoretical basis of nursing.* Philadelphia: F.A. Davis Co., 1970, pp. 41, 44.
10. Kim, M. & Moritz, D.A. *Classification of nursing diagnoses.* New York: McGraw Hill Book Co., 1982, pp. 244-245.
11. Lewis, M. *Clinical aspects of child development.* Philadelphia: Lea & Febiger, 1973, pp. 2-6.
12. Scipien, G., et al. *Comprehensive pediatric nursing.* New York: McGraw-Hill Book Co., 1975, pp. 100-123.
13. Bowlby, J. Maternal care and mental health. In World Health Organization, Monograph #2. Quoted in M. Fry, Ed. *Child care and the growth of love.* London: Penguin Books Ltd., 1953.
14. Winnicott, D. Transitional objects and transitional phenomena. In *Collected papers,* London: Tavistock Publications Ltd., 1958, pp. 229-242.

15. Senn, M., & Solnit, A. *Problems in child behavior and development*. Philadelphia: Lea & Febiger, 1968, pp. 62, 152.
16. May, J.G. Part B nosological diagnosis. In J. Noshpitz, Ed. *Basic handbook of child psychiatry*, vol. 2. New York: Basic Books, Inc., Publishers, 1979, p. 124.
17. Blos, P. The second individuation process of adolescence. *The Psychoanalytic Study of the Child*, 1967, 22, 162-187.
18. Lewis, M. *Clinical aspects of child development*. Philadelphia: Lea & Febiger, 1973, p. 150.
19. Gordon, M.: *Nursing diagnosis, process and application*. New York: McGraw-Hill, Inc., 1982, pp. 127, 192.
20. Hagerty, B., et al.: *Interviewing children: The initial assessment*. University of Michigan: Biomedical Media, 1983, p. 2.
21. Axline, V.A. *Play therapy*. New York: Ballantine Books, 1969, p. 54.
22. Silver, L.B. The minimal brain dysfunction syndrome. In J.D. Noshpitz, Ed. *Basic handbook of child psychiatry*, vol. 2. New York: Basic Books, Inc., Publishers, 1979, p. 416.
23. Rutter, M. *Psychiatry in mental retardation: An annual review*, vol. 13. New York: Grune & Stratton, Inc., 1971, p. 186.
24. Freud, S.: *Three essays on the theory of sexuality* (standard ed.), vol. 7. London: The Hogarth Press, Ltd., 1953.

INDEX